HUMAN RELATIONS IN INDUSTRY

Organizational and Administrative Behavior

HUMAN RELATIONS IN INDUSTRY

Organizational and Administrative Behavior

By

BURLEIGH B. GARDNER, Ph.D.

President of Social Research, Inc.

and

DAVID G. MOORE, Ph.D

Professor and Dean

New York State School of Industrial and Labor Relations

Cornell University

FOURTH EDITION · 1964

RICHARD D. IRWIN, INC.

HOMEWOOD, ILLINOIS

FOURTH EDITION

First Printing, March, 1964

Library of Congress Catalog Card No. 64–17239

PRINTED IN THE UNITED STATES OF AMERICA

PREFACE

Since the first edition of *Human Relations in Industry* was published in 1945, there has been an increasing interest in and concern with the application of the behavioral sciences to business administration. This interest has been accelerated in recent years, particularly as a result of the Ford Foundation and Carnegie Corporation's reports on education in schools of business. What was once of interest only to majors in personnel and industrial relations has now become in many schools a significant part of the curriculum of all students of business administration.

Because of this broader interest, this fourth edition of *Human Relations in Industry* has been written from a managerial point of view. This means that we have focused attention on the role of the business executive and on the contribution which the behavioral sciences make to his decisions and actions. The new approach is reflected in the subtitle of the book—*Organizational and Administrative Behavior*.

Our focus on the executive function has resulted in many unexpected conclusions. We found, for example, that the usual approaches to management were narrowly conceived and related to various assumptions about the organization and human behavior within it. As our analysis proceeded, we found ourselves reaching out for a more realistic grasp of the managerial function in the business enterprise. More and more, we turned to the entrepreneurial functions of management as the starting point for a realistic appraisal of the decisions and actions of the business executive.

The entrepreneurial aspects of business involve exchange relationships among people—relationships which often involve differences in values and interests. These are not differences arising out of personality and status considerations as such, although they may play a part. They are rather differences that are part and parcel of an urban, industrial society in which there is great diversity on the one hand and great interdependency on the other. In this respect, they are "real" differences which cannot be wished away by positive thinking and a pleasant manner.

The concept of co-operation does not seem sufficient to explain the kind of accommodations, compromises, working relationships, and other adjustments made in a complex urban society. We have found the term *coaptation* (fitting together of interests) suggested by A. R. Radcliffe-Brown to be far more useful. It is unfortunate that the term is so similar to *cooptation* which has gained a certain currency in recent years.

As the reader can see from the foregoing, the fourth edition devotes more attention to organizational and administrative theory than did former editions. We do not feel that we have found all the answers by any means. Nor do we feel that what we have to offer is particularly original. We are in so many ways dependent upon our colleagues that we hardly know where their ideas leave off and ours begin. Nonetheless, if we have pushed the theoretical development of the field of management a step ahead, we shall be grateful.

The fourth edition of *Human Relations of Industry* provides much new material but also uses much of the material presented in previous editions. Since the human relations field was generally organized around the notion of interaction, divergent interests and values, and various patterns of human adjustment amidst these divergencies, there is no real break in our current theoretical formulations with previous empirical evidence. Thus, the reader of this text will find himself on familiar ground whenever empirical findings are presented.

The present text can be used in three ways. First, it can be used as an introduction to the behavioral sciences in business administration since it covers the major concepts particularly of sociology and social anthropology and applies these to the analysis of the management function and human relations in industry. Second, it can be used as a beginning course in management, for it represents a realistic appraisal of the management function, reviews management and organizational theory, and provides the student with an understanding of a major aspect of the managerial task, namely, organizational behavior. In its present form, the text fits more neatly into other subject matter of business administration, marketing, finance, business economics, and accounting. It deals with some of the same problems and, therefore, sheds light on the significance and importance of these subjects in executive development. Finally, the text can be used, as it has been in the past, in the more traditional human relations approach.

January, 1964

BURLEIGH B. GARDNER
DAVID G. MOORE

TABLE OF CONTENTS

INDEX

PART I

Introduction and Background

1. INTRODUCTION TO HUMAN RELATIONS IN INDUSTRY

Organization and the Individual

TWO MAJOR themes run through the history of America. On the one hand we are a nation of organizers; we organize a great variety of action systems of enormous technical and human complexity for the accomplishment of many different purposes. On the other hand we subscribe to a deeply rooted philosophy of individualism and have many strong convictions regarding the rights of the individual and his freedom of choice and action. Both themes in our society are powerful forces, and, while they are not incompatible, they often come into conflict. The narrowly defined needs of organizations frequently appear to clash with the more diffuse needs of individuals. Thus a dynamic interplay of individual and organizational demands is set into motion, characterized by an inherent imbalance which keeps the whole system alive, creative, and evolving.

Look at the face of America! You see the outward expression of its great organizations. You see its urban centers, which are no longer communities in the usual sense but gigantic functional and technical systems. You see its massive industries. You see its mammoth governmental institutions. You see its skyscrapers, its communication networks, its educational institutions, its neat geometric patterns. And, if you look closely, you see swarms of men, moving in, out, around, and over these huge structures trying desperately to keep them going, devoting their whole lives, in fact, to keeping them going.

Someone described the U.S.S.R. as a gigantic system of mines, factories, educational centers, and people designed and activated for the primary purpose of sending rockets to the moon. By the same token, the United States might be described as an equally complex system designed for the purpose of getting everyone on wheels, presumably so that Americans can get out each week end and kill each other in fantastic jousting tournaments on the nation's highways. This is one way of looking at modern civilization. Those who are offended by

3

large-scale organization can use even stronger descriptive terms than these. Organized activities are seen as essentially tyrannical, as devouring human dignity, as the antithesis of individual freedom. C. Wright Mills expresses his hostilities articulately and well when he describes the big department store as follows:

In the cathedral, worship is organized; this is the cathedral of commodities, whispering and shouting for its 394,000 assorted gods (not including colors and sizes). In organizing the congregation, the Big Bazaar has been training it for faster and more efficient worship. Its most effective prayers have been formed in the ritual of the Great Repetition, a curious blending of piety and the barking of a circus.[1]

Listen also to his description of the modern office skyscraper:

Each office within the skyscraper is a segment of the enormous file, a part of the symbol factory that produces the billion slips of paper that gear modern society into its daily shape. From the executive's suite to the factory yard, the paper webwork is spun; a thousand rules you never made and don't know about are applied to you by a thousand people you have not met and never will. The office is the Unseen Hand become visible as a row of clerks and a set of IBM equipment, a pool of dictaphonic transcribers, and sixty receptionists confronting the elevators, one above the other, on each floor.[2]

The voice of C. Wright Mills is by no means a lonely one. The criticism of large-scale organization is perennial and follows a fairly consistent pattern. Indeed, each new generation produces its eloquent critics who discover General Motors, U.S. Steel, or some other large-scale organization, which is after all pretty hard to hide, and discourse dramatically either about its soulless lack of purpose or its crushing domination of the individual. The role of the eloquent critic is clear; he is the expression of the important theme of individualism which is so integral a part of the social and political thought of America.

Prior to World War I, large-scale organization, particularly business, was viewed by its critics directly and simply as a ruthless exploiter. This exploitive character gave way in the twentieth century, according to Erich Fromm, to what might be called the principle of manipulation or "the use of man by man." Dr. Fromm says:

Since the modern capitalist "employs" labor, the social and political form of this exploitation has changed; what has not changed is that the owner of capital uses other men for the purpose of his own profit. The basic concept of *use* has nothing to do with cruel, or not cruel, ways of human treatment, but with the funda-

---

[1] C. Wright Mills, *White Collar* (New York: Oxford University Press, 1951), p. 168.
[2] *Ibid.*, p. 189.

mental fact that one man serves another for purposes which are not his own but those of the employer.[3]

He goes on to say:

The use of man by man is expressive of the *system of values* underlying the capitalistic system. *Capital, the dead past, employs labor—the living vitality and power of the present.* In the capitalistic hierarchy of values, capital stands higher than labor, amassed things higher than the manifestations of life. Capital employs labor, and not labor capital. The person who owns capital commands the person who "only" owns his life, human skill, vitality, and creative productivity.[4]

It is undoubtedly true, as Erich Fromm and many others have pointed out, that business was "ruthlessly exploitive" up to World War I or at least, to put it in more positive terms, not essentially aware of the human consequences of mass organization in the rampant quest for profit and economic development. Indeed, it has only been in the past twenty years that business has begun to see the great significance of the human element, not only at the level of labor but at the executive and customer levels as well. Benjamin Selekman says:

It is difficult, if not impossible, for those who have come into adulthood during the past twenty-five years, to appreciate what a radical change this new attitude constitutes in the underlying posture and ideology of business. But to one who, like myself, grew up amidst coal and steel during the first two decades of the century, with short excursions among city sweatshops, the change is a dramatic one indeed. It can truly be said that in those early years business was indifferent if not callous to the welfare of the men and women employed in mines, mills, and factories.[5]

Certainly a change for the better in human relations has come over business. As one man said referring to a particular steel company near Chicago, "They fire them out there better to-day than they used to hire them." He was remembering the old "stockyard" technique of hiring. Applicants would herd together in a yard or large office and sit or stand around for hours until the employment man came out and said, "I want you and you and you. The rest of you can go home." Things have improved. Few who remember industrial life even twenty-five years ago yearn for the good old days unless their nostalgia has addled their reason. Nonetheless, to its critics business is still the same old monster appearing in new manifestations. Instead of pure and sim-

---

[3] Erich Fromm, *The Sane Society* (New York: Rinehart and Company, 1955), p. 93.
[4] *Ibid.*, p. 94.
[5] Benjamin M. Selekman, *A Moral Philosophy for Management* (New York: McGraw-Hill Book Co., Inc., 1959), p. 8.

ple exploitation, large-scale organization is committing even graver sins: it is reshaping the social character of Americans; it is molding our citizenry into men of shallow values and shoddy purposes; it is creating a society of social relativists, status seekers, organization men, and glad-handers whose only measure of achievement is social success in one kind of hierarchy or another. This is obviously an even deeper wrong to the individual because of its subtlety and its pervasive weakening of inner virtue and morality. The basic thesis of William H. Whyte's *The Organization Man* is in this vein. Whyte argues that we are developing a nation of bureaucrats guided by a new ideology which he calls the "social ethic." He states:

With reason it (the Social Ethic) could be called an organization ethic, or a bureaucratic ethic; more than anything else it rationalizes the organization's demands for fealty and gives those who offer it wholeheartedly a sense of dedication in doing so—*in extremis*, you might say, it converts what would seem in other times a bill of no rights into a restatement of individualism.[6]

The thing that galls Mr. Whyte is not that we have bureaucrats but that they like it that way and actually believe that they are expressing individualism within the structure of large-scale enterprises.

Erich Fromm's criticisms are even more damaging in some respects. A humanist and psychologist, he is concerned with the psychopathogenic influences of society. His psychology is a highly developed one in that it relates social organization to the development of personality and character. He was deeply impressed in the 'thirties with the *folie à millions* of totalitarian nations, particularly Nazi Germany, where madness stalked the land, delusions became reality, and paranoia emerged as the national policy. While Nazi Germany focused the madness of modern man in the screaming, grotesque figure of Adolph Hitler and in the incredible inhumanity at Buchenwald, the rest of the world was and is perhaps no less sick, even though its behavior was and is somewhat less destructive. In *The Sane Society*, Dr. Fromm turns his attention to twentieth-century Democracy and its deep characterological and mental illnesses. As might be expected, the old monster, business, rears its ugly head. Dr. Fromm says:

Man has to relate himself to others; but if he does it in a symbiotic or alienated way, he loses his independence and integrity; he is weak, suffers, becomes hostile, or apathetic; only if he can relate himself to others in a loving way does he feel one with them and at the same time preserve his integrity.[7]

    6 William H. Whyte, Jr., *The Organization Man* (Garden City, New York: Doubleday Anchor Books, 1956), p. 6.
    7 Fromm, *op. cit.*, p. 68.

He goes on to say:

It is . . . easy to see that only a sense of identity based on the experience of his own powers can give strength, while all forms of identity experience based on the group, leave man dependent, hence weak.[8]

With this definition of the etiology and sources of mental illness, it is but a small step to the more general condemnation of our entire society which Dr. Fromm levels. Our capitalistic society and particularly its economic institutions are primary factors in the alienation of the individual. Modern man is distinctly isolated, disengaged, uninvolved, and, to use Dr. Fromm's term, alienated. As he says:

Alienation as we find it in modern society is almost total; it pervades the relationship of man to his work, to the things he consumes, to the state, to his fellow man, and to himself. Man has created a world of man-made things as it never existed before. He has constructed a complicated social machine to administer the technical machine he built. Yet this whole creation of his stands over and above him.[9]

These are powerful words and the theme is equally powerful, since it is an integral part of the social and political philosophy of America which is profoundly concerned with the individual, his rights, his development, and his role within the social leviathan. Yet, in spite of the urgency of the message of the Mills, Whytes, Fromms, and others, there are those who look upon modern large-scale organization not only without rancor but even with a certain fondness. They view organized activities in more personal, less alienated ways, as expressions of living, vital human efforts to build a world of physical and, yes, even spiritual comfort, and as an important means of allowing man the freedom and the time which he needs for his creative, aesthetic, and essentially human growth. They are not fearful or even overly anxious in the face of the Golem, since they see it as man-made and, therefore, controlled by man. To be sure, it has unintended consequences; to be sure, also, the management of large-scale organizations requires continuously greater breadth of understanding; but organized effort is not seen as a monstrous, mechanistic superstructure crushing the individual or, even worse, gently enfolding him within the madness of the Great Bazaar, the Enormous File, and the Assembly Line, and feeding his mad delusions with Mass Communications spooned out of the witch pots of Madison Avenue.

---

[8] *Ibid.*, p. 69.
[9] *Ibid.*, p. 124.

Roger Blough, Chairman of the Board, United States Steel Corporation, expresses his more positive sentiments about business organization,
as follows:

I hope that by now these great families of small-, medium-, and large-sized
corporate groups have come alive for you, for they are people and they constitute the economic bloodstream which feeds our free society. These groups are
the providers—the suppliers and the creators of our free markets where customers are constantly deciding which of the groups serve them the better. In
making his selection competitively, the customer pays for a job well done; and
by paying, he directs the flow of production, the use of resources, and he stimulates the ingenuity of competing organizations—he rewards the better providers.
    The whole process is a free society's way of disciplining itself.
    But the heart of the matter is still not as clearly delineated as one would
desire.
    To me the heart of the matter is not that we have certain management tech-
niques which do produce excellent results but that within voluntary groups of
free men lie the genius and the will to originate and perfect those management
techniques.
    To me it is not that these corporate groups are the primary generative source
of the capital formation of our land but that freely formed groups have, through
their own internally directed efforts, the unrivaled capability for capital formation.
    To me the heart of the matter, therefore, is not that corporate groups are the
indispensable providers of the physical elements of our national well-being; the
heart of the matter is that, through these freely formed and constantly evolving
organisms of production, generative forces of great originality rise far above the
individual imagination of any of its members, enhancing the role of *every* man
and giving breadth and scope even to him who may be called the uncommon
man.[10]

Mr. Blough's statement is but one of a current crop of arguments
emerging out of business and is evidence of the growing sophistication
of the business executive in matters of broad policy. Parenthetically, it
is interesting to note that business executives today evince a self-con-
sciousness which their "public-be-damned" forebears would have found
distasteful if not effete. Perhaps the narrow-shouldered, Ivy League suit
has had, through some devious social chemistry, an estrogenic effect.
Be that as it may, William Miller, historian and author, who is no great
lover of the Robber Barons and the excesses of the Gilded Age, has
noted with some dismay the defensive, somewhat apologetic posture
of the modern business executive.[11] One might ask what happened to

---

[10] Roger M. Blough, *Free Man and the Corporation* (New York: McGraw-Hill
Book Co., Inc., 1959), pp 38–40.
    [11] See William Miller, "The Business Elite in Business Bureaucracies," *Men in Busi-
ness, Essays in the History of Entrepreneurship,* Edited by William Miller (Cambridge,
Mass.: Harvard University Press, 1952), pp. 286–305.

Sandburg's industrial metropolis, "Stormy, husky brawling/ City of the Big Shoulders." Have the "hog-butchers" indeed been draped in narrow-shouldered suits?[12]

Whatever the deeper motivations, the current efforts of modern business executives to concern themselves with the essential problem of organization and individual creativity and freedom are laudable and useful. The student of business administration and management should be thoroughly familiar not only with the perceived function of large-scale organizations in modern society but also with the role of the individual within these systems. For these are not considerations of interest only to the ivory-towered intellectual or to the self-conscious businessman; they are fundamental problems of a democratic society. The world is presently confronted with two systems for solving the problems of famine, the material needs of people, and national defense. Both systems are obviously successful at the material level. Differentiation from here on out must be made on achievements at a much higher level than material productivity. Inevitably, these higher-level achievements rest upon the creative integration of the two great themes of organization and individualism. Within America, these two great themes of Western civilization have been sharply focused and eternally conjoined. They are not academic considerations but vital influences in our daily lives and in our daily decisions and must be reckoned with at every occasion when the individual comes into contact with the organization.

The Significance of Large-Scale Organization

No matter what criticisms may be leveled at large-scale organizations, they are undoubtedly here to stay. This is not to say that specific large-scale organizations will enjoy eternal life. Organized activities are, after all, quite ephemeral, even delicate. Chester Barnard, former president of New Jersey Bell Telephone Company and author of the classic study, *The Functions of the Executive*, points out that "most cooperation fails in the attempt, or dies in infancy, or is short-lived. In our western civilization only one formal organization, the Roman Catholic Church, claims a substantial age. A few universities, a very few national governments or formally organized nations, are more than two hundred years old."[13] The mechanistic, inexorable monster of Mills, Whyte, *et al.*, in Barnard's view becomes a flimsy, jerry-built structure

---

[12] Also see James C. Worthy, *Big Business and Free Men* (New York: Harper & Bros., 1959), chap. i.

[13] Chester I. Barnard, *The Functions of the Executive* (Cambridge, Mass.: Harvard University Press, 1938), p. 5.

held together by cotton string, bent paper clips, and the sheer effort and willingness of men to prop up the corners. Take away one necessary support and the whole structure collapses like the crude contraption it really is. Indeed, the survival of modern business organizations depends upon their ability to change and regenerate themselves. They are in a sense in a continuous process of death and rebirth. Whole industries survive today on products and processes which were not even in existence ten years ago.

Nonetheless, the techniques, processes, and structural forms of large-scale organization are here to stay, for it is the primary and basic social invention of civilization. Take away large-scale organization and you are back to living in a cave or mud-hut, eating rutabagas and turnips, and discovering why the Anglo-Saxons invented all those four-letter words, as you try to shoot a racing rabbit with a bow and arrow. It is true that you will no longer be alienated; you will most assuredly be involved; your relation with nature will be intimate and complete. But your concern with that precious little ego of yours and its creative impulse to self-realization will fade into the background, like polite conversation at social teas, as you face the sheer brutality of physical survival.

The world cries for human freedom, but human freedom without organization is a mob in the streets or, worse, a roving band in the jungle. The crucial problem facing the underdeveloped areas of the world is organization and the management of organization. Frederick H. Harbison and Charles A. Myers have recently completed an extensive comparative study of management and organization throughout the world. They say:

In modern society, industrialism is an almost universal goal toward which all nations are marching. The underdeveloped countries are striving to industrialize as a means of accelerating economic progress; the advanced countries seek to broaden and to extend industrialization in order to achieve ever-higher standards of living and greater economic power. In the march toward industrialism, capital, technology, and natural resources are but passive agents. The active forces are *human agents* who create and control the organizations and institutions which modern industrialism requires. They are the ones who build and manage the enterprises which combine natural resources, technology, and human effort for productive purposes.[14]

The "human agents" about whom Harbison and Myers speak are managers or "organization builders":

---

[14] Frederick Harbison and Charles A. Myers, *Management in the Industrial World: An International Analysis* (New York: McGraw-Hill Book Co., Inc., 1959), p. 3.

In the hierarchy of management, the organization builder has a critical role. He may be the owner of the business, a professional manager, or a government official. In any case, he is the top manager who builds the hierarchy. He is the keystone in the arch of management; he cannot be separated from his organization but is fused with it. . . . This is the most difficult of all managerial functions. It requires a concept of organization building and a philosophy of management.[15]

Management, according to Harbison and Myers, is an economic resource, a factor in production, which should be set up alongside the classical economic sources of wealth, namely, land, labor, and capital. As they point out, "A country's economic development may be limited by a relative shortage of this critical factor, or that development may be accelerated significantly by a high capacity to accumulate it."[16] They go on to say, "In many instances, . . . management is an even more critical factor in industrialization than capital, and it is almost always more vital to development than either labor or natural resources."[17]

Harbison and Myers emphasize the role of management resources in the development of large-scale organizations. Their emphasis is an important one; however, it raises questions which we should like to discuss in greater detail in a later chapter. The major consideration which should be grasped at this time is the significance of large-scale organizations whether they arise out of managerial resources or out of the organizing genius of a whole people. The student of business administration should acquaint himself with some of the problems of "getting things going" in an underdeveloped country. He should get a feel for the incredible difficulties of trying to "do things" when no particular talent for organization exists within a society. Only then can he begin to appreciate the political agonies of so many areas of the world and the great gulf in understanding existing between the United States and a number of the underdeveloped countries. Only then can he truly appreciate the significance of large-scale organization.

Human Relations, Organization, and the Individual

Almost a quarter of a century ago, Chester Barnard pointed out the lack of attention of the social sciences to organization "as the concrete social process by which social action is largely accomplished."[18] His views in 1937 were not entirely accurate, as any sociologist hastens to

---

15 *Ibid.*, p. 15.
16 *Ibid.*, p. 19.
17 *Ibid.*, p. 19.
18 Barnard, *op. cit.*, p. 3.

tell us. Alvin Gouldner claims in his article in *Sociology Today* that "Saint-Simon was probably the first to note the rise of modern organizational patterns, identify some of their distinctive features, and insist upon their prime significance for the emerging society."[19] According to Professor Gouldner:

Saint-Simon argued that, in the society of the future, administrative methods would no longer entail coercion or force, and the administrator's authority would no longer be based upon birth or hereditary privilege. The authority of the modern administrator, he held, would rest upon his possession of scientific skills and "positive" knowledge.[20]

Saint-Simon propounded his views more than 150 years ago. More pertinent certainly was the relatively recent work (prior, however, to 1920) of Max Weber, German sociologist, who in his analyses of bureaucratic models of organization delineated the major dimensions of formal organization and the influence of the "office" and the formal aspects of organization on executive and employee behavior.[21] Nonetheless, with one exception, Chester Barnard's views, as expressed in 1937, were essentially correct. Very little was being done in the social sciences toward a more empirical and scientific understanding of organization.

The one exception was the research at Western Electric Hawthorne Works sponsored by that company and the Harvard Graduate School of Business Administration. This research, which was conducted primarily in the late 'twenties and early 'thirties, was actually a whole series of studies beginning with a relatively simple study of working conditions and employee efficiency and culminating in an elaborate social psychological and sociological interpretation of employee and management behavior within the organizational setting. How the researchers got from a simple cause-and-effect analysis of monotony and fatigue at the production worker level to a systematic analysis of the social structure and processes of the modern factory is a story in itself. It is a story of broadening interests as the researchers involved sought to find more satisfactory explanations of employee behavior. It is a story of academic flexibility as the researchers shifted from psychological to sociological analyses of human relations. It is a story above all of a group

---

[19] Alvin W. Gouldner, "Organizational Analysis," in Robert K. Merton, Leonard Brown, and Leonard S. Cottrell, Jr. (eds.), *Sociology Today: Problems and Prospects* (New York: Basic Books, Inc., 1959), p. 400.

[20] *Ibid.*, p. 400.

[21] See Talcott Parsons, *The Structure of Social Action* (Glencoe, Illinois: The Free Press, 1949), p. 506.

of insightful men from many different disciplines who, through a melding of many ideas, tried to develop a useful science of human and organizational behavior.

It is not necessary within this text to review the details of the research conducted at Western Electric. These have been reported in F. J. Roethlisberger and William J. Dickson's *Management and the Worker*, which is the "official" report of the research.[22] Any serious student of business administration should be familiar with this monumental work. Moreover, there are a number of excellent summaries which are available. Reference can be made to Miller and Form's *Industrial Sociology*[23] and especially the recent book of Henry A. Landsberger, *Hawthorne Revisited*,[24] which reviews not only the major findings but also the criticisms of the research. Our concern in this text with the Western Electric study is in the influence which it has had on organization theory and research and on the problems of understanding human adjustment within the organization.

The greatest contribution of the Western Electric research was to demonstrate the complexity of human behavior and to provide a systematic approach to the analysis of human relations in industry. There has been a tendency in management circles to assume a simple, uncomplicated cause-and-effect relationship between conditions in the working environment and employee behavior. This, for want of a better name, might be called the "fallacy of linearity"—the assumption of a direct-line relationship between factors in the work environment and human behavior. Linear propositions follow the form of "if the event A occurs, then the event B will follow." Such propositions are applicable to the physical sciences, since there is no apparent intervening, integrating variable, unless it is God Himself. The relative stability and consistency of physical phenomena make such propositions useful. But, when they are applied to human phenomena, where there is the intervening variable of the human mind with its highly particular integration of past and present experiences, they are often inappropriate and inaccurate.

Nonetheless, management even today bases many of its decisions upon linear propositions which are essentially simple rules of thumb

---

22 F. J. Roethlisberger and W. J. Dickson, *Management and the Worker* (Cambridge, Mass.: Harvard University Press, 1939).

23 Delbert C. Miller and William H. Form, *Industrial Sociology* (New York: Harper & Bros., 1951).

24 Harry A. Landsberger, *Hawthorne Revisited* (Ithaca, New York: Cornell University, 1958).

which hopefully provide guides to appropriate action. Examples of such propositions are as follows:

If employees are given an opportunity to earn more through an incentive plan, they will produce more.

If working conditions are improved, employee morale will improve.

If supervisors follow the "rules" of good human relations, they will develop greater satisfaction among their employees.

If prices are decreased, people will buy more.

For all of these propositions, even though each has a common sensical face validity, there must be added two words of warning—"It depends!" It depends on how people look at the actions and events which have taken place and how they interpret them. We have seen many instances of so-called improvements in working conditions which have in no way affected employee morale or have even affected it adversely. Incentive systems sometimes increase the productive efforts of employees and sometimes cause them to strike. The "rules" of good human relations applied to a group of girls in an office will not be appropriate to a group of longshoremen. And sometimes price increases create more consumer demand than price decreases. It all depends; and it depends on how people interpret the events which are occurring around them.

It is understandable why business management has seized upon "linear" propositions such as these. In any action situation where decisions have to be reached, there is a natural tendency toward oversimplification, the reduction of complexity, and a search for certainty in the face of ambiguity. Management attempts to contend with complexity by breaking it down into simpler components and by developing relatively simple action principles or rules of thumb for dealing with complex events.

It is precisely in this area that the Western Electric study made its most significant contribution. The study in fact might be interpreted as an honest but deliberate effort to highlight the "linearity" and oversimplification of managerial thinking and to direct the attention of management to considerably more complicated, but more appropriate and useful, ways of looking at human relations in industry. The Western Electric research began with a series of illumination experiments, which were not properly an integral part of the research but preceded it and served, therefore, as a point of beginning. These studies of illumination were based upon the simple, linear hypothesis that, if illumination in the workplace is improved, worker productivity will increase. An experimental group was set up as well as a control group. In the experimental group where illumination was increased, productivity went up as expected. However, productivity also went up to about the same extent in the control group where the lighting was not altered. This unexpected result led to more elaborate investigations of the relationship between conditions of work and productivity. There followed accordingly a whole series of experiments in which an effort was made to eliminate variables which appeared to "contaminate" or influence the results. As indicated previously, it is not necessary here to spell out in complete detail the nature of these experiments. Suffice it to say that the very effort to eliminate "contaminating" variables resulted in the wholesale introduction of new influences which really fouled up the research. For example, in the so-called "Relay Assembly Test Room," a small group of girls were separated from their regular work group. Hovering about them were the researchers seeking their co-operation in the experiment. The girls were given periodic physical examinations; they were interviewed; the physical conditions of work, including the temperature and humidity, were carefully watched; professors, management representatives, and visiting dignitaries came in to observe them from time to time. Altogether, the girls had more attention than they would have gotten if they had visited their own grandparents. Small wonder that the results were unexpected and productivity increased from period to period during the experiment.

At first blush, one might brand the Western Electric study as the natural consequence of a group of blundering Keystone cops messing around with social scientific phenomena. This initial reaction, however, is far from the truth. The researchers involved were sophisticated men. Looking back from the vantage point of three decades, one might even suspect that they knew exactly what they were doing. For they were starting essentially from management's own assumptions regarding the linear relationship between working conditions and employee productivity. They hoped to demonstrate for all time that simple, cause-and-effect propositions were not adequate to explain human behavior.

Accordingly, the research at Western Electric moved over a period of years from objective, experimental studies to intensive studies of what might be called the subjectivity of human behavior. The researchers became more and more interested in employee attitudes and the psychological and sociological factors in employee attitudes, sentiments, and beliefs. Some of the earliest work in the application of semantics, nondirective interviewing, and client-centered counseling occurred at Western Electric. Moreover, the researchers entered the area of social research through an historic study of small-group influences on worker behavior. All of these were contributions of the behavioral research team which developed around the Harvard Graduate School of Business during the creative period of the 'thirties. The most important contribution, however, of the Western Electric study was in its development over a period of years of a theory of human behavior in organization. It was a theory which looked in two directions in keeping with the two main themes of American life. It provided on the one hand major insights into the nature of large-scale organizations;[25] and on the other it followed the deep humanistic and individualistic traditions of America in focusing attention on the problems of employee adjustment, growth, and development in large-scale enterprises.

What were some of the major propositions of the theory of organization and human relations which emerged out of the Western Electric study? (We will not analyze these propositions in detail at this time since they will be discussed in subsequent chapters of this text.) However, a few of the key concepts were as follows:

1. The industrial organization should be viewed as a social system. By system is meant something which must be considered as a whole because each part bears a relation of interdependence to every other part.
2. The industrial organization is seen as performing two major functions, that of producing a product and that of creating and distributing satisfactions among the individual members of the organization. The industrial concern is continually confronted, therefore, with two sets of major problems: (a) problems of external balance, and (b) problems of internal equilibrium. The problems of external balance are generally assumed to be economic. The problems of internal equilibrium are chiefly concerned with the maintenance of a kind of social organization in which individuals and groups through working together can satisfy their own desires.
3. The two major functions of organization are interrelated. Employee relations and productivity are intimately related and interdependent.
4. The industrial organization can be roughly divided into the technical organization and the human organization. These are interrelated and interdependent. The human organization is constantly molding and re-creating the technical organization either to achieve more effectively the common economic purpose or to secure more satisfaction for its members. Likewise, changes in the technical organization require adaptation on the part of the human organization.
5. In the human organization we find a number of individuals working together toward a common end: the collective purpose of the total or-

---

[25] The industrial organization should be viewed as a social system. By system is meant something which must be considered as a whole because each part bears a relation of interdependence to every other part.

ganization. Each of these individuals, however, is bringing to the work situation a different background of personal and social experiences. The demands a particular employeé makes depend not only upon his physical needs but upon his social needs as well. These social needs and the sentiments associated with them vary with his early personal history and social conditioning as well as with the needs and sentiments of people closely associated with him both inside and outside the work.

6. The process of social interaction and social conditioning is never ending and continues from birth to death. The adult's evaluation of his surroundings is determined in a good part by the system of human interrelations in which he has participated.

7. However, the human organization of an industrial plant is more than a plurality of individuals, each motivated by sentiments arising from his own personal and private history and background. It is also a social organization, for the members of an industrial plant—executives, technical specialists, supervisors, factory workers, and office workers—are interacting daily with one another and from their associations certain patterns of relations are formed among them. These patterns of relations, together with the objects which symbolize them, constitute the social organization of the industrial enterprise. Most of the individuals who live among these patterns come to accept them as obvious and necessary truths and to react as they dictate. Both the kind of behavior that is expected of a person and the kind of behavior he can expect from others are prescribed by these patterns.

8. In the factory, as in any social organization, a process of social evaluation is constantly at work. From this process distinctions of "good" and "bad," "inferior" and "superior," arise. Each work group becomes a carrier of social values.

9. All the patterns of interaction that arise between individuals or between different groups can be graded according to the degree of intimacy involved in the relationship, that is, in terms of "social distance."

10. Just as each employee has a particular physical location, so he has a particular social place in the total social organization. In any factory there is considerable mobility or movement. Movement can occur in two ways: the individual may pass from one occupation to another occupation higher up in the prestige scale; or the prestige scale itself may change.

11. Any person who has achieved a certain rank in the prestige scale regards anything real or imaginary which tends to alter his status adversely as something unfair or unjust. From this point of view it can be seen how every item and event in the industrial environment becomes an object of a system of sentiments. According to this way of looking at things, material goods, physical events, wages, hours of work, etc., cannot be treated as things in themselves. Instead they have to be interpreted as carriers of social values. It becomes easy to tell a person's social place in the organization by the objects which he wears and carries and which surround him.

12. The behavior of no one person in an industrial organization, from the very top to the very bottom, can be regarded as motivated by strictly

economic or logical considerations. Routine patterns of interaction involve strong sentiments.

13. The social organization of the industrial plant is in part formally organized. The formal organization includes the systems, policies, rules, and regulations of the plant which express what the relations of one person to another are supposed to be in order to achieve effectively the task of technical production. The formal organization of an industrial plant has two purposes: it addresses itself to the economic purposes of the total enterprise; it concerns itself also with the securing of co-operative effort.

14. Many of the actually existing patterns of human interaction have no representation in the formal organization at all, and others are inadequately represented by the formal organization. Individuals in their associations with one another in a factory build up personal relationships. They form into informal groups, in terms of which each person achieves a certain position or status.

15. There is an ideological organization of the plant which cuts across both the formal and informal organizations. This includes the systems of ideas and beliefs by means of which the values residing in the total organization are expressed and the symbols around which these values are organized. Both the formal and informal organizations of a plant have systems of ideas and beliefs.

The foregoing propositions, which have been largely excerpted with only minor modification from Chapter XXIV of *Management and the Worker*, indicate the level of interpretation in the Western Electric study. It is not expected that the reader will immediately grasp the significance of the concepts presented or the framework out of which they emerge. However, from the foregoing, the student should begin to see that the human relations approach is more than an expression of humanitarian sentiments; it involves some highly developed concepts regarding the nature of organized activity. Indeed, the Western Electric research is a pioneering study in organizational and administrative theory and behavior.

The Human Relations Field

The term *human relations* implies to the layman a concern with man's relationship to man. This is a laudable, praiseworthy concern but why study it? Don't we know everything we need to know regarding how we should treat our fellow man? Weren't all the principles of good human relations clearly stated two thousand years ago? Aren't these principles so much a part of our way of life that deep within each of us is the understanding needed to deal with most human problems? On what appear to be perfectly legitimate grounds, therefore, many students leave human relations out of their curricula, firmly convinced that they know all they need to know about "getting along with people."

The student is further confused by the tendency in some circles to equate human relations with a certain kind of orthodoxy regarding employee relations. The human relations approach has been equated with the "happiness school of management"—every worker and executive a grinning, self-satisfied, and above all placid, idiot! More specifically, it has been accused of apotheosizing co-operation. Still further, it has been branded as having a collectivistic orientation, as recommending the submerging of the individual in the group and legitimatizing this submersion by asserting that genuine human satisfaction arises out of group identification, participation, and co-operation.

Most of these difficulties in interpretation arise out of a failure to identify what kind of human relations approach is being discussed. The term *human relations* is too broad and, as a consequence, has become an umbrella under which many somewhat diverse activities take place. For example, there are untold numbers of supervisory and executive training programs being taught in this country under the label of "human relations." Many of these programs are very useful and helpful to the administrator in the field. They call the attention of the administrator to the human problems of his organization and oftentimes provide useful approaches to dealing with these problems. Rather typically, however, they are not designed to teach very much. Their purpose is to reorient thinking, to sensitize the supervisor, and to give him new ways of looking at human relations. Because of the narrow purpose of these programs, they quite naturally appear to overemphasize the concern with human feelings and emotions to the exclusion of other legitimate activities of business which, it might be argued, will have more to do with human satisfactions in the long run than how one treats Willie in the workplace. Furthermore, they appear to be lacking in substance, which of course they are. Finally, they frequently do subscribe to a kind of orthodoxy in human relations with an exaggerated emphasis upon ego involvement, participation, group involvement, and, as Professor Peter Drucker would put it, "Freudian paternalism."[26] Actually, many forget that most of this stuff was originally introduced into these programs as a counterbalance to "first sergeantism," "one-star generalism," and other patterns of local tyranny occurring among men with their first taste of power and authority. When a personnel expert

---

[26] See Peter F. Drucker, *The Practice of Management* (New York: Harper & Bros., 1954), chap. xxi.

of our acquaintance wrote the pamphlet for a supervisory training program some years ago which we recall was entitled, "Sock Him in the Ego," he was writing this as an antidote to the more commonly accepted notion at that time of "Kick Him in the Teeth!"

The human relations approach, as the authors have known it, is nothing more than another name for the application of the behavioral sciences to the study and understanding of management and organization and human motivation within the business setting. The group at Harvard which hammered out much of the Western Electric research and most of the interpretation of this research was a team of interdisciplinary social scientists. Elton Mayo, who provided leadership for the project from its inception, was trained in psychiatry; he was a student of Pierre Janet, famous French psychiatrist. W. Lloyd Warner, an anthropologist fresh from a field study of Australian aborigines, provided much of the sociological and anthropological orientation which gave direction to later developments in the Western Electric study.

The entire undertaking was sponsored by the Harvard Business School. It had the enthusiastic support of Dean W. Brett Donham of that institution, who, with his career as a practical businessman as well as that of an educator and head of a major school of business, saw the importance of understanding society and the relation between business and the broader society of which it was a part. The men who were involved in the studies, not only at Western Electric but later in the related "Yankee City" study, were men of diverse educational, social, and geographical backgrounds. Some were trained in engineering and the physical sciences; others, in liberal arts and in the social sciences. There were those from the established New England upper class and those of immigrant parentage. There was even a Wall Street broker. The research was not formally organized to represent various disciplines. There was no attempt to say "we must have represented in this research the viewpoint of the economist, or the sociologist, or the psychologist, or the practical businessman." Instead there were gathered together a group of researchers of varied background but with no formal commitment to the specific concepts of established disciplines.

As a result, the Western Electric research took on an interdisciplinary character practically from its beginning. The men associated with the research have through the years placed great faith in the notion that men of intelligence who are good observers, accurate recorders, and capable of pursuing theoretical and empirical considerations wherever they might lead are likely to be productive in research and new insights.

They have not typically bound themselves within tight disciplinary boxes but have tended to associate themselves with those academic and business activities which permit a wide range of interest no matter what the established disciplinary lines.

It can be seen from the foregoing that the so-called "human relations approach" has no claim as a field at all; it is nothing either more or less than an interdisciplinary social scientific approach to the study of organization and human motivation and behavior within business. Nonetheless, there has been a certain sense of identification among various scholars and researchers in these areas which marks them off as a group. For the most part, this sense of identification has grown out of various academic associations. A kind of cultural diffusion has occurred through the years as various individuals associated either directly or indirectly with the Western Electric research have moved about the country.[27] In addition, the group has developed a sense of identification because it has been highly interdisciplinary in its approach, representing a kind of melding of clinical psychology, psychoanalytic theory, social anthropology, and functional sociology. Finally, there has been a sense of identification because of the concern of the group with the discovery and understanding of our emergent, present society. All of these factors—the personal associations, the interdisciplinary, somewhat clinical approach, and the interest in our emergent, on-going society—have helped to create an image of a "school" of thinking which is often referred to as the "human relations school."

---

[27] W. Lloyd Warner, for example, moved to the University of Chicago in 1935. There he helped establish the Committee on Human Development and the Committee on Human Relations in Industry. The first executive director of the Committee on Human Relations was Burleigh B. Gardner, who worked with Warner at Harvard on the "Yankee City" study, received his Ph.D. in Anthropology at Harvard, and also served in a research capacity in the counseling program at Western Electric prior to his association with the University of Chicago. Gardner moved on to establish Social Research, Inc., which in recent years has become one of the outstanding research firms in the country, specializing not only in organizational studies and executive appraisals but also in motivation research. Others intimately associated with Warner at Harvard include Conrad Arensberg, Solon Kimball, Allison Davis, Eliot Chapple, Paul Lunt, Leo Srole, J. O. Low, and others. William F. Whyte, who also came under Warner's influence at Harvard, followed Gardner as executive director of the Committee on Human Relations in Industry. Whyte, a sociologist, subsequently moved to the New York School of Industrial and Labor Relations at Cornell University. These three men, that is, Warner, Gardner, and Whyte, have been instrumental in the development of an amazing number of people working in the field of human relations—Leonard Sayles, George Strauss, Chris Argyris, James Abeggelen, Norman Martin, Donald Roy, Melville Dalton, David Moore, Margaret Chandler, Edith Lentz, Orvis Collins, to mention only a few who have written widely in the field. Others associated with the Western Electric and "Yankee City" study also served to diffuse the human relations approach, but the major point is established.

Learning Human Relations

As might be inferred from our previous statements, a student should gain more from a course in human relations than a point of view. This is not to say, let us emphasize once again, that humanitarian sentiments and concern for one's fellow man are no longer virtues. But compassion is the mark of any mature, educated, and secure person; it is a refinement of character acquired through experience, education, and personal development; it is evidence of emotional maturity and a liberated mind. Compassion, refinement, emotional maturity, and a liberated mind cannot be gained through a single three-hour course in a university. You cannot begin uninstructed in humanity and emerge one term later a full-blown humanitarian and humanist.

What, then, should you take away from a course in human relations? In order to answer this question, we have to raise two additional questions: first, what is the present stage of development of the behavioral sciences; and, second, what are the professional needs of the student of business administration? It goes without saying that the behavioral sciences are not exact sciences like physics or chemistry. Human behavior cannot be readily predicted from a relatively few general laws or principles. In teaching the behavioral sciences, you cannot begin with elementary propositions and gradually build up a complex system of interdependent propositions which can be manipulated at abstract, mathematical levels. The behavioral sciences are still in an empirical, observational phase. James B. Conant defines science as "an attempt either to lower the degree of empiricism or to extend the range of theory."[28] The practical arts in this view are almost one hundred per cent empirical; physics, on the other hand, is almost one hundred per cent theoretical—theoretical in the sense that predictions can be made by deduction from general laws and theories. It is apparent that the behavioral sciences will need many years of development before they reach a similar theoretical phase. They are still wrestling with problems of observation and the classification of patterns of human behavior.

There are a number of reasons why the behavioral sciences have developed so slowly. In the first place, it is difficult to deal experimentally with human beings or with human interaction. Laboratory experimentation involves a deliberate control over variables; but, with human beings, the laboratory itself introduces a new and important

---

[28] James B. Conant, *Science and Common Sense* (New Haven: Yale University Press, 1951), p. 58.

variable as the Western Electric researchers found out. Furthermore, it is often unethical, even immoral, to experiment with the personal lives of other human beings. More than this, it is difficult to control subjectivity in the observation of the behavior of others. The observer is always part of the situation which he is attempting to observe. His mere presence alters behavior. But, even more important, he himself becomes inextricably involved with the situation, oftentimes perceiving what he unconsciously wants to perceive and projecting many of his own needs and emotions into his research. It takes a high degree of discipline and self-awareness to become a good observer of the behavior of others.

In the second place, human behavior is complex. It is always the product of an evolving, dynamic, current reality and an equally dynamic, changing interpretation of this reality. It involves the past plus the present plus a perceived future. When you observe a man's behavior, you cannot tell at first blush whether he is reacting to past events, present circumstances, future possibilities, or all three. He has a sense of time; he has memories and anticipations. He is capable of integrating a myriad of experiences from within, from without, from close by, from far away.

In the third place, a human being is not totally a creature of his environment. He integrates his past and present experiences and his anticipation of the future; he perceives and interprets events in terms of his needs and sentiments. In other words, behind his actions and reactions are underlying motives which must be understood if his behavior is to be understood. With people, we must always ask the question, why?

Nowhere is the problem of underlying motives better illustrated than in marketing research. One example of early motivation research involved a study of the reactions of housewives in a particular neighborhood to venetian blinds versus lace curtains. One group of housewives clearly liked venetian blinds; another group was partial to lace curtains. When asked their reasons for choosing one or the other, both groups maintained that curtains or blinds, whatever their particular preference, were "easier to keep clean." Logic tells us that venetian blinds and lace curtains cannot both be easier to keep clean. Obviously, the housewives in this case were not revealing their true underlying motives; they were simply saying what housewives were supposed to say about their behavior. Careful study revealed that the two groups of housewives enjoyed quite different ways of life. One group was older, more conservative, somewhat hidebound; the other group was younger, modern, more liberal. The two styles of window covering symbolized their different ways of life. The venetian blinds announced to the whole neighborhood, "Here lives a modern family." The lace curtains declared, "Here is a conservative family."

Because of the difficulties involved in studying human behavior, the problems of interpretation, the dynamic, changing, evolving panorama of human affairs, and the problems of underlying motivation, the behavioral sciences have progressed slowly. However, over the past twenty years, with the great increase in social research, techniques of observation and analysis have been considerably improved in the human sciences. While there is as yet no generally accepted theoretical science of man, there are useful models of human behavior, both psychological and social; there are insightful concepts which cast light on various aspects of human behavior; there are well-developed methods of investigation; there are improved analytic techniques which provide greater objectivity in the analysis of human affairs; and there is finally a wealth of material describing various patterns of human behavior in diverse settings.

In short, the behavioral sciences have progressed far beyond the commonsensical observations and judgments of the layman. The administrator or student who feels that he has acquired through some natural process all of the insights and skills that he needs to understand human behavior and make judgments about others is fooling himself. Indeed, most people are completely unaware of the limitations of their personal experiences and the highly subjective, class-bound, culture-bound nature of their observations and judgments. Yet, because they have had to come to grips with human relations throughout their lives, they develop a confidence in their judgment which they would never feel in the considerably less complex physical sciences.

The Professional Needs of Students of Business Administration

So much then for the present state of the behavioral sciences! What about the professional needs of the student of business administration? What application can the behavioral sciences have to his career in business? We are not going to invoke the old bromides that "business is people" and that "management is the art of getting things done through people." Business is people all right, but it is a lot more than this. Most behavioral scientists would not be expert in running a business; they would not have the necessary knowledge of the complex technical and procedural systems of business no matter how much they might know about people. Running or participating in the running of a business requires a great deal of specific, detailed knowledge. The vision that many have of the business executive, particularly the top business executive, as presiding over the business enterprise and applying broad, unspecific principles of organization and administration while others do the dirty work is a distorted one. By the same token, the business student who feels that he is on his way to becoming a vice-president by avoiding specifics and keeping his mind clear of particulars which might clutter his freedom to dream as he wishes is not really preparing himself for anything.

The problem of professional education in business is not a question of general knowledge versus specific knowledge. Highly specific knowledge is inevitably required. However, the panorama of business and industrial life in America is so detailed, so complex, and so dynamic that no school of business could possibly undertake to teach the technical, cultural, and behavioral aspects of every corner of the business world. There would not be enough professors to keep up with the constantly changing reality of this unfolding universe. Even if it were possible to provide the student with up-to-date, detailed information regarding all the diverse aspects of the business world, the student would be acquiring a great deal of specific knowledge which he would probably not use. As a consequence, while the student of business administration must acquire the scholarly habit of learning and retaining detailed knowledge, he must gain much of his specific knowledge about business practices, structures, and behavioral patterns after he has left the university and entered business itself.

The key to effective professional education in business at the university level is the development within the student of the analytic and observational skills which will permit him to gain a quicker, deeper, and more useful knowledge of various aspects of business once he is in the field. It lies in the ability of the student to understand complex, interdependent, multidimensional situations. It lies also in the ability of the student to translate his knowledge into useful action, that is, in his ability to make useful, ethically sound, and integrated decisions about the complex reality with which he will, as a business executive, be confronted. The student of business administration with these skills may graduate without highly specific knowledge of many of the actual procedures and practices current in our business society. He may not know the "Five Rights of Merchandising" as they are developed within

Sears, Roebuck and Company; he may not know how airlines schedules are set up within United Airlines; he may be completely unaware of the specific accounting practices of Western Electric; but he will be able to learn about any of these, place them in their proper setting, offer ideas, and undertake new developments in any procedural or practice area in the company of his choice.

What are some of the analytic and decision areas in which the student of business administration should develop great skill? As a business executive, he will be primarily concerned with interacting systems of one kind or another. The business executive is a conceiver, builder, integrator, utilizer, adjuster, and maintainer of dynamic, interdependent systems of human and technological interaction. This concept may be difficult to grasp at first, since it attempts to state abstractly the essential activities of the business executive. Putting it in another way, we can say that the business executive is primarily concerned with structure and the events and especially the relationships among events which must occur if the structure is to come into being and continue to exist. The business executive must develop the skills of understanding large and complex systems of technical and human interaction and of linking together and holding together various and diverse activities and events.

The task of the business executive is not unlike that of the engineer, at least insofar as the form of his activities is concerned. The engineer is concerned with the building of complex machines or extended technological processes from unit-acts or events involving motion, forming, cutting, and shaping operations, chemical processes, and so on. Like the business executive, the engineer builds interacting structures of limited purpose and dimensions; he abstracts out of the total universe of actual or possible events only those which are appropriate to his purposes.

However, the work of the engineer and the work of the business executive differ in certain very important respects. The executive is primarily concerned with the building of human structures and the linking together of existing or possible human actions into complex interacting human systems. This difference introduces a great many new and complex elements into the job of the business executive. The job of the engineer is finished once he has perceived and described the interconnectedness among the events necessary for a particular operation or total process. His problem of linking together various and diverse events and actions ends once he has conceived the essential chronology and order of the unit-events which must occur if over-all purposes are to be accomplished. His task, therefore, at least insofar as binding and linking together events are concerned, is essentially logical and involves time and spatial arrangements only. Back in the World War I days when notions of efficiency were rampant in engineering circles, a common practice among engineers planning plant layouts and technological organizations was to draw a straight line and then to attempt to arrange machines, processes, and work flow along this straight line. They could do this because their problems were essentially chronological and geometric.

In the case of the business executive, the problems of linking together various and diverse human events are enormous. People don't stay put like machines and physical events do. They can be arranged logically, but they slip out of these arrangements. They have their own purposes and motives which must be taken into account. Thus, the business executive must not only conceive structures as the engineer does, but he must simultaneously consider how to link together the various human events which must transpire if the total structure is to be workable. He must bring into his considerations not only the actual or possible human activities which are needed to build and maintain a business enterprise but also the inducements and other binding forces which are necessary to insure that the events occur in the order and at the time required.

One other important distinction between the work of the engineer and the work of the business executive! The engineer's problems of structure are essentially linear. He has clearly in mind an end product. His problem of conceptualizing is typically one of developing an orderly set of events which have a beginning and ending no matter how complex or extended. The business executive is dealing with an interacting system which is essentially circular. It has no beginning or ending. The problem of the Ford Motor Company does not end when the car moves off the assembly line under its own power. Nor does it end when the car is turned over to the customer. Nor does it end when quarterly dividends are declared. Nor does it end when a contract is signed with the United Auto Workers. Nor does it end when the year-end financial report is made. In short, there is no one end product of a business enterprise. It does not exist for any single purpose but has multiple purposes which are at once means and ends. Indeed, it can be said that a business enterprise is a complex, self-sustaining system of human interaction which creates products of psychological, social, and economic value which are in turn fed back into the system to sustain and nourish it. As such, it has organismic qualities in that it is a highly interdependent system of differentiated activities which together create an integrated enterprise which exists for the sake of its own survival and growth. Any of the differentiated, individual activities has no meaning separate from the whole enterprise, but, by the same token, the enterprise has no meaning that can be distinguished from the satisfactions of those who participate in it—more specifically from the satisfactions of investors, customers, employees, management, sources of supply, general public, and so on.

A final distinction between the activities of the business executive and the engineer is the extent of personal involvement of each in the phenomena with which each must deal. The executive is part of the human structure and interaction processes which he builds, develops, and maintains. The engineer, of course, can stand back from the physical phenomena which he brings together. He can view these events more or less objectively. The executive constantly deals with subjective and objective phenomena.

Our comparison of the task of the business executive with that of the engineer is not meant to be invidious or an effort to depreciate the work of the engineer. The point is that the engineer's task is hard enough, but the task of the business executive, properly conceived, is even harder. For his problems of conceptualization are multidimensional and circular; the elements with which he works are dynamic and changing; he must concern himself with processes and techniques by which various events can be bound together in intricate, interdependent relationships; and finally he must do all this when he himself is subjectively and personally involved with the structures which he builds, maintains, and develops. We are all aware of the rigorous education required to turn out competent and creative engineers. It would appear that the education of the business executive should be at least as rigorous, if he is to function at a professional rather than at a routine, conventional, highly empirical level of achievement.

With these considerations in mind, then, regarding the present state of the behavioral sciences and the professional needs of students of business administration, we can gain some insight into what the student should get from a study of human relations and the applied behavioral sciences.

Concepts. At the outset, the student of business administration needs an understanding of concepts which will permit him to view and identify events, patterns of behavior, and relationships in complex, interacting systems of human endeavor. Such concepts are essentially "beams of light," as Professor Herbert Blumer once put it, which can be focused on various aspects of human behavior and, as such, improve our powers of observation.

Functional Analytic Skill. Coupled with his conceptual skill, the student of business administration needs to learn to think in a "functional" way. Basically, this means that he must learn to observe the interdependence of events within a system of interaction, how one event has consequences which are functional or dysfunctional to other events. He should begin to comprehend the great and intricate relational networks which bind together business enterprise and how action in one area of these great and intricate systems frequently reverberates and affects activities which seem far removed from the original area of action. He should acquire the prudence which every administrator should have, searching for unintended consequences.

Value-Formation, Conflict, and Agreement. The student of business administration should have some understanding of the process by which men form values, beliefs, attitudes, and ideologies. This is essentially the process of socialization, the way in which a person develops his own identity, notions regarding his relationship with others, and values and images regarding what the world and especially various aspects of the world should look like. The student should learn how values come together, that is, the great areas of agreement in society, and also how values are differentiated. One of the major skills of the business executive is dealing with differentiated values and bringing people of divergent interests and abilities together into interacting systems of relationships.

Models of Business Organization and Business Enterprise. The student of business administration should acquire the ability to design various models of business organization, business enterprise, and administrative action systems. To be effective in this area, he must develop the almost automatic skill of perceiving and evaluating the assumptions which underlie these various models and designs—the underlying assumptions regarding human behavior and human relations. He should also be able to assess the consequences of various administrative and organizational designs in order to take advantage of the strengths of various models and shore up their weaknesses. Indeed, much of the skill of administration lies in buttressing administrative and organizational designs of limited dimensions in order to mitigate inherent weaknesses.

The Role and Functions of the Business Executive. Since the business executive is himself a part of the systems which he seeks to develop and control, he must have an intimate understanding of his own role, the factors which motivate him, the way in which the executive organization operates, patterns of success and failure in the executive role, and finally the program of personal development which the aspirant to high-level executive positions must set for himself if he is to provide effective leadership within one of the most important institutions in our society.

Human Behavior in Diverse Settings. The student of business administration must become acquainted with human behavior in diverse settings. He needs the comparative knowledge typical of the social anthropologist, since truly insightful "clinical" understanding of human behavior can best be achieved through comparative analysis. When the student can begin to see that event "A" is like event "B" and that process "X" is like process "Y" and when he can draw analogic conclusions from these comparisons, he is powerfully equipped to make adequate judgments and projections from his observations of given situations. At present, as we have indicated, there are a number of excellent case research studies of human behavior in the business setting. The student of business administration should be acquainted with them. Moreover, the student can broaden his understanding of human behavior through the extensive reading of novels, biographies, and history. He should keep in mind in all of his studies of human behavior that he is not simply trying to understand behavior within the business setting inasmuch as this narrows his scope. His objective, at least in part, is to seek out diversity, to achieve a cosmopolitan view, to open his mind to a variety of belief systems. He vitally needs a deliberate extension of his horizons because of the provincialism and localism which naturally occur among those who concentrate their attention heavily upon one institution within our society.

These, then, are some of the skills, understandings, and insights which a student of business administration should gain from his study of human relations and applied behavioral science. It is hoped that this text will start him on the road, motivate him to learn more, and bring him new and exciting prospects in his study of business administration.

2. CONCEPTS IN THE
BEHAVIORAL SCIENCES

WE indicated in Chapter 1 that the student of business administration needs an understanding of concepts which will permit him to view and identify events, patterns of behavior, and relationships in complex, interacting systems of human endeavor. In Chapter 2, therefore, we shall review a number of concepts in the behavioral sciences which the authors have found useful in their own studies of organization and administrative behavior in the business and industrial setting. We do not expect the student to grasp immediately the significance of all of the concepts reviewed, for there is a great difference between intellectual learning and real understanding and application in the field. One can understand cultural differences, for example, at an intellectual level, but not truly understand them until confronted with belief systems which are totally different from one's own. Understanding requires the ability to open one's mind to new beliefs and to integrate these into new perceptions about human behavior. These is accordingly a great difference between "mouthing" behavorial concepts and utilizing them in gaining new understandings. The best training in human relations can be obtained in the field under guidance, because it is here that the student can learn to relate concepts to concrete events. The serious student of human behavior, barring the opportunity for organized field research, can make use of his own daily experiences in applying the various concepts of human behavior. More than this, he will find throughout this text many examples and applications which will help him to relate concrete, familiar incidents to abstract concepts. Still further, he can take advantage of the numerous case-research studies as indicated in the bibliography to extend his knowledge of the dynamics of human relations in the field.

We have been using the term *behavioral science* without defining it. Originally, it was simply a catch-all term referring to the noneconomic social sciences, namely, sociology, anthropology, and psychology. It was not initially intended that the term should refer to an integration of these sciences. Nevertheless, the term has been a useful one to those social scientists who have strong interdisciplinary leanings.

Most of the applied social sciences tend to be interdisciplinary since real-life problems do not ordinarily arrange themselves along neat disciplinary lines. As a consequence, the applied social scientists within schools of business, law, medicine, education, and so on, may sometimes refer to themselves as behavioral scientists to indicate their interdisciplinary orientations. However, the student should keep in mind that the term "behavioral science" does not refer to a field which can be clearly distinguished from psychology, sociology, or anthropology. Furthermore, he should be aware that behavioral scientists, no matter how interdisciplinary, will reflect the concepts, methods, and body of knowledge of their original fields. This, of course, is true of the authors of this book—one of whom is a social anthropologist and the other a sociologist. The behavioral concepts which follow, therefore, reflect these prior interests.

SOCIAL BEHAVIOR

Culture

We shall begin with the concept of culture since it underlies much of the research of the anthropologist. Culture, as the anthropologist uses the term, usually refers to the way of life of a people—the manners, customs, values, and accepted modes of behavior to which people living together in a society subscribe. In one sense of the word, culture can be thought of as the memories of a social group—the accumulated wisdom, knowledge, folklore, techniques, tools, language, symbols, and values which are remembered from one generation to the next but modified and adjusted to meet new challenges, crises, and circumstances. The anthropologist's use of the term *culture* refers to something more than the aesthetic life of a people. It refers to all of the beliefs which characterize a society—its scientific beliefs, its magical beliefs, its religious beliefs, its beliefs about authority, organization, and so on.

An individual is born into a society, which then proceeds to educate or indoctrinate him in the values and modes of thinking and behavior which characterize that society. The indoctrination, of course, occurs through the father, mother, schools, play groups, religious institutions, and other agencies common to every society. Such indoctrination is done both consciously and unconsciously; but, however it occurs, the individual learns what behavior, what ends, and what means are appropriate and accepted within his society. He develops a way of life which clearly identifies him with the society into which he was born.

To the individual, his way of life seems natural and right. Moreover, the society or subsociety of which he is a part supports him in his beliefs. As a consequence, he feels that what he does is reasonable, morally justified, and supported by all "right-thinking" people the world over. If he lives in a traditional, isolated society where nearly all of his behavior is specified, he may not even be aware that other ways of life are possible. If he lives in a modern, urban society, he structures the diverse, complex world of beliefs and behavioral patterns of which he is aware into belief-disbelief continua;[1] thus, he becomes aware of gradations of "right thinking," ranging from those who think as he does to those who are clearly "out to lunch," not "with" it, and sometimes downright dangerous.

Cultural differences can best be observed when we compare our own society with that of a foreign country. People are not the same the world over, but it is one thing to understand this at an intellectual level and quite another to gain a deeper awareness. Cultural differences strike us as essentially odd and deviate, very much as the aberrant behavior of the psychotic impresses us as strange. We are likely, therefore, to attribute cultural differences to some failure of comprehension on the part of members of other societies rather than to our own inability to understand them and the way they think. It is not by chance that the word *foreign* is used as a synonym for the word *strange*. It is not by chance either that many of our efforts to change the beliefs of others take the form of trying to reason with them, for we are making the tacit assumption that their inability to think straight results from some unexplained failure of the intellect.

While we can readily understand, at least intellectually, the differences in values and modes of behavior between, let us say, a society of South American Indians and modern American society, we do not as readily comprehend the cultural differences within our own society. Here we are even more prone to attribute differences in behavior to individual aberrations and deviation. Thus, we are quick to believe that those who do not think and behave as we do are intellectually inferior, morally degenerate, or influenced by rabble-rousers. The factory superintendent complains, "What can I do with the kind of workers we have today?" not realizing that his counterpart thirty years ago was saying the same thing. The older generation asks, "What is the next generation

---

[1] See Milton Rokeach, *The Open and Closed Mind* (New York: Basic Books, Inc., 1960).

coming to?" not knowing that the same question was once asked about it.

The cultural patterns developing in a society or a subgroup within that society are not simply a hodgepodge of ideas and ways of doing things. There is an underlying logic to their development which is based upon the past and present efforts of members of the group to solve life's problems. In the accompanying diagram (Figure 2–1), we have attempted to present schematically the way in which internalized beliefs and externalized action interact with one another in the never ending process of the human adjustment. The diagram, viewed dynamically, shows how beliefs, which in a sense are always emerging out of the past, become embodied in the reality of the present. If beliefs do not work in the real world, they are modified; however, they are not usually modified in a drastic, abrupt way but rather integrated with past ideas and beliefs. As a consequence, beliefs change in an orderly, almost dialectical way, giving the impression of a gradual evolution or unfolding. However, in spite of the ideational, dialectical process, there is a definite reality component to cultural beliefs; they represent an integrated effort to deal with life's problems.

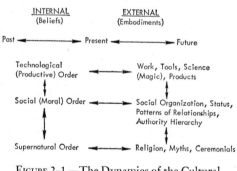

FIGURE 2–1.—The Dynamics of the Cultural
Belief System of a Society

The diagram also shows how the beliefs and activities of a society are related to the three crucial problems of man: wresting a living from nature; providing orderly, reasonably predictable relationships among members of the society; and dealing with the unknown. Thus, every society will have a system of technological beliefs and activities, a system of moral and social beliefs and relationships, and a system of supernatural beliefs and religious and sacred activities in which man attempts to placate or control unknown powers and influences. The beliefs and activities growing up around each of these problem areas also interact and become intricately intertwined in the thinking and behavior of men. Thus, we find that the technological beliefs and activities of a society cannot change without influencing the moral and supernatural beliefs and activities. More than this, if certain beliefs in a society become too rigid and inflexible, little or no change can or will occur without drastic action which changes the entire structure of the society.[1a]

In highly traditional societies, the belief system is unequivocal and prescribed. Everyone knows what behavior is appropriate for any given situation. There are relatively few doubts. However, a dynamic, changing society such as ours is characterized by many beliefs. Appropriate behavior is not clearly prescribed. In many instances, we do not know what to believe. Is the woman's place in the home, or do housewives represent the greatest waste of brain power and ability in modern society? How soon should adolescents be allowed to date? Where are we going and in what can we truly believe? These are questions which deeply concern modern, urban, industrial man. He is forced more and more as an individual to make his own choices or else to organize his beliefs around limited, more narrowly defined segments of the total society.

Value reconciliation is one of the major tasks of a modern, diversified, heterogeneous society. The stability of a society depends upon its ability to organize diverse systems of beliefs. The dynamics of a society depends upon its ability to change—to allow new ideas to come to the surface and to integrate conflicting notions into new syntheses. Value reconciliation and value change are accomplished in a variety of ways in modern society. There are great numbers of organized activities built around the major institutions of our society—that is, the economic, religious, educational, and political institutions—which serve the function of bringing together and integrating diverse values and beliefs. These organized activities take place in a situation where there is an urgent necessity of reaching solutions to current problems, and they bring considerable order out of what could otherwise be a chaos of heterogeneous interests, values, and needs. Dramatic evidence of the reconciliation of divergent beliefs can be found in the conventions of our major political parties where left and right, the most progressive

---

[1a] The influence of W. Lloyd Warner and associates is apparent here. The authors' close association with Professor Warner over the years makes it difficult to identify each point of influence. In this section, and in others, our debt is considerable.

ideas and the most conservative, are brought together under the banner of the elephant or the donkey. In the national conventions, the tactics of value reconciliation are apparent. Power plays an important role. Compromise is the order of the day. There are various kinds of "pay-offs" in terms of patronage and promise of positions in the national administration. Leadership is a very significant element—leadership which rallies divergent interests. Voting procedures, majority rule, also are important. Minority views are given their recognition. All of these tactics are aimed at bringing some kind of unity to the party, so that at the end of the convention, the losers miraculously rally behind the winners.

The reality of the world of values and beliefs is difficult for many individuals to grasp. For this is not an orderly world; it is not a world where the elements fall neatly into place, where there is only one right way. It is by definition an opinionated world, a point-of-view world, a world of subjective motives, group identification, and narrow interpretations. It is a world of conflict, compromise, and political shenanigans. It is a world of horse-trading, bargaining, and transitory agreement. It is a world of influence, persuasion, and manipulation. It is sometimes a world of power and the cynical use of power to gain specific ends. The naive idealist, at his first glimpse of the world of value determination and value reconciliation, is offended by it; it is nothing but politics, persuasion, and power. Instead of grappling with it, he withdraws. "Let me deal with something real," he says, and he turns almost eagerly to procedural and technical matters where there is the neat, step-by-step, reassuring structure of cookbook recipes. What he does not realize is that he will not get very far in our society without coming to grips with the world of values, for value determination is perhaps the most important task of leadership.

What goes on in political conventions goes on in one way or another in all of the major organized activities of our society. In every significant organization in our society, there is a continuous battle of ideas as men seek to structure the emergent reality and gain the ideological foundations and the political support to get things done. This is true not only of our political organizations and labor unions where conflict and the reconciliation of ideas are often highly visible, but also of our business organizations where, to the outside world, things appear to move along in an orderly, sometimes monolithic fashion. The higher one moves in the executive hierarchy in business, or for that matter any other organized activity in our society, the more aware he becomes of the importance of values and ideas. Values, ideas, and beliefs are the basic stuff out of which a modern, dynamic society is forged.

Social Structure

Another behavioral concept which is useful in the analysis of human relations and patterns of behavior is *social structure*. Social structure might be thought of as the anatomy of a society, that is, the various functions and systems of relationships that make up the social body. A society obviously is not just a group of people thrown together in haphazard array. One has only to fly over the country in an airplane to observe some of the obvious aspects of man's design for living—the neat patches and squares of his farms; the geometry of his towns and cities; the connecting rail and highway arteries which proceed purposely and aggressively across plains, across rivers, and over, around, and through mountains; and the corpuscular trucks, automobiles, buses, and trains moving through the arteries from one urban concentration to the next. Even the airplane, flying through uncharted skies, follows man-made, though invisible highways. There is no question that human society is patterned and structured, but from 18,000 feet in the air, we see only the superficial aspects of its design.

Moving closer, we can observe institutions like the family, the school, the factory, the church. We can see neighborhoods which are parts of communities—which in turn are parts of towns and cities—which are parts of states—which are parts of regions—which are parts of nations. We become aware of all kinds of systems of human interaction, all welded together in more or less consistent fashion.

Looking even more closely, we can observe people at work, at play, at home, at school, each performing functions within the larger institutions of our society and related to one another in specific ways. We can see that the members of a society occupy various functional *positions* and that these functional positions are related in various ways to constitute the larger organized activities of a society. The various positions within a society are designated in terms of the technological, educational, political, spiritual, psychological, and social needs of the society. Many of the positions are clearly delineated, such as the occupational positions of the doctor, lawyer, engineer, salesman, professor, and so on. Others are less well recognized but nonetheless important to the survival and satisfaction of a group, such as the "clown" who relieves tension in a group, or the "philosopher" who generalizes about group experiences, or the "taskmaster" who directs the group's attention to the work at hand, or the "humanist" who points up the need to consider human feelings and ideals, or the "devil's advocate" who tests the direction of group interests. Whether formally designated or informally evolved, every society or social group within a society will consist of a set of positions which are related one to another in a structure which is more or less consistent with organizational or group interests.

Social Roles and Expectations

Social structure describes the formal and informal arrangements of people and groups of people as they perform the various functions of a society. It provides the framework around which members of a society organize their lives and activities. Thus, the young man aspires to be a business executive and, although he may bring a great deal to the job, the job in a very real sense existed prior to his entering it. He does not aspire to be a chimney sweep since such a position no longer exists in our society.

Cultural values and patterns of behavior emerge whenever people work together, live together, or otherwise interact over a period of time. Certain ideas will develop with regard to the values and behavior appropriate to the various positions and sets of relationships existing within a society. These notions regarding appropriate values and behavior are called *role expectations*. Role expectations place pressure on the individuals occupying particular positions to adhere to the specified values and behavioral patterns prescribed by society. Thus, the minister is supposed to lead a "model" life, exercising considerable self-discipline over his material and carnal needs. He should not frequent taverns except to "save souls." The high-school teacher is supposed to set an example of mature, disciplined behavior for the students he teaches. The Hollywood actress, however, can bear children out of wedlock without entirely wrecking her box-office appeal.

In a complex, urban society such as ours, the expectations regarding the values and patterns of behavior appropriate to the various positions in the social structure may vary from one segment of society to another. Thus, management may have different expectations with regard to the functional position of the production workers than the production workers themselves. Or one segment of society may have notions regarding the role of the wife in the home different from those of another segment. As a consequence, the individual typically feels under pressure from all sides in the various positions that he occupies. More than this, he is under pressure from his own internalized value system—

his conscience or superego as Freud would call it. The problem of social adjustment is one of resolving these conflicting demands. The resolution and integration of role demands taken together with the emotional needs and internalized values of the individual constitute major aspects of the dynamics of personality development.

Social Character

The term *social character* has come into prominence in recent years. It is a concept which is extremely useful in observing various aspects of human behavior. Perhaps the best way to define the term is to use the words of Professor David Riesman:

> . . . just what do we mean when we speak of "social character"? We do not speak of "personality," which in current social psychology is used to denote the total self, with its inherited temperaments and talents, its biological as well as psychological components, its evanescent as well as more or less permanent attributes. Nor even do we speak of "character" as such, which, in one of its contemporary uses, refers to only a part of personality—that part which is formed not by heredity but by experience . . . : Character, in this sense, is the more or less permanent socially and historically conditioned organization of an individual's drives and satisfaction—the kind of "set" with which he approaches the world and people.
>
> "Social character" is that part of "character" which is shared among significant social groups and which, as most contemporary social scientists define it, is the product of the experience of these groups.[2]

A society tends to develop a more or less dominant character type which is consistent with the society's demands and challenges. Character represents the internalized compulsions which make people "*want* to act in the way they *have* to act as members of the society or of a special class within it."[3] In this definition, it can be seen that social character is in one sense of the word social role internalized; the individual develops a way of behaving, a system of values, and a philosophy of life which fit the various role demands made upon him.

Riesman distinguishes three character types which have emerged under varying circumstances: the tradition directed, the inner directed, and the other directed. The tradition-directed character tends to dominate in a relatively unchanging society. As the name implies, this character type is caught up in the performance of activities which are tradi-

---

[2] David Riesman, *The Lonely Crowd* (Garden City, New York: Doubleday Anchor Books, 1953), p. 18.
[3] Erich Fromm, "Individual and Social Origins of Neurosis," *American Sociological Review*, Vol. IX (1944), p. 380.

tionally prescribed. His life is bound by rituals, ceremonials, and routines, the performance of which leaves him "little energy . . . toward finding new solutions to the age-old problems. . . ."[4] The inner-directed character emerges in periods of great change. In such periods, external conformity and traditionalistic practices are no longer appropriate. The individual is required to adjust to new circumstances. The inner-directed character copes with change by operating on the basis of internalized principles. He moves through life almost deductively or syllogistically, applying his principles to the opportunities and challenges confronting him. He has "incorporated a psychic gyroscope which is set going by his parents and can receive signals later on from other authorities who resemble his parent. He goes through life less independent than he seems, obeying this internal piloting."[5] The other-directed type emerges in periods of abundance when production gives way to marketing and "other *people* are the problem, not the material environment."[6] The major characteristic of the other-directed type is that "their contemporaries are the source of direction for the individual."[7] The other-directed type is more social-minded, paying close attention to the influences of the changing and dynamic world around him. His "control equipment, instead of being like a gyroscope, is like a radar."[8]

Status

Status is used here to mean the hierarchical ordering or ranking of positions in a society. Man somehow is not satisfied simply with recognizing the function of a position; he insists upon ranking it in terms of his notions regarding its relative value to society. The tendency to grade positions in a society is ubiquitous. It occurs in modern society and primitive societies, in executive offices and in the workplace, in monarchies, in the Soviet Union, and in America.

The status system operating in the typical office in modern industry or in the government is readily observable. A single example will suffice to illustrate some of the principal characteristics of a status system. The example chosen is in no way unusual. The accompanying diagram (see Figure 2–2) indicates the layout of a department in a large company.

---

4 Riesman, *op. cit.*, p. 26.
5 *Ibid.*, p. 41.
6 *Ibid.*, p. 34.
7 *Ibid.*, p. 37.
8 *Ibid.*, p. 42.

STREET VIEW

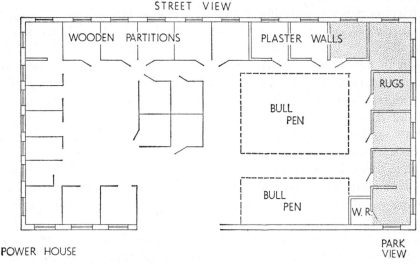

FIGURE 2–2.—The Layout of a Department in a Large Company Showing Status Distinction

Note first the obvious variations in office facilities and location. Some are located along the wall overlooking the park; others along the wall overlooking the street; and still others along the wall overlooking the power plant, which belches forth sooty smoke all day long. Certain of the offices have plaster walls reaching to the ceiling; others have walls of wood reaching to the ceiling; still others have partitions, but they have doors; others have partitions with no doors; still others have partitions with no windows; and finally there are open spaces generally called "bull pens" even though they generally fence off female clerks. Certain of the offices are located in corners; note that the walls in these offices, whether plaster or wooden, all reach to the ceiling. One of the offices has an inside toilet. One also has an inner office for the secretary.

The diagram does not indicate what exists within each office. In several of the offices with plaster walls there are rugs on the floor. Others have linoleum floors; still others have wooden floors. In the office with the inside toilet, the incumbent sits in a large, overstuffed swivel chair, at a very large mahogany table which is perfectly clean except for the papers with which he is working at the moment. Behind him is an equally large desk which is also clean of papers. On the table and desk are a large calendar, an elaborate pen set, framed pictures of a woman, a young man, and an adolescent girl, and four telephones, one of which is an "intercom" which can be used to buzz directly several vice-presidents and key officials of the company. Another of the telephones is a private line which does not go through the company switchboard. There are several overstuffed chairs for visitors and a leather sofa. On the walls are pictures of the chairman of the board, key officers of the company, and former officers. In the office next to this one, connected by a door to the inner office of the secretary, the furniture is of oak, but it is large and massive. The swivel chair is over-stuffed but not the visitors' chairs. You may not know it, but this furniture used to belong to the man in the corner office. On the table and desk are some of the same "trophies" found in the corner office but not all of them. There are three phones instead of four. The calendar is not so elaborate. There are not so many pictures of officers on the wall. As we move through other offices, we find a diminishing number of office appointments; individuality gives way to a monotonous sameness, and every office begins to look alike. We begin to find offices with only one telephone; offices occupied by two people; and finally as we reach the "bull pen," the open spaces so to speak, we find people who sit in rows at desks. But, even here, there are the inevitable differences, since some have phones on their desks and others do not; some have double-pedestal desks, and others, single-pedestal.

Some of the differences described in the foregoing paragraphs can be attributed to differences in the requirements of the job. For example, obviously certain of the executives within the department deal with confidential matters and, therefore, require private offices. Private telephones may be needed for the same reason. But it is difficult for a man to use four telephones at once, and he does not need a massive desk and table to hold the few papers which are on them at any one time. Nor is he more in need of an overstuffed chair than the skinny clerk in the bull pen. Neither can job requirements explain why employees become emotional about the failure of the company to put their names in the telephone book or to give them a private office with a door, or to provide an extra telephone, and so forth.

The status system of an industrial organization reflects both the formal hierarchy of the organization, that is, actual differences in rank in terms of the system of authority, and the informal rankings that can emerge on the basis of seniority, minor differences in skills or job re-quirements, working conditions, pay levels, sex and ethnic differences, and so on. Some idea of the subtle distinctions which can be made among work groups can be gained from the following account reported by Professor William F. Whyte in his study of the restaurant industry:

> The chicken-preparation station was made up of seven workers who did their work at three tables. 1 and her first assistant, 2, who had been with the company for nine years, were stationed at the head of the table that faced the kitchen supervisor's office. The other two tables stood directly behind them. 3 and 4 worked at the table toward the range, while 5, 6, and 7 worked at the table toward the salad station.
>
> 1 and 2 spent most of their time slicing breasts of chicken to be used in the Mammoth sandwich. 1 also cut the wings off the chickens with three deft thrusts of the knife. These two operations were done with great speed, and clearly required more skill than anything else done on the station.
>
> The slices of breast were then piled on a tray and passed over to 3 and 4, 3 standing always on the side toward the range, weighed out the slices and passed them along to 4 opposite her, who wrapped them and stacked them in trays in piles of 100. They were then taken to the service pantries by runners to be used on sandwich stations.
>
> The chicken carcasses, after the sandwich slices had been taken off, were passed along to the other table. There 5, who always stood closest to the head table, picked off the remaining pieces of white meat and passed the carcasses along to 6 and 7, who picked off the dark meat.
>
> There were a number of other operations performed at the chicken-preparation station, but the ones we have described constituted the major part of the work of the station and most clearly outline the status system we found there.
>
> There appeared to be two keys to the nature of this system: skill and type of meat, with type of meat far outweighing skill. While the work of the head table required a fair amount of skill, there seemed no grounds for distinguishing among the other jobs on this basis. Loretta said that the work of weighing and wrapping required speed but no special skill. Certainly picking white meat required no more skill than picking dark.[9]

It is well to keep in mind that status rankings precede the symbols of status, such as location, office facilities, job activities, even pay. In any business organization, management is essentially the arbiter of status rankings, although employees at all levels may play a part in the grading that occurs. Job analyses and classifications reflect status considerations. For example, jobs requiring the use of the mind generally are rated higher than jobs requiring the use of the back. Jobs requiring formal education rate higher than jobs requiring practical, on-the-job knowledge. The status symbols which emerge are typically scarce resources which are distributed in terms of existing rankings. If it is too expensive

---

[9] William F. Whyte, *Human Relations in the Restaurant Industry* (New York: McGraw-Hill Book Co., Inc., 1948), pp. 39–40.

to give everyone a big desk, then such desks are given to those at the top of the status hierarchy. If everyone cannot be allowed to use the company garage to park his car, then this is reserved for "top brass." If everyone cannot sit by the window, then this spot is given to a key employee in the department.

Status symbols also are determined by the objects acquired and activities pursued by those in high positions. If the big boss wears blue suits, others in the organization who aspire to high status will wear blue suits. If the big boss drives a Cadillac, this too may set a style trend among those in lower positions. If the big boss leans toward mahogany in office furniture, a mahogany row might readily develop. In one organization with which the authors are familiar, the big boss liked to collect figurines of elephants, to which animal he himself bore a fascinating resemblance. As might be expected, figurines of elephants were scattered throughout the organization in the offices of lesser functionaries.

Anything might become a symbol of status—common objects like telephones, desk pads, calendars, wastepaper baskets, lamps, colors of walls, cut of suit, and martinis on the rocks made with vodka instead of gin and sherry instead of vermouth and served with anchovy olives in old-fashioned glasses instead of cocktail glasses. Status symbols may be the clubs to which one belongs, the places one goes for a vacation, the music one listens to, the place one lives. There are suburbs, and there are suburbs. One rates higher than another, even though the houses may be approximately the same. These symbols represent ways of fitting people within the total scheme of things.

Social Class

In any society, there are a great number of diverse status systems based on hierarchies of skills, of educational achievement, of artistic achievement, of income, and so on. In many respects, these various status hierarchies are distinct and separate. Thus, a man may, as a professor, rate very high in his field and be accorded many honors in his own profession, but, within his own community, he may not appear so important. Nevertheless, all of these status hierarchies appear to converge in our society into a more or less distinct, over-all status system, which is usually referred to as a social class system.

A number of studies of American communities conducted over the past several decades reveal the major outlines of the class system operating in America. At the top of the heap are the "old families"—the "aristocracy of birth and wealth," as Professor W. Lloyd Warner and associates put it. These are the people whose families have occupied positions of power and prestige in the community for generations. They inherit their status by birth, that is by belonging to the right families. They live in large homes or mansions in the most exclusive neighborhood in town. They go to the church with the highest social rating and belong to the best clubs. They are arbiters in social affairs, and their presence at a dinner party can make it a social success. Altogether, their status and position in the community are assured; although others of lower status may resent them, they nevertheless recognize them as "old aristocracy" or the "social elite." These are the upper upper class.

Below them is another small group of people with whom the old families are willing to mingle but not accept completely. These are persons who have the money and the manners frequently to live like the aristocracy, but they and their families have not been "in society" long enough to rate. They are, in one sense, the "new aristocracy." They represent the lower upper class. Their attitudes are described by Professor Warner *et al.* in *Social Class in America:*

Except that they aspire to old family status, if not for themselves then for their children, these men and their families have a design for living similar to the old family group. But they are consciously aware that their money is too new and too recently earned to have the sacrosanct quality of wealth inherited from a long line of ancestors. They know, as do those above them, that, while a certain amount of wealth is necessary, birth and old family are what really matter.[10]

Clearly separated from the "aristicracy" is another somewhat larger group of "respectable" and relatively well-to-do families composed primarily of executives and professionals.[11] This group constitutes the upper middle class of the communities studied. It is among the wealthiest groups in the community, but it places less importance on family background or lineage. Individual wealth is regarded as far more significant, as is education. These are the "solid, respectable" members of the community who are active in civic affairs and very ofen "front" for the upper classes in community activities.

The three groups just described represent the top crust of the communities studied. Although they include only one sixth, more or less, of the total population, they hold most of the positions of respect, power, and prestige. In some of the newer communities which have

   10 W. Lloyd Warner *et al., Social Class in America* (Chicago: Science Research Associates, Inc., 1949), p. 11.
   11 *Ibid.*, p. 12.

been studied there was no distinction in the upper class between the new families and the old. Because of the relative newness of these communities, it is to be assumed that "old aristocracy" had not yet had an opportunity to develop in these places. Nevertheless, the distinction between a "society" group and the upper middle class was still made.

Below the top crust is the "common-man" level, composed of clerks, small tradesmen, foremen, and a few skilled workers at the top, and then moving down through the "respectable" working class to the very poor and shiftless at the bottom. The top of the common-man level is the lower middle class, which reflects the moral precepts and the way of life of the upper-middle-class group. They think of themselves as being like the upper-middle-class group but lacking the money to live like them. "We poor folks and the other poor folks like us make up the lower middle class. But, it shouldn't be that way," they think. "The people who are up are there mainly because they have money," they insist.[12] Special value is placed upon rigorous adherence to religious and moral precepts, on cleanliness and virtue.

The lower class of all the communities studied was made up of two more or less distinct groups: the "respectable" working class (upper-lower) and the "shiftless no-accounts" (lower-lowers). The "respectable" working class constitutes "poor, but honest" workers—mostly semiskilled and unskilled employees in industry, who work steadily and make a real effort to provide for their families. They are much less likely to ascribe any moral values to the social hierarchy that they observe in their own communities. The people who are "up there" are there simply because they have more money, not because they have worked hard, saved their money, and generally followed the principles of the "Protestant Ethic." Nevertheless, these people have aspirations in the American tradition, if not for themselves, at least for their children. Professor Warner has demonstrated clearly that they have "feelings about doing the right thing, of being respectable and rearing their children to do better than they have."[13]

At the very bottom of the social hierarchy are those persons who are completely economically insecure and lacking in a desire to get ahead. In one sense, they can hardly be regarded as being integrated into the community at all; in fact, they often show a disdain for the

---

[12] Allison Davis, Burleigh Gardner, and Mary Gardner, *Deep South* (Chicago: University of Chicago Press, 1941), p. 68.
[13] *Ibid.*, p. 69. Also see Lee Rainwater, Richard P. Coleman, and Gerald Handel, *Workingman's Wife* (New York: Macfadden-Bartell Corp., 1962).

values of the upper classes and for the government and laws created by these classes.

The class system in America does not appear to be a rigid one. Between one level and the next, there is considerable overlap. Moreover, people move up and down within the social hierarchy. The rich girl marries the chauffeur; the poor boy becomes president; socially aggressive people somehow manage to break into the right clubs. The feudalistic class system which characterized Europe for so many centuries never really caught on in America. Nevertheless, the class structure which has developed is not simply an arbitrary gradation based upon level of income. There are patterns of behavior, values, and relational networks which mark off each class level as a fairly distinctive group. These patterns, while dynamic and constantly changing, must be understood by the business executive, since they have a great deal to do with management-employee relations and with market development. There are genuine value differences which mark off the managerial group from the so-called working class. These differences cannot be entirely attributed to differential attitudes, ideologies, and modes of behavior arising within the business organization itself; they are, in part at least, differences which run deep into the very fabric of our society. The way a boy is brought up, what he aspires to, his way of thinking, his personality, even his apparent intelligence, all are intimately related to his early family life and to familial behavioral patterns which are more or less class-bound. By the same token, the behavior of the customer is not solely related to his level of income but to the way he spends his money—that is, the way he allocates his resources in order to achieve the pattern of life which seems right and appropriate to him.

Social Mobility

As suggested above, a class system may be more or less rigid. Or, to put it another way, it may be either "closed" or "open." If a social class system is entirely closed with no movement from one class group to another, it is a caste system. Ours is, of course, an "open" class system. We refer to the movement which takes place within this system as *social mobility*. Most Americans have during their lifetimes received strong doses of the "rags-to-riches" dream. America, the Land of Opportunity, where the immigrant boy can work his way up from the streets of New York to economic and social success! America, where the Cinderella fantasy is the theme of our "Miss America" contest in

Atlantic City! Much of our escapist literature deals with this theme. It is taught to children in the home, in schools, in churches, in national advertising.

That this sentiment should have an important effect on the thinking of employees and executives alike in business is not surprising. Indeed, there are few situations more frustrating to the average worker in America than the feeling that, no matter what he does, he does not have a chance. By the same token, one of the most powerful motivating forces among business executives is the drive for position, power, and status in the organizational hierarchy. Even those with no particular ambition are influenced by the dominant mobility theme which characterizes America. The most unambitious person still wants to feel that, if he really did put forth the effort, he could rise in the social and economic hierarchy. Many people, though they have no aspirations for themselves, do have hopes for their children. The idea that the children should have more opportunity and success than their fathers is strong in America. It is part of our "third generationalism" which has seen each new generation better integrated into American society than the preceding one.

Our attitudes toward opportunity tie in closely with our feelings about progress. It is accepted in this country that each new generation as a whole should live better than the last. The notion of a constantly rising standard of living is taken for granted by management and worker alike. It is to be expected that each decade should find us with better housing, better refrigeration, better clothes, and more wealth per family at all levels in our society. The idea of a rising standard of living is reflected in the continuous cycle of demands for increased earnings in industry. No one expects our economy ever to stagnate on any one level; the growth curves must be ever upward. The "rising-standard-of-living" idea also emerges in the worker's expectation of constantly improving working conditions. Altogether, then, the notion that each new generation of workers should enjoy better conditions of employment than the preceding one is hardly a radical thought in America.

Social Groups

We must distinguish between two uses of the term *group*. In the first instance, we often use the term *group* to refer to a classification or categorization of people in terms of common characteristics, such as Negroes, ethnic groups, the older workers in a factory, executives, and so on. Because of the common characteristics held by such a group, there may be modal responses to situations that grow out of the particular position that the group occupies in society. Minority groups, for example, may reveal considerable similarity in behavior under certain circumstances because of the common problems which minority groups face in society. This point needs further development, since it is a particularly useful concept to the business administrator. Human behavior and human reaction to challenges, problems, and situations are rarely unique, different, and highly individualistic. Given similar circumstances, the range of possible behaviors open to the average human mind is limited. It is limited by the almost inherent cultural patterns which dominate a society. It is limited by the nature of the human mind. It is limited also by characteristic human emotions. Thus, we can predict that production workers, even though they may have little contact with one another from plant to plant, will express somewhat similar reactions; while they share no communications, they do share similar positions, similar problems, similar demands, and similar expectations.

It is in the analysis of what we might call the *essence* of a social position that a great deal of analogic insight can be gained into the patterns of human behavior from one group to the next. When you can begin to perceive that a given situation is like another about which you have considerable understanding and insight, you can sharpen your observations and, above all, make predictions about human behavior. Analogic reasoning from known social structures and interrelationships to unknown is perhaps the most powerful tool for prediction which the social scientist has. This is why it is exceedingly important for the business administrator to have a thorough and intimate understanding of a variety of human situations. From these, he can move from the known to the unknown; he can begin to make predictions about human behavior.

As indicated previously, there are two uses of the term *group*. We have thus far been discussing group in the classificatory sense. We must, however, distinguish this kind of group from interacting groups or groups in communication. The distinction can perhaps be most readily made by calling attention to the differences between a department in a factory and, let us say, all the older workers. Within the department, employees are usually interacting in face-to-face situations, talking with one another, sharing day-by-day experiences, communicating about these experiences, and formulating attitudes, beliefs, and sentiments. They typically develop a social structure with individuals occupying diverse social positions, playing specific social roles, and organized into some kind of status hierarchy. The older workers, on the other hand, are not ordinarily in communication with one another. They may have a "consciousness of kind" or sense of identity with one another, but they are not likely to come together except in the face of problems inimical to their common interests.

The extent of interaction of a group is, of course, a matter of degree. Interaction may be remote and sparse or immediate and intense. More than this, the kind of interaction which takes place may be *formal* or *informal*. In organized activities in a society, there are formally prescribed relationships which reflect the purposes and objectives of the organization. Such formal prescription permits the development of extended human interaction over wide geographical areas and over long periods of time. Here, one might say the imposed and prescribed system of interrelationships determines the interaction; if the individual follows the system, he will presumably interact effectively with others, at least in terms of the narrow and limited purposes of the system. In formal interaction, only formal and impersonal communications are necessary. Indeed, a characteristic of formal interaction is its impersonality.

A society is characterized not only by formal structures of one kind or another but also by informal structures. Whenever people come together, they tend to create informal structures based upon the needs of the individual and the perceived needs of the group. If the informal structure is a strong one, it will regulate behavior within the group, prescribe roles and statuses, and determine patterns of interaction just like the formal structure does. For example, in many manufacturing plants, indeed in most manufacturing plants, production workers will develop informal systems for regulating production in terms of the group's concept of a "fair day's work," the statuses of various members of the group and what they should earn, and the constant struggle to gain better piece rates from the enemy, namely, the rate setter. Any new employee who comes into such a group will be quickly educated. The informal systems which develop often appear to be antagonistic toward or opposed to management's interests. Since they arise out of individual and group needs, they are frequently compensatory mechanisms designed to protect the individual and the group from the authority and power of management. Without such informal compensation, the imbalance which exists between the power of management and the power of the individual employee would sometimes become insufferable and overwhelming. The informal resistance group would thus appear to be a necessary feature of formal organization, since it permits the individual an opportunity for self-expression, individuality, and personal dignity. He plays the game of revolution and resistance without actually destroying the formal system.

Informal groups, however, do not necessarily have to be inimical to management. Groups form images of themselves which are oftentimes contributory to the organization. Departmental morale is frequently built around a sense of group identification, group purpose, and group superiority. However, it should be observed that high morale is in a sense compensatory, too, so that the same function of compensation is achieved whether or not the informal group which develops is positive or negative from the standpoint of the organization.

Professor Robert Dubin makes a useful distinction between the informal group and informal interaction.[14] Informal interaction refers to any interaction which takes place within a formal organization which is different from the prescribed modes of behavior. As Professor Dubin says: "It would sometimes be exceedingly cumbersome and inefficient to follow . . . prescribed procedures. To overcome that, we 'cut corners' or 'expedite' work or 'see Joe about it' or ignore, in other ways, the requirements of the formal organization."[15] A formal organization or prescribed system of behavior is at best only a general guide to action. Even in the most bureaucratic organizations, action cannot be exactly prescribed in every circumstance. No matter how depersonalized the organization may be, personality enters the picture. Moreover, formal patterns of communication are inevitably tedious and slow. Even more important, most formal organizations are characterized by conflicting policies and pressure from the top for accomplishments which are difficult to achieve. As a consequence of all these considerations, the employee, particularly at the middle-management and supervisory levels, utilizes all kinds of informal techniques to get the job done, to filter information moving up the line, and in general to keep top management off his back.

The Concept of System

The concept of "system" is one which permeates the thinking and research of the social as well as the physical sciences. It also suffuses the thought and action of businessmen who are in one sense designers, builders, maintainers, and developers of technical and human systems.

---

[14] Robert Dubin, *Human Relations in Administration* (New York: Prentice-Hall, Inc., 1951), p. 57.
[15] *Ibid.*, p. 57.

It is important, therefore, that the student of management understand the major characteristics of systems, particularly social systems.

A system can be defined as a combination of discreet units which are related to one another in such a way that the combination results in a whole which is different from the sum of the parts. In other words, the relationship among the units creates a distinctive new object or pattern which has an identity and in a sense a "life" of its own. An example of a system in the physicochemical world is an atom, which is a combination of particles. The particles are bound together in a system of positive and negative electrical charges to create one or another of the chemical elements.

Note here the difference between an aggregation and a system. An aggregation is an assembly of units which can only be described as a sum of its parts like any collection of objects which have no relationship to one another. Consider also the difference between a class of objects or events and a system. A class of objects or events is a categorization based on a perceived similarity as, for example, the zoological classification of animals. A system thus involves a combination of units which are in interaction with one another and are related to one another to form persistent and observable patterns.

Viewed from the standpoint of the over-all system, each part performs a function in the maintenance of the system. It contributes something. However, the significance of the function may vary. In some systems, each part and its function are crucial. A change in any one part results in a change in the total system or pattern. Thus, if you change a particle in an atom, the entire atom changes. In other systems, only certain parts and their functions are crucial. You can remove the wall of a house as long as it is not a supporting wall and the house will remain standing. In other systems, where there is great capacity for adjustment, as in living systems, the system adapts to change and maintains a dynamic equilibrium and balance.

Systems evidence varying degrees of stability and persistence. Some systems may be described as quite unstable with dysfunctional elements contending with functional elements so that the persistence of the system is continually in doubt as, for example, the heavier atoms. Other systems are exceedingly stable and indestructible. Living systems with the capacity for adjustment actively resist destruction. The stability of a system, however, is only a matter of degree, and, in examining any system, the functional elements must be examined against a backdrop of the destructive, dysfunctional elements.

Systems are more or less integrated. Some are tightly bound together, each part dovetailing with every other part like an intricate set of gears. Others are diffuse with more remote, tenuous relationships among the parts like, for example, Western civilization.

Systems become unit parts of other larger systems. In the physical universe, for example, small systems are compounded into bigger and bigger systems in an orderly, hierarchical procession. Thus we start with positive and negative electrical charges, which becomes part of an atomic system, which in turn becomes part of a molecular system, and so on. Ultimately, we end up contemplating the universe and the majestic sweep of its galaxies, too vast perhaps for human comprehension.

It can be seen that a system can exist for its own ends, that is, its own continued existence, and at the same time play a part in still larger systems and thus exist for ends beyond itself. A rose, viewed as a distinct and separate entity, exists out of the needs of a plant species to survive; it exists for itself. In the larger order of things, it exists so that a florist can make money, a lover can woo, or a husband can mitigate feelings of guilt.

Social Systems

The concept of system has been applied to the analysis of society and persistent social groups particularly by the social or functional anthropologists, such as A. R. Radcliffe-Brown.[16] A society, too, can be viewed as a "combination of discrete units (people) which are related to one another in such a way that the combination results in a whole which is different from the sum of the parts." It can be viewed as a structure or pattern of relationships which precedes the individuals who enter into it. The behavior of each individual within the society thus contributes to the persistence and maintenance of the social system and can be said to be *functional* in terms of the persistence of the system. This by no means suggests that the individual performs like an automaton within a society and that individual acts have no personal reference. However, it does indicate that individual acts do have a social significance along with whatever personal value they may have to the individual performing them. The notion of social system, therefore, focuses attention upon the significance of human behavior to the

---

[16] See A. R. Radcliffe-Brown, *A Natural Science of Society* (Glencoe, Illinois: The Free Press, 1957).

persistence and maintenance of the social systems in which human beings participate.

Closely related to the concept of system is the notion of functional analysis, an analytical tool with which every budding executive ought to be familiar. In functional analysis, the question is asked, "How does this event, act, or expressed attitude, interconnect with other events, acts, or attitudes and contribute to the persistence or maintenance of broader systems of relationships?" Or, "What is the significance of this event, act, or expressed attitude in terms of the broader systems of which it is a part?" Questions such as these reveal underlying social motivations which are not ordinarily apparent, just as the psychoanalyst's awareness of the unconscious brings to light hidden motivations and meanings in individual behavior. Thus, in analyzing events within the typical office, we can observe the telephone, on the one hand, as part of a communication system and, on the other hand, as part of a status system. Without such probing of the meaning of objects and events, their total significance cannot be readily understood.

Prof. Robert K. Merton, sociologist, has provided a critical review of the application of the concept of system to the analysis of society.[17] While he takes exception to certain of the assumptions of the social anthropologists, he considerably enhances the utility of the social-analytical approach, particularly in his distinction between *manifest functions* and *latent functions*. Merton defines *manifest functions* as "those objective consequences contributing to the adjustment or adaptation of the system which are intended and recognized by participants in the system."[18] He defines *latent functions* as "those which are neither intended nor recognized."[19] Thus, in the case of the telephone previously mentioned, the manifest function is the contribution the telephone makes to the communication system, while the latent function concerns the status system operating in the typical office. The distinction made here is similar to that made by psychiatrists with reference to conscious and unconscious motives; the conscious motives are those readily expressed by the patient, while the unconscious motives, of course, refer to the unexpressed or underlying meaning of events.

Prof. Merton also distinguishes between functions and dysfunctions

---

[17] See Robert K. Merton, *Social Theory and Social Structure* (Glencoe, Illinois: The Free Press, 1957), chap. i.
[18] *Ibid.*, p. 51.
[19] *Ibid.*, p. 51.

in a social system. In any society, there are both centrifugal and centripetal elements, forces, on the one hand, which tend to integrate and hold the society together and forces, on the other hand, which tend to pull it apart. Social anthropologists, concerned as they are with primitive, preliterate, small, homogeneous societies, have tended to emphasize the so-called functional or contributory elements of the social system, those forces which tend to hold the society together. However, particularly in societies undergoing change, such as the dynamic modern industrial world, there are bound to be dysfunctional elements or even nonfunctional aspects (those which are irrelevant, or extraneous to the system).

The major significance of the systems approach and functional analysis for the study of management is the emphasis which they place on the interconnectedness of events. As we shall see in Chapter 4, a business enterprise is a system of interconnected events of human and technical character, involving persistent and recurrent patterns of behavior and complex reciprocal relationships. The business organization is also a system of interaction, although it is a system in which management can exercise a higher degree of control than in the enterprise aspects of business.

Understanding business administration is primarily a problem of understanding the kinds of interconnectedness and relationships which underlie both the enterprise and organizational systems of business. It is a matter of understanding the properties of the various socioeconomic groups which constitute business, the various occupational groups, the technological systems, the financial systems, and all the other patterns of behavior that are brought together in business enterprise and organization.

INDIVIDUAL BEHAVIOR

Thus far, we have been discussing behavioral concepts which are useful in understanding social phenomena, that is, patterns of human interaction and relationships. In this section, we shall discuss concepts which may be useful in understanding the inner man, so to speak. It is difficult to separate the inner man from his social environment. The line of distinction between what is social and what is individual is fuzzy at best. The social reality exists both within the individual and outside him. Thus, we can speak of Sears, Roebuck and Company with its particular character, policies and values, structure, and technology as a reality in itself. It is a reality which is embodied in buildings, merchandise, green neon signs, blue and yellow trucks, arrangements of work activities, status systems, symbols, and so on. People come and go, but the system precedes and outlasts them. Yet, if individuals did not internalize the values, the patterns of behavior, the customs and usages of Sears, or at least that portion of Sears in which they are engaged, the system would disappear overnight. It is the individual, therefore, which is the ultimate reality—the socialized individual who perceives existing events, integrates and interprets these, and acts in accordance with their meaning to him.

The Socialized Individual and Belief Systems

The individual is born into an existing society and educated over a period of years to the values, beliefs, and expected patterns of behavior of that society. In this process of education, the individual moves through various stages of psychophysiological growth and a progression of social structures. He is in turn an infant, small child, school-age child, adolescent, young adult, mature adult, and older person. Each of these psychophysiological phases of development involves changes within the individual which can have an effect upon his outlook and understandings. In addition, the individual, as he grows up, moves from the intimate relationships of the family, to play groups, to organized educational activities, to work, to the establishment of a new family, to positions of responsibility, and so forth. Thus, each phase of psychophysiological growth involves learning how to function within more and more complex social structures. The individual's thoughtways and beliefs develop in an organic, integrated fashion; that is, each new experience is integrated into the old. The individual mind is always an historical, genetic phenomenon. Basic and primitive generalizations or premises about oneself and one's relationship to others are laid down early in life, so that the individual appears not only to learn with each new experience but also to reveal through his interpretations of new events the inner meaning of his personality. This is not to say that the individual cannot grow, develop, and change; it does mean, however, that his values, beliefs, and modes of behavior are patterned, relatively consistent, and integrated with his past.

The individual rather early in life develops a consciousness of self or an awareness of his inner integration. He gains a sense of uniqueness and individuation. He also typically enjoys a feeling of growth, a kind of unfolding of the self, a sense of progress toward something. If his sense of personal development is blocked, the individual often becomes uneasy, frustrated, and unhappy. Conversely, a sense of personal growth and development is one of the most powerful motivating forces. A man who feels that his experiences are truly contributing to his personal growth is a man with high morale and a sense of purpose.

What is personal growth? Viewed intellectually, personal growth means an ever increasing understanding of the complexities of the surrounding world; it means a deeper, more inclusive integration of events into a meaningful whole. Viewed from the standpoint of inner character and self-discipline, it means control over one's baser motivations. Viewed from a psychoanalytic standpoint, it means the gradual elimination of mean, destructive, infantile thoughts and actions and the sublimation of basic drives into useful, constructive behavior: hate gives way to love, and rigidity gives way to positive action and creativity. Interestingly enough, personal growth means something of the same thing whether it is viewed from a religious, psychoanalytic, intellectual, or humanistic standpoint. There is inevitably the implication of greater control over oneself and one's environment; there is always the implication of self-discipline. Rather typically, every society has its characterological models which serve as standards of individual achievement. Usually, these models have deep religious and humanistic significance. The models, however, can change as social expectations and demands change.

Most people search for some objective referent, some revelation from the outside regarding their inner worth and virtue. It is difficult, if indeed not impossible, for an individual to judge himself distinct and separate from society or at least some segment of society. As a consequence, he tends to seek out objective confirmation of his worthwhileness. A society such as ours provides resources and supports for almost any adjustment which the individual wishes to make. However, there are dominant values and more or less acceptable standards of achievement and success. Dominant values in our society tend to be determined and set by organizations of one kind or another. Thus, the individual in modern, urban society seeks self-realization, personal growth, and successful achievement primarily within organized activities of an industrial, educational, ecclesiastical, political nature. His measure of success and, to a very considerable extent his own personal appraisal of himself, depend upon the position which he occupies within organizations.

Status Seeking and Status Anxiety

It is easy to see how the search for individuality and personal growth often becomes transmuted into a quest for position within a social organization. The individual is motivated to achieve objective confirmation for himself and his activities within the organized setting. He actively seeks status, and the organization provides a ready-made structure through which he can realize his personal ambitions. By the same token, frustrations within the social structure create status anxieties which are the source of many of the compensatory kinds of behavior typical of organized activities. Thus, the man at the bottom attempts to "prove" that he is worthwhile by aggressively asserting in a variety of ways that he is "as good as anyone else!" Much of the compensatory behavior in the international arena can be attributed to status anxiety.

Status seeking smacks of the reprehensible since it appears somehow detached from individually determined values and deep, inner virtues. The status seeker is seen as essentially shoddy, superficial, and shallow. Yet, put another way, trying to get ahead and achieve success is one of the notable American virtues. Much depends on your definition of success and the particular organized activity in which you seek it. No one truly gains status except as he gains recognition and prominence in his particular field of endeavor. He may strive to be the best family physician, the best engineer, the best father, the best punch-press operator, the best administrator. There is nothing wrong with this kind of status seeking. However, if the organized activity in which he seeks status and success is lacking in humanistic virtues and intellectual, aesthetic, and spiritual qualities, then he is truly lost. The story of Adolph Eichmann, as it appeared in *Life*, is a case in point.[20] In Eichmann's words:

But to sum it all up, I must say that I regret nothing. Adolph Hitler may have been wrong all down the line, but one thing is beyond dispute: the man was able to work his way up from lance corporal in the German army to *Führer* of a people of almost 80 million. I never met him personally, but his success alone proves to me that I should subordinate myself to this man. He was somehow so supremely capable that the people recognized him. And so with that justification I recognized him joyfully, and I still defend him.[21]

Individual Beliefs

What an individual believes depends, as we have indicated, upon what he has been taught and upon his own dynamic integration of

[20] *Life*, November 28 and December 8, 1960.
[21] *Life*, December 8, 1960, p. 161.

present reality with his existing beliefs. Included in his present reality are his own experiences and his interpretation of these as well as the interpretations of others whose word he accepts. The latter consideration is extremely important, for what we know of the world mainly depends upon what other tell us. As Professor Milton Rokeach says: ". . . no person can hope to form . . . a picture all by himself. Authorities are the intermediaries to whom we turn for information to supplement what we can obtain for ourselves."[22]

Looking back for a moment to our previous formulation of the dynamics of the development of the culture of a society, we can see that something of the same process occurs in the development of individual beliefs. The individual through his actions embodies his beliefs in the real world. The consequences of his actions are perceived by him, and he directly modifies his beliefs in terms of his perceptions. However, what he perceives depends upon his existing beliefs so that there is a continuous process of integration of present reality with past notions and ideas. The adult individual believes and acts in a complex, multidimensional society, where his involvement with many institutions that affect him tends to be somewhat indirect and remote. His contacts with the larger world are almost entirely through the intermediary of social structure and co-operative systems of one kind or another. In short, his position within various social organizations within the greater society largely determines the nature of his behavior, the personal experiences which he will directly be able to observe, and those authorities upon whom he will depend to guide him in his understanding of events with which he has no direct contact. Likewise, his efforts to embody his own personal beliefs (that is, to take purposeful action) will be constrained and limited by the existing social structure in which he seeks to act. The individual learns that doing something rather typically involves influencing and changing the beliefs of others. In his efforts to realize himself and exercise his own judgment, the individual finds himself seeking a position within the social structure which permits him to act with less outside constraint. Hence, the search for freedom and liberty on the one hand and power and control on the other! This quest ranges all the way from the demands of the unaggressive individual simply to be left

---

[22] Rokeach, *op. cit.*, p. 42. Much of what we have to say in this section is based on the outstanding research of Professor Rokeach. His formulation of the concept of belief-disbelief systems is particularly useful to the sociologist and anthropologist who is concerned with cultural beliefs and values as they are related to social structure and social behavior. Inasmuch as we are not following Professor Rokeach exactly in our presentation, any additions or errors in interpretation rest with us.

alone to the drive of the aggressive individual for a position of influence.

Perception and Beliefs

What a man perceives will be strongly influenced by his existing beliefs. Two people can look at the same event and come up with a totally different interpretation regarding its meaning and significance. The mind continuously filters the flow of information impinging upon it. It is selective; but, not only does it select, it interprets; it almost deliberately reaches out and alters reality like an invisible ectoplasm. Much depends upon whether there is a positive or negative affect toward the phenomenon observed. If you like someone, you not only tend to see only his best qualities, but you interpret positively qualities which others might see in a negative light. For example, a group of employees who like their supervisor may regard him as something of a leader, decisive, willing to take on responsibility, and able to give direction—a man, in brief, who knows where he is going, lending strength and conviction to the activities in which he is engaged. The same supervisor may be regarded by unfriendly subordinates as an autocrat, a man who makes all the decisions himself without reference to the group and its needs. Same qualities, different interpretation! By the same token, one group might view the boss as democratic; another may see him as a "buck-passer" incapable of assuming leadership on his own.

Professor Rokeach has done extensive research on what he calls the "open" and "closed" mind.[23] The "open" mind, as the name implies, is one which is capable of receiving new information and new beliefs and integrating these into its existing belief structure. The "closed" mind serves the dual function, as Professor Rokeach points out, of giving the individual a sense of understanding the world around him but at the same time protecting him from the insecurity of grappling with new beliefs and reorganizing his basic understandings. Thus, deep anxiety and fear seem to lie behind the constriction of the human mind, at least in our kind of society. Psychoanalytic thought is predicated on the findings that anxiety stemming from unresolved early conflicts proves constricting and crippling. The gaining of insight and resolution of conflicts releases energy as it diminishes anxiety. Modification of attitudes occurs, as does learning.

An interesting segment of Dr. Rokeach's research suggests that the so-called "open" mind is better able to conceptualize and make sense

---

[23] See Rokeach, *op. cit.*

out of new events, particularly those events where new and basic beliefs about reality must be assimilated. This shows a significant relationship between the ability to think in an integrative way and the belief structure of the human mind. His studies suggest that the ability to organize reality effectively can best be developed by "opening" the mind, which can best be achieved by the reduction of basic fears and anxieties and, to add still another dimension, through education, that is, exposure to many ideas and beliefs and to diverse knowledge and information. The implications for training for business leadership, or, for that matter, leadership in any of the major institutions in our society, are suggestive and exciting.

Feelings and Emotions

We cannot understand attitudes and behavior without some understanding of the nature of feelings and emotions. Feelings and emotions are not products of the intellect; they are visceral, psychochemical, and not readily subjected to control. Feelings and emotions are prime movers in human behavior; they are the sources of human drives and motivations.[24] Without feelings, employees would never become hostile to management, would never restrict output on the job, and would never develop grievances. Without feelings, also, employees would never have the ambition to succeed, would never invent new ways of doing things, and would never co-operate wholeheartedly in the achievement of the over-all goals of an enterprise. Feelings and emotions can be harnessed for constructive ends but can never be denied successfully. One cannot live by intellect alone but must incorporate his emotional drives and energies into his life's activities.

The formally organized activities of our society, such as business, tend to be highly intellectualized pursuits with an emphasis upon rational procedures, purposeful, objectified activities, and logical, efficient, and measurable performance. In such organized efforts, feelings and emotions are denied or at the minimum relegated to the lowest level of priority. People are not supposed to become angry or frustrated or, for that matter, hilarious or euphoric. They are not supposed to exhibit human frailties. More than this, they are not expected to bring any personal interests into the job situation. Yet, the underlying motivating forces in all human behavior, including business, are feelings and emotions, the ambitions of young executives to achieve, the sense of justice

---

[24] See Sidney J. Levy, *The Meanings of Work* (Chicago: Center for the Study of Liberal Education for Adults, 1963), for a discussion of the varied meanings and motivations involved in work.

in the older executive, the antagonisms between management and union leadership, the desire of the customer for material possessions, the drive for power, money, social prestige—all of the drives and motives that keep the wheels turning in our business society. To deny that feelings and emotions exist is to miss the truly significant factors in business enterprise and organization.

Just as feelings and emotions can be harnessed by the individual and directed toward constructive social ends, so can the feelings and emotions of people in groups be channeled into useful, organized pursuits. This is the essential task of management both in the entrepreneurial and organizational phases of business. The age-old notion, however, that reason is supposed to rule emotions still militates against effective motivational efforts on the part of management. Feelings and emotions are too often regarded as evidence of human incapacity and weakness rather than as a great source of potential energy. A false dichotomy is too often made between "cold, hard reason" on the one hand and "irrational emotionality and sentimentality" on the other. This kind of polar thinking leads some executives to believe that concern for human relations is "Sunday-school stuff." To these men, a soft heart means a soft head. By the same token, motivation research and a concern for the deeper emotional and sentimental aspects of consumer buying are regarded as so much nonsense. The point is that there is no dichotomy between emotions and reason. The two are a necessary part of human behavior and cannot be so neatly separated. Many of the mistakes and missed opportunities in business management are based upon a lack of understanding of nonrational motivation and behavior.

Recognition of Feelings and Emotions

Feelings and emotions are not readily understood either in ourselves or in others. Because of the psychophysical origin of emotions, they are essentially primitive and infantile, particularly when observed in the raw, stripped of all the socially acceptable behavior through which we have learned to express ourselves. Viewed in our most immature state, we lust, we cry for mamma, we yearn for recognition, we express curiosity, we search and fumble. When needs have not been gratified satisfactorily, they press to the fore. Then, in the adult, we find the immature, big baby, attempting to break through the shell of outwardly socialized and mature behavior. Infantile emotionality is unacceptable to the adult. Moreover, crude and primitive expression of desires and drives are unacceptable to a socialized individual. As a consequence, we repress, deny, rationalize, distort. Our needs can thus rise up within us, ill-defined, unstructured, and shapeless, but powerful.

Recognition and identification of feelings in others can also be diffi-cult, although it is easier to observe and identify nonrational behavior in the other man than in ourselves. Difficulties arise, however, for a number of reasons. First of all, each of us tends to be somewhat self-preoccupied. As a result, we fail sensitively to perceive what is hap-pening to others. Even if we are psychologically capable of being observant of the feelings of others, we can be diverted by our interests of the moment and our concentration on other matters. The executive who fails to say, "Good morning," to the employee he meets in the hall may not be by nature an unfriendly or discourteous person but may be simply concerned with other things and fail even to see the employee, let alone observe his concern about being snubbed by one of the big bosses. In this connection, the importance of the other person can make a big difference in the sensitivity of our feelings to others. The plant manager, as he walks through the plant, often is hardly aware of rank-and-file employees. However, if the corporation president walks into his office, he will become keenly sensitive to the behavior of the boss, to even the subtleties and innuendoes of his behavior.

Probably the biggest reason why many of us pay little attention to the feelings of others is that we are simply not trained to be alert to them. In fact, in business, we are often trained to a directly opposite point of view. Business is generally regarded as "practical and logical" and outside the realm of personal feelings and emotions. Being "busi-nesslike" means keeping one's attention entirely on the formal aspects of doing business and not permitting oneself to become diverted by personal needs and the "perversity" of human nature—even in our-selves. This kind of thinking has a long history in the business world; it has become so ingrained in management's thinking that it constitutes one of the most significant barriers to the development of good human relations in the industrial world.

It is possible, in spite of the natural difficulties, to sensitize ourselves not only to our own feelings but to those expressed by others. We must first learn how to ask the question, "What emotions underlie the par-ticular behavioral acts?" At a very elemental level of interpretation, we can identify whether the underlying feelings expressed are essentially positive, essentially negative, ambivalent, or neutral. The employee who says, "This place is run democratically," is expressing positive feelings about the company. The executive who says, "Employees just aren't as good as they were twenty-five years ago," is expressing negative feelings toward the present work force. The student who says, "I like the lectures, but they give us too much work to do," is showing ambivalence. Finally, the meteorologist who says, "It will rain this afternoon," is expressing no feelings at all, at least insofar as we are able to judge from his overt behavior.

Negative, positive, and ambivalent feelings can be expressed in nonverbal ways, too. The executive who greets his visitor by standing up, walking toward him, grasping his hand, waving him to a seat, and offering him a cigar is expressing positive feelings. The purchasing agent who greets the salesman by turning his swivel chair away from the door, busying himself with papers on his desk, and leaving him standing is expressing essentially negative feelings. Common gestures symbolize feelings which are readily recognized. The clenched fist is a symbol of aggression and is essentially negative. The open hand is receptive and positive. The smile is positive; the frown is negative.

Within this admittedly elemental framework, the individual can be viewed as a kind of "hedonistic calculator" registering positive, negative, ambivalent, or neutral reactions to the various symbolic objects, people, and events taking place within his perceived environment. Underlying and stimulating these reactions are the deeper emotional sets of the individual, his conscious and unconscious perception of himself vis-à-vis the other person, both generally and in that specific context; his physiological state, his emotional needs, and his realistic demands or expectations of the situation.

Not all positive, negative, or ambivalent expressions or actions necessarily reflect deep emotional states within the individual. Much of what we do and say is derived from others. Our reactions, for example, to a political candidate may simply reflect the fact that we are either Republicans or Democrats. In other words, we react to things not only in terms of our own emotional needs but in terms of the needs of the various groups with which we are identified. The needs of the group, however, can be used by the emotionally charged individual as a convenient and socially acceptable means of projecting his own needs in a situation. The individual who is essentially hostile toward authority may conveniently identify with the underdogs in a situation and utilize their needs and frustrations as an excuse for expressing his own deep hostilities.

In this connection, it may be useful to describe some of the common ways in which individuals attempt to deny unacceptable feelings or emotions. A common technique is to "rationalize" one's feelings. This involves providing a socially acceptable explanation for these feelings. In one sense of the word, any intellectual argument is basically a rationalization of a position. The opinions and views held by all of us are rationalizations of physical, psychological, and social needs and interests which we have developed throughout our lives and which constitute our personalities. In this sense, we are all living arguments for our own particular ways of life. This is the very essence of individuality, and there is nothing wrong with rationalization supporting our own particular integration of the world and the experiences which we have had in it.

Rationalization can become destructive, however, when it impairs an adequate perception of and response to reality. Thus, a constructive defense can become crippling if neurotically extreme. It should be pointed out that rationalization can occur at the level of the individual or at the level of the organization. Organizations such as businesses or labor unions typically represent relatively narrow, segmental interests in our society. They, too, develop values, beliefs, and ideologies, and they, too, act on the basis of these orientations. Justification is frequently sought for the particular organizational orientations in rationalizations of one form or another. Oftentimes, these rationalizations are consciously sought as, for example, in effective public relations programs. Businesses and other organizations in our society produce their apologists who "explain" the beliefs and actions of their organizations to the general public, that is, the rest of society.

Sometimes, such rationalizations become so much a part of the thinking and ideologies of key members of the organization that they influence objectivity and the ability of executives to cope with reality; or they may even become a cover-up for unpopular and unconstructive organizational behavior. Some executives, union officials, political leaders, and other institutional officials live in a dream world of rationalization, apologia, and ideological cant which seriously limits the ability of their organizations to adjust to reality. On the other hand, the business organization's values and ideologies and the way these are rationalized can become a constructive force in motivating the members of the group to live up to these values. On the whole, the value systems of organizations in our society tend to reflect and support those of the total culture, so that they are in turn a constructive force in maintaining our system.

Another technique for the avoidance of recognition of unacceptable emotions is through "projection." Here the individual attributes his own feelings to others. Projection often occurs with hostile feelings. The individual fails to understand his own underlying hostility and sees the world around him as made up of people who are "out to get him." This type of projection can occur with any of us on occasion. However, when an individual consistently reacts in this way, he develops what is ordinarily called a "persecution complex." In some cases, the "persecuted" individual is passive, absorbing imagined punishments sadly and perhaps even inviting a few "swings" at him by others. These are the "sad sacks" of our world. In other cases, the projection of hostility upon others is used as an excuse for the expression of hostility by the individual. Indeed, sometimes you can find the passive-active quality in the same individual, and you occasionally find that wistful, quiet boy murdering his grandfather, much to everyone's dismay—"He was such a nice boy."

The hostile individual who seeks justification for his own inner anger and resentment in the world around him can cause havoc in an organization, particularly in power-centered organizations like business where aggressive acts against the individual are not uncommon. In such instances, the hostile individual literally invites hostile actions against him so that what started as a delusion ends as a reality. Again, projection can occur both at the psychological and at a social level. An entire nation can project its own hostility upon other nations; indeed, this is one way that wars can start. Management can project its hostilities upon unions; and unions can project antagonisms on management. Since one hostile act tends to breed another, no one knows exactly how chronically hostile situations begin. It is always easiest to project feelings upon those whom we know the least. We can more readily hate people we don't know. There are individuals in our society who perceive the whole world as made up of in-groups (us) and out-groups (others). The out-group is blamed for whatever frustrations and dissatisfactions the in-group may suffer. The fascistic mentality tends to follow this pattern. To the in-group are attributed all the finer values and purposes—ideal and pure characteristics—while the out-group has all the depraved qualities of mankind. The social madness to which this kind of thinking can lead was too starkly illustrated by Nazi Germany.

Then there is the technique of simply reversing one's emotional set. The individual finding that hatred is unacceptable to him unconsciously reduces his anxiety by convincing himself that his feelings are positive. We are familiar with the individual who protests too much; indeed, we are frequently suspicious of the individual who loves everybody and everything. What's he trying to hide? Why the unbalance, since everything is not that good? Hate and love are intricately intertwined. In one sense of the word, we can only hate those things or those individuals whom we are capable of loving. As a consequence, the fact that love can emerge as hate and hate can emerge as love is not as inconceivable as it might sound.

Regression is still another mode of avoiding unacceptable emotions. In this instance, the individual avoids grappling with his emotional conflicts in a mature and adult way by reverting to basically childish behavior. Thus, we find individuals who maintain a childlike dependency upon authority figures. We find individuals who are essentially squalling babies, demanding attention, demanding that the world come to them, beating their little spoons on their high-chairs or stamping their feet in temper tantrums. It is interesting to observe infantile behavior in connection with the serving of food. Any waitress can tell you about customers who literally want their bibs tied on for them and symbolically spit out their food and throw their utensils on the floor if they don't like the dishes served to them. It is an unpleasant experience to sit through a meal with an individual of this type who complains that the soup is too hot or too cold, the steak is not properly cooked, isn't the one that he ordered in the first place, the coffee is too bitter or too weak, and the service generally inadequate.

Any one of us is capable of regressive behavior under pressure. Wartime experiences have demonstrated that strong men can be reduced to squalling infants when under fire. Milder forms of regression are very common in any tensional situation. The employee who is treated as inadequate within an organization may very well become inadequate because of regressive tendencies under pressure. The pariahs of our society, the downgraded minorities, can literally take on social roles within a society which are childlike and dependent. Think of some of the qualities often attributed to the southern Negro for example—his love of song, his childlike dependency upon white folk, his masochistic shuffling gait, his hat in hand, polite approach to his "superiors," and his simple, uncomplicated, irresponsible handling of life's problems. These qualities are not just stereotyped notions; they become real for people who might, under different circumstances, be mature individuals in their own rights.

There is a special form of aberrational or emotional thinking which occurs often enough in business organizations to be noted here. We are referring to what Elton Mayo called "obsessive thinking" or "morbid reverie or preoccupation."[25] A basic characteristic of obsessive thinking is that the individual starts with erroneous assumptions and reasons logically to necessarily illogical conclusions. Another important characteristic of obsessive thinking is its compulsive aspect in which the individual keeps going over a particular line of thought. He thinks, rethinks, and overthinks; he becomes in a sense obsessed and unable to shake free from his morbid preoccupation. All of us have had experience with obsessive thinking, particularly when we have insomnia; in such instances, our minds run over and over various depressing thoughts and events, and we seem unable to control the somewhat morbid trend of our thinking. Roethlisberger and Dickson have described the key characteristic of obsessive thinking as:

. . . a tendency on the part of the complainant to project all his troubles on one object and in such terms to overthink his situation. This morbid overelaboration of an oversimplification in fact was considered . . . to be one of the chief characteristics of what [might be] called "obsessive response." Such situations as these generally revealed an habitual chain of preoccupation which persisted long after the provoking occasion had passed.[26]

Roethlisberger and Dickson go on to point out that obsessive thinking is not always a deep psychopathology but is subject to amelioration and cure through relatively slight improvements in the social conditions of work.[27]

There are several factors which can contribute to obsessive thinking in the workplace. First of all, obsessive thinking is most likely to occur in situations where there is an opportunity for reverie or daydreaming. Repetitive, routine work sets up ideal conditions for reverie, since the worker's mind is only slightly bound to the work at hand and is free to move from one preoccupation to the next. Under these conditions, the employee has an opportunity to dwell all day long on events that transpire in the workplace—the way the boss looked at him, the emergency staff meeting in the front office, the fairness of the incentive rate, the girls who handle the nuts and bolts on the assembly line, and most anything else that comes into view.

Another factor contributing to obsessive thinking is the relatively suspicious, punitive atmosphere which can prevail in certain organizations. Let's face facts: people do get stepped on, are treated unfairly,

---

[25] See Elton Mayo, *The Human Problems of an Industrial Civilization* (New York: Macmillan Co., 1933).

[26] F. J. Roethlisberger and W. J. Dickson, *Management and the Worker* (Cambridge, Mass.: Harvard University Press, 1939), p. 313.

[27] *Ibid.*, p. 314.

are forgotten, and are subjected to aggressive actions in the typical industrial organization. After all, a factory is essentially an authoritarian organization in which the bosses command, expect results, and concentrate on matters of business enterprise and productive efficiency. It is relatively easy for the employee to be mistreated in terms of his personal needs. This is not to say that the average industrial organization is a cruel and threatening environment and that the employee is typically treated in a shoddy manner. But nonetheless things can happen and they do happen often enough to provide much food for morbid preoccupation.

Still another factor which can contribute to obsessive thinking is the relative lack of social interaction occurring in the typical industrial organization. Factories are noisy, busy places; more than this, some supervisors do not permit employees to socialize on the job. As a result, there is no interruption of the daydreaming and reverie that can occur, no opportunity to test one's thinking, and no chance to break up one's morbid trend of thought. Finally, jobs which are frustrating for any reason can cause paranoid projections like those found in obsessive preoccupation. The production worker who finds himself in a low-status, dead-end job can readily project his own personal frustrations and dissatisfactions upon various people and events in the work environment. Employees at higher levels, for example, engineers or even professors, are capable of projections of this type. Indeed, it is possible to find entire organizations which are neurotic, blaming factors in the work environment which have nothing to do with their frustration, seeking scapegoats, and striking out in emotional and irrational ways.

We have spent several pages discussing feelings and emotions, but this is a large and complex subject. It is one also where a little knowledge is a dangerous thing. There is perhaps too much of a tendency for individuals to pick up some of the language of psychology and psychiatry and to apply it without a more fundamental understanding of personality dynamics. It is best, therefore, in analyzing the emotional aspects of behavior to stick to those facts which can be readily observed. Perceiving positive, negative, or ambivalent feelings is not difficult. One may enhance perception through understanding, while leaving diagnostic labels and therapy to the relevant experts.

Interaction Patterns and Personal Behavior

While emotions can be felt by the individual and are very real phenomena, they cannot be observed directly by an outsider. We understand feelings and emotions only by deductions from observable behavior. If an employee who comes into our office is shifty-eyed and awkward in manner, and is hesitant in his speech, we ascribe his behavior to some inner anxiety, but we do not observe that anxiety directly. Actually, all we can directly observe about human behavior is what people say and what people do. We can observe what they say by listening to them talk, by reading what they write, and by analyzing how they respond to questionnaires and tests. We can observe their actions directly with reference to various objects in the environment and various people or indirectly by analyzing the products of their efforts and activities. In the study of personality and small-group behavior, one very useful and interesting approach has been the analysis of patterns of interaction. There are various approaches to the study of interaction. You can study, for example, the positive and negative effect existing within a group and the configuration of interrelationships indicated. This technique is called "sociometry." It was used originally by Dr. J. L. Moreno in the study of group interrelationships in a reformatory.[28] It has since been applied to the study of work groups.

Dr. Eliot D. Chapple has been one of the outstanding proponents of the interaction approach in industry. His concepts and methods have influenced the work of Prof. William F. Whyte, Prof. Conrad F. Arensberg, who collaborated with Chapple in the development of the framework of theory and method utilized in interaction analysis, Dr. F. L. Richardson, Dr. Leonard Sayles, and a number of other behavioral scientists in business administration and industrial research.[29] Professor Arensberg outlines the basic theory and method utilized in interaction analysis, as follows:

[The interaction approach] holds that group life is the outcome of interaction (communication in biology) among animal organisms (including men). These interactions (communications) are events of stimulation and response between one animal and the next, taking place in time, one animal initiating or originating (either in reaction to the environment or acting spontaneously from internal physiological stimulation) the behavior of such an event, the other(s) responding to the prior behavior, thus "terminating" the event with behavior of his own. Such events give one's definition of the social; they are thus a particular class of happenings in the life of living beings, conditioned by the properties of the

---

[28] See J. L. Moreno (ed.), *Sociometry and the Science of Man* (New York: Beacon House, Inc., 1956).

[29] See Conrad M. Arensberg and Eliot D. Chapple, *Measuring Human Relations* (Provincetown, Mass.: The Journal Press, 1940); W. F. Whyte, *Street Corner Society* (Chicago: University of Chicago Press, 1943); F. L. Richardson and C. R. Walker, *Human Relations in an Expanding Company* (New Haven: Yale Labor and Management Center, 1948).

organisms and their environments, but still a demarcatable class of natural phenomena.

These events have properties which yield universal operations for describing and comparing them. The simplest and most general of such operations, thus the basic ones of social science, are:

(1) *Identification and enumeration of the actors;*

(2) *The establishment of the order or sequence of the activity in the event among them* (whether the one or the other[s] acted first, or second, in time);

(3) *Statement of the frequency through the time of observation with which the events, or the orders, took place.*[30]

The "interactionists" focus their attention upon the actual interaction taking place between and among people, the duration of these interactions, who initiates the interaction, the number of interactions taking place among the various actors in the group, and so forth. Interaction at this level of analysis, the interaction that takes place between and among people, can be precisely and tangibly described, that is, it can be counted and measured. The principal tools of the interaction analyst, therefore, are the tally sheet and the stop watch or chronograph.

Communication

All societies, all organizations, and all co-operative efforts depend upon the ability to communicate. In fact, communication can be thought of as the binding force which makes human organization possible.

Human communication is a product of the ability of man to use symbols and to attach meanings to symbols whether they be words, pictures, gestures, or objects. Professor Martin Scheerer described the symbolic behavior of man exceedingly well when he said:

Man no longer deals with things themselves but with self-produced symbols of things and of signs. Man alone has created symbolic systems as a new dimension of behavior. This new reality transcends the visible signals of the physical world. It is an ideational, artificial medium which man has interposed between himself and the things of nature.[31]

Everything in man's environment that he perceives has symbolic value to him. This means that he is literally surrounded by communica-

[30] Conrad M. Arensberg, "Behavior and Organization," in J. H. Rohrer and Muzafer Sherif (eds.), *Social Psychology at the Crossroads* (New York: Harper & Bros., 1951), p. 345.

[31] Martin Scheerer, "Cognitive Theory," in the *Handbook of Social Psychology* (Cambridge, Mass.: Addison-Wesley Publishing Co., Inc., 1954), pp. 125–26.

tions of one kind or another. Anything of symbolic value communicates something to him. This point is being made because of the tendency to limit the concept of communication to verbal or written communications. Actually, other kinds of communications may be equally or even more important. For example, in the workplace, the time clock communicates to the employee his status in the organization either as a man who has the responsibility to "keep his own time" or as a man who has to be checked in or out and is paid for the "time that he puts in." The job communicates his relationship to the organization. If it is a routine, repetitive activity requiring physical effort only, the average employee doesn't need a written communication to know that he has been hired for his strong back, certainly not for his strong mind. The old saying, "actions speak louder than words," is an important adage to remember in the analysis of communication.

At the most elemental level we associate meaning with symbols through direct experience. The baby learns the meaning of the word "chair" by experiencing the sound associated with the object. However, most of our knowledge of verbal meanings comes not through actual experience of this type but through symbolic communications in which the meanings we have already acquired are used to give us new meanings. When we look up a word in the dictionary we are relying on our ability to gather meanings from the words without actual experience with the referent itself. In the same way we can "learn" about new products from pictures, or we "know" the lay of the country from looking at maps.

The most matter-of-fact symbols, *i.e.*, the word "dog," or a picture of a car, while clearly referring to an object, also may evoke a whole set of other feelings and ideas.

These evocative or emotional meanings not only convey ideas but will often create feelings or moods unrelated to the rational intentions of the communication.

To maintain the operation of any business requires a constant flow of symbolic communication ranging through accounting records, work orders, instructions, reports, complaints, and so on. Unless there is common understanding of what is conveyed by these communications, difficulties constantly arise.

In addition, the modern large corporation must rely on communication, largely advertising, to bring it and its products to the minds of the public. In all cases, these advertising communications try to accomplish two things:

1. They seek to teach the public about the product or the company.
2. They seek to develop a favorable set of mind which will increase the probability that the public will buy the product.

SUMMARY

We have attempted in this chapter to provide the student of business administration with some understanding of the behavioral concepts which the authors have found most useful in analyzing human behavior at the social as well as the individual level. There has been no effort to present an exhaustive or systematic listing of all the concepts developed in the behavioral sciences. Furthermore, the student reading this chapter is not expected to have competency in utilizing behavioral concepts in the analysis of business enterprise, administration, and organization. However, he will have made a start, and as he proceeds through the remainder of this book in which the concepts presented in this chapter are applied to various business problems, he should find that his understanding will increase.

Actually, the most important understanding which the student can derive from Chapter 2 is a particular point of view. This point of view involves, first, an awareness that human behavior, variegated and complex though it is, can be understood; second, that we must look below the surface and perceive the underlying meaning of human behavior both at the social and at the individual level; and third, that there are patterns of human behavior, that is, systems of interrelationships, which serve to explain human activities and that these systems can to some extent be controlled by man's efforts in the utilization and shaping of human endeavor for the ultimate betterment of mankind.

PART II

Organizational and
Administrative Theory

3. REVIEW OF
ORGANIZATIONAL AND
ADMINISTRATIVE THEORY

THEORIES of organization are not particularly new, being of special concern to sociologists since Auguste Comte, not to mention the highly developed social and political theories of the ancient Greeks. The United States was founded on theories of organization which grew out of the views of Hobbes, Locke, Rousseau and other political and social philosophers of the seventeenth and eighteenth centuries. Even in the narrower field of business and industrial administration, most developments from Frederick W. Taylor on have involved implicit and occasionally explicit theories of organization. Indeed, it can be said that all men of action in all periods of history have sought out philosophical and rational bases for the political and social organization of human activities.

Interest in Organizational Theory

In recent years, there has been a rather considerable preoccupation with organizational theory.[1] If organizational theory is not particularly new, why then the sudden concern? Some of the interest can be attributed to stylistic trends. Current patterns or modes often serve to influence those who write books, even textbook writers, just as styles shape the female silhouette. Writing theory is *au courant, à la mode;* accordingly, a number try their hand. But more than style trends lie behind much of the recent interest. Any science tends to develop dialectically. There are periods of consolidation and integration which represent the theoretical phases. There are also periods of search, trial and error, and differentiation which represent the empirical phases. The empirical phases in the development of a science are often stimulated by the development of new methods of observation as for example the

---

[1] See Mason Haire (ed.), *Modern Organization Theory* (New York: John Wiley & Sons, Inc., 1959); James G. March and Herbert A. Simon, *Organizations* (New York: John Wiley & Sons, Inc., 1958); William F. Whyte, *Man and Organization* (Homewood, Illinois: Richard D. Irwin, Inc., 1959).

microscope in biology. They may also be stimulated simply by a rejection of orthodox theory (some people get bored with the ritualism and compulsion of existing notions); or they may be stimulated by new theories, facts, and methods entering the field, through cross-fertilization, from other sciences or disciplines. However the empirical phases develop, they usually require a new integration of existing theory or the formulation of new theories. In part, then, the current demand for a new integration of organizational and administrative theory grows out of the need to consolidate a great amount of empirical knowledge which has developed in the behavioral sciences over the past thirty years. But there are other considerations.

One of the requirements of "good" theory, at least in modern science, is that it leads to research—that is, it generates strategic hypotheses or propositions which can be tested. Much of what has passed for organizational and administrative theory does not measure up to this fundamental requirement. Most of the "traditional" management theory which has gained wide acceptance in business circles is at best quasi-scientific. It is "scientific" in the sense that it aims at the development of general propositions, but it is "unscientific" in that its propositions are not well-developed hypotheses which can be tested. The underlying propositions or principles of "traditional" management theory are typically not made explicit; as a consequence, the propositions dangle and fail to provide an adequate basis for further testing and research. We can attribute much of the current concern with "new" organizational and administrative theory to efforts to develop more adequate foundations for present and future research in organizational and administrative behavior and action.

Still another factor which has helped to stimulate the current interest in theory in schools of business and industrial administration throughout the country has been the growth and development of organization and administration as a distinct field of inquiry in business administration. This trend constitutes a new thrust in business education. It alters the present structure of the business school, which has been organized along so-called "functional" lines, that is, around the functions of marketing, accounting, production, finance, and so on. The challenge of this new thrust requires that it be thoroughly justified, that the new directions which it proposes be argued effectively and well. Some of the recent theory accordingly can be attributed to efforts to justify a new approach to business education. Just as in any new field, there is great concern with the appropriate boundaries of the new discipline not only as it impinges upon the provinces of the existing "functional" fields in business, but also as it invades the borders of the more basic social sciences, particularly sociology and psychology. Academicians can become quite basic, philosophical, and theoretical as they skirmish at the disciplinary borders. Powerful theory strengthens and bolsters the new disciplinarians and justifies their efforts. The authors of this text support the view that any efforts which stimulate extended and sustained inquiry into organizational and administrative behavior are to the good. Whether these efforts are made within already established disciplines or within new disciplines is of small consequence.

One other consideration which should be mentioned concerns the relationship between concepts regarding the role of the administrator and organizational theory. The two obviously go together. We cannot talk about what the administrator or business executive does without relating his behavior to a well-integrated set of assumptions regarding the nature of the organization and the administrator's role within it. The modern business school is emphasizing the development of executive skills and abilities. There has been an almost precipitous movement away from so-called vocational training (sometimes called "professional" training to make it more impressive) toward executive development.

This trend is all to the good, but public pronouncements and the simple act of appending the word "management" to traditional courses do not change reality, although they may provide directions for change. If indeed business schools are training executives and administrators, there must be an underlying science or set of interrelated sciences, as in medical schools, which provide a basis for education in administration of a truly professional character. Professional training for administration cannot rely on an unintegrated smorgasbord of "functional" offerings from the several departments or areas of the traditional business school. Hence the current push in many circles for more fundamental theories of business enterprise, organization, and administration and the active quest for more powerful analytic tools such as mathematics, statistics, economic analysis, and clinical and other behavioral techniques.

The Requirements for an Adequate Theory of Organization

Brief attention should be given to the requirements for an adequate theory of organization. Many students, particularly those concerned with "practical" matters draw back from theoretical considerations as inconsequential abstractions. A theory is nothing more than a plausible explanation of an event or set of events. All of us, no matter how practical we may think ourselves to be, engage in theoretical speculation about the world in which we live. Similarly, in business, marketing strategies, organizational models, accounting procedures, and administrative action are all based upon implicit theory and assumptions about the nature of business, the nature of human behavior, and ethical considerations regarding man's relationship to man. It has been aptly said that a good theory is the most practical tool available to the administrator.

It is apparent, however, that theory can range all the way from folklore to science, from myth to objectively based, logico-experimental concepts. What is plausible or acceptable in theoretical speculation depends upon the culture or subculture of which you are a part. What makes sense, what seems reasonable, is a function of your existing beliefs. When the Irish countryman attempts to cure the sickness in his cow or children by heating a plowshare, he is behaving to his neighbors in a perfectly plausible way.[2] When he rationalizes the therapeutic value of heated plowshares, his theory is quite reasonable in his own social circle. He may even reject modern medical theory on the grounds of its implausibility. When Hitler accused "international Jewry" as the source of all evil, all problems, economic and social, his theory seemed plausible to great masses of Germans who were emotionally thwarted by a combination of nationalistic pride, deep sense of persecution, and economic depression. Wild though his speculative rantings in *Mein Kampf* may appear today, they made sense to a large group of Nazis at one point in history. We must distinguish, therefore, between scientific plausibility and other kinds of plausibility.[3]

An adequate scientific theory is one which lends itself to objective testing. Its major propositions must be confirmed or at least confirmable by objective facts. In the social sciences, however, it is difficult to obtain completely objective facts. Accordingly, the social-scientific investigator is distinguished by his quest for objectivity, by his efforts to separate fact finding from interpretation, by his slowness in leaping to conclusions, by his frequent unwillingness to offer easy generalizations from insufficient evidence. The social scientist often appears pe-

---

[2] Conrad Arensberg and Solon Kimball, *Irish Countryman: An Anthropological Study* (New York: Macmillan Co., 1937).

[3] For a whimsical account of cross-cultural differences in beliefs, see Aubrey Menen, *A Prevalence of Witches* (New York: Charles Scribner's Sons, 1948).

destrian and uninspired when compared with those who never allow
facts to interfere with their unhampered quest for conclusions. This is
not to say, of course, that men should not seek ideas, alternative solutions to problems, even without all of the evidence; but this necessary
and continuous search for policy and direction is not strictly scientific
but involves religious, cultural, aesthetic, and ethical considerations as
well as scientifically based evidence.

Without belaboring the point, we can say that a useful, scientific
theory must meet the following conditions:

1. *Objective referents.* The terms used must have objective referents; that is,
   they must refer to events, the existence of which or the degree of existence
   of which can be observed and measured.
2. *Explicitly stated assumptions.* The basic assumptions underlying specific
   propositions must be explicitly stated. Without such underlying "explanations," propositions "dangle."
3. *Supporting evidence for assumptions.* Assumptions must be either self-
   evident, that is, confirmed by everyday experience, or else proven by
   scientific evidence, which may incidentally run counter to everyday common sense.
4. *Rules of logic.* Deductions from basic assumptions must follow the rules
   of logic. Logic is the powerful servant of science.
5. *Testable hypotheses.* The theory as a whole should provide testable
   hypotheses which, if proven or denied, prove or deny the theoretical or
   conceptual framework or at least require its modification. The strategy of
   any science is in the development of critically significant propositions
   which lend themselves to testing in the real world.
6. *Completeness.* The theory as a whole must account for observable events,
   that is, those events which are known. Oftentimes, the test of the adequacy
   of a theory or conceptual framework is its completeness and breadth, its
   ability to account for a wide range of known events.
7. *Predictability.* The theory should permit prediction with a high degree
   of probability.
8. *Simplicity and coherency.* By all odds, that theory is best which meets
   the above conditions in the simplest and most understandable way. There
   is no earthly reason why theory has to be incoherent gobbledygook, re-
   plete with newly invented terms and sentences qualified and requalified in
   the German tradition. While a kind of multisyllabic validity may result,
   obfuscation of this sort is unnecessary and impresses only the uninformed
   who equate a labored search for meaning with depth and profundity.

The preceding eight conditions of truly scientific theory represent
an ideal which is seldom completely met even by the most meticulous.
Moreover, judgment must be used with respect to how far one should
go in the development of a theory. The compulsive theorist, particularly those who tend to be strongly positivistic in their approach, can

unnecessarily belabor the obvious, developing all sorts of overcomplicated circumlocutions to explain relatively simple events. Theory must necessarily spare others and leave something to the reader's own insight and interpretation.

Organizational theory must not only meet the requirements for scientific theory in general but also give us a basis for organizational design and administrative action. Organizational theory concerns systems of action. It must include, therefore, what the sociologist calls *normative* considerations; or, to put it another way, it must be concerned with action models which are appropriate and effective in terms of specific norms. This means that organizational theory and its counterpart, administrative theory, must do more than simply describe organizational and administrative processes; it must point the way toward more appropriate and effective action. Herein, as we shall see, lie many of the problems of developing adequate organizational and administrative theory, since the most normative of the approaches generally are gross oversimplifications and the most accurate from the standpoint of empirical considerations are simply descriptive and provide little or no direction.

Models of Organizational Analysis

In the past, there have been a number of distinctive efforts to analyze the nature of business enterprise and organization and the proper role of management in business. The two major thrusts which can be noted are the "principles of management" approach and the "human relations" approach. By far, the so-called "principles" approach has been the most significant and important. It has for many years served as the basis for the development of the field of management in business schools. It has provided the structure and implicit theory out of which has emerged a "managerial" approach to personnel, marketing, finance, production, and other functional fields. The "human relations" approach has been influential but has generally been relegated to a secondary role in the business school, appearing to some extent in the personnel management course or in a senior course in human relations. It has been a kind of afterthought which has been given consideration and attention after the main show. It has come into the picture mainly as a word of warning to the budding young business executive not to forget the human equation as he deals with the more "important" problems of economic analysis, cost accounting, and money and banking. The impact of human relations has been, interestingly enough, far greater in business circles than in business schools. Our observations regarding the relative significance of the two approaches should not be taken as a complaint but simply as a statement of fact.

The Scientific Management Movement

Inasmuch as the so-called "principles of management" approach owes its beginnings in part to the scientific management movement, a brief description of the basic tenets of scientific management is necessary.[4] The theories of Frederick W. Taylor, founder of the scientific management movement and often regarded as the father of modern management theory, reflect both mechanical and biological analogies. Taylor made his contribution to management thought in the last decade of the nineteenth century and the first decade of the twentieth. This was a period in which there was great interest among physiologists and psychologists in individual differences, especially the measurement of individual differences. It was also a period in the industrial history of the country in which two very significant events were occurring—the rise of mass production and the emergence of professional management. Taylor himself was a compulsive, somewhat rigid, practical engineer who, when faced personally with the problem of supervising production workers, found himself seeking, with considerable ardor and motivation, an objective basis for making demands on employees. Basically, he sought to develop standards which could serve as established, irrefutable measures of job performance. In other words, he attempted to remove job standards from the capricious realm of either management's or the worker's notions of a fair day's work and to place them rather in the realm of objective measurement and scientific evidence. Thus, he focused attention on job design, standardization of tools and machines, machine speeds, measurement of the worker's capabilities, and the "proper" integration of man-machine-tools-job.

While the original motivation for the development of scientific management probably arose out of Taylor's personal needs to develop objective standards of performance in order to overcome restriction of output and soldiering among production employees, he accomplished far more than satisfying his own compulsions. First, he provided a basis for the management of production. With the rise of mass production, new managerial models were needed; Taylor provided a formula for administrative action in the area of production which was powerful

---

[4] For a complete review, see George Filipetti, *Industrial Management in Transition* (rev. ed.; Homewood, Illinois: Richard D. Irwin, Inc., 1953).

enough to persist to the present time. Second, he clearly distinguished a significant, professional role for management. In a period when a new class of professional, nonowner management was developing, any distinctive formulation of a managerial role was likely to gain wide acceptance. Taylor's ideas, while limited primarily to production, served as a major impetus in the search of the new managerial class for a proper and significant role. Taylor provided a rational and objective basis for management which was distinct from ownership.

As indicated previously, the Taylor model of organization and administration reflected both mechanical and biological analogies. First, he believed that the brains should be separated from the brawn in industrial organizations. This view is based upon assumptions of functional differences drawn in part from biological models where the brains (or sometimes spinal ganglia) make all decisions and the muscles perform the functions for which they are best adapted. It is also based on notions of individual differences which in Taylor's time were of special interest to psychologists who were bent on the discovery, description, and measurement of individual differences in traits and abilities both at the physiological level and at the mental level. It is not by chance that industrial psychology and industrial engineering for many years developed along parallel lines, since both are derived from the same general assumptions and related research.

A second assumption of Taylor was that there was one best work system bringing together the man and the job in the most efficient possible way. This assumption was based in part on a deep scientific conviction of a natural order. It also was founded on the notion that man can be viewed as a physiological mechanism like a machine which can be integrated with nonhuman machines. Thus, Taylor viewed man as a machine of given power and capabilities which could be analyzed like a punch press or milling machine and fitted appropriately and efficiently to a particular task just like any other machine. All of the elements of production, that is, men, machines, tools, and materials, were subject, therefore, to the same kind of scientific scrutiny and all of them could be integrated into one "best system." Taylor's emphasis on careful observation of machines, tools, processes, and worker capabilities, his objective analysis of data, his search for the one best method for a given task, and his belief in the ultimate morality of objective, scientific determination of work standards are all important features of his science of management. Taylor's concern with the worker as a physiological machine led to the notion not only of *one best way* to do the job but *one best man* to do it. He believed in the square peg in the square hole. As he put it with his inimitable objectivity, "No one would think of using a fine trotter to draw a grocery wagon nor a Percheron to do the work of a little mule."[5] His interest in how much of a horse-power is a man clearly shows his physiological, mechanistic interests and biases.[6]

A third assumption or set of assumptions in Taylor's theory concerned worker motivation and control. He assumed an underlying rationality in the worker's decision to work as the worker faced limited alternatives of reward and punishment. Even though he thought many workers at the lowest level were patently stupid, he nonetheless placed considerable faith in logical argument and the ability of the worker, even the least intelligent, to understand a rational presentation of the "facts."[7] Indeed, Taylor sincerely believed that the development of scientific standards of work performance should constitute an over-whelming tour de force both among production workers and in management circles as well. Again, we find the emphasis on a rational, objective consideration of the facts. In this respect, Taylor differs little from those who perceive motivation, persuasion, and influence as an essentially intellectual process.

Employee training in Taylor's formulation followed the same rational, intellectualized model. It meant primarily indoctrination in the scientific, right way to do the job. Training thus was an intimate part of Taylor's broader notions regarding control and discipline.

Altogether then, Taylor had a well-developed theory of organization as a system of work and efficiency. He believed that, if you designed the job properly, selected the right man to do it, trained him in the proper methods, and rewarded him for his adherence to the job routines set up for him, you would develop the most efficient organization. While Taylor's assumptions were oversimplified and somewhat harsh, nonetheless they were explicitly stated and open to examination. He truly believed in the notion of individual differences particularly the differences in brains and brawn among men. It was to him a great waste not to apply individual capabilities at all levels to their appropriate tasks.

---

[5] Frederick W. Taylor, "Shop Management" in *Scientific Management* (New York: Harper & Bros., 1947), p. 27.
[6] Frederick W. Taylor, "The Principles of Scientific Management" in *Scientific Management* (New York: Harper & Bros., 1947), p. 55.
[7] Taylor's famous conversation with Schmidt, the "dumb" Dutchman, illustrates his faith in logical argument even though he perceived Schmidt as truly dim-witted. See, "Principles of Scientific Management," *ibid.*, p. 44.

Because of the simplicity of Taylor's thinking, his consistency, the appeals that he made indirectly to natural managerial prejudices regarding individual differences, and the "brainy," professional role assigned to management, his theories have had wide influence. Indeed, the Taylor model has had a very strong influence on personnel management. Examination of a standard textbook in this field will show how personnel management developed out of the Taylor model.[8]

Principles of Management

Taylor evolved certain notions of management from his mechanistic model of the production organization or work system, particularly his ideas of functional foremanship, standardization, and management by the so-called "exception principle." However, it remained to others to scrutinize the role of the manager and to attempt to evolve basic principles of management and organization at a broader level. Early efforts in this respect probably received some impetus from the scientific management movement; at least, they occurred during a period when management was becoming more conscious of its role and was searching for a rational base and a body of guiding principles. The work of Henri Fayol, French industrialist, who wrote in 1916, is an outstanding early effort to develop managerial and organizational principles.[9] Lyndall Urwick has had a good deal of influence not only in Great Britain and overseas but in this country as well. But there are many others who have written in this area; indeed, most of the major texts in management fit the Fayol-Urwick framework although we hasten to point out that the "principles of management" movement does not by any means owe its origins in this country to Europeans.

Urwick's little book *The Elements of Administration*[10] is an excellent presentation of the key ideas in the principles approach. Here he summarizes the work of Fayol, Mary Parker Follet,[11] J. C. Mooney and A. C. Reiley,[12] Taylor, and his own ideas. He develops not only the basic framework of the principles approach but also adds considerable

---

[8] Personnel management is typically concerned with job analysis, selection, training, wage and salary administration, and supervision. The close relationship of these interests to the Taylor model is immediately apparent.

[9] Henri Fayol, *General and Industrial Management*, trans. Constance Storrs (London: Sir Isaac Pitman & Sons, 1949).

[10] L. Urwick, *The Elements of Administration* (New York and London: Harper & Bros., 1944).

[11] Mary Parker Follett, *Dynamic Administration* (New York and London: Harper & Bros., 1941).

[12] J. C. Mooney and A. C. Reiley, *Onward Industry* (New York: Harper & Bros., 1931).

wisdom all within the short space of 132 pages including the index—a major achievement in what has become a wordy field.

The principles approach begins with what amounts to an analysis of the manager's job. In this respect, the principles approach is not unlike Taylor's effort to analyze and describe a job at the production level. There is the same assumption that the job can be broken down into its component unit-acts. Management is rightly conceived by Fayol *et al.* as a cycle of thought and action, since all purposeful, goal-directed human action, whether you are running General Motors or shopping in the local grocery store involves thought and action. The phases of the thought-action cycle can be broken down into substages something perhaps as follows:

1. *Identification of occasion for thought and action.* If we follow through on our shopping analogy, this is the phase when mother opens the refrigerator door and finds the shelves empty.
2. *Searching for alternative solutions to the problem.* Mother develops a number of possibilities, such as, letting the family starve, eating out, or going to the store and buying something.
3. *Narrowing the alternatives and choosing a course of action.* Mother considers the various alternatives and their consequences. She decides that going out shopping would be the best choice; she reaches closure.
4. *Detailing the plan of action.* Mother sets up her shopping list and decides where she should shop. She organizes the step-by-step procedure for accomplishing her goals.
5. *Acting to achieve objectives.* Up to this point, mother has been thinking; now she reaches the action phase. Here she needs motivation, discipline, ability to communicate, ability to command, and in general the ability to interact with the market and various individuals in the market to achieve her purposes.
6. *Control and feedback.* Throughout the entire action phase, she seeks information regarding the effectiveness of her prior plan. When she finally returns home, she thinks about what she has done and resolves to learn from experience and modify her plan accordingly the next time she goes shopping.

Management's job can be variously broken down into something of the same phases. Henri Fayol saw the job of management as that of forecasting, planning, organizing, commanding, and controlling. There are modifications of this basic framework, but in general they all amount to the same thing—namely, an analysis of the thought-action cycle under the assumption of an orderly and rational relationship of means to ends.

March and Simon point up that scientific management as developed by Taylor and others is essentially a technique rather than a set of propositions. As they put it:[13]

> Taylor's principal prescriptions were three: (1) Use time and methods study to find the "one best way" of performing a job. By the best way is meant the way that permits the largest average rate of production over the day. (2) Provide the worker with an incentive to perform the job in the best way and at a good pace. In general do this by giving him a specified bonus over day rates if he meets the standard of production. (3) Use specialized experts (functional foremen) to establish the various conditions surrounding the worker's task—methods, machine speeds, task priorities, etc.
>
> It can be seen from these prescriptions that Taylor's contribution was not a set of general principles for organizing work efficiently, but a set of operating procedures that could be employed in each concrete situation to discover the methods that would be efficient in that situation and secure their application.

While it is true that Taylor emphasizes the process or procedure for analyzing the problems of co-ordinating men and machines, his assumptions about the mechanistic nature of man and about the significance of time and motion dimensions as the measure of productive efficiency make his procedure applicable in the real world.

The description of management's job as a thought-action cycle also places emphasis on process. It, too, like scientific management represents a procedure for analyzing management's task. As such, it provides an obvious but useful chronology in that it urges management to think before it acts and to think after it acts. This is excellent advice to those caught up in action situations, who oftentimes have little occasion to think, so intensely are they involved with the routine performance of day-by-day activities. The importance of feedback, analysis of consequences, and afterthought is worth repeating many times over. But obviously something is missing. What is missing are clear-cut and applicable dimensions such as Taylor's operational definition of efficiency as time and motion economy. This is where the so-called "principles of management" come in, and, as might be expected, they are a key aspect of the principles approach to an understanding of management.

The principles of management, as they have developed in the principles approach, range all the way from truisms like "think before you act" through tautologies like "responsibility should be commensurate with authority and vice versa," through simple descriptions of current modes of organization in business like "there should be unity of command," to observations reflecting the wisdom of experience such as

---

[13] James G. March and Herbert A. Simon, *Organizations* (John Wiley & Sons, Inc., 1958), p. 19.

found among others in Urwick's little book previously mentioned.[14] Premature and inadequate though they might be, the "principles" at least focus on the toughest problem of all, namely, what ought to be the guiding norms and rules of conduct for management as it deals with complex co-operative systems within the dynamic environment of business.

The analysis of the thought-action cycle as found in the principles approach follows the analytic framework of rational psychology, which centers on the conscious, rational aspects of the human mind. It is a highly intellectualized approach dominated by the notion that the human mind has the capabilities of deducing "proper" modes of action from limited assumptions about human behavior. This model of the managerial role fits, as we shall shortly see, a rational, impersonal model of organization. It is also suffused with the idea of the dominance of mind over body, that is, reason over emotions, a dichotomy which has plagued intellectualizers for centuries. From the standpoint of its rational, intellectual orientation, the principles approach shares something in common with theoretical economics. Both represent a rational approach to the determination of norms and directives in human behavior. Both constitute an effort to think through the problem of rational behavior within models of limited dimensions. Both are aimed at rational understanding and control of man's social and economic destiny. However, the principles approach all too frequently stops short of full theoretical development; the underlying assumptions and the logical development of corollary propositions from these are often not made clear and explicit. Under such circumstances, there is real danger that the field of management can become more ritualistic than logical, more folklorish than scientific, more a matter of form and etiquette than the application of basic generalizations and principles to an evolving, changing world.

The principles of management approach, as previously suggested, develops norms or directives for administrative decision and behavior largely based upon an impersonal, instrumental model of organization. The organization is a means or instrument for the accomplishment of specific objectives. In such a model, the goals or objectives of the organization must be explicitly stated and the various activities of the organization geared efficiently to the accomplishment of the prescribed objectives. The ideal organization thus is seen as monolithic, task-ori-

---

[14] For a criticism of typical "principles" of management from a logical point of view, see Herbert A. Simon, *Administrative Behavior* (New York: Macmillan Co., 1949).

ented, impersonal, highly controlled, and disciplined. Any activities outside the "official," prescribed duties are viewed as bad, wasteful, or in need of correction.

In this impersonal, task-oriented, goal-directed, instrumental organizational model, the managerial role emerges as one which is primarily concerned with such aims as the clear definition and communication of directives, unity of command, careful and precisely defined division of labor, commensurate responsibility and authority, narrow span of control, and highly disciplined adherence to established plans. The prescribed role gives the manager a sense of purpose and control. He develops a sense of command not only of himself but of others. Hence the appeal! Proponents of this approach can say to you in so many words: Plan ahead; get the facts before you act; once you have decided on a course of action, stick to it. But all that is being said is, what you need is more discipline, and there isn't one lazy slob among us who can't agree. In any action situation, concentrated, single-minded, disciplined effort is inevitably more effective than willy-nilly, scattered attention. More than this, it gives one a sense of being master of his own destiny—a sense of initiating his own action as opposed to having it initiated upon him by outside pressure and circumstances.

One trouble is that anyone who behaved in this disciplined, duty-bound way all of the time would look something like Al Capp's "Fearless Fosdick."

But a more important difficulty is that exhortations regarding the need for discipline do not necessarily give us a sense of direction or purpose. A definition of ends can never be achieved by a concentration on means. This is precisely where the principles of management approach breaks down. The objectives of management are never clearly defined. This lack of definition results in part from the efforts of adherents to this approach to deal with organization and the managerial role in the abstract. Nothing is said about the nature of business or what it is all about, since the business organization is seldom viewed in its broader socioeconomic setting. Moreover, nothing or very little is said about the social role of the manager as part of the organizational structure itself. Thus, the business organization is viewed neither in terms of the socioeconomic processes of which it is a part nor in terms of its own internal processes. What the manager is actually doing is, therefore, unclear. We know that he is supposed to be using his head and exercising discipline over himself and others but for what purpose escapes us. Strict adherents to the principles approach thus find themselves defining and redefining management's functions and activities within a tight, narrowly defined system, which in itself cannot generate new information, insights, or understandings. The entire undertaking becomes a compulsive exercise where you are always on the verge of "discovering" the secret of effective management but somehow it always escapes you.

Present-day experts in the field of management who have grown out of the traditional principles approach have attempted to break out of the narrowness and rigidity of the approach by accepting the general framework but by carefully avoiding the ascription of universality to the so-called "principles." Thus, the principles are watered down and oftentimes simply indicate areas where management decision is required. This permits greater flexibility in interpretation and allows common sense pragmatism and wisdom to come in, but it does not add to our scientific understanding of the nature of organization and the administrative role.

Bureaucracy and the Approach of Max Weber

It is possible to examine the impersonal, rational model of organization in a scientific, objective way and within a broader framework of analysis. In a sense, the work of Max Weber bridges the principles approach and the human relations approach and thus places both within a more comprehensive setting. Max Weber was a German sociologist, economist, and historian who wrote about the same time as Taylor and early students of management. Weber was a man of great scholarship and among the most eminent educators in Germany prior to and during World War I.[15] He was also a man of stern conscience and ascetic disposition, which perhaps accounts for his interest in ascetic Protestantism, its underlying ethos, and its effect upon modern social organization, particularly rationally organized bureaucracy. Weber believed "the central feature of rational bourgeois capitalism to be the 'rational organization of free labor.' "[16] The characteristics of this type of social organization, which Weber calls "bureaucracy," is described as follows:[17]

Bureaucracy, as Weber uses the word, is a rather complicated phenomenon. It involves an organization devoted to what is from the point of view of the par-

---

[15] See H. H. Gerth and C. Wright Mills, *From Max Weber: Essays in Sociology* (New York: Oxford University Press, 1958), which includes a biography of Weber.

[16] Talcott Parsons, *The Structure of Social Action* (Glencoe, Illinois: Free Press, 1949), p. 506.

[17] *Ibid.*, p. 506.

ticipants an impersonal end. It is based on a type of division of labor which involves specialization in terms of clearly differentiated functions, divided according to technical criteria, with a corresponding division of authority hierarchically organized, heading up to a central organ, and specialized technical qualifications on the part of the participants. The role of each participant is conceived as an "office" where he acts by virtue of the authority vested in the office and not of his personal influence. This involves a clear-cut distinction in many different respects between his acts and relationships in his official and his personal capacity. It in general involves separation of office and home, of business funds and property from personal property, above all of authority in official matters from personal influence outside the official sphere.

A central feature of rational bureaucratic organization is its focus on the impersonal office. Duties, responsibilities, and authority are seen as residing in the office, not the person. Indeed, the individual sees the job as a vocation or profession, an activity devoted to impersonal, social, political, or economic ends, in which personal satisfaction, status, and reward can be gained through the achievement of greater and greater proficiency. Thus, the bureaucrat sees the job as a career to which he devotes a great portion of his attention and energy. His career depends upon the judgment of higher authority, which in turn is based upon various considerations not the least of which are technical and demonstrated competence in the job.

When the impersonal, task-oriented values of bureaucracy are generally accepted, it becomes possible to plan the organization, divide up the labor so to speak, and allocate duties, responsibilities, and authority prior to staffing. In other words, the organization can be designed around impersonal, objective ends without reference to the individuals who will occupy the various positions thus created. Weber points up indirectly the powerful influence of formal organizational structure upon human behavior and activities in our kind of occupationally oriented society. Note, however, that this kind of impersonal organization would not be effective, and this is a central preoccupation of Weber, if our values were different.

We cannot fully appreciate the significance of the rational, impersonal, bureaucratic organization characteristics of Western industrial society until we compare it with organizations based on different themes and ethics. A recent study by Dr. Frank X. Hodgson of the modifications of a typical Western, bureaucratic organization in Iran is an excellent case in point.[18] The structure of most American organizations tends

---

[18] Francis X. Hodgson, "A Cross-Cultural Study of Management" (Ph.D. dissertation, Michigan State University, 1961).

to be bureaucratic, that is, organized around functions, authority, and impersonal relations. This is not to say that personal, nonfunctional elements do not enter into the picture. They do; but the basic, intended framework is largely bureaucratic.

Quite a different situation prevails in Iran, according to Dr. Hodgson. Here the basic framework of organization follows the status, kinship, tribal structure of the broader society. One interesting result is the lack of career orientation among Iranians, who tend to conceive of success as "status in the bazaar" rather than occupational status. This is difficult for Americans, particularly middle-class Americans to understand, for they are strongly oriented toward careers, and conceive of success as related to occupational achievement.

It can be readily seen that the rational, impersonal, instrumental, bureaucratic type of social organization is the basic model perceived by the adherents to the principles of management approach. While Weber agreed that this type of organization was by far the most efficient, he nonetheless placed his views within a broad context in which other modes of social organization were clearly recognized. In other words, he did not seek universal principles in the bureaucratic type of organization, for he clearly saw that its existence and successful functioning depended upon existing human values.

Inasmuch as Weber perceived rational bureaucracy as the central feature of bourgeois capitalism, he plucked this out for special analysis and emphasis. As a result, he tended to overemphasize the rational, impersonal characteristics of this type of organization. However, the functioning of the modern business organization is far more complicated than this and contains many unintended, informal aspects which are crucial to its survival and growth.

The Human Relations Approach

The principles of management approach begins with the manager and, through a priori reasoning, analysis of experience, and tacit assumptions about epistemology, human nature, and the nature of cooperative systems, attempts to develop a reasonably consistent set of guiding principles or norms which serve as directives to management in the performance of its recurrent functions. The human relations approach rather typically has begun with the employee or groups of employees and has viewed their manner of behavior and adjustment within the already existing organization. Because of this focus of attention on the underdog, so to speak, the human relations approach in the past has made its greatest contribution in the areas of employee motivation and adjustment. Whenever the human relations expert has attempted to deal with problems of management as such, he has tended to view the manager primarily as a co-ordinator, leader, change-agent, and "clinician." He has been inclined, therefore, to overemphasize management's problems of co-ordination and employee morale occurring as a consequence of disequilibrium in the organization, usually created by change of one kind or another. The manager's business or enterprise role has been neglected and, as a result, the human relations interpretation of the managerial function has sounded unreal to those who perceive management's role from a strictly business standpoint. Actually the same criticism can be leveled at scientific management and the principles approach since these, too, fail to give attention to management's enterprise functions and concentrate on the production and bureaucratic aspects of organization. However, with human relations, there is a strong tendency to view co-ordination and internal equilibrium as an end in itself, almost as though management's role was the essentially clinical one of maintaining individual and group satisfaction and, above all, peace and quiet. Human relations in this narrow form has been criticized both by those who take a hardheaded business view of management and by labor leaders—the first on the grounds that human relations directs management's attention away from the significant, tough, entrepreneurial problems of business and the second on the grounds that management has no right to be messing around with human adjustment problems.

The Social System of the Modern Factory

While it is the point of view of this text that the behavioral sciences have a more important role in business administration than employee relations as such, the student should have a good grasp of the human relations approach as it developed in the years after the publication of *Management and the Worker.* Many of the concepts implied or explicitly developed in the early studies are useful in the analysis of the broader aspects of the management function and of business administration in general.

It is important, first, to perceive the significant difference between the normative approach of scientific management and principles of management and the empirical approach of human relations. The first two are concerned with the essential problem of how the organization *should* be set up and what management's role *should* be. The emphasis, therefore, is on prescriptions for action. The human relations approach has been primarily research-oriented and concerned with how organizations actually do function; there has been considerably less emphasis on what management should do. Too often, management has been left floundering with lots of information and data about its employee morale, while the "human relations" expert walks off shaking his head. The particular approach characterizing the human relations study in its quest for an understanding of the dynamics of organization has been to view the organization as a "social system," that is, to see the meaning of organizational situations and events in terms of their meaning to employees playing various social roles within a formal and informal social structure. This approach has been a powerful one, inasmuch as it reveals many new and sometimes hidden influences affecting employee motivation, behavior, and adjustment. It provides a deeper understanding of the dynamics of organization and gives management more realistic information and a considerably more adequate basis for evaluating employee behavior and planning both the structure of the organization and appropriate administrative action.

There is nothing very complicated about viewing an organization as a social system, although understanding its significance and meaning to employees at various levels and in various functional activities requires considerable personal and field experience. This is why education in the human relations approach has typically followed the pattern of getting the student as quickly as possible into the field. Indeed, it is still true that understanding of human behavior can best come from deep, empathetic contact with people in various situations and circumstances. In the "Yankee City" study previously mentioned, the field researchers were carefully trained in the then current methods of the field anthropologist. However, it was not a matter of training first and research later. As each member joined the project, he was expected to get into the community and start collecting data immediately. His training then went along with actual doing; it was on-the-job training in a very real sense. As a field anthropologist, he had to learn a number of things:

1. He had to learn to be a good observer. If he attended a meeting, for example, he had to be able to report how many attended, who attended, particularly in terms of sex, age, occupation, and other major structural features of our society, how they arrived and found their places, what seating arrangements occurred, and what happened at the meeting from beginning to end.

2. He had to learn to be a good interviewer, how to establish rapport, how to get people to discuss in depth the latent or nonpublic meaning of events, and to probe into the underlying sentiments which guide human behavior and determine reactions.
3. He had to learn the importance of detail, meticulous detail, even if he was dealing with the commonplace. He had to dispense with high-flown theories and to separate observations from analysis.
4. Finally, he had to learn to be a good reporter, carefully recording for future analysis the observations which he had made. This of course required the development of his memory for details, structure, and events.

In observing the modern business organization, the human relations researcher first noted its obvious structural features. The organizational structure was broken into its "formal" and "informal" patterns of positions, roles, and relationships. The "formal" patterns concerned the anatomical features of organization growing out of its technological arrangements and its hierarchy of authority and communication. Thus, in the first edition of *Human Relations in Industry*,[19] Burleigh B. Gardner states:

A factory is a co-ordinated system of activities directed to the production of goods. It is like a machine of which the component parts are both objects and people, in which each part operates in a very definite and circumscribed way, but in which all parts combine to perform the functions for which the machine was built. It is like the physical structure of a living organism, in which the objects and people may be seen as the cells variously grouped to form different parts, with each having characteristic functions and activities. The composite of all the cells forms the total organism and their combined activities make it a living whole. In such a system each individual fits into a definite place within the total pattern. He has his job and his duties; he has his physical location; he is brought into contact with certain other people and objects; he has his circumscribed round of activities. In such a system, too, the individual is important only in terms of his activities and the way he fits into the activities of others. To put it another way, the whole forms a system of relationships in which each individual fills one position and must function according to the needs of that position.

The gross anatomy of the social structure of a factory forms a rough pyramid with the workers forming a broad base level and the president or plant manager at the top. In between there are a number of layers which make up the supervisory hierarchy and which form a basic status system, with those at each particular level having the same rank in the structure. This structure is linked together from top to bottom by a series of superior-subordinate or man-boss relations. These linkages running from top to bottom form the lines of authority by which the man at the top directs and controls the entire organization.

---

[19] Burleigh B. Gardner, *Human Relations in Industry* (Homewood, Illinois: Richard D. Irwin, Inc., 1945), p. 4.

Besides the supervisory hierarchy and the lines of authority, there are vertical groupings or lines of cleavage which split the organization into units. These are best shown in the typical organization chart on which the various segments are represented with titles which indicate the differences in function of such units as engineering, manufacturing, and accounting. On such a chart, which is in effect a map of certain aspects of the social structure, we do not see the individuals but only the positions which they occupy and the way their positions fit into the various lines of authority and into the supervisory hierarchy.

Up to this point, Gardner has been describing the gross, formal structure or anatomy of the business organization with some suggestion that it is an interacting system. But he is talking primarily at this point of the "bones"; he begins to get to the "meat" of the human relations approach when he says:

A person's position in this structure determines to a large extent his behavior and his relationships with others and even the way he thinks about his job and the organization. Thus the engineer acts and thinks differently from the accountant, the foreman is different from the worker, and the office worker is different from the shopworker.

The individual employee is seen as adapting his personal interests and behavior to the demands of the functional roles (or jobs, if you please) within the formal structure of the organization. But the point is that he does not make an impersonal adaptation but becomes subjectively involved. In fact, it becomes apparent that the organization could not function without his personal involvement. If a man did not personally identify with his occupation and career, the motivation, devotion to duty, and specialization necessary for the successful functioning of the bureaucratic organization would be lacking.

There are two key considerations most frequently of concern to the human relations expert. One is occupational identification, the tendency of employees to become personally involved with the particular tasks which they are called upon to perform; the other is status, that is, a sense of hierarchical position within the organization. Both of these tendencies represent an adaptation to the existing formal, bureaucratic structure of the organization. But, once established, they become in a sense a new structure superimposed upon the bureaucratic structure; and they either facilitate the functioning of the organization or, as is frequently the case, they appear to impede and hamper its operation. Thus, in any organization, we find a formal, bureaucratic organization which oftentimes merely represents a paper organization describing how the organization presumably functions; but in addition we find a somewhat less public social organization in which employees at various status levels within the structure and identified variously with diverse interests and objectives are interacting, adapting, and adjusting their behavior and attitudes. Indeed, to many behavioral scientists who actually observe real-life behavior in the business organization, the social system appears to be the reality and formal, bureaucratic structure merely a starting point for further analysis.

Status behavior and status symbols are obvious indicators of the social system operating in the typical bureaucratic, hierarchical organization. In the first edition of *Human Relations in Industry*, Gardner gave considerable attention to the hierarchical and status structure and employee behavior within it. This approach represents a particularly useful starting point for the student of human relations. By examining the status system of an organization, he can begin to get the feel of the purely social, human aspects of organization. He begins to see how the commonplace in human desires, interests, and emotions affect behavior in the most formal settings.

A major analytic difficulty in the earliest approaches to the study of human relations in the workplace was that observations were confined primarily to the lowest levels of the organization. Thus, the formal organization was more or less accepted as the inevitable backdrop against which the human relations drama was taking place. This limitation was not due to any particular narrowness in viewpoint but resulted rather from the interest in employee relations and management-labor relations during and around World War II. Subsequent developments in the human relations field has seen an increasing interest in the executive role, the nature of business organization, and the broader socioeconomic setting.

Recent Organization Theory

Recent organization theory focuses more directly on the nature of the organization, the functions of the executive, particularly in the area of decision making, and employee needs, with special emphasis upon character formation and mental health. Much of what is being done represents a refinement of previously existing approaches. For example, the recent works of William F. Whyte, E. Wight Bakke, Douglas McGregor, George Homans, F. W. Richardson, Chris Argyris, Eliot Chapple, Leonard Sayles, and others, all are representative of a new sophistication in what began as the human relations approach. In addition, several new breeds have entered the field, starting for the most part from the highly systematic work of Chester Barnard and Herbert

A. Simon and also emerging out of the field of cybernetics, the research of the Cowles Commission at Yale University, the development and application of game theory as a mathematical model for examining problems of strategy, operations research, and other sources. These approaches represent a new effort to understand the rational aspects of organization and decision making. They are concerned with various models of organization of limited dimensions and a rational analysis of "optimum" decisions within an established framework of assumptions. In this respect, the treatment tends to be mathematical and logico-deductive.

However, the Carnegie School,[20] which has been extremely creative and insightful, has been attempting to bring together the systematic, theoretical thinking of the economist with the empirical knowledge of the behavioral scientist. This melding is accomplished by examining problems of rational decision where the decision-maker is limited both in knowledge about, and his ability to solve, problems and where emotional, subjective considerations are accepted as part of the general analytic problem. It is obvious to the authors of this text that there will be a gradual integration and fusion of the various social science fields. But, at the moment, universal men like Aristotle and Leonardo da Vinci are needed.

The Rational and Natural-System Models of Organization

It can be seen from the foregoing that two basic themes have run through the analysis of organization. An examination of these two basic themes will serve as a fitting summary and end to this chapter. Alvin Gouldner in his article "Organizational Analysis,"[21] calls attention to the so-called "rational" model of organization and the "natural-system" model. In the rational model, organization is viewed as a means to an end; it is, as Professor Gouldner points out, an "instrument" for the accomplishment of goals. However, the instrumental nature of the rational organizational model does not quite define its essential characteristic. There is a more basic underlying assumption that the activities of an organization can be structured and co-ordinated to accomplish the over-all goals of the organization in the most direct and efficient way. It is further assumed that the most efficient structuring and

---

[20] The Graduate School of Industrial Administration, Carnegie Institute of Technology.

[21] Robert K. Merton et al. (eds.), Sociology Today (New York: Basic Books, Inc., 1959), p. 400.

co-ordination of the diverse activities of the organization are fundamentally logical, that is, subject to reason and to neat syllogistic analysis.

Thus, in the rational model of organizational analysis, we start off with a precise definition of the goals of the organization and everything else seems to fall neatly into place as we translate goals into major functions and major functions into specific work tasks. The major concern of organizational analysts who subscribe to the rational model is the search for the most efficient possible arrangement of activities in terms of the achievement of specific, prescribed goals. The search may be based on a priori reasoning, that is, on arrangements which somehow *seem* logical, or it may be founded on careful observation and complex mathematical and statistical analyses. But, however it is done, the search is based on the assumption that there is an underlying logic and that it can be discovered, described, and taught.

There is nothing wrong with the application of reason to the analysis of human affairs. However, it is well to keep in mind that the logic of any analysis is limited to the particular dimensions which are being considered. There is a logic of cost and efficiency which can be fruitfully applied in the analysis of business organization. But in addition there are other logics; there is, for example, a logic of human motivation which does not follow the cost and efficiency model; there is a logic of creativity which seldom parallels the efficiency model; there is a logic of status and mobility which makes perfectly good sense but is seldom considered by "efficiency" experts. Human behavior, when it is not entirely impulsive, is based upon logical reasoning of lesser or greater intensity, but it is often a logic of compromise, a logic of power, a logic of personal reward and satisfaction, a logic of double talk, but nonetheless a logic which is perfectly plausible once the fundamental dimensions of human behavior in various situations are understood.

The term "rational" is frequently misused. Being rational means being consciously aware and capable of providing plausible reasons for one's ideas or behavior. Plausibility in academic or intellectual circles means following the rules of reason, that is, the rules of logic. Plausibility in business circles most frequently means being profit-minded and cost-conscious. Plausibility in union circles means being security-minded and consciously aware of and reasonable about employee needs and interests. Any particular point of view can be argued well or poorly; any action can be more or less capricious or firmly based on considered judgment and analysis. But logic in itself is not sufficient to reconcile the myriad of interests and considerations which enter into human affairs. A logic based on limited dimensions and interests will inevitably be an oversimplification of reality. The worst thing about it is that the more logical you become, the greater is the tendency to limit the dimensions which you are taking into consideration. The tightest systems of thinking always develop within systems of limited dimensons—for example, in mathematics where pure reason is developed to its highest point.

The so-called "rational" model of organization and administration is an oversimplification. It considers primarily the technicoeconomic dimensions of business enterprise and organization and is accordingly limited to the logic of machines and technical processes and to the logic of cost and efficiency. For control of the human element in organization, it depends upon legalistic devices, authoritarian control, and the acceptance of the fundamental "logic" of its position. It is accordingly a useful "ideal type" in the area of production where technical and cost factors loom as major dimensions, but it is peculiarly ill-adapted for analyzing what business enterprise is all about, human adjustment within the organization, and in general the dynamics of human behavior and relationships not only within the organization but in the broader society of which business is a part.

In the so-called "natural-system" model, organization is viewed as a natural phenomenon—something which like Topsy "just growed." This model emerged primarily out of the work of the social anthropologists and functional sociologists who examined business organizations primarily from the standpoint of human needs and behavior. To this analysis, the anthropologists and sociologists brought assumptions about social systems developed primarily out of the observation and study of primitive societies and other types of social organizations. These assumptions included such notions as the following:

1. A social organization is a system of interrelated activities.
2. Each of these activities is functional to the continued existence and growth of the social organization.
3. The social system is tightly integrated such that a change in one part will result in changes in the whole system.
4. The system tends toward equilibrium so that adjustment to change is internal to the system and, as Professor Gouldner puts it "spontaneously and homeostatically" achieved.
5. The system serves the interests of those who participate in it; it also, however, influences and determines the participants' goals and expectations so that, as these become internalized, the system becomes an end in itself.

Goals thus emerge out of the needs of the system for survival and growth which are as much internal as external if indeed not more so. In short, a social system is seen as a natural, superorganic phenomenon adjusting both to its internal needs and to its external environment.

6. The focus of attention, therefore, as Professor Gouldner aptly points out is on "disruptions of organizational equilibrium, and particularly on the mechanisms by which equilibrium is homeostatically maintained." In other words, behavioral scientists subscribing to the natural-system model of organization see equilibrium and the co-ordination of the various parts of the system as "healthy" and "good" and disequilibrium and lack of co-operation as essentially "unhealthy."

The interpretation of the social system of the modern factory as described in Roethlisberger and Dickson's *Management and the Worker*[22] is a good example of the natural-system model.

Inasmuch as a business organization, particularly in a highly developed and mature business, tends to be a tightly integrated system of production, motivation, communication, authority, and control, the natural-system model, which was originally developed for the analysis of primitive, traditional societies, is peculiarly well adapted to the analysis of modern, large-scale organizations. It reveals especially the close and intimate relationship between the social system of the modern organization and its technological and economic functions and activities. It demonstrates clearly that these various orders fit together and that business management must take into account the social and psychological systems operating within the business organization as well as the technicoeconomic systems.

The natural-system model of organization, however, tends to overemphasize the unintended and socially "unconscious" considerations in social organization. It has not yet given rise to an adequate theory of management, simply because it has difficulty in making room for conscious, deliberate, goal-directed behavior. In fact, if the rational model tends to overemphasize the role of a thinking, consciously aware, rational management, the natural-system model leaves no specific function for management at all. Management per se is just a prestigeful role, which like any other role is very much a part of the total system. It is the system that is all-important not a small, oligarchical group deliberately and consciously exercising power and influence over others. Thus, in natural-system circles, there has been little effort until recent years to develop administrative theory beyond the notion that effective administration is the art, or conceivably clinical science, of helping the

---

[22] *Op. cit.,* see chap. i.

organization to adjust to change, that is, helping the organization to achieve equilibrium in the face of disruptive forces.

The point of view of this text is that business organizations reflect both "rational" considerations and "natural" influences. Many aspects of organizational behavior are very much a part of human nature. It is natural for human beings to work reasonably effectively in formal work structures, responding to the demands of higher authority and working co-operatively with their fellows. It is also equally natural for humans to perceive the social significance of various events in the workplace, to observe differences in status, to identify with particular work activities, to compete, to form resistance groups, to restrict output, and so on. As we shall see later in this text, all of these modes of behavior are natural. But business activities also lend themselves to thought and rational judgments. A business which depends entirely on "natural" homeostasis and adjustment is doomed to failure, for we live in a rapidly changing world, which will belong to those with the foresight to see down the road, those with the knowledge to know what can be done and what the probable consequences of alternative modes of action are, and those with the judgment to pick the right directions.

While there is much about business decision and action which is simply trial and error and much also which grows almost unconsciously out of social and organizational processes, nonetheless purely capricious behavior can be reduced and administrative errors can be lessened by forethought, knowledge, and judgment. Logical and intelligent thinking are as much a part of human nature and of man's behavior as sentiments, emotions, and social and psychological processes. Indeed, man's ultimate control over his own affairs rests upon his ability to think intelligently. The test, however, is not whether he thinks or not, but what he thinks about. If his comprehension of reality is narrowly defined, conventional, and restricted, his thoughts will reflect these limitations. If his conceptions are negative and essentially hostile, his ideas will be destructive and antagonistic. If, on the other hand, he has a broad understanding of human affairs, a deep sensitivity to the consequences of his actions for him and for others, and the ability to conceive new possibilities which are both integrative and humanly constructive, then his thoughts are worth listening to.

4. DIMENSIONS OF
BUSINESS ENTERPRISE

MOST theories of business administration are deficient because they are
built on assumptions about business organization rather than upon
assumptions about business enterprise. This failure to relate organizational events to the outside world results in unrealistic conclusions about
the functions of the executive and the nature of the business organization. If we eliminate in this way the entrepreneurial functions of the
business executive, his administrative activities become little more than
a bureaucratic exercise, reflecting a kind of organizational introversion
in which internal processes alone have significance and meaning.

In this chapter we shall attempt to develop a theory of business administration based on entrepreneurial rather than bureaucratic dimensions. We shall begin with an analysis of the entrepreneurial network
or matrix in which a given business grows and develops. Here we shall
focus attention on the pattern of human relations existing in the entrepreneurial matrix. We shall view this pattern realistically as a system
of exchanges and transactions. We shall give special attention to the
way in which exchange relations are conceived, developed, and maintained; of particular interest will be the manner in which diverse interests and values in our business society are reconciled and secured
through time. We shall view the business executive, first, as a rational
decision-maker and actor who consciously and deliberately intervenes
at as many points as possible in the total system of entrepreneurial exchange in order to increase the number and improve the quality of exchanges taking place. We shall view the business executive, second, as
an ordinary human being trying to make the best of an exceedingly
complex situation. Finally, we shall examine the business organization
as an important structure within the entrepreneurial matrix.

Our analysis should be regarded as mainly exploratory. This is not
an effort to develop a tight, rigorous theory but is rather a search for
interesting new dimensions which can lead to a more realistic evaluation
of the functions of the business executive.

THE ENTREPRENEURIAL MATRIX

Every business enterprise regardless of type operates within a larger environment. The environment of business can be examined at two levels: first, the level of society itself with all of the beliefs and activities which constitute it; and, second, the entrepreneurial level or the level of business and industrial beliefs and activities. We are concerned here with the second level, namely, the entrepreneurial level, which we shall refer to as the *entrepreneurial matrix*. We shall use the term "matrix" in both its biological sense of "a place or medium in which something is bred, produced, or developed" and its mathematical sense of "a rectangular arrangement of quantities."[1] The first meaning indicates the significance of the entrepreneurial environment to the development of an individual business enterprise and the second meaning implies structure and a high degree of interdependence. The term is a better fit for our purposes than the more common sociological term "milieu."

The entrepreneurial matrix is a network of interrelated activities. The events taking place there are intricately intertwined and interconnected. Professor Arthur H. Cole, entrepreneurial historian, emphasizes the interconnectedness of entrepreneurial events in the following words:[2]

A composer or a baseball player might possess exceptional talent, but his contribution to the entertainment of the nation would remain rather minor if his performances were restricted, respectively, to his family parlor or his own sandlot. Music as a social phenomenon nowadays means, when viewed realistically, everything from symphony orchestras to arrangers of FM broadcasts, and from publishers of musical scores to manufacturers of disc recording apparatus. And correspondingly baseball means all sorts of supporting and fulfilling elements: producers of equipment, talent scouts, architects of baseball parks, schools for umpires, and what-not. So, likewise, with entrepreneurship.

A major characteristic of the entrepreneurial matrix is that it involves exchange. Resources are created, used to develop new resources, and used again in a never-ending process. The exchanges which take place involve three classes of events:

1. Physical objects—materials, tools, and other physical resources.
2. Human acts—work effort, skills and know-how, social and psychological events.
3. Money—a common denominator for equating values.

---

[1] *The Oxford Universal Dictionary* (London: Oxford University Press, 1955), p. 1218.

[2] Arthur H. Cole, *Business Enterprise in Its Social Setting* (Cambridge, Mass.: Harvard University Press, 1959), p. 76.

Events of one class or another are in constant process of exchange among individuals or groups playing various socioeconomic roles such as customers, investors, employees at various levels, suppliers of goods and services, and owners. The series of exchanges can be likened to a great circle, such that one man's end-product becomes another's resource. Products and services move in one direction and money, the common medium of exchange that presumably equates all value differences moves in the other. Professor George Stigler calls this great circularity the "wheel of wealth" (see Figure 4–1).[3]

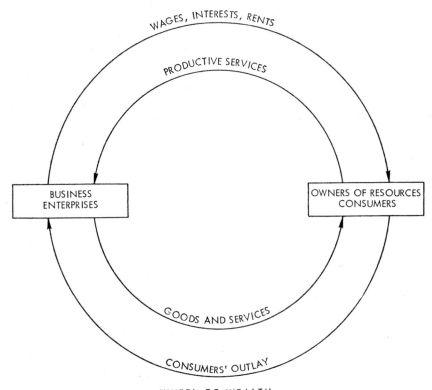

WHEEL OF WEALTH

FIGURE 4.—The Wheel of Wealth

(This obviously is an oversimplification of the exchanges taking place in the entrepreneurial matrix.)

Time and Change

The entrepreneurial matrix is in a continuous state of flux through time. The activity within the system is in fact generated through its

---

[3] George J. Stigler, *The Theory of Price* (New York: Macmillan Co., 1952), p. 6.

basic imbalance or disequilibrium. It is a structure which is never completely built, where gaps occur which are linked together by entrepreneurial effort only to give rise to new hiatuses which require further rearrangements. Thus, the entrepreneurial matrix moves through time with the entrepreneur striving to meet challenges and solve problems as they arise—always hoping to achieve a more stable, homeostatic balance but inevitably faced with new imbalances and the need for novel adjustment and innovation.

Professor Arthur H. Cole likens entrepreneurial activity to a stream. He sees business as a flow of events in which there is constant change and adjustment—where the present decisions of entrepreneurs emerge out of past considerations and have their effect on future events. The entrepreneurial role is like that of the logger riding his log raft down the river, constantly beset by new and unexpected eddies, rapids, and twists and turns, striving to maintain his balance and keep his raft intact, sometimes riding through unscathed and other times ending up a jumbled mess at an unexpected elbow in the river.[4]

We can envision entrepreneurial activity as a matrix of interrelated events and a system of linkages, moving through time and change, coming together, dissolving, and reassembling into new patterns. Each business presides over one or more of the links in the entrepreneurial matrix but never over all of them or, for that matter, over a large number of them. The individual business enterprise constitutes a link or set of links in the larger entrepreneurial network or matrix. Conceiving of a business means conceiving of a potential link in the existing framework. A gap occurs which in a sense the entrepreneurial system itself creates; a business or industry moves in to fill the gap. It may be a gap between one industrial activity and another or between industry and the ultimate consumer. The linkages may be of a minor nature such as providing a routine service, or they may be of major importance and give rise to a whole new set of potential linkages such as developing a new consumer product or a significant new process or new basic material.

Structure and Function

The establishment of a link in the entrepreneurial matrix is essentially an act of structuring; that is, it involves an awareness of structure, of existing structural gaps, and of new structural possibilities. The activities of modern men consist of a never-ending process of structuring component parts and then reassembling these into larger and more com-

---

[4] Cole, *op. cit.*, p. 76.

plicated structures. At the physical and technological level, this process is readily observed. Here we find men refining and restructuring metals and organic materials for use in manufacturing. We see them shaping the restructured materials into parts for ultimate assembly as consumer products. We see the consumers acquiring these products for reassembly in their homes as an integral part of their ways of life. We can observe the whole panorama of human enterprise as men reach out, sometimes routinely, sometimes creatively, and act on the world around them to shape and structure it into forms which for various reasons are more pleasing, satisfying, or useful to them.

This never-ending process of structuring and restructuring must be understood, since it helps resolve some of the major dilemmas of organizational and management theory. First of all, at an abstract level, it will be observed that the component parts of any structure exist for the structure itself. Or to put it another way, the structure defines the purpose or functions of its unit components. Thus, if we ask what is the purpose of a carburetor, we have to say its purpose is to perform a function within a broader structure called a gasoline engine. If we wish to go further than this, we can view the gasoline engine as a unit component within a broader structure, let us say a water pump. Still further, we can see the water pump as part of the plumbing of a farmhouse and so on. The purpose of any unit component, therefore, must be considered from the standpoint of the larger system or structure which it serves. It would appear, then, that we should drop the term "purpose" or "objective" from our vocabulary when considering business management and use the term "function" instead, since this draws attention to the broader structure or structures which business activities serve.

The significance of this observation can be best understood when we consider the amount of wasted energy that has gone into efforts to define the so-called objectives of business. Some say the purpose of a business is to make a profit; others say its purpose is to serve the customer; still others maintain that the purpose of business is its own survival as an institution and activity. None of these defined objectives means very much until we begin to consider the broader systems of relationships which the various activities of business serve.

Another terminological difficulty in business which a functional approach helps to resolve is the presumed distinction between "production" and "consumption." In our terminology, "production" is the creation of structure out of unit components. "Consumption," interestingly enough, is the same thing. It all depends upon whether you want to look at the end product or the process of utilizing component parts. We cannot, therefore, talk of business as producing for consumption as though there were some ultimate act of oral ingestion in which its products were consumed. Its products are not consumed but reused in new activities and in new systems of relationships. Products may wear out, requiring maintenance and ultimate replacement; but, in the process of aging itself, they become unit components of the junk industry or the antique business or museums. Thus, aging itself can become a productive process, depending upon the vantage point from which we wish to view it. The main point, however, is that the activities of business are part of a broader stream of events which are intricately blended and not easily separated into a distinct chronology.

Again, the significance of this observation can best be understood when we consider the energy wasted in some circles on the question, which is more important—production or marketing? In the entrepreneurial matrix, there is no such thing as production which is not intimately related to consumption or at least hoped-for consumption. By the same token, there is no such activity as marketing unrelated to product. Indeed, we can go further than this. The concern of the production expert with costs and efficiency is essentially a concern with marketing considerations and the willingness of the customer to buy and use the company's products. The so-called marketing function of distribution and transportation could readily be regarded as production functions since they are part of the total task of creating an end product and assembling it in time and space. The distinction between production and consumption is at best a matter of convenience if you keep in mind the underlying references. Better terms would be "resource creation" or development and "resource utilization" since these refer outward to the broader system of relationships of which a given business is a part.

The entrepreneurial role in business requires a deep understanding of the structure of the entrepreneurial matrix, not only the existing structure but how that structure is changing. It is a matter of perceiving existing gaps in the structure and correctly assessing where gaps are likely to occur. But even more, it is a matter of acting effectively to fill existing gaps, to implement and take advantage of change, and to improvise and innovate when the directions are unclear and the future foggy.

The Entrepreneurial Matrix as a Technological Structure

An important and obvious feature of the entrepreneurial matrix is the technological structure which appears to provide the basic pattern around which individual businesses are organized. The high degree of interdependence in the technological order can be readily observed. One business produces steel, which it supplies to another business that produces machine tools, which in turn are sold to still another business that manufactures cans, and so on. The technological order is an intricately organized procession of events which begins with the earth's raw materials, then moves through various processes, and emerges finally as useful products or resources. Laid out as an exhibit in a science museum, the entire procession seems intricate but orderly.

Technological necessity, however, is only one of the bonds that link businesses together. While technology determines in broad outline the links which a given business must establish with other businesses in the industrial world, it does not specifically prescribe *which* other businesses. In other words, General Motors may appear to be technologically bound to the steel industry, but there is no absolute technological reason why it has to do business with the United States Steel Company. There are other competitive alternatives. Moreover, there is not even the absolute necessity that it use steel at all since there are other substitute materials available. It is obvious that considerations other than technology enter into the determination of the particular exchange relations which develop in our business society.

Later, when we discuss the beliefs and values of scientists and engineers,[5] we shall see also that what appears to be "technological necessity" is sometimes only a reflection of the socially derived beliefs and values arising within a particular technological segment of our industrial society. A given technology is often as much an art as it is a science. An art typically involves an element of tradition, a sense of form, and beliefs about the rightness or wrongness of various techniques or approaches. Accordingly, steel might be used in certain technological processes, not because of any inherent advantages of this material over other alternatives, but simply because this is the material that has always been used. Or it might be used because it fits the techniques and knowhow of "forming and stamping press" engineers who find it difficult to conceive of any other process.

---

[5] See Chapter 13.

Technology and Society

The technological structure is one aspect of the network of relationships which constitute the entrepreneurial matrix. However, technology unrelated to social organization is meaningless. Modern civilization is not so much a result of technological development as of social and organizational changes.

V. Gordon Childe, Professor of Prehistoric European Archaeology at the University of London, describes three broadly defined stages in the chronology of man's social and economic development.[6] The first of these, called "savagery" by Professor Childe, refers to the simple food-gathering of the Paleolithic period, that is, hunting, fishing, and berry gathering. At this level of economic development, there can be no division of labor. As Professor Childe says:[7]

... since every adult must be contributing directly to the food-supply, there can be no true division of labour, no full-time specialists. No one, for instance, could live by making stone tools to barter for game, fish, and fruits caught or gathered by his fellows, for there is no guarantee that the latter would be regularly so successful as to keep him supplied.

In such an economy, human survival needs are so completely front and center that there is no question of the relationship between technological resources such as stone axes, spears, and knives and human demands for food.

The second stage of economic development is called "barbarism" by Professor Childe. Barbarism begins with the so-called Neolithic revolution, which ushered in the agricultural period of farming and stock breeding. The significance of an agricultural economy is that it "permits and indeed requires the regular production of a social surplus."[8] With such a surplus, according to Professor Childe, full-time specialists can be supported and trade and exchange can begin. However, in a "hypothetical pure Neolithic economy, there could be no full-time specialists. Trade, even if fairly regular, would be confined to luxuries."[9]

In this connection, we are reminded of the pattern of trade in the Trobriand Islands, a modern Neolithic society, where there is a highly

---

[6] V. Gordon Childe, "Early Forms of Society," in Charles Singer *et al.* (eds.), *A History of Technology* (New York and London: Oxford University Press, 1954).
[7] *Ibid.*, p .42.
[8] *Ibid.*, p. 43.
[9] *Ibid.*, p. 44.

developed system of exchange called *kula*.[10] Here, the Melanesians on the various islands trade armlets for necklaces—the armlets moving around the islands in one direction like George Stigler's "Wheel of Wealth" and the necklaces moving in the opposite path. The items which are exchanged are not necessities or of practical use but are more of the nature of trophies. Moreover, exchange is not based on notions of material equivalence but rather on ideas of social prestige.

Where there is technological interdependence, then trade, even in Neolithic societies, apparently takes on a more characteristic form. The earliest systems of interdependence were doubtless related to raw materials. We sometimes forget that stone-age societies were as much dependent on particular types of stone as our society is on metals, especially steel. Some sense of the trade in stone in Neolithic societies can be gained from the following account of trade among North American Indians before the coming of the European:[11]

With the West there was a heavy trade in stone, both as artifacts and as raw material. Brown pipestone from the Chippewa River and red pipestone from the Minnesota came by way of the Lakes into Ohio and New York as far east as Onondaga and Oswego, and thence north into Canada. Flint from Ontario went west in the shape of "blanks"; and the finished points, traveling into Saskatchewan and Alberta, and north of Ontario, tipped the weapons of the Algonquin hunters. Obsidian from the Rocky Mountains, which was widely used in Ohio, was imported both as raw material and as artifacts; deposits of several hundred pounds have been found in the Hopewell mounds. There were evidently tribes who did nothing but manufacture even in that early day, for Tonty found that the Natchitoches and the Nasoui of the Red River "did no work except making very fine bows, which they make a traffic with distant nations."

This account of trade in North America before the European conquest suggests quite extensive systems of exchange, and indeed in some instances, full-time specialization. However, as Professor Childe points out, the main characteristic of the Neolithic economy was self-sufficiency—"homemade products of local materials."[12] This extensive localization of resource development and resource utilization indicates a close and intimate relationship between technology and human needs during the period of barbarism.

The third stage of economic development was the "urban revolu-

---

[10] Bronislaw Malinowski, *Argonauts of the Western Pacific* (London: Routledge, 1929).

[11] George T. Hunt, *The Wars of the Iroquois* (Madison: University of Wisconsin Press, 1960), p. 18.

[12] Childe, *op. cit.*, p. 44.

tion." According to Professor Childe, this phase involved a very radical change "both in social structure and in psychology, as well as in economy."[13] Detailing his argument, Professor Childe goes on to say:[14]

The author is inclined to doubt whether a mere multiplication of the deviations observed in Neolithic or barbarian societies would be sufficient to produce the final result. That result required a very unusual conjunction of circumstances, which occurred at most five times—in the Tigris-Euphrates delta, in the Nile valley, in the Indus basin, in Central America, and perhaps in Peru.

Key elements of the urban stage were "the conversion of luxuries into necessities" and "an increase, and above all a concentration, of the social surplus."[15] Professor Childe suggests that the conversion of luxuries into necessities must have been very difficult, something like trying to "make a peasant so much want a more efficient agricultural machine, electric light, a bath, or air-conditioning that he will regularly work harder to get it."[16]

More important than this type of conversion, indeed necessary to it, was the concentration of social surplus which Professor Childe relates to the development of the city. Thus, we see that urbanization and division of labor, full-time specialization, and technological interdependence which we think of as civilization are all closely connected. It is not by chance that the words *city* and *civilization* have the same root.

According to Professor Childe, the city developed in at least two ways. Cities, for example, in Mesopotamia grew up around temples.[17]

To secure the maintenance of the favour of the deities, (the people) paid tribute from the produce of their labour. These revenues were used not only to provide the gods with gigantic feasts and ample supplies of beer, but to support a corporation of priests, who acted as ministers of the gods, and a variety of specialist artisans, who provided for the equipment of the temple and also for the more efficient working of the temple estates. A portion was used to pay for the importation of raw materials for the adornment of the gods' houses, the enjoyment of the ministers, and the better equipment of their tenants.

In Egypt, cities developed through a concentration of social surplus as the result of conquest. One clan conquered the whole Nile valley and thereby secured the right or privilege of receiving "as tribute the sur-

---

13 *Ibid.*, p. 45.
14 *Ibid.*, p. 45.
15 *Ibid.*, p. 45.
16 *Ibid.*, p. 47.
17 *Ibid.*, p. 49.

plus produce of the whole valley."[18] Once again, the surplus was used to pay new classes of full-time specialists.

These early trends toward urbanization started "the change of Sumerian and Egyptian society from a mechanical aggregate of persons, all doing the same things but held together by feelings of kinship or some other emotional bonds, into an organic unit whose members perform complementary functions and are united by the mutual benefits thus conferred."[19]

From the foregoing observations of Professor Childe, we can gain a better understanding of the relationship of technology, specialized division of labor, and social organization. What happened in the urban revolution was not so much a change in technology. After all, most of the techniques of the early urban period were well known to Neolithic cultures. The change was in the organization of society itself from an undifferentiated collectivity to a highly differentiated, interdependent social structure characterized not only by specialization of resource development but by an increasing diversity of demand and resource utilization.

Two Patterns of Social Cohesion

Professor Childe's analysis highlights two major patterns of cohesion found everywhere in human society. One pattern occurring typically in undifferentiated collectivities arises from emotional and sentimental bonds—a consciousness of kind, a sense of collective identity, camaraderie, brotherhood, and so on. This pattern of cohesion depends on human feelings which lie very deep within the species; assuredly, they are the very source of human gregariousness.

The other pattern occurring in urban, differentiated societies arises out of the necessity for interdependent behavior and human exchange. This pattern of cohesion depends less on emotions and sentiments and more on the conscious, deliberate efforts of men.

The distinction made here is very important for an understanding of human behavior and particularly the different points of view regarding human behavior. It also explains to some extent the diverse theories regarding the role of the business executive; for he is sometimes conceived as a social leader, providing integration and a sense of morale and collective identity, and at other times he is viewed as a strategist engaged

[18] *Ibid.*, p. 50.
[19] *Ibid.*, p. 52.

in a game of put-and-take and utilizing various techniques and influences to gain his ends.

Émile Durkheim, French sociologist, to whose ideas Professor Childe has already alluded, pointed up the sharp differences between the two patterns of social cohesion when he distinguished between mechanical and organic solidarity. "Solidarity" was Durkheim's word for "cohesion." About mechanical solidarity, Durkheim said:[20]

The social molecules which can be coherent in this way act together only in the measure that they have no actions of their own, as the molecules of inorganic bodies. That is why we propose to call this type of solidarity mechanical. The term does not signify that it is produced by mechanical and artificial means. We call it that only by analogy to the cohesion which unites the elements of an inanimate body, as opposed to that which makes a unity out of the elements of a living body.

About organic solidarity, referring now to highly interdependent social organizations, Durkheim said:[21]

It is quite otherwise with the solidarity which the division of labor produces. Whereas the previous type implies that individuals resemble each other, this type presumes their difference. The first is possible only in so far as the individual personality is absorbed into the collective personality; the second is possible only if each one has a sphere of action which is peculiar to him; that is, a personality. It is necessary, then, that the collective conscience leave open a part of the individual conscience in order that special functions may be established there, functions which it cannot regulate. The more this region is extended, the stronger is the cohesion which results from this solidarity. In effect, on the one hand, each one depends as much more strictly on society as labor is more divided; and, on the other, the activity of each is as much more personal as it is more specialized.

Durkheim's choice of terms seems rather poor until we realize that he is referring to the structural characteristics of social organizations and especially the degree of interdependence and specialization of roles within the social structure. Under these circumstances, the terms "mechanical" and "organic" by analogy at least, are acceptable.

Of particular interest to us is the way in which Durkheim relates the personality of the individual to the social structure. The two obviously go together. With mechanical solidarity, the individual presumably loses his identity in the society; he is simply one undifferentiated unit among many. So complete a submergence of the individual does not appeal to us, socialized as we have been in a highly individuated

[20] Émile Durkheim, "On Mechanical and Organic Solidarity" in Talcott Parsons et al. (eds.), *Theories of Society* (New York: Free Press, 1961), p. 212.
[21] *Ibid.,* p. 213.

society. Yet, we should not lose sight of the basic appeal that lies in a sense of fellowship with others. There are deep satisfactions to be gained in feelings of brotherhood around a common purpose or symbol of identity. Primitive Christianity developed a deep sense of fellowship, interestingly enough without loss of individuality.[22] Indeed, the assumed loss of personal identity may be a matter of definition, for awareness of self in the ultimate analysis may be only a consciousness of one's similarity to, and differences from, others.

In highly differentiated social organizations, the individual would appear to be considerably more autonomous. He has a sphere of action and influence. At the same time, he is aware of his utter dependence on others and, therefore, acts to maintain his relationships. Thus, the greater the autonomy, the greater the need for interdependent action. The sentimental ties of the undifferentiated social organization are "gut reactions," while the bonds of organization in complex, urban societies would appear to be a function of the conscious, rational mind. This is not to say that the individual in a highly differentiated society is consciously aware of all of the relationships which bind the society together. Rather typically, the individual knows only a piece of the reality; he has a particular task or set of tasks which he tends to perform in a rational, conscious manner; he has the faith that, if others do likewise, his needs will be satisfied.

Professor Childe in his analysis suggests a clear-cut break between the two patterns of social cohesion as society has moved historically from the undifferentiated collectivities of the Neolithic period to the differentiated structures after the urban revolution. Durkheim, however, is keenly aware that the two types of solidarity exist in the same society. The modern society represents a complex intermeshing of emotional and sentimental bonds, which are part of the nature of man and of conscious and rational ties, which are equally a part of human nature. While there appears to be an inexorable trend toward the more rational, interdependent modes of social organization, from "sacred to secular" societies and from agricultural to urban, industrial societies, nonetheless modern man like his caveman counterpart still searches for ties with his fellows and still relates to others partly on the basis of sentimental rather than purely rational considerations. Assuredly, many of the conflicts arising in modern society are explained by these different modes of social cohesion.

---

[22] Ernst Troeltsch, *The Social Teaching of the Christian Churches* (London: George Allen & Unwin, Ltd., 1950), p. 55.

The Entrepreneurial Matrix as a Social Organization

It goes without saying that the entrepreneurial matrix reflects the characteristic pattern described by the urban revolution. It clearly is characterized by a concentration of "social surplus" or capital, full-time specialization or division of labor, a high degree of interdependence, and a concomitant individuation of needs, interests, and demands. It is a social organization in which "organic solidarity" based primarily on rational considerations is the dominant mode of cohesion.

This last point needs further clarification. It would be an easy matter to ascribe the integration of the modern, highly specialized, urban society to a superorganic mystique of some sort. In an advanced industrial society like ours in which people function within an elaborate, highly evolved structure and have internalized the complex beliefs necessary for interdependent modes of behavior, the relationships in the entrepreneurial society seems "natural" and "untouched by human hand" so to speak. The entire system appears to take on a superorganic character, functioning in terms of a transcendent design, over and above the acts of individuals. The "free enterprise" system is sometimes given this transcendental quality. Such a view, however, diverts our attention from a consideration of the agents, agencies, and other social devices and techniques in our society which hold it together, keep it working, and maintain it through time and change.

Our own view is that the integration of the entrepreneurial matrix, and the implementation of, and adjustment to, the changes occurring within it, result directly from the efforts of men: men pursuing their own personal interests or the interests of their reference groups in part, but men also who are at least sometimes aware of the broader system of relationships which characterize the modern industrial society. In short, the entrepreneurial matrix does not occur by chance, or because of some superorganic design, or as an unexpected social consequence of the rabid pursuit of self-interests as Adam Smith suggested, or even because of broadly shared beliefs and values. All of these influences play a part but beyond them are the rational, deliberate, often insightful acts of men at all levels who have occasional glimpses of the total system of action and contribute their efforts to these broader ends.

Functional Differentiation and Problems of Linkage

The foregoing observations indicate that our analysis will proceed along fruitful lines if we view the organization of the entrepreneurial matrix and the integration of its many diversified segments as something less than a highly articulated, self-perpetuating social organism. In fact, the importance of the acts of individuals will stand out more clearly if we regard the entrepreneurial organization as essentially crude and holding together because men strive to make it hold together.

It is apparent that full-time specialization, increasing interdependence, and individuation of needs and interests create differentiation. As the entire system of specialized activities and diverse interests develops, the lines drawing together the various elements become more complicated and tenuous, have more intervening variables, and are considerably less direct. In times of depression when the whole system of activities seems to atrophy, the complex nature of the entrepreneurial matrix becomes very evident indeed.

Nowhere are the relationships in the entrepreneurial matrix more tenuous than in those existing between the technological order of our society and the life style order. As we have already indicated in our discussion of Professor Childe's observations, a key characteristic of the periods both of "savagery" and of "barbarism" is the intimate connection between technology and the needs of people. In a primitive society, the technological activities, whatever they are, and the direct utilization of the tools and resources produced by these activities for the satisfaction of human needs are integrated and one. There may be a minor separation of functions, such as the "old lady" tending the yam patch while the men sit around contemplating a "big deal" like a canoe foray to the next island, but this functional differentiation is incidental to the main theme.

"Natural" integration of technological skills and human resources does not occur in modern society. There are many intervening variables between the manufacturing organization of a business and the activities of the consumer in the home. Technology and resource development have become highly complicated activities requiring not only specialized knowledge and skills but also expensive apparatus and facilities. At the same time, drastic changes have occurred in the way people live. As a consequence, our society appears to be broken into two great segments—a scientific, technological order and a life style order. Although neither makes much sense without reference to the other, each appears to be a separate social organization obeying the influences of its own inner dialectic and surrounding environment. This separation is recognized in William Fielding Ogburn's notion of "culture lag,"[23] which may not be a "lag" at all but simply divergence. It is also recognized

---

[23] William Fielding Ogburn, "Culture Lag as a Theory of Social Science," *Sociology and Social Research*, Vol. 41 (January-February, 1953), pp. 167–74.

in the average man's view of science and technology; they seem to him to be a distant world, something "out there," where knowledge is pursued and things discovered often without particular regard for what the average man wants or the directions in which he wishes to move. The distinction and separation are seen from the other side, too, as scientists and technologists wonder about the strange world of human needs and expectations and the antics of people as they live their lives in terms of social, emotional, and sentimental influences which may escape the attention of the physical scientist.

The important separation that occurs between technology and life styles in the entrepreneurial matrix is illustrative of other cleavages in interests and activities that occur—among various occupational groups, for example, or between unions and business management, or among stockholder-owners, investors, customers, employees, business management, and other socioeconomic groups contributing to and making claims on business enterprise. Viewed from this standpoint, the entrepreneurial matrix and the individual business units of which it is constituted are in a constant state of flux and essentially more volatile than stable. When a business executive says, as many have, "A business must keep moving, growing, developing or it will die," he is clearly recognizing that he exists in a changing world—one which will pass his business by if he fails to keep up, to perceive changes, and to innovate.

EXCHANGE AND TRANSACTIONS

To the business entrepreneur, the entrepreneurial matrix in which he operates is a complex system of linkages which must be secured, maintained, and developed through time. These linkages are essentially points of exchange and transaction in which the entrepreneur seeks to exercise influence and control insofar as he is able. The entrepreneurial matrix thus is bound together by the efforts of individual business enterprises to secure, develop, and maintain exchange relationships through effective transactions. It is important, therefore, that we understand the nature of human exchange, relationships of reciprocity, and the transactions undertaken in these relationships.

We shall begin by defining more precisely some of the terms to which we have referred. We shall think of *exchange* as meaning any relationship of reciprocity. It may be a reciprocal relationship in which goods are bartered, or goods traded for money; or it may be reciprocity in which verbal noises are passed back and forth, or even physical blows are traded. Relationships of reciprocity underlie all social structures. Whether they are positive as in relationships of mutual aid or negative as in relationships of conflict, interaction binds individuals together into interdependent social structures of short or long duration.

A *transaction* we shall take to mean the act of developing a relationship of reciprocity or a relationship involving an exchange. A transaction is not the exchange itself but the development of the necessary agreements and reconciliation of values necessary for an exchange to take place.

A. R. Radcliffe-Brown uses the term "coaptation" to describe the actual fitting together of interests, the correlating of divergent interests on the basis of socially derived notions of equivalence. We shall find this term useful to us since it describes a successful transaction—one in which there has been a successful correlation of needs and interests culminating in an exchange.

With these terms in mind, we can now turn to an analysis of the elements of human interaction in the entrepreneurial matrix. These are as follows:

1. Human demands for outside resources
2. Differential valuation of resources
3. Differential possession of resources
4. Transactional processes and ways of reconciling values which include:
    a) Transactional structures
    b) Coaptive norms

Obviously, this is a large and complicated area of inquiry. Accordingly our major interest is in setting forth the major dimensions which must be taken into account.

Human Demands for Outside Resources

A totally self-sufficient individual has no need for outside resources and, therefore, is not involved in exchange relationships. Obviously, such complete self-sufficiency occurs only rarely if at all. However, there are relative degrees of self-sufficiency ranging all the way from those who through their own efforts supply most of their personal needs to those, more typical of modern, urban societies, who are almost totally dependent on resources from the outside.

The entrepreneurial matrix, of course, depends for existence on a high rate of exchange activity. Acquisitiveness is, therefore, a necessary factor in the development of the entrepreneurial matrix. This means something more than a reduction in self-sufficiency; it involves an absolute increase in desire. Indeed, for the entrepreneurial matrix to grow and develop, people have to want more and more. From the standpoint of a traditional agricultural society where the farmer's tastes are simple and he supplies his own needs, the modern, industrial society may appear to be highly materialistic, avaricious, and greedy.

What are some of the factors in decreasing self-sufficiency and increasing acquisitiveness? We have already discussed the significance of the urban revolution in the "translation of luxuries into necessities." Full-time specialization automatically places the specialist in a position of being dependent on others. Of course, others become more dependent on him in their turn. Nonetheless, he must be sheltered, fed, and clothed by other specialists so that he can pursue his specialty. Moreover, his family must be supported in the same way.

In addition to personal and family demands, full-time specialization results in new occupational demands for tools and materials. Thus, simultaneous with the development of a consumer (life style) market, there develops an equally important industrial market.

Full-time specialization also has the effect of increasing the total supply of given resources. Greater availability increases demand, at least up to a given point (no one knows exactly where), because availability enhances the prospect of possession; it broadens the potential market. More and more people look forward to the acquisition of a resource, previously denied them as a result of scarcity.

The superiority of resources created through specialization adds to the general increase in demand. The effect of European trade on North American Indians is a case in point. The Europeans had no difficulty in getting the Indians to engage in the fur trade; in fact, they fought among themselves for the opportunity. As George T. Hunt points out:[24]

. . . the European trade instantly divided the tribes into highly competitive groups, and the competition for trade was, or soon became, a struggle for survival. The native who had known and used the keen steel tools of the white man was unlikely to renounce them and was shortly unable to do so, so swiftly did the skills of the Stone Age vanish.

Thus have human beings over and over again demonstrated their willingness to give up low-level self-sufficiency for better resources, even though it made them more and more dependent on others.

Democratization plays a very important part in the absolute increase in demands in a society. Egalitarian feelings in the political area often

---

[24] Hunt, *op. cit.*, p. 19.

carry over into the economic area as well. As a consequence, the masses aspire to luxuries and come to expect them as their right in a democratic society. One of the authors recalls an occasion in which he attempted to advise a production worker on budgetary matters. The worker owned a new medium-priced car which was costing him in time payments alone almost half of his take-home pay. When it was suggested that he get rid of the car, he exploded.

"Who are you to tell me what I should buy or shouldn't buy," he said more in the form of a statement than a question.

He was right, and the discussion was quickly terminated. Certainly, the rapid development of the entrepreneurial matrix in the United States was as much a function of mass demand and mass expectations as it was of the importation of the industrial revolution from England. The two influences obviously developed together.

Social changes bring concomitant psychological changes. Industrial societies often enhance the individual's desire for acquisition and spending for its own sake. Like an electrical current, the desire to buy flows through one channel after another, seeking paths of least resistance. In some, it builds up like an electrical charge, a detached, undischarged force searching for an outlet. When we say, "Money burns a hole in his pocket," we are referring to this unresolved build-up of energy. The individual, thus charged, literally goes shopping to *find* something to buy, enjoying relief only after a purchase has been made. The "Five and Ten" used to provide a wonderful place to go when buying impulses built up; with no article costing more than a dime, you could clearly limit your expenditures.

Change becomes a factor in demand particularly where free-floating desires to buy already exist in a society. Thus, notions of newness, novelty, the latest model—the one with the gadget on it that lights up when you open the door—become important influences in the creation of demand. Styles clearly play a part in the way people live and in the housing and furnishings as well as clothing which they deem appropriate. The fine appointments of yesterday become today's junk, but the elegant antiques of the day before yesterday are coveted by many. Some people can hardly get rid of the old junk before they are reacquiring it as antiques.

Individualism, Dependency, and Symbolic Demands

As we have already seen in Chapter 1, one of the major conflicts in a highly interdependent industrial society is that which develops between the sense of personal identity of the individual and his equally compelling feelings of dependency. Other prior references indicate that full-time specialization and interdependency are accompanied by an increasing individuation of needs and interests. This augmented consciousness of individuality results in demands for self-realization and self-fulfillment.

The quest for self-realization can take a number of forms.[25] Often, it is transformed into a quest for status and recognition from others. The individual develops a consciousness of the kind of person he is, where he fits, and what he should expect from those in higher positions, positions of equivalence, subordinates, and the world in general. Frequently, there is pressure for enhancement of one's status—a demand for a constantly improving situation. This doesn't mean that everyone wants to be president; nonetheless, there are high expectations in our society that things will get better and better.

In the community, status demands take the familiar form of expectations for a particular standard of living in keeping with one's station in life. The various resources sought and gained are symbolic expressions of status. The young wife accordingly wants a washing machine not only for what it can do in the laundry, but because it is part of a "package" of appliances, all neatly boxed and wrapped in a suburban ranch house, which she has come to expect. Symbolic considerations reflecting both the social and the psychological needs of people become increasingly complex and important in interdependent, abundant societies. Unraveling the tangle of buying motives is no easy task, as the marketing experts can tell us.

What is happening in the home and community is also occurring, as we shall see, in the workplace. Employee demands are not just a reflection of their work and occupational activities; they are certainly more than a concern for wages, although these are important; they reflect also the symbolic needs of the individual as he and others like him seek out their identity and expectations in a changing world.

Differential Valuation of Resources

Thus far, we have been discussing human demands in broad outline, as a kind of "surge" or "current" running through a group and arousing a general desire for outside resources. As we attempt to become more specific about the nature of human demands, we must take into account the different interests of people and the different priorities

---

[25] For a fuller development of this point in another context, see Chapter 2.

which individuals assign to the resources they covet. Exchange of a positive kind would be impossible if everyone's interests were alike and especially if they assigned the same urgency to the demands they shared.

Many areas of interests are broadly shared. Physiological needs and the deeper psychological needs are obvious examples of common interests. In addition, human beings typically share with others the culturally based demands of their society. However, outside these rather basic considerations, the interests of people, especially in highly developed societies, become more and more individuated and differentiated. The interests diverge for at least three related reasons. First, the division of labor in a complex society creates many specialized activities; people have many different jobs to perform. Different activities mean different demands. Second, the hierarchical ordering of a society places people at different levels. Things look different to those down in the valleys and those breathing the rarified atmosphere on the tops of mountains. Third, they look different to those rolling down the sides of the mountains and to those making the arduous climb upward. For our purposes in this text, occupational activities, social class characteristics or status rank, and status mobility will be very important considerations in delineating the differences in interests and demands among employees.

Even where demands are grossly similar, there are usually marked differences in the urgency with which people hope to satisfy them. This is essentially a problem of priorities. Even more specifically, it is a problem of comparison. Human beings make their judgments largely on a comparative basis. They bring a limited number of alternative demands into their fields of thought and then make their assessments.

In considering the assignment of priorities, we must add to our consideration the negative aspects of demand. We have been considering up to now only those demands which apply to the acquisition of positive resources of "goods." We must now take into account the human demands which apply to the avoidance of "bads." Certain events are regarded as punishing, painful, or unpleasant. Physical danger or harm is an obvious punishment, but there are more subtle pains and unpleasantness in our society which people strive to avoid. In a society as affirmative as ours, it is hard to believe that threat of unpleasantness plays an important part in human exchange. Yet, large segments of the exchange activities of our society are motivated primarily by avoidance demands. For example, our entire defense establishment, the huge tax burdens borne by our citizens to support it, even a major part of our so-called foreign aid program, spring primarily from avoidance demand and fear of military aggression. At less dramatic levels, union contracts are signed for fear the workers will strike or for fear the employer will take a long strike; employees in too many cases do their jobs for fear the boss will "get on their necks"; and executives limit their actions for fear they will make a mistake and get fired.

While there is some general agreement regarding the "bads" in this world, particularly at the physiological level and at the level of deep psychological offense against the integrity of the individual, the problem becomes quite sticky as we move from these more basic levels. We must regard the evaluations which people make of various "goods" and "bads" as a continuum ranging from events which practically everybody except "some kind of nut" would want to avoid to those which practically everybody except another "kind of nut" would want to gain. With this sort of gradation in mind, it can readily be seen that what is "good" is relative and what is "bad," equally relative. It's like the young college student coming home for the first time. His mother greets him effusively and then, leaning back and holding him in outstretched arms, asks eagerly, "And how is my little boy?" "Relative to what," says her now educated son. Or better still, another version has a friend asking, "How's your wife?" And the other responds, "Compared to whom?"

As one thinks about the question of priority of demands, other considerations come to the fore. It is interesting to note that our concept of *costs* is based on a comparative analysis of the "goods" and "bads" in a given situation. The question confronting us is typically, "If I seek this, I can't seek that; which is more important to me?" Or, "If I go for that, I will suffer the following consequences all of which are 'bad.' How can I proceed in order to gain something that I want and at the same time limit my losses or costs?" In any exchange-situation, we are inevitably confronted with the problem of giving up something in order to gain something; there are always costs which, as we have seen, can range all the way from direct punishment to lost gains.[26]

The adjustment possibilities in exchange situations involving gains and costs or even losses are also interesting to consider. The creative, highly integrative individual can bring his full abilities to bear on considerations such as these, as he strives to take a stance which will bring

---

[26] For a fuller development of ideas about exchange situations, see George C. Homans, *Social Behavior: Its Elementary Forms* (New York: Harcourt, Brace, & Co., Inc., 1961), especially chap. iii.

him the greatest return for the payments that he will have to make. The complex mind can deal with the various alternatives presented to him in combinations of intricate design. Indeed, the business enterprise itself can be viewed in part as an effort to introduce this kind of complexity into the exchange situation. The simpler mind will deal with his gains and losses as clear-cut alternatives here and now. The simple, uncluttered mind sometimes can do better in an exchange situation than the mind which has become so complex that it is no longer capable of taking a stance on any issue. This is particularly true over the short haul, or in situations where immediate action is more important than long-range thinking.

As we might expect, there is a great deal of compensation that takes place in exchange situations. As a person faces possible punishment as the price he must pay for achieving a particular objective, he sometimes learns that he didn't really want that anyway. Typically, the whole process of stabilizing social interaction is a matter of adjustment along these lines as people learn what they are capable of accomplishing and what they must settle for in this competitive world.

The whole issue of the level of compensatory adjustment which is "mentally healthy" is an important one and one which has been given a great deal of attention, particularly as more is understood about the dynamics of the individual personality. Professor Chris Argyris, for example, has centered his attention on the problems of frustration created by the conflict between the "mature personality" and the dependency demands of the typical organization and especially of the management which shapes and controls it.[27] Assuredly, there is great tension in this situation as individuals strive to "stand on their own two feet" and the organization and its management insists on compliancy and dependence.

Closely related to the foregoing considerations are the efforts of men, particularly in an abundant society where many things are possible, to seek out an identity and posture which will give them a sense of direction and purpose. It is interesting to note that, as aspirations move to higher levels and more things become possible, the individual often becomes more uneasy and less sure of himself. Oftentimes, it is almost a relief to face a crisis where the issues seems clear-cut; good is good, and bad is bad. You know what you have to do and don't have to "stew"

---

[27] Chris Argyris, "The Individual and Organization: Some Problems of Mutual Adjustment," *Administrative Science Quarterly* (Ithaca: Cornell University), Vol. II (June, 1957), p. 1.

about it. We have known executives, for example, who more or less drifted when things were going well, but could nonetheless still rise to a crisis, like old warriors. The search for a stance is a crucial one in our abundant society; at least, people think it is. It may not, however, be as important as some believe. The world is a changing, relative thing in which ultimate solutions to the problem of evaluation and priorities are not likely to occur. In this connection, we like to distinguish between those who think in terms of ideologies or ultimate systems of values and those who think in terms of problems and meeting these with the best solutions available now and in the foreseeable future. In a society as complex as ours, ultimate systems of value, rigid ideological dicta, except as they relate to the deeper human needs, seem nonsensical. We call your attention in this connection to the work of Milton Rokeach, discussed in Chapter 2, regarding the "closed" mind.

The trend in our society is toward an elimination of "low priority" items from exchange consideration. This is certainly one of the basic aspects of the dynamics of the abundant society. The trend toward greater and greater concern with human relationships and with the individual personality is evidence simply that other considerations are no longer issues. We are not, for example, debating the issue of the industrial revolution or the factory with its advanced technology as it was debated and fought, for example, by the home weavers, carders, and spinners in Devon in the eighteenth century. We are no longer debating the issue of bare subsistence pay on the grounds that the masses will only work up to a certain point once the grim physiological incentives to eat and drink have been satiated. Our entire economy is geared to abundance—an abundance shared by all the people. Under such circumstances, personal and relational issues loom larger and larger.

Differential Possession of Resources

If all resources in demand were possessed by everyone, obviously there would be no need for exchange. People would be completely self-sufficient and in no way covet the possessions of others. *Possession* should be taken to mean *control*. John R. Commons, who many years ago analyzed the social economy around the concept of transactional relations, pointed up the importance of the meaning of property in transactional relations.[28] To Commons, property rights were derived

---

[28] John R. Commons, *The Economics of Collective Action* (New York: Macmillan Co., 1951). Included in the appendix is an excellent summary of Commons by Kenneth Parsons who helped edit the book.

from the state and reflected through the law. The law and the meaning of property has changed through the years. Kenneth Parsons in his summary of Commons' ideas states:[29]

Commons has traced out, especially in his *Legal Foundation of Capitalism*, the long, halting judicial procedure by which the meaning of property has been changed. In the original common-law conception, property meant a physical corporeal thing held for one's own use. Gradually, property came to mean the sale or exchange value of the thing rather than the physical object. This shift from things for use to rights of sale changes the meaning of property from things to expected behavior regarding things. Thus Commons concludes, "The term 'property' cannot be defined except by defining all the activities which individuals and the community are at liberty or required to do or not to do, with reference to the object claimed as property."

Business, according to Commons, could not exist as a "going concern" without some guarantee that expected behavior would in fact occur. "Property" thus becomes a system of expected duties and obligations in transactional relations.

Extending Commons' thinking further, we might even conceive of possession or property rights as social power—a privilege granted by society to control and exchange resources of various kinds. This is something far beyond simple notions of private property. After all, the people of the United States *own* TVA; yet, it is set up as a distinct and separate corporation and has rights of control and power over its disposable resources. The same is true of business corporations, as Berle and Means pointed out many years ago.[30] Here, too, power is not concentrated in the hands of the owners (stockholders) as such but is more frequently possessed by management.

The concentration of machinery and capital necessary for full-time specialization and the co-ordination of effort required makes for the development of corporate bodies which have not only technological significance but political importance as well. The superiority of this mode of organization is unchallenged. As a consequence, the major material resources in our society are controlled by large-scale organizations, not only in the business and economic areas but in educational, religious, and other areas as well.

This concentration of power is controlled, however, in a number of ways in a democratic society. First, the charter of the large-scale organization is limited. A democratic society is marked by an aversion to

---

[29] Kenneth Parsons, "John R. Commons' Point of View," *ibid.*, p. 357.

[30] Adolph A. Berle and Gardiner C. Means, *The Modern Corporation and Private Property* (New York: Macmillan Co., 1932).

monolithic organizations; we are essentially pluralistic not in the sense of individual anarchy but in the sense that our major institutions are confined to particular functions and limited objectives. Not only are religious, educational, business, and governmental organizations in broad competition for support, but, within each area, there is competition. Thus, one business with the same charter competes with another. How much competition is needed to secure the most effective use of power for the greatest good is a moot question and one which is constantly deliberated. Certainly, the trend at the moment is toward greater and greater concentrations of power through mergers and combinations of great and complex scope.[31]

It must be remembered that corporations are creations of government. Power is, therefore, limited by direct governmental control at all levels. This control, however, is not of the nature of specific directives regarding how and what resources are to be created and how they are to be distributed. They are rather legalized rules of conduct which define what cannot be done—that is, when someone is "off-side" and when a "personal" foul has been committed. As a consequence, there are many gray areas which business management brings into focus and assesses for itself.

The business enterprise itself thus becomes within limits an autonomous center of power, setting its own rules, determining its own beliefs and values, and deciding on particular actions. As Berle and Means said:[32]

The institution here envisaged calls for analysis, not in terms of business enterprise but in terms of social organization. On the one hand, it involves a concentration of power in the economic field comparable to the concentration of power in the mediaeval church or of political power in the national state. On the other hand, it involves the interrelation of a wide diversity of economic interest,—those of the "owners" who supply the capital, those of the workers who "create," those of the consumer who give value to the products of the enterprise, and above all those of the control who wield power.

Later, they said:[33]

In direct opposition to the . . . doctrine of strict property rights is the view, apparently held by the great corporation lawyers and by certain students of the field, that corporate development has created a new set of relationships, giving to the groups in control powers which are absolute and not limited by any implied obligation with respect to their use.

---

[31] See especially W. Lloyd Warner, *The Corporation in the Emergent American Society* (New York: Harper & Bros., 1962).

[32] Berle and Means, *op. cit.*, p. 352.

[33] *Ibid.*, p. 354.

There has been much water over the dam since these words were written in 1932. Certainly, the average business executive does not feel that his powers are absolute. Nonetheless, it is important that we analyze the organization of business at all levels and especially at the management level as a moral order and as a system for reconciling differences in the beliefs and values applying to the use of resources and their allocation. Inasmuch as the major activities of our society are carried on through large-scale organizations, it is exceedingly important that we understand how these work as systems of power and morality. Moreover, we should understand how hierarchical organizations function as systems of control.

Quest for Power

From the foregoing, we can begin to understand how human exchange can be translated into relationships of power. For often the outcome of an exchange depends upon who holds the most power—that is, who possesses the most resources of a positive and negative variety. Securing and threatening to use negative resources are an easy way to resolve an exchange situation. You simply threaten to "kick a man in the teeth" if he doesn't comply. There can be, of course, and usually are, more subtle ways of using power over negative resources to accomplish one's ends; but, whether in blatant or subtle form, the "mailed fist" frequently reveals itself. In fact, behind the power of every government is the control exercised over the use of arms to gain one's ends, the privilege of forcibly making someone comply if he is unwilling voluntarily to do so.

Much of the chatter about tough-mindedness and soft-mindedness revolves around this issue of use of negative resources to gain over-all objectives. In other words, it is, at least in part, an argument about "goods" versus "bads" and their efficacy in human exchange. Looked at in this way, it can be more readily understood why tough-mindedness is often self-defeating. The use of negative resources only breeds in the other man a quest for control over equally powerful forces. It also creates a desire for revenge. We shall have much more to say on this subject throughout this text.

Concept of Social Property

We should point out, if indeed it has not already been implied, that property or possession over resources is not limited to physical events. Many of the satisfactions which human beings seek are not physical at all but psychological and social. It is interesting to note that social recognition, status, and the sense of self-fulfillment are all satisfactions which must in part be secured from others. This means that the control over these satisfactions are inevitably possessed by others. Thus, every human being has "social property" which can be utilized in human exchange. A smile, a friendly gesture, or the withholding of these are valuable resources in human exchange.

However, "social property" can be something more than the social niceties or personal offenses which every human being can turn off or on. Social organizations create by their hierarchical structures differential status opportunities. Hierarchical organizations thus come to "possess" status rewards and punishments which are powerful influences in the exchanges taking place between management and employees. We like friendly gestures from anyone; but, if they come from someone who possesses status, they are far more significant to us. Gaining position and the security, recognition, and status derived from organized activities are major factors of motivation in the modern society. They are exceedingly important in binding the individual to large-scale organizations.

Transactional Processes and Reconciling Values

Transaction requires communication. We are very much aware of the significance of communication at the international level. The structural agencies for establishing communication are limited, although we are far better off than we were before World War II. In business, communication is established through social structures of one kind or another, sometimes called markets, sometimes the "collective bargaining table," and sometimes organizations. John R. Commons distinguishes three types of transactions which imply the different structural arrangements in which bargaining can take place. The three types of transactions are bargaining, managerial, and rationing. Quoting once again from Parsons' excellent summary of Commons' ideas, we find: [34]

Bargaining transactions occur between persons who are legal equals; in case of dispute the adjudicator holds them equal before the law. If they are economic equals, the negotiators reach agreement by the mere persuasion of personality; if they are economically unequal, there may by coercion, as in the case of the disparate withholding power of a workman bargaining with a corporation over a job. The subject matter of a bargaining transaction is the familiar price of the market, although more precisely it pertains to alienation of ownership.

The managerial transaction occurs between parties which stand in the legal

---

[34] Kenneth Parsons, *op. cit.*, p. 352.

relation of superior and inferior; it represents a command-and-obedience relationship. The typical situation includes a foreman and a workman. One orders; the other obeys. In terms of subject matter managerial transactions pertain to the processes of physical performance, as the construction of a machine, or the physical delivery of goods.

It is evident that bargaining and managerial transactions are interdependent and not clearly separate in fact. They are related as limiting and complementary factors. "As a bargainer, the modern wage earner is deemed to be the legal equal of his employer, induced to enter the transaction by persuasion or coercion; but once he is permitted to enter the place of employment he becomes legally inferior, induced by commands which he is required to obey."

The third type of transaction, the rationing transaction, also pertains to persons in the legal relationship of superior-inferior. However, the rationing is done by means of negotiation and agreement among persons who have been authorized to apportion the benefits and burdens. The allocations of tax burdens has long been the typical rationing transaction between the concern and the general politico-economic organization.

The distinctions made by Commons are primarily concerned with legal and economic differences in transactional structures. Our interest is perhaps less analytic and more empirical. A company transacts its business in a variety of structures depending on the nature of its industrial and commercial activities. Each of these structures constitutes a kind of subsystem with a set of beliefs regarding how business is to be conducted, what roles the various participating parties should play, a status structure, rules of conduct, and so on. In other words, a transactional structure is truly a social system just as real as the family or the community. It may be a relatively loose, informal structure in which the rules of conduct and patterns of expected and accepted behavior have arisen more or less naturally. Or it may be a tightly controlled structure with a central administration supported by legal authority which carefully defined what relationships will prevail among the participants. But, however it shapes up, it still evidences all of the characteristics of a social system.

Knowing how to operate within a particular transactional structure requires that the participant has assimilated the beliefs, rules of conduct, and expected patterns of behavior of the structure. Moreover, he must know what his own expected role is and have the ability to perform it. Within limits depending on the structure, he can add his own individual variations—grace notes if you will to the basic melody; but he cannot stray too far without danger of alienating himself from the system. Like all structures, however, in our society, transactional subsystems are continuously in process of change. The participant not only must keep up with and take advantage of change, but he has the opportunity himself of being inventive and visualizing new possibilities. Herein lies one of the important challenges of business—namely, the opportunity for new techniques and new approaches to transactional relations.

The importance of the social system which operates in the transactional structure cannot be too strongly emphasized. The transactional structure not only serves the function of establishing the possibility of communication and exchange but prescribes how this communication will take place, who will play what roles, what conduct is regarded as acceptable, who has what power in the bargaining situation, the importance of influentials in determining behavior, and so on. When we think of the housewife entering the shopping center, she is there obviously to buy and sell. She must learn and enact a particular role. As a matter of fact, she literally becomes an employee of the supermarket, pushing her little basket about and picking her own order. If it weren't for a few dishonest people in this world, she could check herself out, ringing up the cash register, and giving herself the trading stamps. More than this, she has to learn how to be a "good" shopper. She is taught by the market system itself and by her informal associations with fellow-shoppers and other influentials.[35] If she moves from one type of market structure to another, she has to alter her behavior. There is a remarkable difference in prescribed behavior in different kinds of markets, even those that are entirely within the retail system. For example, in a fixed-price retail operation, when the salesclerk says, "The price is seventy-five cents," you don't respond with, "I'll give you fifty!" Yet, in a haggling market, this kind of behavior is perfectly appropriate. The difference in digging through the dress racks in J. C. Penney's and buying at Blum's Vogue is not just a difference in cost consciousness on the part of the buyer; it is a difference in learned behavior regarding the role of the seller and the role of the buyer.

The transactional structures of our society are well understood as legal and economic systems. However, studies of the social influences operating within these structures are sorely needed. Exchange seldom takes place totally within the sterile, rational atmosphere of economic considerations. While these are taken into account to a greater or lesser extent, depending on the patterns developing within the various structures, the influences of social role, status, traditional practices, rules of conduct, all play an important part. Even in those markets consciously

---

[35] Elihu Katz and Paul F. Lazarsfeld, *Personal Influence: The Part Played by People in the Flow of Mass Communication* (Glencoe, Ill.: Free Press, 1955).

and deliberately set up as rational economic models such as the stock market, the process of trading and exchange takes place within a social context and is influenced thereby.[36]

While the myriad of buying and selling markets are of great interest to us, the transactional structure which most concerns us in this text is the hierarchical and functional organization of a business. Ordinarily a business organization is viewed as a monolithic structure which is highly co-ordinated and integrated around specific goals and objectives. This image is true of the production and operational aspects of business, particularly in manufacturing, but a major feature of the organization is its transactional structure. A significant deficiency in current organizational theory is the focus on business organization as a single, unified, integrated system of action. From this view, it is easy to draw the analogy that the business organization is a kind of superorganism complete with brains (management), nervous system (chain of command), muscles (workers and machines), and need for survival and homeostasis. We submit that the typical business organization is a lower form of "animal" than this and more useful, viewed as a tenuously linked, transactional system involving divergent beliefs and actions, sometimes coming together for more or less brief periods of time and sometimes flying apart. The business organization is somewhat integrated, to be sure, around various operations and processes; furthermore, it develops habitual modes of behavior, occupational identification, rules of conduct, and other accommodations. But these controls are no different in kind from the controls that develop in market structures and other competitive transactional systems.

If we view the business organization as a transactional structure rather than a goal-directed system of production, we can begin to understand the role of the business executive as he operates within a complex transactional system which not only extends outward into the money markets, raw-material markets, tool machines markets, industrial markets of all kinds, and the myriad of consumer markets but also extends downward and outward into the organization itself. Thus, he finds himself in a competitive, transactional relationship with his own boss and colleagues in mahogany row; he thinks of this as the good old American pattern of getting ahead, getting his fair share of the resources of the business, pushing his ideas and the functions of his particular division or department. He also finds himself continuously negotiating with his

---

[36] See Ira O. Glick, "A Social Psychological Study of Futures Trading" (unpublished Ph.D. dissertation, Department of Sociology, The University of Chicago, 1957).

subordinates; he thinks of this as motivating his employees, planning and developing better production methods to get more work out per unit of cost, introducing efficiency, building morale, making a better world, and providing leadership. But all the while, he is engaged in a highly dynamic, transactional process in which he is trading his own efforts for status, prestige, and financial rewards and trading financial and nonfinancial incentives with his subordinates to gain greater productivity, loyalty, and support.

Executive behavior and human relations at the lower levels cannot readily be understood without introducing the note of volatility implied in a transactional structure. Sociologists used to talk about competition as a universal pattern of interaction. Conflict, accommodation, and assimilation came about as a result of conscious awareness of competition and the need either to dominate the other fellow, adjust one's interests to those of the other person, or else knuckle under and accept his domination. These social processes of interaction are all at work in the typical business organization. The stability which does exist is a consequence of considerations of mutual aid, sense of interdependence, and sociability and of willful efforts to seek integrative solutions to problems involving real conflict in interests. But the underlying, inherent volatility remains and indeed is necessary to the adaptation of the business to its constantly changing environment.

The reconciling of values is the critical aspect of the transactional process. For exchange to take place, there must be agreement among the transacting parties. As we have seen in the previous section, the situation or structure in which transactions take place are major determinants of transactional values and beliefs. What goes in one situation may not be at all acceptable in another. There are several key dimensions which identify most transactional situations. The first of these has to do with the extent to which there are commonly shared beliefs and values. In a situation in which there are clear-cut guide lines, such as in highly traditional societies or in some industrial bureacracies, then transactions take place easily, without overt conflict, and, we might add, without change. All societies have commonly held rules of behavior governing interaction. Some of the more obvious of these have to do with social courtesies—like saying, "Good morning," when someone says, "Good morning," to you. But many reciprocities which are almost habitual in our society have considerably more significance than this—as, for example, the reciprocities which develop between the boss and his employees. The authority structure of business largely depends on commonly shared values which define the relationship which ought to prevail between the supervisor and his charges.

Those habitual or traditional reciprocities often take place at an *unconscious* level. Indeed, when we begin to think consciously about transactions and what we are getting for what we are giving, the chances are that we are in a situation where there are few, if any, commonly shared beliefs regarding how differences in interest can be reconciled. In short, when reconciling differences is a matter of *conscious* negotiation, the values which ought to prevail are likely to be rather ill-defined. A society, however, could not endure for long if all of its reciprocal relationships were negotiated each time there was a difference in interest. Even labor-management negotiations are conducted within a broad framework of mutual accord and commonly shared beliefs. Moreover, such negotiations result in a contract, supported by law, which guarantees accord over a relatively long period of time.

The so-called "rational" aspects of business decisions and actions are concerned with the conscious negotiational interest of management as it deals with the demands of employees, unions, stockholders, customers, government, and sources of supply. Here we find an effort to calculate costs and values, maintain a systematic accounting of gains and losses in given transactional situations, and search out more profitable exchanges. Nonetheless, in spite of this "intended rationality," as Professor Herbert A. Simon once put it, all sorts of unconscious, vaguely defined, and more broadly shared beliefs and sentiments come into the picture and guide business behavior. Indeed, some exchanges may not readily lend themselves to objective calculation at all, since they involve deeper emotions and sentiments which are sensed only as generalized anxieties or satisfactions as the case may be. All of this is evidenced by the fact that we can hardly put into words the profound emotional satisfactions gained out of intimate personal relationships. Any social system, business included, is bound together by deep emotional and sentimental ties.

Another dimension which is crucially important in transactional situations concerns the relationships of the transacting parties in the hierarchical authority and status structures of society. All societies develop patterns of "higher," "lower," and "equal" around which men organize their relationships. There is a tendency to think of reciprocal relationships as relationships between equals. However, George Orwell's observation that "All men were born equal, but some were born more equal than others" suggests the reality of social arrangements in all societies. Thus, we learn to behave one way with those in higher positions, another way with those who are subordinate to us, and still another with our colleagues. So subtle are our changes in behavior as we move from one situation to the next that we are hardly aware of how our actions are modified to meet the shifting demands. In fact, knowing how to behave in our society is essentially a matter of knowing how to adapt to the give and take of various social situations. Thus, in business we learn to treat those in higher authority with deference. We know, whether we like it or not, that we can't deal with the boss as though he were one of the boys. In the same way, we acquire a pattern of reserve in dealing with subordinates. We know that unbending too much may alter the relationship and thereby influence transactional results.

Those in a higher position in our society obviously have certain advantages in transactional relationships. Indeed, the term *higher* could readily lend themselves to objective calculation at all, since they in a higher position possesses more tangible and social property and, accordingly, is in a better position to grant or withhold both rewards and punishments. A person has power when, for any reasons, social, psychological, or economic, he possesses the right, within varying limits, to reward or punish, that is, to grant or withhold resources. The withholding of reward can be thought of as punishment, just as the withholding of punishment under certain circumstances can be regarded as reward. The wife who gets beaten by her drunken husband every Saturday night might think true love is dawning when he starts beating her only once a month. In punishment-centered bureaucracies, considerable motivation might be generated among subordinates by the withholding of punishment. The employee who knows that he will be "eaten out" or even fired if he does not toe the mark may regard himself as quite well off if the boss gives him nothing at all. Nothing is better than something in this case. But the employee in another organization may feel very unhappy because the boss never tells him how well he is doing and seldom praises him for his good work. Here, nothing becomes a real punishment.

In an egalitarian society such as ours, there can be anxiety on both sides in any unequal transactional situations involving differences in power and status. Those who are out of power tend to feel anxious and sometimes hostile towards power figures. One of America's heroic types is the aggressive underdog who kicks authority or power and prestige in the teeth. Various kinds of compensatory behavior appear in relationships of inequality—informal resistance groups, critical attitudes about the bosses, usually out of earshot, depreciating nicknames for those in authority like "Tweedledum" and "Tweedledee," and other devices for "equalizing" relationships. Nevertheless, it is not just among the underdogs that status anxieties exist in our society. Oftentimes, the "bosses" wear their mantles of authority with considerable uneasiness. There is a certain sense of guilt engendered in relationships of inequality —relationships where one can demand more from others than one gives. Again, all kinds of compensatory behavior appear. In some cases, there are intermittent symbolic practices communicating the essential egalitarian nature of the relationship. For example, the general occasionally visits and sits with the privates in the foxhole. The big boss unbends a little at the company picnic and makes an ass of himself trying to play first base in the softball game. Or the chairman of the board goes into the shop and talks to some of the boys on the assembly line. At a more subtle level, the boss attempts to explain the inequality of his relationship with subordinates by attributing his power and authority to the business organization. His right of decision and command thus becomes part of a larger, objectified system. It is not something within him, although he may secretly think of himself as a leader of men, organizational structure or not.

The projected image or idea of an organization is an important factor in transactions. A man at any level can find himself giving his "all" for an abstract idea of an ongoing organization—the ivy-walled university or good old Sears with its catalogues, sprawling warehouses, and dynamic retail stores. Psychologists speak of such relationships as "personifications" or sometimes "reifications." The individual makes the abstract real, so real in fact that some of his deepest emotions are tied up with his interaction with his own projected ideas of the organized activities of which he is a part. Symbolic attachments become extremely important in such relationships. For example, in the song "America, the Beautiful," the words have to do primarily with a physical reality: "O beautiful for spacious skies, for amber waves of grain, for purple mountain majesties above the fruited plain." The words mean nothing in and of themselves. To describe America as uniquely beautiful because of its skies, mountains, flat lands, grain fields, and orchards is patently ridiculous. Lots of countries display these same features. Symbolically, however, invoking an image of the land arouses deep emotions within every American, for the image is associated with home, brotherhood, history, loyalty, and love of country. The same kind of symbolic attachment occurs in other relationships between the individual and organized activities. The ivy walls of our alma mater might invoke memories of a positive or negative nature depending upon our personal experiences. But the ivy itself really only means that the building is old, the brick probably crumbling, and the university sorely in need of more donations from loyal alumni in order to get rid of the old firetrap which looks so picturesque on the dean's Christmas cards.

Some of the best and the worst features of man's nature are revealed in his associations with abstractions and in the emotions which he projects upon organizations. It is probably true that no organized activities could exist if man did not have the capabilities of interacting with abstractions. If every commitment depended upon the quality and consequences of interaction between individuals, society and large-scale organizations would be in a continuous state of flux and characterized by considerable instability. More than this, man is typically at his best when he commits himself to ideals which are somehow greater than he; in this way, humankind rises above itself. Yet, chauvinism, blind organizational loyalties, identification with "we-groups" and rejection of "other-groups," "tribal incest" as Erich Fromm has called it, all of these have led mankind down the road to war, conflict, racial tensions, and blind hate. Thus, we find society depending for its stability upon the tendency of its members to commit themselves to abstract organized activities and discovering that its worst sicknesses are somehow related to the same fundamental human characteristic.

Still another set of dimensions influencing the way differences are reconciled in transactional relations revolve around the degree of formality or informality characterizing the situation or the degree to which the situation is regarded as impersonal or personal. It is, of course, extremely difficult to separate the personal from the formal and official. We can recall the president of a company a number of years ago with whom we were discussing an employee attitude survey. He said, "I am all for the survey but I want you to deal only with facts. Just leave personalities out of this!" We said then and we would say to him now, "But it is impossible to deal with human relations without taking into account the personal side." Nevertheless, the way a man strives to behave in an official, formal role or capacity is quite different from his manner in personal situations. He might in the name of his occupation apply certain values which he would find unthinkable in other circumstances. For example, in business, he would automatically expect a return on any loan which he made. Yet, he would lend his lawnmower to his neighbor without thought of gain. Formal transactions inevitably appear to be more selfish and narrow than informal transactions. The man of business in that role is not a whole man when he is acting in an official capacity; he is a limited-purpose man.

Closely related to the above are the differences in transactional relationships occurring in face-to-face situations and those where considerable spatial as well as social and psychological distance is involved. In face-to-face situations where individuals are directly and personally engaged, it is difficult if not impossible to operate entirely in an official, abstract way. But where others are remote and there is no intimacy, any action is possible. Indeed, some of the worst crimes against humanity have been perpetrated in just such circumstances. Yet, insulation from face-to-face relations may be necessary for executives attempting to make decisions in limited-purpose organizations as long as such decisions are accompanied by a sense of deep compassion and humanity. True justice requires broad understanding and integrative thinking, which may sometimes be hampered by the immediacy of the demands of face-to-face relationships.

Social Norms and the Principle of Justice

From the foregoing we can begin to grasp the complexity of the transactional relationships characterizing our business society. We can sense the difficult task not only of the business executive who has primary responsibility but of others in the organization as they seek to understand their own interests and the interests of the other guy; strive to gain their own ends; and yet, at the same time, secure the support from others necessary in the intricate system of reciprocities constituting a modern, highly interdependent society. In this task, as one might well expect, there are selfish, ego-centered individuals who seek always to gain their own interests. Such men are blocked and hemmed in by a competitive order, a moral order, and a legal order. Counterbalancing the selfish ones are a certain number of altruists who for reasons of guilt, compassion, masochism, lack of ego-development, or true Christianity "turn the other cheek" or allow themselves to be "taken." Finally, there are the great majority of individuals who give and take, sometimes gaining, sometimes losing, but hopefully batting .500.

It is dramatically apparent that the reconciliation of values in transactional relationships is fundamentally a moral issue. The moral order of a society is shaped within the framework of transactions in which it engages. In our society, the entrepreneurial matrix, together with the individual enterprises which compose it and the market structures of all varieties in which transactions take place, is one of the principal arenas in which our beliefs about man's relationship to man are shaped.

While it is true that moral codes and ethical principles are functional to the particular activities and pursuits of men and, therefore, often relative, nonetheless, deep within human society, perhaps the basis of society itself, is a more or less universal principle of justice which guides human interaction. So fundamental is this principle that it is the very core of humanity and the source of all stability as well as adjustment in human society. Professor A. R. Radcliffe-Brown once said, "The nearest I can come to what I could call an abstract structural principle, which I believe is characteristic of all social systems, is the principle of justice."[37] Justice means what is fair and right in human exchange; every society develops norms, rules, and laws regarding exchange ranging from primitive laws of retaliation—*lex talionis*, an eye for an eye— to the complicated systems of justice in modern courts of law. The notion of justice not only applies to positive exchange—the exchange so to speak of goods, but to negative exchange—the exchange of beds. But basic to both is the principle of equivalent return, that is, giving what you get. In less highly developed societies, this takes the form of direct exchange. Professor Radcliffe-Brown points out that the "principle of equivalent return" takes three forms.[38] First is the "law of talion." "*A* injures *B*. The justice steps in and says *B* is now entitled to receive satisfaction for the injury inflicted upon him. *B* is entitled to injure *A*." The second form is what might be called the "law of equal benefit." "*A* benefits *B*, whereupon *B* is under obligation to benefit *A*, and *A* can expect a benefit of equivalent value." A third form of the "principle of equivalent return" is the notion of indemnification for an injury. "*B* now compensates for the injury he has inflicted on *A* by paying an idemnity." It will be noted that equivalent return inevitably involves the complex question of equal value. Professor Alvin W. Gouldner says:[39]

Equivalence may have at least two forms, the sociological and psychodynamic significance of which are apt to be quite distinct. In the first case, heteromorphic

---

[37] A. R. Radcliffe-Brown, *Natural Science of Society* (Glencoe, Ill.: Free Press, 1957), p. 131.

[38] *Ibid.*, p. 133.

[39] Alvin W. Gouldner, "The Norm of Reciprocity," *American Sociological Review*, Vol. XXV, No. 2 (April, 1960), p. 172.

reciprocity, equivalence may mean that the things exchanged may be concretely different but should be equal in *value*, as defined by the actors in the situation. In the second case, homeomorphic reciprocity, equivalence may mean that exchanges should be concretely alike, or identical in form, either with respect to the things exchanged or to the circumstances under which they are exchanged. In the former, equivalence calls for "tit for tat"; in the latter, equivalence calls for "tat for tat." Historically, the most important expression of homeomorphic reciprocity is found in the *negative* norms of reciprocity, that is, in sentiments of retaliation where the emphasis is placed not on the return of benefits but on the return of injuries, and is best exemplified by the *lex talionis*.

Whether or not the exchange involves equivalent acts or events, the underlying principle is equivalent return. Thus, in human society everywhere there is a constant movement towards equivalence in exchange and equality in relationships—the inexorable, continuous search for what is fair and right under various transactional circumstances. The search goes on in courts of law, in the market place, at the bargaining table, in the day-by-day activities of men as they work and play together.

SUMMARY

This entire chapter is a summary of key dimensions and ideas regarding business enterprise, organization, and administration. We have covered a wide area, pursuing concepts that seemed significant in gaining a deeper understanding of the functions of the business executive. We have attempted to place the business executive within the complex entrepreneurial and exchange environment in which he operates. Our main purpose has been to paint a picture of business which realistically reflects the true complexity of the business world. If the student at this juncture feels exposed to a myriad of elements, buffeting him on all sides, that is precisely the way we want him to feel.

In the next chapter, we shall center our attention directly on the executive within the business complex.

5. THE MANAGEMENT FUNCTION

WE HAVE BEEN discussing the entrepreneurial matrix and the characteristics of the exchange and transactional relationships in a business society. It now remains for us to discuss the role of the individual business enterprise and the function of management within it.

An individual business enterprise is simply one phase of a much larger system of exchange; each enterprise is so dependent on other business and industrial activities and so enmeshed in the larger system that it can hardly be regarded, from one point of view, as having an independent existence. Yet, from another standpoint, it is distinct and self-contained. What makes it self-contained is the fact that each business is itself a focal point of exchange relationships. A business enterprise is a particular convergence of resources and interests involving stockholder-owners who contribute seed money or services and are interested in capital gains and dividends; investors who contribute capital and seek interest earnings; employees who contribute skill and labor and seek wages, career opportunities, and security; customers who pay money for goods and services which they can use in their own pursuits; and so on.

The exchange system of a business is not a unitary, highly controlled structure of action organized around a single objective. It is instead a pattern of exchanges in which the bond or cohesive force is, at least in part, mutual advantage or usefulness and in which there are as many objectives as there are identifiable socioeconomic groups participating. It is a system in which the actors must not only be aware of their own demands but of the demands of others. It is a system of human relations in which one man's objectives and interests are set against another's and in which some kind of adjustment, coaptation, or equilibrium must be established among the contending demands. It is a structure characterized, as we have already indicated, by flux and change and recurrent states of equilibrium and disequilibrium.

It is clear that management sits in the midst of this complex of demands, counterdemands, and activities. It is management's primary job to bring together human resources into relationships of mutual usefulness. This means that management must be capable first, of perceiving mutually useful relationships and second, of mediating differences in values and interests so that advantageous relationships can be established, maintained, and developed. In concrete terms, this means that management must have the vision to perceive the potentiality of new scientific and technological developments in satisfying human needs, the human skills and energies that can be put to work for useful purposes, the allocation of capital resources for fruitful ends, the challenge and opportunities presented by changes occurring everywhere. It means also that management must have the skill, moral judgment, and influence to create, develop, and maintain mutually useful relationships.

That management is dealing with complex problems hardly need be said. They are so complex in fact that many executives retreat from complexity by developing oversimplified ways of dealing with problems and challenges. Yet, in a highly developed, industrial society, we can no longer depend on oversimplified judgments. Our relationships have become increasingly governed and managed, and, as we have become more and more dependent on management, our standards of managerial performance have gone up. Robert Redfield has said about the urban revolution:[1]

This is the period in which the moral order becomes managed by an elite, or functional class, and in which the reflection and systematization accomplished by the literati have added a new dimension to the ethical and intellectual life. The moral order has now a public phase connected with deliberate policy. . . . It is the presence of two things—the state and speculative thought—and of two new types of men—the statesman and the philosopher—that distinguishes this period, this later institutionalization of moral order.

We can see that the task of management, properly conceived, is an intellectual and moral job of the highest order. It is not a job which can be performed by following a few simple rules. Nor is it a task which can be handled on the basis of personality alone or simply by being a good fellow and getting along with one's associates. Indeed, the task is so complicated that, in large companies, it is typically broken up and distributed to specialized members of the management team. Thus, we find at the top of every large-scale business organization specialists in labor relations, personnel, finance, production economics, sales, product development, and so on. In this way, the executive can concentrate on one primary set of exchange relationships. As we shall see later, this

---

[1] Robert Redfield, *The Primitive World and Its Transformation* (Ithaca: Cornell University Press, Great Seal Books, 1962), p. 65.

focus of attention creates new problems of exchange. Sometimes, the executive loses sight of the total system of relationships constituting the business.

The over-all task of management can be subdivided into a number of identifiable activities. Some of these activities involve information seeking; some involve strategic judgments; some involve transactional skills of various kinds.

INFORMATION SEEKING

Information about Exchange Relationships

A major activity of the management of any business organization is gathering information about the various exchange relationships with which the business is involved. Effective management requires a thorough knowledge of the needs and interests of the socioeconomic groups participating in the business. Product design and development, for example, must be related to the needs and demands of the customer. Management must also be interested in the needs and interests of employees, investors, stockholders, sources of supply, and all of the groups with whom the company maintains exchange relations. A deep understanding of human needs and demands among these various groups gives management real insight into the tangible and intangible resources which it can use to strengthen relationships and develop positive motivation in all of the diverse transactions and exchanges which must take place if the enterprise is to survive and grow.

Management must have insight into the changes in needs and interests occurring among the various groups with which it deals. Understanding the dynamics of change and directions in which changes are taking place is one of the keys to successful business performance. It is often through timing and successful anticipation that real gains in business performance are achieved.

Successful management also requires an understanding of how human needs and interest can be shaped, directed, and controlled. While it is probably impossible to shift the interests of people drastically— that is, to make water flow upstream—nonetheless, it is possible to help people define their interests and specify them. Success in transactions is often a process of helping the other person move from vague desires to specific interests and demands.

Finally, management needs to understand its own interests and desires in business. Management is in a sense the transactional agent of business presiding over all transactions and mediating exchanges. The objective function of management is to ride above the particular interests of the various transacting groups and to attend the total system of transactions necessary for the survival of the business. Nevertheless, management itself is part of the transactional order; and the needs and interests of management clearly must be taken into account in the transactions which take place in business.

Information about Resources

Resources refer to the "properties" possessed by the transacting parties, the granting or withholding of which is desired in transactional relations. Resources can be tangible or intangible, and they can be negative or positive. It is important for management first of all to have an understanding of the various resources which it possesses and the extent to which these have either negative or positive value to others. The value of various resources at management's disposal will differ from one transacting group to another. For example, management's status position within the organization and the power it can exercise over subordinate employees may not have any value in dealings with suppliers or stockholders. The ability to produce a usable product may be of value to the customer but of no direct value to stockholders as stockholders.

Management also needs to know how to shape and control the resources of others in order to enhance these and make them more valuable to the business. This consideration is one of the most important of the management's skills and understandings. It is one of the truly creative aspects of business management. Successful business management is capable of taking relatively unskilled human labor and, by relating this to machines, turning out fine products in large quantities. Successful management is also capable of taking invested capital and putting it to work in more effective ways. All along the line we see business management developing the undeveloped resources of others. Interestingly enough, as management develops the resources of others, it enhances the value of their contribution. Thus, unskilled labor, which in a sense has little value separate from the productive apparatus of business and industry, organizes into unions and makes demands on management for a higher valuation of its efforts. Management sometimes thinks labor is ungrateful, but this is the nature of the system.

Business occupies a central position in our society because it is capable of utilizing and placing a value on human resources. Its role in our society will diminish when and if it ceases to be a dominant employer of such resources. At first blush, this point may seem academic. However, with automation, manufacturing, which is a major segment of our business society, may fall behind as did agriculture as a primary employer of labor. From a profit and efficiency standpoint, automation may appear to be the right approach; but, from the standpoint of power in our society, it may be wrong. Manufacturing has been an exceedingly important developer and utilizer of human resources and, as such, has been a principal factor in the valuation of human contributions and in the distribution of salaries, wages, and other income. If manufacturing ceases to exercise this function, other types of enterprises will take over as dominant organizations in our society.

It goes without saying that the central position which business presently occupies in our society places heavy moral responsibilities on management. Business can literally create or eliminate human resources. A modern, industrial society, the directions which it takes, and the character of its citizens are all intimately related to the value which management places on various human resources and the way it develops these. A major contribution of modern business has been its ability literally to put people to work in more and more effective ways. Obviously, as a society, we do not want to lose the positive affirmation of human capabilities which this spirit implies.

Ways of Seeking Information

Management strives to gain information in a variety of ways. This usually takes the form of examining cost figures gathered by the accounting department, looking at sales figures, reading information presented in trade journals and provided by trade associations, listening to speeches, conversing with associates on the job, listening to intelligence reports provided by spies and stool pigeons, attending meetings of the local Chamber of Commerce, Manufacturers' Association, personnel directors, purchasing agents, accountants, and so on, and generally picking up whatever scuttlebutt is available. Beliefs about what is happening are all too frequently formed on the basis of very informal and usually inadequate information. However, most businesses are not universities seeking the ultimate truth; moreover, except for the largest corporations, most of them can hardly afford to spend very much time or money on information gathering. As a consequence, the majority of businesses operate pretty much on the beliefs formulated by the top manager and his key staff. The quality of these men determines the quality of the actions taken by the business.

A major characteristic of large-scale organization is its proliferation of information-gathering activities. While the beliefs of top management still are crucial to the ultimate decisions made, now their thinking is supported and enhanced by top-level staff executives, intellectuals, consultants, and research institutions of all varieties, who really dig in and gather information through massive research efforts. The large-scale organization has its scouts out watching all sorts of events, searching out ideas about the present reality and emerging reality of the future. Some of the most important of these scouts are representatives of top management itself, who through their personal connections as powerful figures in our society are able to glean information about unfolding events, history in the making, directly from those who are responsible for these events. The advantage gained from direct contact with the history makers can hardly be calculated.

It is interesting to consider the various procedures which might be followed in gathering information about exchange situations. One procedure is to grant this responsibility directly to business management and to give it the authority to sift, sort, and assess the evolving human interests and needs and the emerging resources of our economy. Another is to set up associations such as unions which will presume to represent the exchange interests of the various socioeconomic groups. Still another is to rely on the assessments and judgments of experts, such as economists, sociologists, accountants, and other professionals. Finally, the government can attempt to interpret unfolding events and control the sources of information about the social and economic reality. Actually, in our complex and hopefully pluralistic society, all four procedures are used. However, it is important to observe that control over information and especially the authority to interpret information are basic political problems related to the fundamental question, who knows best what's going on? The only observation that we wish to make on this subject is that the future clearly lies with those with information, insight, and knowledge, whether they are representatives of business, government, unions, or universities. We are becoming increasingly a problem-solving society rather than a society of ideological contention. Certainly those who have the insight to identify problems and challenges in a complex world and, more than this, have the ability to deal effectively with them, will play increasingly important roles in our society.

Measurement

Measurement of course is simply another aspect of information seeking. It is so much a part of the management function, however, that it deserves special mention. Transactional activities raise questions of how much we are giving for what we are getting. As a consequence, one can say that the management of transactional relations really begins with measurement. The modern era of business was truly ushered in with double-entry bookkeeping.

Measurement requires, first, an operational definition of a dimension and, second, units of measurement along the dimension. Obviously, measurement can be most easily applied to physical objects which exist in time and space. When it comes to the measurement of complex phenomena such as value or success in transactional relationships, the problem becomes more difficult. In business, the problem of measurement is partially resolved by reducing as many events as possible to money value. By assessing all transactions in terms of the income and outgo of money, measurement at least appears possible. However, reducing all events to the common denominator of money is a difficult and, in some cases, almost impossible task.

Our economic society is characterized by all sorts of devices for equating human events to their money "equivalents." Thus, we have stock markets, metal markets, grain markets, and so on for assessing the value of certain key commodities. The major function of the stock market is determining the money value of business property. Interestingly enough, the stock market does not of itself create new capital; even a new stock issue merely transfers money from one owner to another. In the field of labor, collective bargaining determines, at least in part, the value of labor. In the consumer market, there are many social inventions for evaluating the price of products. All of these procedures have the primary function of reducing human events to their money equivalents, thus making it possible in our society to exchange all kinds of diverse products. But, in addition, the common denominator of money makes measurement possible and provides business management with a yardstick for measuring its transactional success or failure. Nonetheless, the student of business administration should never forget the underlying complexity of value determination; he should look beyond money to the underlying reality of business and recognize that money has symbolic meaning only.

The heart of the measurement system in business is the accounting department. Accounting is an orderly way of keeping track of the results of transactional relationships. The operational definition of transactional success is an excess of money retained over costs at the end of a designated accounting period. However, accounting is much more than this. Considerable judgment and business acumen enter into the assessment of the financial position of a business enterprise. Simple accumulation of money or objects with money value is not sufficient; the business must be assessed as a viable enterprise. Thus, accounting moves very quickly from records and simple summations to complex qualitative judgments. Accounting, however, is fairly narrowly confined to money considerations. Inasmuch as all relationships of reciprocity involve norms and values which are of social and cultural derivation, we need broader and more complete measures of transactional relations.

In addition to the measures of value undertaken by the accounting department, business management seeks to evaluate other intangibles. For example, there is a continuous effort to assess executive capabilities. At lower levels, there are various programs of merit rating and performance review. Selection involves measurement, as the employment manager attempts to select new employees who can fit into the company and the job. Most of the so-called personnel techniques characteristic of modern business are techniques of measurement. Here, of course, the dimensions being measured are complex, and the measurement procedures are exceedingly crude.

Profit Seeking

Measurement and the conscious calculation of costs are obviously closely related to the notion of "advantage" in entrepreneurial exchange. What is "advantage" in exchange situations? Some would simply indicate that a business is in business to make a profit and consider this the last word to be said on the subject. But what indeed is this so-called "profit" which every businessman is supposed to be pursuing? Is it dividends for stockholder-owners? Capital gains for speculators? Stock options, retirement plans, bonuses, and high salaries for management? Is it wages, Christmas bonuses, and fringe benefits for employees? Is it surplus which can be used for research and development of new products, capital investment, or expansion? Is it a reserve for future contingencies? Is it extra money for donating to universities or charity

or other public causes? Is it reduced price or improved quality for consumers? Is it money, power, personal satisfaction, or what?

Actually, an "advantage" or "gain" in an exchange relationship is
anything that we believe it to be; it depends on our evaluation of the
resources gained in the exchange and how much it cost us to secure
them. But, as we have already learned in the preceding chapter, such
evaluation is based on many considerations—personal interests, comparisons with other alternatives, social norms, one's appraisal of oneself
and of what one deserves in this world, and so on. To make things
even more complicated, the evaluations that are made typically involve
clusters of factors. For example, the worker evaluating his job views a
whole array of resources offered to him for his work effort—the pay,
the security, the status and recognition, the personal satisfaction gained
from the work itself, the quality and friendliness of supervision, the
relations with fellow employees, his image of the company, and its
management and policies. At any one point in time, any of these resources can loom larger than the others. More than this, he considers
them in various combinations with reference to an equally complex
array of personal and family interests at both practical and symbolic
levels of expression. Still further, he can make his evaluations in terms
both of short-run and long-run considerations.

It goes without saying that the assessment of "advantage" in exchange relationships is an exceedingly complex problem. One way to
resolve complexity is to oversimplify and this is exactly what happens.
For the average person, the process of evaluation is not systematic at all
but is rather a crude reckoning of events against general expectations—
pretty much at the level of vague feelings about how things are going.
The individual feels good or bad about an exchange relationship more
often than not without knowing why. This is especially true where
there are no outstanding features in the exchange relationship which
are obviously advantageous or disadvantageous.

Thus, the concern with the assessment of advantage is transformed
into positive and negative attitudes and beliefs about exchange situations. The individual assumes an attitude, sometimes on the basis of his
own experiences and feelings and more often on the basis of what others
tell him, and he acts accordingly. This is not to imply that there is no
reality and that all evaluations of events are hit-or-miss, unsubstantiated
opinions. It is only to suggest that the reality is so complex that the
human mind must make its determination in devious ways. Public opinion may not always be based on the "facts," but it has an accumulated

validity which is more frequently correct than not. If morale in an organization is poor, there are usually good reasons for the negative feelings expressed. If customers have a negative attitude toward a particular store, the development of their feelings can be traced and understood.

Another approach to simplifying the complexities involved in the assessment of exchange relationships is to limit the factors taken into consideration. This is what happens in business, of course. Here we find an assessment of exchange relationships on the basis of monetary considerations only. The value of all resources is translated into a single unit of account, *viz.*, money. With the value of all events in business exchange thus equated, it is possible to make comparisons of costs, calculate gains over costs, and in general introduce highly systematic ways of evaluating gains and costs in exchange relationships. Measurement of this kind and conscious, strategic calculation go hand in hand. When you can measure events, you can begin to calculate the advantages of one set of actions over another. You can begin to assess what you are getting or going to get for what you have to give.

As we have already suggested, the focus on monetary measurements is indeed an oversimplification. Every accountant knows that some of the most important resources in business exchange cannot be assigned a monetary value. For example, the "good will" of a company may be crucial to its success and yet its value cannot be readily calculated. In fact, no value can be assigned to any resource until it is bought and sold. Yet, there is no market place for buying and selling some of the most important resources on which a business enterprise depends, for example, the motivation and creative ability of management, the loyalty and support of employees, and the positive attitudes of consumers.

Yet, there are certain very real advantages in systematic measurement of this kind, even though it does represent an oversimplification. For one thing, accounting focuses the attention of management on the end results of business exchange. Thus, the value of a resource is what it sells for in the market place. You may think your product is the finest in the country and worth many more dollars than your competitor's product. However, if you can't sell it at any higher price or sell more of it at the same price, for all practical purposes it is not worth more. You may think that your relations with employees are an outstanding example of managerial leadership and organizational morale; but, if the end result is a product that costs more to make and does not compete effectively in the market place, your good human relations have had no entrepreneurial value to you.

STRATEGIES AND ACTION PROGRAMS

It is not enough simply to have information about exchange relationships; management must take action. One of the major functions of management, accordingly, is to come up with ideas for action. These are not just any old ideas but ideas about how to build new exchange relationships or improve existing ones. We can think of such ideas as essentially strategic, since they imply conscious and deliberate intent.

Much executive activity revolves around the generation of strategic ideas and programs of action. Some of these ideas catch on and become basic premises on which the business operates, but most never get beyond the "drawing board." The growth and development of a business can be fruitfully examined by studying the history of its basic strategies. In its initial phases, a business enterprise typically emphasizes the special interests and orientation of the founding father. Thus, if the entrepreneur is essentially a craftsman (which incidentally many are), the activity which is most strongly emphasized is that of production. Such entrepreneurs view business basically as a problem of creating products or services. Their basic strategy is building a better mouse trap and waiting for the world to beat a path to their doors.

If on the other hand the founding father is a sales promoter like Richard W. Sears, founder of Sears, Roebuck and Company, he conceives of his business in the narrow framework of developing a market and generating sales. The story is told of the running argument between Richard Sears and Julius Rosenwald, president of the company, at the time of the 1907 depression. Sears felt that the problem of shrinking profits should be handled through greater promotional effort rather than through a more effective and efficient consolidation of the business.

Narrowly conceived business enterprises rather typically remain undeveloped, since the full potential is not being realized. In our studies of entrepreneurial activity, there seems to be a sharp distinction between these more narrowly conceived enterprises and those which have broadened the base of exchange activity and have developed effective relationships on a wide front. These are the businesses which have not only developed a product or service but have also done something about the market, sources of supply, financing, and methods of handling all of the other relationships typical of a modern business. When there is active intervention by management at all points in the exchange relationships characterizing a business, there is considerably greater opportunity for growth as well as economic stability.

As the business grows and problems of getting the work done increase, a new stage is reached—that of organization. The excess work and new functions created by the extension of active intervention in all phases of the exchange relationship must be accomplished through people and machines. At first the organization may develop in a haphazard fashion; an employee or machine is introduced here and there to handle a specific activity or function. However, at some point in the growth of the business, the organization itself is conceived of as part of the exchange relationship. Problems of efficiency, effective structure, and notions of managerial leadership and employee morale begin to develop. The organization itself is conceived as an important strategic device in business relationships.

A mature, established business organization develops, over a period of years, a set of strategies[2] for dealing with all of the important elements of the socioeconomic environment. Certain strategies have to do with the way the organization fits into the chain of economic and technological events which mold and process the materials of the earth and distribute the product of these efforts to the customer. A business or industrial organization must maintain and develop its relations with those socioeconomic groups which precede it in the economic chain— that is, its sources of money, machines, tools, and materials—and those which follow it—that is, its customers. These strategies have to do with the economic metabolism of the organization, its intake and output. They also define the particular technological or commercial activity of the organization—what it does for a living, so to speak. For want of a better designation, we can refer to these strategies as the *external economic strategies* of the organization.

Other strategies concern the relations which the organization maintains with the broader community, including the general public, government bodies, organized charities, schools, and so on. Here we view the organization as a social entity having certain rights and privileges, duties, and obligations. These strategies we call *external social strategies*.

Finally, there are strategies which have to do with the way in which the organization does its job; the way in which employees are motivated, co-ordinated, and controlled; the technology and use of machines and tools; the division of labor; the hierarchy of authority; and so on. These are the strategies of management with which we are pri-

---

[2] *Strategy* refers here to a norm or guiding principle which is regarded as especially effective in achieving successful exchange relationships. "Satisfaction guaranteed or your money back" is such a norm. Company policies often take the form of exchange norms.

marily concerned in this book. We call them the *internal organizational strategies*.

The norms and principles of exchange which develop in a company for dealing with its external and internal relations are many and varied but reasonably consistent. New principles of action are built on the old and made consistent with the company's past experiences and previous modes of behavior. Most companies are perceived as having a business "character" or "personality" which differentiates them from other companies.

For example, one of the national airlines operates on the basic belief that success in this business depends upon maintaining quality service which attracts first-class customers. The management of this company believes that cheap air transportation means a sloppy and unsafe service which ultimately will weigh against the competitive advantage of air speed. This basic view of management influences many other aspects of the business.

First, the major emphasis of the company is on passenger service. Stewardesses are very well trained. The food, of which the company is very proud, is excellent and prepared by Swiss chefs. Second, the company is never first, but always a close second, in introducing new equipment. It prefers to let its competitors try out new equipment and iron out the "bugs" which might exist. Third, it regards "coach" or "air tourist" service as unsafe, particularly when passengers are crammed into planes with narrow aisles and poor opportunities for escape if the planes should catch fire. Moreover, it feels that coach service does not attract new passengers but merely takes customers away from the first-class flights. Fourth, it regards too much competition as ruinous and tending to down-grade the kind of passenger service which should be provided. Fifth, it sees the primary use of air transportation in long flights. Sixth, it has developed an organization which emphasizes specialization of functions. In this respect, it sacrifices co-ordination in order to achieve perfection in the specific functions performed. Seventh, it has one of the finest maintenance bases in the airlines industry. In these and other ways, this company has made a consistent effort to develop a "quality" service, aimed at attracting first-class customers.

Another example of consistent character development is a large merchandising organization which acts on the principle that people, if given the "right" opportunity, will respond in the "right" way without coercion or manipulation. This fundamental idea emerges in a variety of ways in this company. In dealing with its customers, it follows a "low pressure" merchandising pattern. It believes that customers will buy if given an opportunity to purchase good quality merchandise at the lowest possible cost. It attempts to educate its customers through careful labeling of the merchandise. It has developed techniques of buying and selling which have materially reduced the cost of distribution. It has a definite policy of customer satisfaction. There is little or no hedging on this policy because of the belief that most customers are fundamentally honest.

Internally, this company is operated on a highly decentralized plan with delegation of authority to the lowest possible levels. Employees are given maximum freedom on the job. Supervision is exercised with a minimum of overt authority. There is an active policy of promotion from within. The company has a longstanding profit-sharing plan through which it distributes a large share of the profits to employees. At present, approximately one-third of the company is owned by its employees.

It is apparent from the examples given that the strategies of management imply certain assumptions about the probable behavior of customers, employees, stockholders, and other groups participating in the enterprise. In the case of the airline, it is assumed that it is primarily the "higher class" customer who travels by air. The "higher class" customer likes good food, service, and attention. He must be weaned away from first-class rail travel by guarantees of safety and assurances of speed as well as comfort. In the case of the merchandising organization, it is assumed that people, if given the "right" opportunity, will respond in the "right" way without coercion or manipulation. The assumptions about human behavior underlying the strategies of the management of any company reflect a variety of influences. Often they are shaped, at least in part, by the needs, interests, personalities, and ideologies of top management. In the examples given, there is some evidence of a "class" versus "mass" ideology reflected in the thinking of the two management groups. It is possible to point to a number of companies where the personality and emotional needs of a dominant management figure have molded the strategies of the entire organization.

The strategies of a company are also determined, in many cases, by imitation of the successful actions of others. Large, successful companies serve as models for smaller enterprises. If Sears, Roebuck and Company has a policy of decentralization, then other companies adopt this administrative pattern simply because it appears to have been successfully utilized in Sears. Management groups like to keep in "style" and follow the fad of the moment as much as any other human group. Indeed, the itinerant management consultant often acts as a communication link from one company to the next, carrying the news about the latest trends in administrative styles.

It is apparent, without pursuing the subject further, that the strategies of an organization are influenced and shaped in the same way as any other human behavior. The influences operating range from purely emotional factors, through social factors, to rational, scientific efforts to analyze and understand human behavior. More and more, business management is attempting to develop its key strategies on the basis of a thorough understanding of the social and economic world in which the business exists. There is a growing recognition of the importance of a broad knowledge of human nature and human behavior in various settings and relationships. It is no longer possible to operate a well-established, successful company, which is fulfilling all of its social and economic responsibilities, with limited and ill-conceived notions about society and the human beings within it. Chester Barnard, formerly president of New Jersey Bell Telephone Company, has said:[3]

A need of the executive of the future is for broad interests and wide imagination and understanding. Whether or not narrowness of interest has limited present-day executives in their contribution to the general society which impinges on all their immediate activities and has also thereby restricted the performance of their direct duties is a matter of opinion. At any rate, nothing can be done about them now. However, there is a narrow-mindedness associated with the concentration heretofore deemed indispensable. In the future it would seriously limit the capacity of men to serve effectively both in the major and in the intermediate executive positions of large and small organizations. The emphasis I am placing here is upon the so-called humanities and also upon science as a part of general education. It is an emphasis that applies not merely to instruction in the schools but also to pursuits after graduation. I hope it needs no argument that persons occupying positions of leadership in the community need an understanding of what goes on in the world and of the nature of the interests served by and underlying its activities.

TRANSACTIONAL SKILLS

We use the concept of transactional skills broadly to include the activities of management which have to do with the actual consummation of exchange relationships. These include such activities as shaping the productive efforts of employees, negotiating with unions, selling

---

[3] Chester I. Barnard, *Organization and Management* (Cambridge, Mass.: Harvard University Press, 1948), p. 195.

the customer, buying from sources of supply, dealing with the board of directors and stockholders, and so on. In each of these relationships, certain kinds of transactional skills are required, mainly those having to do with setting up transactional structures and communication.

We have already discussed transactional structures in the preceding chapter. The design of such structures defines the way people are brought together in transactional relations and the rules of conduct which guide them. Much of the discussion about organizational and administrative patterns are related to this area. For example, when we discuss centralized versus decentralized management, we are really discussing two models of transactional relations between management and employees.

In addition to structural arrangements, successful transaction requires effective communication among the parties to the transactions. It is apparent that an important factor in communication is meaning. Misunderstandings arise because of direct failures in verbal or oral expression. Even more important, however, are the latent and symbolic meanings which come into the picture, often unintentionally, and alter the manifest communication. Effective management must be keenly aware of the communication process at all levels, the factors which facilitate or block the communication process, and especially the varieties of symbolic communications which frequently have more meaning than the words that are spoken or written.

The successful executive must learn to communicate demands. Surprisingly enough, management frequently fails to make its demands clear. It does not let employees know what it wants, sets no standards of performance, and drifts along indecisively, vaguely hoping that employees will by themselves come to know what is expected. On the listening side, there are also failures. This is especially true because so much is communicated in symbolic ways which sometimes escape the attention of all but the keenest observers. Accordingly, management must learn not only how to interpret symbolic events and their meaning but also how to develop the skills of helping the other party express his interests and desires in more understandable ways.

Communication skills also should be regarded as including the skills of motivational leadership. Leadership is successful communication. It is the successful management of impression. It involves the creation of a psychological and social climate in which exchanges occur easily and with a minimum of conflict and negotiation.

Implied in the above but deserving special emphasis are the norms of reciprocity and coaptation which are an essential part of our society and the various subsocieties that constitute it. Not only must business management have a keen knowledge of the rules of conduct and norms of the various transactional structures in which it operates; it must also have a deep understanding of the nature of our society, its principles of justice and equity, and its deep philosophy regarding the relationship of the individual one to the other and to large-scale organizations. There are many gray areas in human relations where no directives are provided regarding the propriety of various modes of conduct. It is in such areas, where temporizing is required, that the true moral character of executive decision and action emerges.

SUMMARY

In this chapter we have analyzed the tasks of management as an organizing and mediating agency in a system of exchange and transaction. We have viewed the manager's job around three key activities, namely, information seeking, strategic judgments, and transactions. In the next chapter, we shall examine the influence of social organization and the way in which it affects the job of management.

6. THE BUSINESS ORGANIZATION AND MANAGEMENT

IN BUSINESS CIRCLES, there is continuous reference to the *business organization*, the *company*, the *firm*, or the *corporation* as though these terms were accurately defined. We often speak, for example, of "organization objectives," "company policy," or "corporate needs." It is assumed that these references are well understood by everybody. Yet, is the picture clear? What picture really comes to mind when we invoke the image of a company? Often, we think only of its physical paraphernalia—its accumulation and concentration of visible property, buildings, machines, desks, tools, and neat mesh fences that mark off its property lines. All of these are tangible evidence of a company's existence and, as such, are frequently mistaken for the business itself. When we think of a specific business like Sears, Roebuck and Company, we think of its stores, warehouses, and central offices, all of which carry signs clearly labeling these as Sears. It may come as a surprise to the reader that most of these buildings are not even owned by Sears; they are leased. In fact, what we think is Sears is actually someone else's business.

If visible property is not the company, then what is the company? The next easy solution is that the company or business organization is management and employees. But, how can we limit the company just to these groups? Where do the stockholder-owners fit in? Aren't they really the company? After all, they own the business. Or, for that matter, how do we really exclude the customers—all of those nice people "out there" who support the business? Aren't they part of it? In fact, managerial and employee activities are geared in large part to satisfy consumer interests.

How, then, do we draw a line around specific activities or relationships and say that these are clearly the *business organization* or the *company?* Actually, we can resolve our problem of definition in two ways. First, we can view business, as we have been doing, as a coaptive system of exchange involving the interests and resources of various socioeconomic groups. In this view, the hard core of the enterprise is that group of people who are concerned broadly with the total system of exchange relationships constituting the enterprise. This is the group which actively seeks to build exchange relationships, mediate transactions, and reconcile interests and values. Quite obviously, we are speaking of the management group. In most companies, management, at least from an entrepreneurial point of view, *is* the company. We say "most companies" because there are some companies where employees down the line are broadly concerned with entrepreneurial affairs and others where stockholders play an active part. But, for the majority, only management really worries very much about the varied interests and resources involved in the exchange relationships of the enterprise. Most typically, stockholders seek only dividends or capital gains and would gladly sell out whenever better prospects are presented to them. The same is certainly true of customers. They may develop sentimental loyalties to particular companies or brands, but these are not so much an interest in the company as such as they are a symbolic expression of their own psychological and social needs. Employees, too, view the enterprise in narrow terms, seeking to satisfy their own interests through their involvement in its activities. This leaves only management to tend the store and, even here, as we shall see, many distracting and narrowing elements enter into the picture.

There is a second way of defining the business organization. Around any continuous human activity, there is a tendency for people to form ties and to think of themselves as an entity. Management and employees are thrown together in continuous, close relationships. They occupy the same space. Together, they look out into the outer world through the same windows. From their vantage point, they begin to think of "insiders" and "outsiders"—those who gather together each day under the same roof and those on the other side of the steel mesh fence. This kind of group identification is a major part of what we think of as *social organization*. Professor Ralph Linton defines a *society* as "any group of people who have lived and worked together long enough to get themselves organized and to think of themselves as a social unit with well-defined limits."[1] His definition applies exactly to the pattern of organizational identification and social structure which arises in the typical company.

What unity does exist in the business literally grows out of the social and psychological meaning ascribed by human beings to the activities

---

[1] Ralph Linton, *The Study of Man* (New York: D. Appleton-Century Company, 1936), p. 91.

and relationships in which they are engaged. In other words, a business organization in the usual view is an organization *only* because a social system develops in and around business activities. Thus, the social system is not just an excrescence, an interesting but relatively unimportant aspect of the business organization; it *is* the organization.

The Social Organization of Business

The social organization of a business develops as a consequence of several factors. First of all, the ongoing, regular routines of business bring together a number of people who are thrust into daily and regular contact with one another. Social proximity and regular patterns of interaction typically give participants a sense of ongoing structure—a feeling of being part of something larger than themselves. Second, the tendency to identify with the activities with which one is engaged—to gain a sense of direction and purpose out of one's occupation—heightens the feeling of being part of a larger system of relationships. This is particularly true in the operational occupations which are fitted together around technological or procedurally based processes. Third, the hierarchical structure of business, its characteristic pyramidal shape, focusing upward to a chief executive and a small coterie of top-management personnel, provides a sense of purpose and ultimate ends. Fourth, the projected images of the business as an integrated entity adds to the idea of unity. The imagery is coupled with a tendency toward oversimplified reifications. The company is often perceived as a great, big man or superman, with an identifiable character and social personality, just as the rustic, sometimes wise, sometimes duped figure of Uncle Sam represents the United States. Fifth, the mere fact that employees at all levels are housed in buildings identified as belonging to a particular company further reinforces the sense of being part of a larger, integrated system of action. Sixth, the memories of participants, the sense of history, and the feeling of identification developing among those who have gone through similar experiences also augments feelings of being part of a larger unity.

In Chapter 4, we distinguished between two patterns of social cohesion. One pattern, which is deeply human, arises from emotional and sentimental bonds—a consciousness of kind, a sense of collective identity, a feeling of being part of a larger unity. The other pattern emerges out of the complex interdependence of a modern society and requires deliberate and conscious effort to build, maintain, and develop interdependent relationships of exchange. Our society is an intermeshing of these two structural patterns. The social organization developing in business, the sense of identification, the feeling of being part of something, the idea of common purpose, and the status and role structure are all a reflection of the profound social needs of man. At the same time, the more conscious, deliberate efforts to develop effective exchange relationships, to negotiate differences, and to reconcile values result from the second structural pattern—the need to develop and maintain an ongoing complex of interdependent exchange activity.

Bureaucracy, Career Orientation, and the Social Organization of Business

In Chapter 3, we discussed the Weberian view of the rationally organized bureaucratic form of organization which characterizes modern business. We should like to return to this concept now and consider it in light of some of the ideas presented in intervening chapters. The bureaucratic organization is merely a type of social organization, reflecting the unity and sense of common purpose of any social organization. It, too, is bound together by sentimental bonds, even though these appear to be rationally conceived and objectively oriented. The bureaucratic organization is not imposed on employees; they accept it and regard it as "right and proper" in a place of work. Indeed, modern business as we know it today would be literally impossible if most people rejected it and the values on which it is based. The surprising thing about the modern business organization is not so much the breakdowns in human relations which occur as the relative stability which it has achieved. Millions of people every day rise groaning from their beds and drag themselves off to another round of relatively impersonal activities to which they have apparently no heavy commitments. Our attitude surveys conducted over a number of years in many industries suggest that at least one third or more of the nation's working population enjoy little if any positive motivation in their work. Yet, business organizations manage somehow to hold together. They hold together not because business executives provide outstanding personal leadership, but because bureaucratic organizations are part of our way of life and because certain dominant beliefs and values about work have infused our society and penetrated it from top to bottom.

As a people, we accept bureaucratic modes of human relationships, primarily because they fit our notions regarding the social organization of work. Two subsidiary beliefs appear to underlie our broader sentiments about limited-purpose, work activities. First is our acceptance of hierarchical authority structures. The psychologists tell us that men typically project on their bosses their feelings about their fathers and mothers and other authority figures with whom they have had experience early in life. In other words, the boss is a surrogate father image or in some circumstances a mother image or perhaps even an old schoolteacher image. Whatever the boss is from a psychological standpoint, we can be certain that childhood and even infantile experiences with authority figures largely determine the character of our behavior in hierarchical structures as adults. We are thus preconditioned to respond in certain ways to those whom we perceive as stronger, bigger, and more powerful than we. The hierarchy of authority in a business organization, no matter how hard we may try to make it out to be simply a division of functions, is a hierarchy of power and authority. That most of us clearly understand this is reflected in our reference to the "big boss." He may actually be only five feet, four inches tall and completely cowed by his burly wife at home; but, from the vantage point of the human pyramid in the factory, he gains deference, respect, and ready response to his commands as though he were seven feet tall and a veritable tiger in all of his relationships.

Our ascription of authority depends upon our views regarding how authority and power are legitimated. The important fact about our kind of society is that authority is granted not because of inherited right but presumably on the basis of the man's ability and achievements. The bureaucratic organization provides this kind of legitimation. Occupational validity at least in part underlies the boss's claim to authority. When we say that the boss has a right to issue orders because he "runs the place," we are underscoring his occupational authority. We are not thereby extending his authority, however, to other areas. We subordinate ourselves and defer to him as a man of status and power only in the work situation. Indeed, if he tries to extend his authority into our personal lives outside the "legitimate," work areas, we typically resent it.

In addition to our acceptance of bureaucratic patterns of authority, there is a second, subsidiary set of beliefs which reinforces and supports the bureaucratic mode of social organization. This is our occupational and career orientation. The social world to most of us is a structure of jobs. We live in a great, interdependent system of work in which our status is determined largely by what we do for a living. The best way we have to place someone in our society is to find out what his job is. Where he works and what he does are much more important than his family connections or his religion or even where he is from.

The occupational orientation of Americans coupled with the dream of equal opportunity to rise in the social structure makes the hierarchical, impersonal structure of the bureaucratic organization even more legitimate and attractive. Here is a social structure in which a man presumably is judged on his ability to produce in a job. Personality considerations, family background, and nepotism are of less importance than a man's own effort and personal achievements. This is an American notion which is not without some foundation, for men really do move up in bureaucratic hierarchies on the basis of their own abilities. This is not the whole of it of course, but hard work and successful achievement continue to play an important part.

Those without social connections or who for reasons of personal conviction reject nepotism and sponsorship will regard the impersonal, bureaucratic organization as a social organization of high moral quality. Thus, the rational structuring of job relationships around objective ends, the depersonalization of the job to a set of specific functions, and the elimination of personal considerations in the carrying out of job duties and responsibilities are all appealing ideas to those who must rise or wish to rise on their own work efforts.

For these and perhaps other reasons, rational bureaucracy is the characteristic pattern of organization in our society, especially for structuring the relationships among employees and between management and employees around work activities. It represents a dominant belief pattern reflecting our notions about what is right and proper in human relations on the job. We need not emphasize here how strong the feelings are in this regard. We write treatises and set up manifestoes about equal opportunity; indeed, equal rights is often translated to mean equal opportunity to rise in an occupational hierarchy. Occupational achievement and utter devotion to one's job are among the highest virtues of our citizens. Willingness to play one's part within a structure of activities once directions have been set is often regarded as the height of personal responsibility. With values and beliefs like these, the typical bureaucracy seems as natural and acceptable to many of us as the kinship, tribal organization of the precivilized.

The Structure of Human Relations in Business

The acceptance of the bureaucratic pattern does not negate consideration of the concrete reality of business as a system of exchange and transaction. Actually, three influences are always at work in management-employee relations. First, there is the influence of bureaucratic beliefs and sentiments. Second, there is the influence of more personal sentiments, as men inject into the formal, impersonal relations prescribed by bureaucracy the more informal, personal considerations of human relations. Third, there are the profound influences derived from the exchange and transactional order of business. Thus, for every man in business, management and employees alike, there are the compelling, formal demands of the bureaucracy for unselfish devotion to duty and to the common purpose, whatever it is perceived to be. At the same time, the less objective, personal needs cry for satisfaction; the limited, impersonal roles prescribed by the bureaucratic model are thus altered to fit the "whole" needs of man. These alterations for the most part are minor deviations from the dominant bureaucratic pattern but are nonetheless important in understanding human behavior in the workplace. Finally, there are the inevitable pressures of the system of exchange and transactions around which business activities are organized. Because of these three influences, management can look at an employee, all at the same time, as an integral member of a co-operative, work system, subordinated to the common purpose, as a person with broad human needs and interests which ought to be met, and as a party to an exchange relationship which must be continuously negotiated.

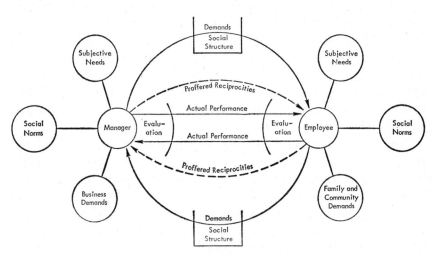

FIGURE 6-1.—Dimensions of an Exchange Relationship

Management and Employee Relations

With these ideas in mind, we can now indicate some of the key characteristics of management-employee relations in an organized setting. The diagram in Figure 6–1 represents the elements of an instance of exchange between a manager and an employee. The diagram is highly simplified but highlights some of the main elements of exchange and transactional relationships. Management's demands on the employee are determined, first, by business demands coming on the manager, second, by social norms and rules of conduct prescribed both by the broader society and by the social organization of business, and third by the subjective needs of the manager himself. These demands are communicated through a social structure. In business, the social structure is hierarchical and may involve a number of layers of supervision. The communication of demands to the employee include both intended meanings and unintended overtones.

The employee in his turn is communicating demands to the manager. His demands are also determined in part by the demands of his family and community, in part by social norms, and in part by his subjective needs and interests. Once again, the communication of demands occurs through a social structure, and there are manifest tones as well as latent overtones.

Both parties to the exchange not only make demands but also proffer reciprocities if the demands are met or not met. These reciprocities take the form of positive or negative resources. In the case of management, this might include payment of wages, incentive payments, and offers of promotion and personal recognition on the positive side and withholding of rewards, punitive action, and personal criticism on the negative side. For the employee, the proffered reciprocities might include on the positive side greater work output, willingness to adjust to change, and loyalty or on the negative side restriction of output, sabotage, threat of strike or work stoppage, and disloyalty.

Both parties to the exchange evaluate the demands against proffered reciprocities. This evaluation is based on considerations of what might happen if the demands are met and what might happen if they are not met. Once again the various possibilities are set against the individual's expectations and needs. In addition, consideration is given to the ability and willingness of both parties to perform as indicated. Talk is one thing but actual performance is another. Can and will the parties to the exchange actually follow through on the reciprocities which have been indicated? This represents an assessment of the power and resources which each has at his disposal and of his willingness to use them.

Out of this evaluation, a decision is made and the actual performance follows; or, to put it another way, the exchange occurs. Evaluation also continues after the actual exchange, as the individual learns what to expect in the future and resolves either to continue his present patterns of behavior or to change them in future exchanges.

Now, put in more concrete terms, we can observe the exchange, let us say, occurring between the employment manager of a factory and an applicant. The employment manager has certain requirements, based on the needs of the factory organization, for an employee of particular skills and abilities. The requirements include not only the ability to fit into a technological system but also the ability to get along in a bureaucratic, co-operative system of relations. In addition, there are certain requirements based on labor costs and how much can be spent for an employee of particular skills and abilities. Still further, the employment manager himself has certain subjective needs and interests which cause him to reject applicants of a particular ethnic background or to accept others because of the way they part their hair. All of these demands emerge as demands on the applicant. He hears them as the employment manager describes the job opening and requirements.

At the same time, he hears the proffered reciprocities if he accepts the job and if he does well in the job. The employment manager tells him what the job will pay, what benefits will be available to him, what the future might hold, and what kind of social climate exists in the plant. The applicant obviously must judge the ability and willingness of the company's management to deliver on its promises.

The applicant also has demands based on his needs and expectations. He too has to be assessed in terms of his ability to perform if his demands are met.

If everything works out, the new man is offered the job and accepts it.

SUMMARY

In this chapter, we have introduced the dimension of social organization into our analysis and indicated the various perceptions of management regarding the employee as a member of a social organization and as an element in an exchange situation. Finally, we examined the elements of exchange relationship, reducing the whole concept to simple analytic terms. This mode of analysis can be applied to the descriptive material which follows in Part III of the text as we consider various groups of employees in their relation to the organization and to each other. It can serve as a framework for discussion of the various human relations situations described in Part III.

PART III

Employee Behavior in the
Industrial Organization

7. THE FACTORY

ORGANIZATION AND

DIVISION OF LABOR

WHEN we examine the normal factory organization we see a general structure and typical patterns of behavior related to that structure. This structure and behavior all can be viewed as:

1. A system of exchanges (transactions) between the company and the people and also between the people.
2. A sociological system in which people fit into various roles and relationships.
3. A co-ordinated production system in which people, machines, and processes form an integrated whole designed to accomplish the work of the company.

One of the most significant aspects of the modern factory is the division of labor and the multiplicity of different skills and activities which are co-ordinated to form a working whole. This occupational structure of business is a direct reflection of its broader system of exchange and transaction. It reflects management's efforts to build, maintain, and develop an intricate system of exchange relationships. However, the structure takes different forms, as we have already suggested, depending on the phase of the exchange process in which various segments of the structure are engaged. In the following pages, we shall analyze the occupational structure of a typical manufacturing organization, but the student should keep in mind that there are many variations from this pattern from one business to the next. The method of analysis, however, can be adapted to other types of organizations.

DIVISION OF LABOR AND THE OCCUPATIONAL STRUCTURE

The Structure of Technological and Operational Activities

The bulk of the work force of the typical manufacturing organization is engaged in operations of one kind or another. The operational activities are concerned with the utilization of resources (raw materials, machines and tools, and human labor) in the creation of new resources for exchange in the industrial market, wholesale market, or directly in the consumer market. They are organized around technological processes or other agreed-upon procedures, which typically are broken down into a series of predetermined operations.

From a technological point of view, the only structural principle which must be followed is chronological order. In other words, certain events in the process must precede others; you can't assemble a product until the parts are made. Thus, we can think of technological activities, following Richardson and Walker, as a workflow.[1] This is a useful concept, since it emphasizes the movement of work-in-process through successive operations. Richardson and Walker state:[2]

A workflow system in any factory may be compared to a river stream. The raw materials, the order, the engineering blueprints all start, so to speak, from the headwaters of the workstream. Unfinished parts flow downstream from operator to operator, section to section, division to division, until they are assembled, packed and shipped at the stream's end. Such a concept and image has several advantages. It enables one to visualize clearly, and also to plot graphically whatever a department or an individual contributes to the workflow at the physical spot where his contribution is made—whether, for example, he is a production planner who processes the papers necessary for planning the flow of parts or a machine operator, processing the actual parts planned.

The workflow or productive activities of a typical manufacturing organization is shown in Figure 7–1. The diagram is highly simplified

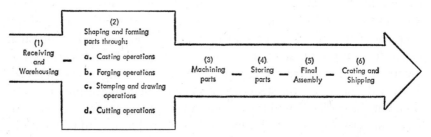

FIGURE 7–1.—Workflow of Typical Manufacturing Organization

and shows only the actual operations involved in the manufacturing workflow. However, coming in like tributaries into the mainstream are all kinds of supportive and control activities particularly out of engi-

---

[1] F. L. W. Richardson, Jr., and C. R. Walker, *Human Relations in an Expanding Company* (New Haven, Conn.: Yale Labor Management Center, 1948).

[2] Charles R. Walker, *Modern Technology and Civilization* (New York: McGraw-Hill Book Co., Inc., 1962), p. 188. With all of the analogic references to the river, the student must be beginning to think of business as "old man river."

neering and its auxiliary functions. Thus, engineering activities flow into the mainstream at every point—initially in the form of product design and specifications, then in the form of tool and die blueprints, process design, and ubiquitous inspecting operations. Engineering might be conceived as a great lake with many outlets flowing from it into the mainstream. A smaller lake, connected by a wide channel with engineering, is made up of skilled tradesmen, manufacturing tools, fixtures, and dies, setting up and maintaining machinery, and in general providing the machinery and tools needed by the production operations of the factory.

The distinction which we have made (following Richardson and Walker) between the mainstream and the so-called tributary activities is only one of convenience. Engineering and the skilled trades are primarily concerned with organizing, setting up, and maintaining the production process. The actual running of the apparatus is done by operatives and semiskilled or unskilled workers. There is, however, always some contention regarding the design and control of the production process between engineering and manufacturing supervision. Both groups have knowledge of how to set up production and each thinks it knows how best to get the job done.

Transactional Influences on Technological Processes

We have already pointed out that the only structural principle guiding the arrangement of technological processes is chronological order. When we introduce, however, transactional considerations, other elements enter the picture. For example, if we consider transactional factors like cost and efficiency, we find ourselves very much interested in the arrangement of processes to insure the least waste of time. It is not sufficient to lay out operations in terms of simple considerations of chronology. Now, they must be dovetailed and integrated to insure that all machinery and human labor are fully used, that there is no idle time, and that subassemblies and parts do not gather dust in storerooms waiting on the completion of other pieces of the total assembly. Idleness of parts means idle capital; idleness of machinery and employees means waste; unnecessary storage means money tied up in empty, useless space.

When we introduce the additional consideration of employee relations, the problem of arrangement of operations becomes even stickier. Now we cannot be concerned just with the physical dimensions of time and space but must take human feelings and attitudes into account. What may look perfectly logical from the standpoint of physical arrangement may have real disadvantages from a psychological or social point of view. Jobs can be set up—indeed, have been set up—which no one can perform without great psychological duress either in the form of monotony or in the form of great mental pressure. Methods engineers can sit up nights devising new and more efficient procedures only to see them fail because of lack of support from foremen and employees in the shop.

The mind of the human being is exceedingly complex. What may appear to be completely illogical from an engineering standpoint may be perfectly plausible to employees. Even more important, if employees truly support a particular arrangement of operations, they can literally make it work in spite of its deficiencies. The studies at Western Electric demonstrated this phenomenon years ago when employees showed that they were capable of maintaining a high level of production when the lighting on the job was reduced to ten candlepower, which is about as much light as the full moon sheds on a cloudless night.

There is much discussion in the management literature regarding organizational principles and structural arrangements.[3] Some of these have to do with the requirements of any process-mediated, co-operative system. For example, great emphasis is placed on the importance of setting clear objectives and analyzing the various functions which must be performed in order to accomplish the predetermined end result. The notion that the organizational structure must be built around the process rather than around the individuals performing the tasks also grows out of the obvious requirements of process-determined activities. Some of the organizational principles and structural arrangements are concerned with the transactional and exchange relationships between management and employees. For example, the so-called *scalar process* involving "graded steps of responsibility" is simply another name for the chain of command or hierarchy or authority in the organization which serves the transactional function of communicating management demands to employees, negotiating differences, and exercising authoritative control. The principle of *control* is another aspect of transactional relations and calls attention to the need for checking activities to insure that management's demands are being met. The concepts of *span of control* and *unity of command* also represent assumptions about how best to secure effective exchange relationships with employees.

---

[3] We aren't going to take the time to present the principles of organization ordinarily described. For a review of typical organizational principles and techniques, see Henry G. Hodges, *Management* (Boston: Houghton Mifflin Co., 1956), chaps. vii and viii.

We take the view that there are a few principles of organization, but not many, which are inevitably true for all process-mediated, co-operative systems. What is true, however, is so self-evident that it seems almost fatuous to mention them. For example, the nature of the technological process itself determines the following:

1. The technological process clearly must be related to the technological objectives. If the process isn't appropriate, the objectives won't be accomplished. If the objective isn't clear, you won't know what you're doing and everything will be out of whack.
2. The technological process must be arranged in chronological order to insure that first things come first and last things, last. You can't build an automobile without wheels. The production of wheels accordingly must precede the final assembly.
3. Regardless of what organizational arrangements are made to accommodate the interests of employees and management, the tasks prescribed by the technological process must somehow be accomplished. In other words, if you're manufacturing can openers, it may be that employees would be happier if they weren't required to operate punch presses. But, if the presses don't operate, there will be no can openers. The process has primacy but the arrangement of the process-activities is another matter.

With regard to the transactional considerations of cost and efficiency in technological operations, the following seems to us to be self-evident:

1. Planning the work to eliminate idle time is a must. Idle machines, employees, or work-in-process cost money.
2. Reducing the time and expense of moving materials from one production station to another saves time and money.
3. Greater production for less cost is the abiding concern of production management whether these results are obtained through changes in the technological process, layout and design of the organization, production machines, tools, jigs, and fixtures, or efforts of employees.

All of the preceding observations are self-evident. They are simple and uncomplicated, because they have to do with simple and uncomplicated physical considerations. When we consider, however, the direct transactions and exchanges taking place between management and employees around technological operations, the number of self-evident truths diminishes to zero. There are no principles which are inevitably true of all human relations. Unity of command, scalar process, limited span of control, specifically assigned job responsibilities, and specialization, all of these must be qualified and related to the concrete reality of the situation. What works with one management-employee group doesn't work with another.

There are, however, certain broadly accepted notions about the design of process-mediated, co-operative systems and bureaucratic structures which have wide currency both among managers and employees. Some of these are as follows:

1. Impersonal organized activities typically are controlled by a hierarchy of authority. Having a boss is not totally untenable in our society; in fact, it is very much a part of our way of life and is generally expected.
2. The idea that the boss "runs the place" and prescribes the tasks to be performed is also more or less accepted.
3. A man should have a reasonably clear idea about the requirements of his job, its duties and responsibilities. If no one tells him what is expected, he cannot be blamed for the consequences.
4. Specialization is very much a part of the occupational and career orientation of Americans. Having a job and the identity attached to occupations is an integral part of the social structure of our society. To be unassigned or floating, itinerant labor is no mark of achievement in America.
5. Being part of a larger structure of activities is also a widely accepted notion. Working together with others in process-mediated, co-operative systems is practically a way of life to many people.
6. Performing one's tasks in terms of job requirements, that is, impersonally and without injecting one's own personal needs and interests, is for many a perfectly acceptable way to orient oneself toward the job.
7. Accepting the primacy of scientifically validated technological process over human needs, particularly those which are more or less immediate, is a broadly held idea. Many people truly believe that there is no such thing as technological unemployment over the long run. More important, it is generally accepted that science and technology can and will change our way of life and that such change is inevitable.
8. The concept of efficiency is a well-accepted belief in our society. This view is coupled with the notion that work should become less and less demanding of the employee, at least at a purely physical level of effort, and that there should be a constant up-grading of jobs.

There are no doubt a number of other widely held beliefs which lie behind the characteristic bureaucratic form which most industrial organizations assume. However, broadly held attitudes and beliefs are not immutable principles of organization; they are subject to change, continuous alteration, and local adaptation.

The Structure of Transactional Activities in the Business Organization

The technological apparatus is a large and visible part of the manufacturing organization. It is typically what you see when you take a plant tour. However, other important events are taking place in the typical manufacturing organization which must be examined. A business enterprise, as we have learned, is primarily a system of exchange among several socioeconomic groups. At each point of exchange, specialized activities have developed. These specialized activities are built mainly around the rules of conduct, norms, and subcultures characterizing the various market structures of our society. Thus, we find experts in finance who have a highly specialized knowledge and ability to operate effectively in the money market of banks, investment firms, and other fiduciary structures. We find experts in public relations who have great knowledge and skill in dealing with the mass media. We find marketing experts of all kinds, experts in union relations, experts in various buying markets, and so on.

The technological structure of the business is a subsidiary part of the business enterprise. Its function is to create resources for exchange in the consumer market. Thus, product development is clearly a transactional activity and requires constant reference not only to the emerging technology but also to the evolving needs of customers. A good product from a business standpoint is not just one that is technologically feasible but one which will sell. A product for most companies thus represents a coaptation of the interests of research and development engineers, the manufacturing organization, and the sales and marketing organization. We have heard of companies in which the sales manager has been put in charge of research and development; this may not be as farfetched as it may at first seem.

Once the product has been determined, the technological process which is largely designed by engineers becomes a set of job demands which management makes on manufacturing employees. From a strictly engineering standpoint, these demands take the form only of certain task requirements and quality standards. However, the exchange value of the product can be enhanced by cutting the cost of its production. New demands enter the picture. Cost figures are gathered by the accountants; budgets are set up; and these become a new set of demands which management makes on manufacturing employees. Indeed, a great portion of the activity of manufacturing management is concerned with demands for greater efficiency and lower production costs.

The technological process also creates very specific demands on the purchasing activities of the company. The process determines the specific requirements for machines, materials, and parts. In addition, the cost and efficiency demands generally imposed on the manufacturing organization are also imposed on purchasing. Most of the activities of purchasing accordingly are related to the problems of buying various commodities of the right specifications but at a reduced cost. Savings can be achieved not only through direct bargaining on price but also through inventory reductions, out-of-season buying, buying of distressed merchandise, acquisition and direct control of sources, and so on. Purchasing is, however, not just concerned with costs; a steady source of supply is also a factor. The purchasing agent sometimes finds himself hanging on the horns of a dilemma, knowing full well that one chiseling act may cost him the friendship he needs to guarantee the service he expects on a particular commodity. He may make an immediate gain; but in a world of exchange sometimes the other party will have the upper hand. Perhaps a good principle of exchange for the student of business to remember, if he must have principles of human behavior, is that memories in business circles are usually elephantine.

Within the organization itself, the authority structure or chain of command is basically a transactional activity. It is essentially a social device for securing the effective exchange of productive labor from employees for wages, salaries, and other rewards which the organization can grant. The authority structure introduces new elements into the transactional relationship—elements inherent in the notion of authority and power. The authority structure in a sense reduces, although it does not entirely eliminate, the necessity for constant bargaining and bickering, since at the crucial points "rank" can be pulled and commands issued.

The executive organization, viewed as a decision-making structure, is also a transactional system involving a competition of ideas and proposed actions in which the contending parties are negotiating in a sense for the resources of the organization. We shall discuss the executive organization later and, therefore, will give no further attention to it at this point.

Around the measurement activities of business, as we have already indicated, a number of jobs develop. The most important of these are, of course, the accounting jobs which constitute the largest segment of the office activities of most companies. In recent years, electronic data processing has given a considerable impetus to the measurement activities of business and in its wake has created a whole new collection of jobs. More than this, a great portion of management's time is spent in evaluation and assessment of a more qualitative sort. Indeed, it is possible to classify the major strategies of business management in terms of what various executives regard as key dimensions in business transactions and how they go about evaluating these. There are certain executives in every company, generally regarded as practical and down to earth, who evaluate everything against a cost-and-efficiency yardstick—"How much does it cost and what are we going to get out of it?" There are those who evaluate events against standards of product quality—"If the product is good, everything else will take care of itself!" There are those who evaluate only the quality of relationships in business—"If they love us, little else matters!" There are those who look only at the quality of management, or the plant housekeeping, or the total sales and how they look compared to last year's.

It can be seen from the foregoing that a business organization is a complex of transactional activities related not only to "external" exchanges with customers, sources of supply, and money markets but to "internal" exchanges as well. Indeed, the activities of the business organization can be best thought of as a replication of the total system of exchanges in which the enterprise is involved. The business organization expresses through its activities the convergence of the demands and resources of all of those who are party to the total system of exchange of the enterprise. The sales department thus reflects the problems and challenges of the exchange relationship between the company and the customer. The accounting department reflects the exchange relationships between the company and all other parties in the enterprise where monetary considerations are involved. The personnel department expresses the challenges and problems of management-employee relationships, and so on. As the various interests represented by these diverse occupational groups conjoin, they come into conflict. There are real differences in interest which must be worked out and coapted. When the various conflicting interests are resolved, exchanges are consummated. The actual process of exchange is the level of work where metals are shaped and assembled into products, goods are transported from one place to another, checks are written and payments made, and foremen attend courses in "good human relations."

The foregoing suggests a classification of the transactional and exchange activities of a business in terms of the relationships of the enterprise to the various socioeconomic groups participating in the enterprise. This is the familiar "functional" division of labor characterizing most businesses and practically all business schools. In this view, when we think of a business organization, we think of the activities of the marketing and sales department, the accounting department, the manufacturing organization, the personnel department, the purchasing department, finance, and so on. In a previous edition of this text, we divided the various functions of a business into three groups: "external" functions, "internal" functions, and "auxiliary" functions. We regarded the "external" and "internal" functions as major or primary activities. The "auxiliary" functions were seen as supportive activities. The so-called "external" functions were regarded as those which had to do with the external relations which any business must develop and maintain if it is to survive—relations with customers, stockholders, sources of money, sources of supply, unions, governmental agencies, and the community. The "external" functions of a typical manufacturing company are shown in Figure 7–2.

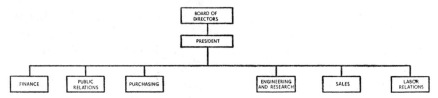

FIGURE 7-2.—"External" Functions of Typical Manufacturing Company

The "internal" functions had to do with the internal processes of the organization through which it produced salable goods, services, or ideas. These primarily had to do with the manufacturing function as shown in Figure 7–3.

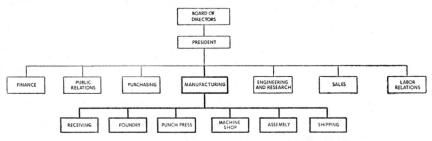

FIGURE 7-3.—"Internal" Functions of Typical Manufacturing Company

Finally, among the "auxiliary" functions, we lumped all of the "administrative control" and "centralized service" activities such as accounting, maintenance, employment, warehousing, and so on. These are shown in Figure 7–4.

A "functional" classification of organizational activities has the advantage of surface simplicity. Everything seems to be in place. However, it seems to us now that a more useful classification of activities

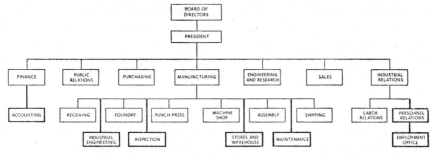

FIGURE 7–4.—"Auxiliary" Functions of Typical Manufacturing Company

can be built around the elements of the transactional process. While specialized knowledge of the various exchange and transactional relationships in which a business is engaged is needed, nonetheless the process of relating effectively to customers, stockholders, employees, and all the other contributing and claimant groups is not too different and for the most part involves the same activities. Moreover, in the day-by-day activities of the business, the various transactional considerations do not fall neatly into departmental and divisional boxes. The manufacturing organization, whether it knows it or not, is continuously transacting business with stockholders, customers, employees, unions, other departments and divisions of the company, and even the broader community. So is the sales department and the finance department and the industrial relations department. All of these have a total job to do— a total system of exchange relationships to build, maintain, and develop.

OCCUPATIONS AND HUMAN RELATIONS

One of the important significances of the division of labor is that it places employees in a special set of relations with one another. Employees are bound together by mutual needs and by the demands they make upon one another, growing out of the jobs that they are called upon to perform. The production worker, for example, by the very nature of his job wants the necessary materials to perform his job efficiently when he needs them. Already you can see that he will be making demands on the floor boys or central trucking or the supervisor to secure for him the things that he requires. If there is a breakdown in the flow of necessary supplies, he will react to it in one way or another. Likewise, the production worker wants efficient operating tools and equipment at all times. He is, therefore, continuously making demands on the maintenance workers and the setup men. Also, because of the nature of his work, the production worker is interested in securing a rate on his job which will permit him to earn a "fair" return on his efforts without "killing himself." A certain set of relations, therefore, builds up between him and the rate setter.

Stresses and Strains

Every job, every department in an organization, by the very nature of the functions which it is called upon to perform, develops a certain set of demands on other jobs and departments in the organization. Out of these demands grow many of the stresses and strains and the potentials for conflict which are characteristic of industrial organizations. In addition to worrying about the flow of work in the organization, management should also be concerned with the flow of demands, for it is out of these that most of the potential for conflict among employees will arise on all levels in the organization.

Studies by William F. Whyte of the restaurant business demonstrate clearly the significance of flow of demands to potential conflict among employees.[4] In his *Human Relations in the Restaurant Business*, Professor Whyte points out that the demands in the restaurant start with the customer, flow back from there through the waitress and pantry, and ultimately reach the kitchen. At each point along this chain of demands, friction can develop. It can develop between the customer and the waitress, the waitress and the counterman, the kitchen runner and the cook. If the personal needs of employees along this chain do not permit acceptance of the formal, organizational demands being made upon them, open conflict will develop and the efficiency of the organization will suffer. Thus, Whyte shows that the efforts of the waitresses in one large restaurant to initiate action and make demands on the men working on the counter resulted in conflict because the men, who were trained socially and culturally not to accept orders from women, had difficulty in adjusting to the demands made upon them by women in the work situation. In the same way, the kitchen runners, who were of very low social status in the restaurant, came into continuous conflict with the cooks who were of very high status. The cooks simply could not accept a low-status youngster shouting orders at them no matter how dire the need was from the work standpoint.

As the division of labor in an organization becomes more complex,

---

[4] William F. Whyte, *Human Relations in the Restaurant Business* (New York: McGraw-Hill Book Co., Inc., 1948).

it can be seen that the demands become correspondingly proliferated and intense. To take an example again from the restaurant business, the small lunch counter, compared to the large restaurant, has practically no problem of co-ordination. In the small lunch counter the cook, counterman, and waiter are all one and the same person. In the larger restaurant, there may be four or more job positions between the cook and the customer. Furthermore, each one of these positions may be occupied by five, ten, or more different personalities. The individuation of interest is multiplied tremendously. In the small restaurant, there is no difficulty in seeing the relation of the demands of the customer to the activities of the organization. In the larger operation, however, the original demands of the customer come through so many hands that they become confused with other demands operating in the organization.

It is apparent from this that the differences in values and interest of employees increase with the complexity of the technology and the size of the organization. In both cases the division of labor is increased and the demands intensified. Evidence of the effects of size and complexity upon the morale of employees can be found in morale surveys conducted by the authors and by others. In these studies, size alone was especially significant, larger organizations of the same type tending to have lower morale than smaller organizations. Complexity of technology and division of labor seemed even more important. In our surveys, factories generally had lower morale among employees than retail stores. Certainly foremost among the factors causing these differences in feelings and friction among employees was the greater problem of coaptation of interests which existed in factories as compared with retail stores. In retailing, the manager only has to be concerned with the co-ordination of merchandising activities and with operating. In the factory, the manager must be alert to the problems and demands of manufacturing, engineering, methods, maintenance, inspection, sales, purchasing, personnel, and research. He must be able to co-ordinate these demands to develop effective relations. In effect the retail store manager is running a two-ring circus, while the factory manager is confronted with six or more rings. Unfortunately, also, he often is not sufficiently well trained to administer as complex an organization as this. However, given the same caliber and quality of management, employees of retail stores will always have higher morale than factory workers simply because the problems of accommodating diverse interests are so much simpler.

Types of Relations among Departments

Important also to the development of different interests and values among employees are the types of relations which exist among departments. Several dimensions are important here. One is the actual extent of interrelationship which exists. It is apparent that some departments or groups of jobs are in continuous relations with one another and that others practically never come in contact. We have seen some organizations where departments exist side by side but with no functional relationship between them at all. The need for adjusting differences in interest in such cases is, of course, practically nil. Other organizations constitute an intricate web of relations so that each department is variously related to practically every other department in the organization. The need for adjusting differences in interest here is considerably incremented.

The nature of the relations which exist between departments is also exceedingly important to the kinds of relational problems which will arise among employees. The authors have been able to distinguish four such relations which appear to characterize all organizations. These will be discussed in the following paragraphs.

LINE RELATIONS

The line organization of any company is usually thought of as that department or set of departments which is involved directly with the principal functions of the company. In a factory, the production departments represent the line organization. The sales department may represent another line. In a retail store, the merchandising and selling functions are the line activities. In a restaurant, the flow of work from the kitchen to the customer is the line. All other activities in the organization are more or less built around the main line of work and are auxiliary to it. However, the distinction is not always clear. A developmental engineering department may, in one sense, constitute a line activity even though it is generally thought of as a staff activity. The development of new products is, of course, an important and direct function of any manufacturing organization; as such, it is not auxiliary to the production departments, and therefore is a line function. In general, a developmental engineering department is set off by itself in the organization. It comes into contact with the line only during the period of initial construction of the new product.

Another difficulty in defining line activities is that, within a staff department, there may be activities which constitute a line function for that department even though the department as a whole is an auxiliary activity. In a personnel department, for example, the employment procedure may be a line function within that department. The relations between employees working along that line will be similar to those between production workers. In the same way, in an accounting department, there is a line of activity which will relate employees in a certain way, one to the other. The important thing to remember here is that we are discussing the relations that exist among various jobs and departments. Whereas the department as a whole may be a staff activity, nevertheless, within it, there may be activities which are related as in any line organization.

The line organization develops a special orientation toward the rest of the organization because of the nature of its activities. Perhaps this orientation can be described best by saying that employees in the line at all levels feel that they are "doing all the important work" in the organization. Most other activities in the organization are thought of by this group as service activities of varying degrees of value to the line. What happens between various service and administrative control departments and the line organization will be discussed elsewhere. In this section, we are primarily concerned with what happens between line organizations and within a single-line organization.

Relations between Line Organizations

It can be readily seen that the principal source of difference between members of rival line organizations revolves around the question of who is doing the most important work. Since each line organization feels that its work is the most important, difficulties can arise whenever one makes demands on the other. The conflict which often develops between the sales and production departments of a factory is a good illustration of this. From the production department's standpoint, the sales department is forever going out and making promises to customers, either in regard to the construction of a product or to delivery dates, which "no self-respecting person, if he knew anything about production" would ever do. From the point of view of the sales department, the production and manufacturing divisions of the organization are always giving them a hard time because "they don't seem to realize that if the company doesn't get sales, there just won't be any production to holler about." And so goes the argument swinging back and forth, very often depending on how prosperous the times are—that is, if times are bad, sales are regarded as most important; if good, production gets the nod. Very often, too, the resolution of conflicts such as this one depends on the orientation of management. Studies have shown that some management is sales-minded and some production-minded, with very definite effects on the nature of the business that develops. It has been found that production-minded management is particularly interested in securing large, long-term contracts with big merchandising firms. This solves the sales problem for them and, at the same time, permits the operation of a relatively stable and efficient production organization. Sales-minded management, however, is not at all interested in large, long-term contracts but prefers smaller contracts with many customers. The reason for this is simply that the executive enjoys sales contacts. The more, the merrier! As one said, "If I had to give up selling, I'd just die." By the same token, such a company is less concerned with stable, efficient production.

Differences in interests can also develop between developmental engineering departments and production departments. Here the difference is not so much a question of whose activity is the most important but of who knows the most about production. The engineer's knowledge is highly specialized and professional, generally gained through formal education and training. He is trained in general principles, while the shopworker has the know-how that comes from actual and direct experience in the factory.

In retailing, the two principal line activities are merchandising and operating. The merchandising organization is concerned with the problem of buying the right goods and selling them. The operating people are responsible for all the other activities of receiving and shipping the merchandise, control of store equipment and properties, problems of personnel, and so on. There are differences in values and interests between these two line organizations on all levels in the store where the cleavage exists. The buyer, for example, may decide that he needs four more display tables and an additional employee in order to achieve the sales quota that he has set for himself. The operating manager, however, may decide that the store cannot spare him four additional tables and, furthermore, cannot increase its payroll costs at this time. So, the conflict starts—where it ends depends again on the orientation of management and on the economic times. Retailers tend to follow bullish and bearish trends like the market. In good times, any "wild" scheme in merchandising goes. But, in bad times, the close, tight operators reign supreme.

It can be seen that differences between rival line organizations can arise over the two questions, "Who is doing the most important work?" and "Who knows more about the work that is being done?" Now we will turn to a discussion of what happens among employees within a line organization.

Relations among Employees in the Line

The essential feature of line activities is the flow of work. One person performs one operation and passes on the products of his efforts to someone else. The activities of these workers are generally logically connected, at least in terms of the job to be done. The separate operations constitute a series of interconnected steps leading to a final product. In relatively simple organizations, the employee can see the relation of his work efforts to the creation of the final product. He knows that he must receive work in process from his fellow workers, perform certain operations on it, and pass it along to the next person. He knows that he must keep up with the others or they will all fall behind. He sees the importance and significance of working together as a team. The work makes at least some sense to him.

It can be seen that, in simple organizations of this type, there is a potential for co-operation on the job. The problem of co-ordination is reduced considerably, particularly if the breakdown of jobs along the production line is necessary and sensible. However, in many organizations, the line is not nearly so simple and uncomplicated as this. The original self-explanatory logic of the line, which is understandable to everyone involved in it, becomes lost in a maze of complications. This can happen in two ways. First, the line of activity can become so long and the steps along it so minute in importance that the employee feels only his complete insignificance in the total effort. He is no longer working on a significant unit of production. Moreover, he shares his responsibility with so many others that his job seems small indeed. The logic of the line and the need for co-operation is, therefore, lost to him.

However, mere extension of the line and the overelaboration of steps along it are not nearly so bad as the complete elimination of the logic of the line. In a number of organizations, this has been done, leaving the individual worker isolated and performing completely meaningless activities. Perhaps the best way to describe this situation is by means of diagrams. In the set of diagrams shown in Figure 7–5, Diagram I represents a simple straight-line production setup. In Diagram II the organization has been increased in size so that each step in the production

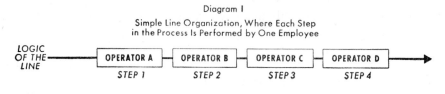

Diagram I

Simple Line Organization, Where Each Step
in the Process Is Performed by One Employee

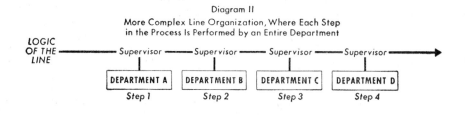

Diagram II

More Complex Line Organization, Where Each Step
in the Process Is Performed by an Entire Department

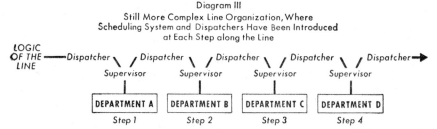

Diagram III

Still More Complex Line Organization, Where
Scheduling System and Dispatchers Have Been Introduced
at Each Step along the Line

FIGURE 7–5.—Logic of Line Tends to Be Lost as Organization Becomes More Complex

process is now performed by an entire department of employees. It can be seen that the logic of the line has been moved up to the supervisory level. The employees no longer participate in it; the potential for co-operation which existed when only one man occupied each step in the process is gone. Now the co-operation of employees at each step along the line must be secured by constant explanation of the logic of the process to them by the supervisor and by plain and fancy urging. The problem of co-ordination has been considerably increased.

Diagram III represents another complication of the line. Here the logic of the line has been broken still further by the introduction of dispatchers who guide and control the movement of raw materials and work-in-process through the line. Under these circumstances, the supervisors themselves begin to wonder what is going on. It can be seen that, in this way, the logic of the line can be complicated to the point where the activity of the organization makes sense only to top management. Employees down the line work almost in isolation, hardly realizing that the job they are doing is part of a great co-operative effort. In such a situation, management is faced with the prospect of trying to create team spirit among employees when the obvious and apparent need for co-operation and co-ordination of efforts has been taken away from them.[5]

ADVISORY AND STAFF ORGANIZATIONS

In all organizations of any size, various auxiliary departments are set up as an aid to the line. Among these auxiliary departments, we shall consider first those which give advice to the line and attempt to help with difficult problems where specialized assistance is presumably needed. Personnel departments and engineering departments partially fall into this category. The members of these departments are regarded as advisory experts from outside the immediate shop organization, who come in either when difficulties arise or when changes are contemplated. However valuable and necessary they may be, therefore, they are not the ones who ultimately have the responsibility for getting the work out. And as a rule, the more efficient the shop organization and the better it handles its own problems, the less need there is for the technical staff. Setups of this type almost inevitably lead to friction between the advisory and line organizations.

Each advisory or staff organization is prone to see the work of the line in terms of its own special functions and to be very critical of any failure of the line to follow its suggestions or directions. The engineer has an eye out for any possible improvement in equipment or methods, and complains that the shop foremen and workers are ignorant, stupid, and unco-operative about such changes. The personnel man is always on the watch for improper treatment of employees and complains, no doubt with some justification, that shop foremen are indifferent to the workers or object to following correct practices in hiring, firing, and promotion. Thus each directs his attention to only a limited aspect of shop activities, and each is looking for trouble or chances for improve-

[5] For an excellent study of the relation of work effort and level of co-ordination to employee morale, see Richardson and Walker, *Human Relations in an Expanding Company* (New Haven: Yale University, Labor Management Center, 1948).

ment, since it is largely through such changes that he justifies his existence.

People in the shop, on the other hand, feel, with equal justification, that the staff members are all riding their own special interests, that they are more concerned with making a showing personally than with helping to get the work done, that they do not realize the pressure the shop is under, and, all in all, that they are not as smart as they think they are. The shop foreman has to deal with the job as a whole. He has to get the work out; and, by the way, he has to struggle with technical difficulties, enforce safety rules, and take into account dozens of other factors in everything he does. It is not surprising that he often resists suggestions from staff members and is annoyed when they seem to expect him to drop everything else when one of their specialists comes around.

Engineers and the Shop

Between the engineering organization and the shop, differences in interests and values are especially common. The engineers usually look down on the shop workers as being of lower status, uneducated, and "sot in their ways." The shop employees consider the engineers too theoretical, filled with book learning, very impractical, and altogether obnoxious with their superior airs. When the engineers have the responsibility for developing better products or manufacturing methods, they are in the position of imposing changes on the shop almost constantly. Every time they make any improvement, it is likely to mean that the shop people have to learn new work habits or change their accustomed routines, and the established status systems and systems of interaction between workers may be upset. For example, an improvement in method which would eliminate certain skilled jobs would mean that some workers would have to change to other jobs perhaps at lower pay, and at the same time it might remove the goal that some of the younger men were working toward. Another change might result in new and tighter rates, which would mean either harder work or lower earnings for the group.

The various functions of the engineer all put him in a position superior to the shop people. He is either proposing changes which may be rammed down their throats whether they like it or not, or he is finding things wrong with the way they do their job, or he comes in with his superior knowledge to straighten out things that have gone wrong. Even if he is acting as trouble shooter, they would much rather handle the problems themselves than call him in, since they feel that too much reliance on him may be interpreted by their bosses as meaning that they cannot handle their jobs. (An engineer who sits around waiting for the line supervisors to call on him for help is usually not kept very busy.)

We do not mean to imply that there is always conflict and antagonism between engineers and the shop, because in many instances there are cordial and co-operative relations. In any shop group, however, there are innumerable tales, or we might say myths, illustrating the ignorance and impracticality of engineers, and frequent complaints about the new ideas the engineers dream up. On the other hand, every group of engineers has its own tales about the stubbornness and lack of co-operation in the shop. There is so much of this that we may conclude that there is inherent in the relation between an engineering organization and a shop organization a basic conflict, so that members of each group identify themselves with their fellows and are opposed to the other group.

Not just with engineers but in their relations with staff experts generally, the shopworkers and foremen are usually on guard. Even when maintaining friendly and co-operative attitudes, they are often on the alert to protect themselves against undesirable changes and resent any attitude of superiority. In many cases there is open hostility toward a staff man which shows itself in a negative attitude toward all of his suggestions, covering up anything which he might criticize, or finding reasons why co-operation is impossible. Sometimes the resistance to him takes the form of putting off the execution of any of his ideas, of not wanting to try things out, or of refusing to do anything except under direct orders from their superiors. At best, a staff man is in a difficult position. To get things done, he must always work through the shop organization, and especially through the foremen, who are the ones to put his ideas into practice. And, no matter how good his ideas may be, their success or failure often hangs on the willingness and ability of the shop foremen and workers to carry them out in actual practice. There are, in fact, plenty of cases in which sound ideas failed because of the indifference or opposition of the shop organization. And when he meets with active opposition, the staff man's position becomes even more difficult. He often feels blocked in everything he attempts; everything moves terribly slowly; and he finds himself in an agony of frustration.

An Outsider in the Shop

Another factor which adds to the difficulties of the staff representative is his position as an outsider in the line organization. Because of this he is always under suspicion. If he is coming right into the work situation, watching the work and the workers, in touch with what is going on, he is a potential threat, since he provides a channel of communication upward which is not controlled by the line. As a part of a staff organization, he can effectively short-circuit the line and carry criticisms of the line organization up to the top of the structure without detection. This is a very real problem to the staff specialist, too, because he must not only get his ideas across to the line but must keep his own boss informed of his activities and show what a good job he is doing. This means that he has to report on the problems of the line organization to show how he is spending his time. Inevitably, then, he becomes a channel through which shop problems are passed up through the structure and are short-circuiting the line. For example, a foreman finds that a certain process has gone wrong and he calls in an engineer to help straighten it out. The difficulty seems to lie in some short cuts which the workers have been trying to get away with, and the foreman would hate to have his boss find it out, as he would be blamed for laxness in his supervision. So the foreman says nothing up the line and hopes that he can get by. The engineer, however, tells his boss what he has been doing. They discuss the cause of the difficulty, and his boss complains that they are spending too much time fixing up things that would never happen if the shop foreman followed the engineering instructions. The next day, in talking to the superintendent of engineering, he uses the incident as an illustration of the kinds of unnecessary difficulties they have to deal with. The superintendent of engineering, when lunching with the manufacturing superintendent, asks him why he cannot make the foremen follow instructions, and recounts the incident. The manufacturing superintendent then puts his subordinates "on the pan," first for letting such a thing happen, and second for not keeping their superiors informed on what is going on so that he has to learn about his own job from outsiders. Such a situation seems to justify shop suspicion of staff experts and shows just how much of a threat to the shop they may be.

Justifying Staff Activities

The problem of justifying their existence, of showing that the work they are doing is actually worth the expense, is often a serious problem, especially with large staff organizations. The individual members, as well as the organization as a whole, often show concern as to how management evaluates the organization or how the superiors judge the individual. An engineering organization may be judged by the number and value of the improvements they introduce, or by the number of problems they solve. A safety organization may be judged by the decrease in accidents. And since much of the showing they make depends upon the acceptance of the shop organization, they are likely to feel that their success is blocked by the indifference and obstinacy of the shop. In some cases the relations with the line are seriously affected by the manner in which the staff people are judged either by their immediate superiors or by top management. For example, an engineer whose job is evaluated on the basis of the improvements in shop equipment and methods which he develops may find that he is competing with shopworkers or foremen. Engineers are often accused of stealing bright ideas from shop people and presenting them as their own; and engineers say that the shop people do not have the technical knowledge to make even a really good idea work and that their ideas would never amount to anything without the engineers. In one instance a shopworker developed a simple but important improvement, submitted it through the plant suggestion box, and received considerable recognition. The engineer who had been assigned to developmental work in that department was called in by his superiors and bawled out for not making the improvement himself. As he told it to a friend, "I was told that it was my job to make these improvements, and I shouldn't let the shop have all these bright ideas. It made our organization look bad, especially when such obvious improvements got by us." Inevitably, such attitudes lead to conflict and failure to develop mutually useful relations.

Desire for More Authority

Because of these conditions, the staff experts are apt to feel that they should have more power and authority to force the shop to accept their ideas. They are also prone to react to resistance by "going up the line" with complaints and demands for co-operation. Almost every staff man at times dreams of being able to demand the co-operation of the shop foremen and workers. And almost everyone has at times been guilty of going over the heads of the shop foremen with complaints and criticisms. Unfortunately, there is no authority that can force a reconciliation of values, and any such attempts to force it tend to increase the difficulties. An example of this was seen in the case of a very unpopular safety engineer who always had an authoritative manner toward the shop foreman. He would inspect a department, list everything which he could find wrong, and then, instead of taking it up with the foremen and letting them straighten things out, he would go higher up and report on the terrible conditions. He himself was always complaining about the unco-operative attitude of the shop. He complained that there had to be a club over the foremen to get the safety rules enforced and that he could not understand why management did not back him up more. As a result, the entire shop organization disliked him. They did not want to have him around; they never asked his advice or told him anything. On one occasion he brought a division chief down to inspect the shop on a Saturday morning when the place was shut down and the foremen were not present. Apparently the division chief felt that he could not refuse; so he accompanied the safety man, who listed every instance of poor housekeeping, safety hazards, improper machine guards, and so on. On Monday morning the division chief had told them that he understood the situation and was not criticizing them, that he was just cautioning them to try to improve conditions before they all got in trouble. They felt very strongly that the safety man had been snooping behind their backs and had not given them a chance either to correct or to justify the conditions before calling in the division chief. This is a good example of a transactional failure.

While the desire for more authority is especially strong at the lower levels of the staff organization where members are in direct contact with the shop, there are similar feelings at all levels. There is a tendency, therefore, not only on the part of the individual experts but of the whole organization, to be pressing management constantly for more and more authority and power as an easy solution to their transactional problems. Then, too, since each organization is concentrating on its own specialty, all are constantly struggling to increase their effectiveness in their own field. This often results in a tendency for each staff group to try to increase its size, to add more and more specialists, and to impose more and more of its point of view upon the entire company. This leads to a lot of competition between staff groups, even though they have quite different functions. Each is likely to be critical of the others, skeptical of their value, and jealous of any group which seems to be getting unusual recognition or growing rapidly.

Internal Structure of Staff

In their internal structure the staff organizations tend to be quite different from the ordinary shop organization. Even in very large plants the staff organizations are much smaller than the shop units and usually have a shorter supervisory hierarchy. Individual engineers, for example, may report directly to a department chief without the intervening supervisory level, or the department chief may report directly to the plant manager. Furthermore, the number of individuals reporting to any one department head are much fewer than in the shop, so that each individual has much more contact with his immediate superiors and even with higher levels. This has the effect of bringing the individuals closer to the higher supervisory levels, often develops feelings of being close to management and of identification with management and its objectives, and generally adds to their feelings of superiority.

Because of the nature of their work, the staff men are apt to have more formal education than people at comparable levels in the shop organization. They often have college educations and even graduate training and are generally looked upon as being superior in intellect to the foremen and workers. The need for special technical training means that people are usually recruited for staff jobs from outside the plant rather than from the shops. As a result, there is no channel through which the shop people can rise from the ranks. This means that the staff organizations are differentiated from the shop not only by their functions but also by the kind of people who are selected to perform these functions.

This selection process tends to bring in at the bottom of the staff organizations a group of young college graduates, often with degrees in engineering or science, thoroughly drilled in the logic and point of view of their particular field. These newcomers often run into difficulties in their relations with the shop. There are the young engineers, for example, often fresh out of college, who are in constant contact with the shopworkers and supervisors and who try to give them technical assistance. And there are the young personnel men, often without actual factory experience, who try to tell the old-time shop foremen how to handle personnel problems. Being young and ambitious to make a showing and get ahead, these young experts tend to become very aggressive toward shop people, to be critical, and to indulge in pleasant daydreams of having the authority to "tell that stubborn old so-and-so in charge of the X Department just what he has to do and no back talk." Inevitably the experienced shop people look upon these as "not-yet-dry-behind-the-ears youngsters," long on book learning and short on judgment, who are more interference than help. In their turn, the young people feel constantly frustrated in their efforts to put their knowledge to use; and in their attempts to get the shop to change its ways, they feel that they are beating their heads against a stone wall.

They look upon themselves, furthermore, as future executives, as the cream which is bound to rise to the top. This tends to strengthen their feeling of being part of management and their acceptance of management's aims and point of view. At the same time, it makes them impatient with the shop people, those "unintelligent" people who do not accept the ideas and reasoning which to the young experts are so clear as to be obvious. They are often impatient, too, with the slow processes of advancement and part of their feelings of frustration are translated into antagonism toward the shop organizations which block their ideas and prevent their getting suitable recognition.

In some staff organizations which have been well established over a long period of time, there may be two groups of people at the lower levels. One is a group of older people who have been in the organization a long time but who have no college training. Often these people have been brought in from the shop in the early development of the staff organization because of their practical knowledge of shop work. They may be experienced mechanics, tool- and diemakers, or others with extensive practical knowledge and skill. Their limited technical training, however, in many cases serves as a barrier to further advancement, and they remain for years at the lower levels in the staff jobs. The other group is composed of young people like those just described above, highly trained specialists, often just out of college, who start at the same level as the old-timers. They usually advance rapidly because of their education. These two groups are generally mutually antagonistic and split the organization in two. The noncollege old-timers feel that their practical knowledge is not given adequate recognition, and the college group are scornful and impatient of them because "they don't know anything and haven't gotten anywhere." The older group tends to be antagonistic to management—or at least toward the top of the staff organizations—and does not share in the feeling of identification with management and acceptance of its logic to the same extent as the younger fellows. Often they identify themselves much more with the shop and sympathize with its general antagonism to "the young punks out of college who don't quite know what the score is."

Personnel and the Line

The personnel department often finds itself in somewhat the same position as the engineering staff in its efforts to have its ideas and suggestions adopted by the line organization. Like the engineering people, personnel representatives deal with a special problem which is just one of the concerns of the line supervisor. Furthermore, because of their specialized training, they can observe all sorts of personnel mishandlings in the line organization. They are, therefore, considerably troubled about the lack of ability shown by line supervisors in their handling of human relations. These same supervisors, however, feel that the personnel department wastes its time with "Sunday school stuff" and has no awareness of the practical problems of running an organization.

In some respects, the personnel department is in an even more difficult spot than the engineering department. The work it is doing is usually less well established in the thinking of top management. As a consequence, it is much more concerned with its status in the organization as a whole. Much of the work of personnel departments is designed to impress management that it has a job to perform. This work takes the form of projects of various kinds so that something can be shown management whenever questions about personnel activity arise. Whether or not these projects contribute in any way to the over-all efficiency or well-being of the organization is often not a consideration.

Like other staff departments, personnel departments frequently attempt to take over various functions of the line in order to insure that personnel matters are handled correctly. Very often this usurping of line functions is accomplished by the establishment of red tape and procedures covering personnel handling. When everything of this nature must clear through the personnel department, the line becomes saddled with red tape and loses its ability to make important decisions with reference to the employees that it is supervising. The personnel department under these circumstances ceases to play an advisory role in the organization and is actually performing administrative functions for the line.

SERVICE ORGANIZATIONS

Nature of Service Organizations

Service departments differ from advisory departments in an organization in that they perform some direct and needed service for the line; their work is tangible and necessary. Unlike advice, these services cannot be turned off and on by the line. The line has to have them. A department like the maintenance department in the factory falls into this category. Employment activities in the personnel department are of a service nature, and the purchasing department is also a service organization. Warehousing, customer delivery, mechanical repair units, receiving—in fact, practically all nonselling departments—are service activities in retail stores.

It can be seen from the nature of service departments that differences of various kinds can arise between these organizations and line departments. A number of these differences hinge on the fact that the line departments initiate action for, and make demands on, the service organization but, at the same time, do not have authority over it. Although the service organization must meet all reasonable demands made upon it and cannot easily refuse a request for service, nevertheless it can decide when it will meet these demands. Many intense conflict situations in industry revolve around this crucial issue. Because the line cannot obtain services when it feels that it needs them, it accuses the service department of hampering and bottlenecking production. It takes the attitude that the service organization does not have the interests of various line departments at heart. The service department, on the other hand, is of the opinion that the line department has an interest only in its own problems and is not at all concerned with the over-all problems of the organization.

Problem of Scheduling

The proper scheduling of service is, as a matter of fact, a real problem for service departments. It actually is difficult to determine which department has the greatest need for service and should come first. There are various ways of handling this problem of scheduling. The simplest is, "First come, first served!" But there are always special requests, and handling those is usually a headache. Very often, the determination of who should come first is made in terms of the relationship between the service department supervisor and the supervisor making the request. If this relationship is friendly, then the service department supervisor is likely to give his friend priority. Cries of favoritism are thereupon heard ringing throughout the line organization. Another basis on which priorities are granted is in terms of who screams the loudest. Under such an arrangement, the supervisor who is most capable of dramatizing his need for service and who shouts loudest for help gets what he wants. This situation lends itself neither to good feeling nor well-balanced service activities.

Management on higher levels is in a position to gain priority for its pet projects over any lower-level demands. Top-level administrators, as a consequence, are often impressed with their own leadership ability because they can get things done so easily while lower-level supervisors struggle around with the simplest of problems. One manager thrived on this evidence of his ability. "Why can't these foremen get anything done around here?" he was frequently heard to say. "I told Pete two weeks ago to get that junk cleared out of his end of the department. Today, I finally had to do it myself. Called the maintenance department, and they had it out of there in two hours. You'd think these foremen would exercise a little initiative." Of course, the facts of the matter were that Pete had made the same request of the maintenance department on three occasions, and had practically pleaded on bended knee; but all he had gotten were promises which were never fulfilled.

Because service departments are on the receiving end of the demands constantly being made in the organization, a certain frustration develops. No one likes to be told incessantly to "do this and do that." It is like living with a nagging wife; even the most docile husband will snap back on occasion. Very often service department employees are quite critical of the line organization. This is true because usually the service employees are experts in their own field, and they can see careless mistakes and poor planning in the line organization which result in more work for them. "Why don't they take care of this equipment? They must beat this stuff with sledge hammers," is one remark not infrequently heard. Or else, "You'd think they'd plan their work better. They wait until the last minute and then expect us to pull them out of a hole."

Effect of Different Lines of Authority

The problems of reconciling the differences that develop between service and line organizations are considerably enhanced and magnified whenever each organization reports through a different line of authority. Under these circumstances the line department cannot easily get the help of higher authority in securing services which it feels are necessary. Furthermore, the service department is not close enough to the line department to understand its problems fully. In one manufacturing organization, the maintenance department reported directly to the general manager of the factory. The plant superintendent had no authority to demand service for the production departments. Actually, the relationship which developed was unfair to both supervisors involved. Throughout the line departments, there was considerable criticism of the maintenance superintendent. They felt that he played favorites, continuously and unfairly criticized the line, and carried stories to the general manager. In one sense, these criticisms made by the line organization were true. The maintenance superintendent was in a position to observe many of the mistakes and problems of the line organization. Furthermore, he was in a position to carry his views direct to the top man in the organization who, in his turn, was eager to receive them and use them to stimulate line supervisors to greater effort and improved skill on their jobs. The pattern was not, however, organizationally sound and was finally resolved by placing the maintenance department under the direct supervision of the plant superintendent, who was also in charge of manufacturing.

A similar situation occurred in a merchandising organization. The functions of this organization were to buy, receive, store, and distribute —at the proper time and in the proper quantities—soft-lines merchandise to retail stores throughout the country. Most of the lower-level activities in the organization, of course, were devoted to the receipt, storage, and distribution of merchandise. Originally, each merchandise department was set up to mark and ticket its own merchandise, then to store it, and finally to assemble it for distribution to the various stores in accordance with a centralized distribution plan and also in accordance with special requests from the stores. Under this setup, the merchandise department was able to work together as a unit in meeting seasonal demands and any special requests from the stores.

However, the operating division of the organization sold management on the idea of centralizing all marking and ticketing operations. This was going to improve the efficiency of these activities by bringing all employees performing the same functions together in one place, scheduling their work more intelligently, and utilizing their time more completely. When this was accomplished, the new marking and ticketing department became a service department with reference to the original merchandise departments. On routine orders, all went well; but the moment the merchandise departments started making demands for merchandise out of its proper order, the fight started.

Usually the requests for special handling were made by one of the girls from the merchandise department involved. These girls were placed in the position of attempting to initiate action for the supervisor of the new service department. The results were appalling from a human relations standpoint. First, the supervisor did not, under any circumstances, like to have his system for handling incoming merchandise disturbed. Special requests meant bringing in merchandise out of order, with all the extra work and diminished efficiency that this involved. Second, he certainly did not intend to have his neat, well-organized department thrown out of gear on the say-so of some little "pipsqueak" from another department. After all, he reported through the operating department, which was primarily concerned with efficiency and saving money, "If you let the merchandising departments push you around, why, they would be asking for special handlings all the time," etc., etc. The end result was that the girl went sobbing back to her own supervisor and he emerged forthwith to do battle for the honor of his departmental womanhood (not to mention his departmental needs). The argument that followed, and the shouted accusations and counteraccusations which accompanied it, was dramatic evidence of the problems which line departments can become involved with in their relations with service departments.

CONTROL ORGANIZATIONS

Activities and Functions

Accounting or cost control, rate setting, and inspection comprise another group, which may be thought of as control functions. Except in large concerns, these are not usually set up as three separate and distinct organizations. On the basis of their functions, however, we shall discuss them here as three types of control systems, without regard to their exact positions in various plant organizations.[6] These control organizations do not actually control operations in the shop directly, but they supply the basis for management's evaluation and control of shop performance. The accounting or cost control organization, for example, is constantly checking up on the performance of the shop and reporting to higher executives about it. Management relies on its reports to judge how well the shop is performing in terms of production and costs. The piece-rate organization has the responsibility of setting the rates which serve as a control over labor costs and which are another standard by which management evaluates the shop.[7] The inspection department must pass on the quality of the products, and its reports serve as still another measure of shop performance.

All these various reports on costs, quality, performance, earnings,

---

[6] Almost invariably, even in small plants, there is an accounting system which is separate from the shop organization. Inspection, however, is usually part of the shop. Rate setting usually comes under the accounting or engineering organizations, and only rarely achieves the status of a separate organization.

[7] The functions and problems of rate-setting organizations will be discussed in a later chapter on wage systems.

and so on, serve to pull together in a highly condensed form certain information concerning the way the shop is operating, for the use of higher supervisors and management. On the basis of their interpretations of these reports, management judges how things are going, puts pressure on the shop organizations, and makes decisions regarding shop activities. The proper interpretation of such reports is one of the skills that executives must develop, since it is important for them to understand just what the figures mean in terms of the way the shop actually functions.

Anticipating Control Reports

Since it is evaluated largely on the basis of these reports, the shop is inevitably concerned about them, how they will be interpreted, how management will react to them, and what the consequences will be. Shop supervisors want to be able to anticipate all such control reports. They want to know, at least approximately, what is going to go up the line, especially for those reports which are most used by management. Supervisors are also interested in understanding the methods by which the figures are gathered, so that they may keep alert for any errors and, when possible, control the figures themselves. In other words, the shop bosses want to know just what the reports will mean to them and how to beat the system. As we shall see in a later discussion of piece rates, the foreman often tries to control the job in order to maintain straight-line earnings, as a means of protecting himself from criticism or questions from above. The same is true of any other report which goes up the line; if it is used as a control report by management or if it is examined and questions asked about it, the foreman tries to see that only harmless figures go up. In the case of reports which go in on regular dates, for example, such as monthly reports, a foreman likes to know about where his department stands before the report is compiled, so that he can try to correct any adverse conditions. If a company is trying to cut down on raw-material inventory and places great stress on monthly reports of raw material on hand by departments, then just before the inventory period each foreman starts keeping his own private check on raw materials and tries to reduce his stocks to a minimum. Once safely past that period he will let his stocks build up again.

If the foreman can anticipate any such reports, he can not only plan his work so that the figures will be what his superiors like, but, in case of adverse changes or any conditions which might be questioned, he can prepare his answers safely in advance. Thus, if he sees that his group will show a drop in piecework earnings which he cannot avoid, he will have his explanations prepared even before the earnings report is released. In many cases, he not only prepares his story but passes it up to his boss, so that he, in turn, knows what to expect and what answer to give. In fact, it is considered very important that the foreman warn his boss of any important changes which will appear on any reports. This is then passed up the line for at least a few levels, so that when the big boss gets the report, everybody is ready for his questions. In that way all levels can show that they are on top of their jobs and know what is going on in their organizations.

This need to anticipate the reports often leads to a lot of informal record keeping on the part of the foremen. In some cases a foreman himself may keep a few records which give him the needed information, but on other jobs there may be so much work that he has a clerk just for this purpose. In one company where piecework earnings reports were used as an important control, it was informally expected that the foremen pass on their estimates of the earnings for their groups a few days before the actual accounting figures were released. A study of this company showed that every foreman had some form of informal records, usually duplicating in a rough way the actual accounting records and requiring as much as the full time of one clerk for each department. In other words, there were two sets of records of piecework earnings, one the extremely accurate accounting figures and the other the rough records from which the foremen made their estimates. While the informal records seemed rather unnecessary and quite expensive, the foremen felt that they needed them in order both to control their groups and to warn their superiors as to what to expect at the end of the month. These needs are so great that there is probably no way to eliminate completely this kind of informal record keeping.

Accounting and Cost Control

The systems of accounting and cost control arise directly out of the economic logics. These systems provide a method by means of which practically everything—the buildings, machines, tools, materials, labor, and so on—is reduced to a common denominator of dollars and cents. Thus they provide a basis for comparison of the most diverse activities or for combining them in various ways. In effect, they provide a means for adding horses and cows to bushels of oats and bales of hay, or for comparing one to another. Thus, through a cost report, management can compare the performance of the department making heavy castings with that of the final assembly department, or it can combine them all into one report to show the performance of the entire plant for any given period. This seems rather obvious and is usually taken for granted, but back of all cost control lie a number of assumptions which have their effect upon the way people act on the job.

Because cost reports are frequently used as a sort of score sheet for the shop organization and its segments, the supervisors tend to run their jobs with one eye on these reports. If labor cost per unit of output appears on the reports, the foreman watches his labor costs; and as long as they stay within limits acceptable to higher management, he feels at ease; when they go beyond those limits, he tries to dig up an acceptable excuse. Thus such reports set the operating goals for the shop and set the standards of proper performance. As a result, we see foremen and higher supervisors devoting their attention to meeting the requirements of the score sheet rather than to actually improving the job. As long as these requirements are met, they seem quite willing to coast along keeping everything stable. In fact, we may conclude that the average shop organization tends to seek stability—to level off and hold everything steady—and does not have within itself the pressure to lift performance to higher levels. Top management, however, as we have seen, is always concerned with raising the level of performance and uses the cost reports as a pressure device to stimulate the lower supervisors to this end. These supervisors, in turn, often react by working out devices to protect themselves from this pressure with a minimum of disturbance to the equilibrium of their organizations. For example, we see foremen juggling the records or shifting people around to cover up, when one part of their job is "going in the hole." Often the supervisors are not primarily concerned with doing the job the best or cheapest way, but with doing it in the way that will look best on the reports.

Although cost reports are a useful tool for management, it must be remembered that they provide an oversimplified picture of what is going on. To have a report showing that the cost per unit of output has increased 1 per cent over the preceding month may provide management with something very concrete and simple with which to put pressure on the manufacturing organization. Nevertheless, behind such figures lie all the problems and difficulties with which the organization has to struggle, all the delays beyond their control, as well as all their own mistakes in judgment. And if top management takes the cost reports as the sole measure of performance and gives no consideration to all the difficulties which may arise, the lower levels feel unfairly treated.

This is generally recognized by top management; they know that to interpret the reports properly and to be fair in their demands upon the shop, they must be able to read between the lines and not just take the reports at their face value. This usually means that they must have some acquaintance with the way the shop works and with the difficulties it faces, and must keep informed as to changes in its situation.

Many companies use a budget system in which they make an estimate of the needs of each department and set up a budget based on these estimates. Thus, they make an over-all estimate of the needs of the business and the funds to be spent during a period, and then distribute the funds to the various departments. This may be further broken down into details of the way in which the funds are to be spent, such as: so much for direct labor, so much for indirect labor, so much for materials, tools, repairs, and so on. Under such a system, and especially where there is a detailed breakdown of the budget, each department operates within a framework of anticipated expenditures which do not always fit changing conditions. When management readily approves variations from the budget, this does not present much difficulty; but when it tries to adhere pretty closely to the budget, many problems arise. For example, if a punch press department has almost exhausted its monthly budget for tool repairs, it may be forced to delay necessary repairs until the next month. This often results in makeshift repairs by the department itself in order to save sending the tools to the regular toolroom, or it may mean using tools beyond their period of efficient operation. This, in turn, may decrease the output for those tools or increase the defective parts. This may lower the earnings of the operator or cause him extra trouble with the job, which, in turn, annoys him because he can see no reason for not having the tools repaired when needed. Also, such makeshifts often result in things being done in more expensive or less efficient ways, even though it does keep the budget looking right. In any case, having to subordinate the needs of the job to the needs of the cost control system is always annoying to the worker and the foremen, who are acutely aware of the inefficiency and waste of such practices.

While the whole system of cost control and its reports is a constant threat to the peace of mind of shop supervisors, there is rarely open antagonism and conflict between the two organizations. The cost control procedures are highly systematized and reduced to simple routines of paper work, much of which is done by clerks. These systems depend very little upon personal contacts between foremen and accounting people for the collection of data, which frees them of one source of possible friction. As a result, because there is little personal interaction, there is much less friction between the shop and the accounting organization than between the shop and the average staff organization. In some cases, however, the way the cost control system is set up gives rise to friction between segments of the shop organization. For example, where there is strong emphasis upon scrap losses, there is always argument as to who is responsible. Often defective work in one department may not appear there, but may cause work in some other department at some later stage to be junked. In such cases, there is always the argument as to who is actually responsible and to whom it should be charged. And each department is always suspecting the other of trying to do a little "chiseling" by passing on defective work rather than junking it when found, or by trying to pass the blame back to someone else. Thus, it is often found that the particular cost control system, or the emphasis it places on various items, has far-reaching effects upon the attitudes of the workers and the relations between various departments.

Since the accounting and cost control system, especially in large plants, involves a great deal of routine clerical work, these organizations are usually larger than the staff organizations and often parallel the shop organization in number of levels. In the large accounting organizations where much of the work has been reduced to simple routine operations, no great skill or understanding of accounting methods is required of the clerks. In smaller organizations, there is less routine work, and even the clerical workers may need to have an understanding of the system as a whole. In either case, the average clerical worker needs to know little beyond the mechanics of the accounting system itself.

The accounting organization offers opportunity for many of the younger people from worker families to move to the often-coveted white-collar or office status. Many of the jobs can be handled by any alert high-school graduate, and others may require moderate skill at typing or operating business machines, such as comptometers, calculators, or adding machines. This makes it relatively simple for any ambitious youngster either to start directly in this work or to prepare for it through brief evening-school courses. In the past, the desire for these jobs has been so great that most accounting organizations, as well as most office work, have a starting rate no higher, and sometimes even lower, than the starting rate in the shop.

To the youngster with college education, however, especially if trained in accounting, the average accounting organization is discouraging. If he comes into a large organization, he is thrown into a lot of routine work which others with no college education can perform as well as he, and he feels that his talents are wasted. Furthermore, he is sometimes working under supervisors who have little or no theoretical training but who have grown up in the organization and know its routines thoroughly. This gives him a feeling of isolation, of not having opportunity to display his learning and talents. A small organization is often more satisfactory, since it offers more variety of activity and more opportunity for contact with higher levels, which relieves some of the feeling of being completely lost in a huge organization.

Inspection

Inspection is another type of control which is also important to the shop and with which it has considerable contact. The inspector's job puts him in the position of telling the shop what is wrong with its work. He points out mistakes and defects in the products and reports such mistakes to his superiors; and, in a piecework system, he directly affects the pay envelope. Also, in many plants his reports on quality are one of the control reports which top management watches closely and which are, therefore, a threat to the shop.

Because of these functions, there is likely to be a sharp cleavage and considerable friction between inspection and the line organization. The workers and shop foremen rarely regard inspection as a friend; they are apt to be critical of the way it does its job; they argue over its standards and disagree with many of its judgments. This is especially apparent when inspection involves the judgment of the inspector rather than precise standards of measurement. In such cases the shopworkers and foremen are likely to complain that the inspector uses poor judgment, that he discards parts which to them appear perfectly adequate, or that he is trying to hold them to standards that are impossible to maintain. Of course, when inspection is primarily a matter of the inspector's judgment, he can be tough or easy on the shop; and, unless they question every judgment, they have a hard time defending themselves. A case of this was described by a foreman of a finishing department, who said:

We once had an inspector in here who was a terrible grouch and always made it as tough as possible. Once we had a job putting a baked enamel finish on some metal panels about five feet long and a foot wide. We would spray the enamel on one side, rack them up flat on a truck, and shove the truck into the baking oven. When they would come out, this inspector would tilt each one up to the light, and if he would see even one dust speck, he would send it back; said the specifications called for perfectly smooth finish. Well, our spray room and oven weren't in too good shape and it was almost impossible to get one completely dust free. It was crazy to be so strict; it was only a protective enamel for an inside surface that was never seen, but this guy didn't care. Finally we got the engineers to look at the job and they told him it was good enough the way we were doing it.

Inspectors sometimes feel superior to shopworkers and express attitudes of superiority, which increases the friction between the two groups. Most inspection people feel that they are always fighting with the shop in order to maintain the quality of the products and the reputation of the company. They feel that the shop people are only concerned with their own selfish interests and want to make a showing in output or earnings at the expense of quality and that it is up to the inspectors to keep them in line. Furthermore, they often feel that the shop is not to be trusted but must always be watched with suspicion—attitudes which are often shared with other groups, such as safety engineers, cost control people, and rate setters.

The shop cannot feel that they are through with any job until it has been passed by inspection; but, once passed, their responsibility is ended. In many cases, they feel no concern for their work beyond getting it past inspection. If inspection is lax and passes products that will not work, that is no concern of the shop and may even be their good fortune. If they can "pull a fast one" and sneak some defective parts past inspection, that may even be considered a good joke on inspection. As a result, we often see considerable scheming by the workers, and even foremen, to "beat" inspection. When the quality reports are used by management for control, it becomes important for the shop to keep defective work down. One way to do this is to see that defective work does not go to inspection but, rather, that it is either repaired or junked before inspection sees it. Sometimes the department maintains its own informal inspection of the work either by the workers or by the foremen. For example, the foreman may make a rough check on the work, either during processing or before it goes to inspection, and, if there seems to be a lot of defective work, he may go over the whole job carefully. Sometimes he will sort over a bad lot of parts and send only the good ones up to inspection. In these ways he can keep his workers on their toes with regard to quality and keep some control over their quality reports.

Under individual piecework, inspection has an important influence upon the earnings of the individual worker. The work of each individual must be counted, and the inspector's records become part of the accounting routine by which the worker is paid. This tends to increase the possibilities of friction between the inspector and the individual worker and stimulates the worker to try to figure out ways of slipping poor work past inspection. The functions of piecework as a wage system and the problems involved will be discussed in some detail in a later chapter.

If, as sometimes happens, the inspectors and shopworkers are on friendly terms, the inspectors may help the shop make a good showing by turning back defective work without reporting it. In such cases the inspectors will call the workers' attention to any recurring errors, will send defective parts back for repairs or to be junked by the shop, or may even make slight repairs or readjustments themselves when they have time. These inspectors are always well liked by the shop and usually have little difficulty in getting the shop to accept their judgment. Sometimes this sort of alliance between workers and inspectors goes on even without the knowledge of the shop foreman and serves to protect not only the shop organization but also the individual worker from his boss. The extent to which such co-operation can flourish, however, is usually limited by the way the inspectors are judged by their own supervisors. In many cases the work of the inspector is judged by his reports of defectives found and by spot checking his work to see if defectives are getting past him. If he does not report any defectives, the assumption is either that he is not doing his work carefully or else that the shop is turning out such perfect work that it does not need inspection. If check inspections show that there are not any defectives, then they may decide either to do away with that inspection or put it on a sampling basis in which only so many pieces out of every lot are inspected. If they find the inspector has been working closely with the shop and turning back all the defectives without reporting them, they feel that he has somehow betrayed his own organization and superiors. In any event, he has to report some defectives in order to keep his boss from looking too critically at the job he is doing.

In general, inspectors rank somewhat higher than shopworkers; and inspection organizations, as a whole, have status superior to the shop organization. This probably arises partly from the fact that the worker is, in a sense, directly subordinated to the person who checks his work and decides whether it is good or not. Also, most inspection jobs are lighter and easier than the shop jobs, so that the inspectors can dress like the office workers. Because of this superior status, inspection work often offers a chance for a minor degree of mobility from the shop. It does not ordinarily rank high enough to attract people with special training or with a desire for office status, however, since its work is done in shop location and to the office people it still ranks with the shop.

INFORMAL RELATIONSHIPS AND ORGANIZATIONS

So far, we have been considering the groupings, divisions, and relationships which grow out of the formal organization and are largely defined by the way the organization is put together. In addition, there is the more spontaneous type of groupings which arises out of the daily contact of people. This "informal" organization is an important element in the whole structure and is one of the major objects of the social environment in which each individual spends his days.

Patterns of Interaction

When we speak of a factory as a system of human relations, we mean, in part, that the individuals in the system are brought together into frequent interaction with each other. This interaction is not a matter of random contacts but, to a large extent, has a definite pattern, and may even be a habitual routine. Thus, every person has a fairly definite pattern of interactions which relate him to certain others in the structure. Contacts outside of this pattern are generally infrequent and limited. Of course, much of the interaction is determined by the work itself, as, for example, the contacts between superior and subordinate for the purpose of giving instructions or communications regarding the work, or contacts between helper and machinist as a result of their working together. On the other hand, there are innumerable contacts which are not directly necessary to the work, such as morning greetings, chatting about outside affairs, joking and "horseplay," and gossiping about what goes on around the plant. These all go to complete the pattern of daily contacts and interaction which help make the factory an integrated social system.

When we look at all the human relations in a factory, we see that each person fits into a pattern in which he has a lot of contact with a few people, a little contact with some more people, and practically nothing at all to do with most of the others in the plant. In other words, people fit together into groups. Within a group there is a lot of interaction, and between groups there is little. Thus we can think of any organization as being broken up into a myriad of groups of workers— some large, some small, some following formal organizational lines, some groupings of people who work together every day, some groups-within-groups, and some embracing a whole plant division of workers. An individual usually has some feeling of belonging or identification with the group or groups into which he fits. He may hold attitudes of antagonism or friendliness toward certain other groups, or he may express beliefs and sentiments which are common to his group with regard to the work, the company, or anything else in the work environment. Thus we find that much of the work behavior of the individual is an expression of his place in the group or groups to which he belongs.

These groups are not all clearly defined or separated from one another, by any means, and there is a great deal of overlapping. For example, the six girls who work side by side on the assembly conveyor form a work group, and four of them may be a social clique who get together outside of the factory. At the same time, they all probably have only very limited contacts with people in other departments. Going still further, they all probably feel themselves members of a still larger group composed of all shopworkers, as opposed to office workers.

Formal Organizations and Informal Relations

In talking to the members of each division of the organization, it is seen that each member has feelings of identification with his own particular division, usually has a high degree of interaction with his fellow members as compared with members of other divisions, and may express fairly uniform attitudes toward the functions and behavior of the members of others. In many cases, well-developed patterns of antagonism are found between such major divisions, with each being very critical of the others and defensive of their own organization. Generally, there is a sharp cleavage between the staff and line organizations, growing out of their difference in function.

Within each of the larger organizations, too, there are further subdivisions which, in turn, are groups. The maintenance department, for example, feels itself different and separate from either production or inspection, and usually has quite definite attitudes toward these other groups, although all are part of the production division. At this level in the organization, there is likely to be conflict between the production and inspection departments, arising out of the fact that inspection must pass on the work of the production department and decide whether it is acceptable or not. This frequently puts inspectors in the role of critics, and nobody loves his critics.

In one small factory some of these conflicts, antagonisms, and cleavages along organizational lines were observed in extreme form. An observer described the factory and some of its groups and discords as follows:

The organization described is one that has grown over a long period from a small beginning to a present group of about 400 employees. . . .

There are several vice-presidents in charge of departments, and some men heading up smaller departments who have not yet been given any title. . . . The many departments making up the organization are like separate nations, the department executives standing against each other, demanding more in the way of salaries for their people, and more in the way of service from other departments. This causes friction and rivalry between heads of departments and constant problems for the office manager and personnel director. . . .

Mr. K. is a vice-president in charge of the largest department—65 men and women. He does not seem to consider that he is vice-president for the whole organization; his department is all that matters. His people are higher paid than those in other departments. He thinks the service departments—typing, dictaphone, filing, mailing, etc.—operate for his benefit alone; and if their results do not suit him, he does not hesitate to tell them so, in no uncertain terms. The result is that there are really two organizations—K.'s department and the rest of the office. To illustrate, this year his 65 people are having their Christmas party on the twentieth by themselves, and all the other departments—300 people —are having theirs on the twenty-second. Mr. K. explained: "Mr. X. [the president] knew I wanted a separate party, so he didn't insist on a general office party." The office manager commented: "K. could sell X. a gold brick any day. . . ."

Then there is the little vice-president who started as an office boy forty years ago. Great rivalry exists between this one and Mr. K. as to whose department makes the most money, which is closest to Mr. X., etc. For weeks they are not on speaking terms, and the slightest concession from Mr. X. to either of them is likely to start another war.

Even when conflicts and antagonisms do not actually exist, lines of cleavage tend to develop between organizations, so that their members remain as distinct groups. For example, in one instance two separate organizations each occupied half of a large room. In the center of the room, members of each organization were seated back to back at adjacent rows of desks, only a few feet apart (Fig. 7–6). In spite of the physical proximity, there was very little interaction between these individuals beyond a polite good morning or occasional comment. Almost never were there any long conversations or gatherings between mem-

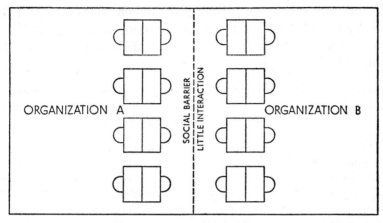

FIGURE 7-6.—Floor Plan of a Workroom

bers of the two groups. Within each group, on the other hand, there was a great deal of interaction both on the basis of the work and for purely social conversation. In this case it was apparent that the formal organization itself set up a wall between the two groups in spite of the fact that there was no apparent feeling of conflict, antagonism, or defensiveness. Furthermore, there was nothing in the attitudes of the superiors in either organization to prevent them from mingling. There seemed to be merely a distinct feeling of indifference of the members of each organization toward the others, with the result that there was very little interaction of any sort.

When there is conflict or competition between supervisors or superiors in different organizations, as, for example, in the case of the vice-presidents described above, the barriers between the members at the lower levels are strengthened. In such cases, subordinates tend to have feelings of anxiety over any contacts with the other organization. They wonder what their boss will think if he sees them talking to someone from the other group; they avoid social contacts which might be observed by the superiors; or they feel it necessary to explain any such contacts to the boss. The result of this is to limit all forms of interaction and to isolate the groups from each other, even though they may be seated almost side by side.

Cliques

Within the nonsupervisory group in any organization, there are forces acting to split it into smaller groups, too. Often such lines of cleavage may follow functional lines, as in the case of a clerical organization in which typists formed one group and file clerks another. In one study, by Roethlisberger and Dickson,[8] of fourteen men in a small work group, it was found that the group was divided into two cliques. This was described as follows:

On the basis of the material just reviewed some conclusions can now be drawn as to the informal organization of this group of workmen. In the first place, it is quite apparent that the question raised at the beginning of the pre-ceding section must be answered in the negative: these people were not inte-grated on the basis of occupation; they did not form occupational cliques. In the second place, it is equally apparent that there did exist certain configurations of relations in this group. With one exception, every record examined seemed to tell something about these configurations. Whether the investigators looked at games, job trading, quarreling over the windows, or friendships and antago-nisms, two groups seemed to stand out. One of these groups was located toward the front of the room, and the other toward the back. "The group in front" and "the group in back" were common terms of designation among the workmen themselves. The first of these groups will be designated as clique A, the second, the group toward the rear of the room, as clique B.

What was the membership of these two cliques? This question can be an-swered only approximately. Clique A included W1, W3, W4, S1, I1, and clique B included W7, W8, W9, and S4. W5, S2, and I3 were outside either clique. With W2 and W6, however, the situation was not so clear. W2 participated in the games of clique A, but beyond this the similarity of his behavior to theirs ceased. He entered very little into their conversation and tended to isolate him-self from them. Much of his behavior suggested that he did not feel his position in the group was secure. He was the only wireman in soldering unit A who traded jobs with S4, the solderman in clique B, and he traded jobs with his own solderman more than anyone else. In so far as the social function of job trading was to differentiate wiremen from soldermen, this could be interpreted as mean-ing that W2 felt rather keenly the necessity of constantly emphasizing his posi-tion by subordinating the soldermen. Taking all the evidence into consideration, then, it may be concluded that W2 was not a bona fide member of clique A. W6 tended to participate in clique B. He was continually "horsing around" with the selector wireman and had relatively little to do with the members of the clique A. That he was not entirely accepted in clique B was shown in many ways, chief of which was the way in which clique B co-operated in resisting his attempts to dominate anyone in their group. Yet he participated in clique B much more than W2 did in clique A. It may be concluded that although W6 tended to participate in clique B, he was still in many ways an outsider.

As a means of summarizing the results of this inquiry, Figure 45 [Fig. 7–7] has been prepared to represent diagrammatically the internal organization of the observation group. The soldering units into which the members of the groups were divided are shown by the three rectangles. The two large circles demarcate

    [8] F. J. Roethlisberger and W. J. Dickson, *Management and the Worker* (Cam-bridge, Mass.: Harvard University Press, 1939), pp. 508–10.

the two cliques. There were three individuals, I3, W5, and S2, who were clearly outside either clique.[9] The line around W6 has been made to intersect that of clique B to indicate his partial participation in it. The instability of W2's position is indicated by the broken circle around his number.

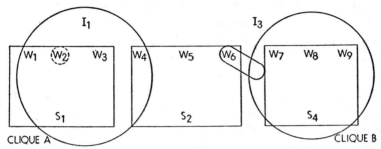

FIGURE 7-7.—"The Internal Organization of the Group"
"Bank Wiring Observation Room"

That the members of clique A regarded themselves as superior to clique B was indicated in many ways. Clique A did or refrained from doing things which were done by clique B. They did not trade jobs nearly so much, and on the whole they did not enter into the controversies about the windows. Clique A engaged in games of chance, whereas clique B engaged often in "bringing." Both groups purchased candy from the Club store, but purchases were made separately and neither clique shared with the other. Clique A bought candy in small quantities, whereas clique B bought a less expensive kind in such large quantities that W9 one time became ill from eating too much. Clique A argued more and indulged in less noise and horseplay than clique B. The members of clique A felt that their conversations were on a higher plane than those which went on in clique B; as W4 said, "We talk about things of some importance."

Horizontal Cleavage

In many cases, too, we see horizontal lines of cleavage between the vertical levels within an organization. The most common point of cleavage of this sort is between workers and supervisors. This separates them

---

[9] "Perhaps a word of caution is necessary here. When it is said that this group was divided into two cliques and that certain people were outside either clique, it does not mean that there was no solidarity between the two cliques or between the cliques and the outsiders. There is always the danger in examining small groups extensively, of overemphasizing differentiating factors. Internal solidarity thus appears to be lacking. That this group, as a whole, did have very strong sentiment in common has already been shown in discussing their attitudes toward output and will be brought out more clearly in the next chapters. It should also be said that position in the group is not so static as one might assume from this diagram. Had the study continued longer, membership in the cliques might have shifted. Also, if the group had been larger, or if the group had been allowed to remain in the regular department, it is quite probable that the people who appear as outsiders here would have formed cliques with others who had similar sentiments" (*ibid.*, p. 510, n.).

into two antagonistic groups, with the workers feeling that it is necessary for them to unite in defense against excessively critical or demanding foremen or other supervisors. This defensive attitude of the workers causes them to avoid contacts and interaction with their superiors, makes them withhold information, cover up mistakes, restrict output, and devise a variety of protective measures. Foremen usually respond to such behavior by critical attitudes, avoiding social conversation, and restricting contacts to those required by the work. In such cases, we find contacts are kept at the "strictly business" level, and then they are filled with feelings of suspicion and criticism, so that the contacts are uncomfortable for both sides. Such horizontal cleavages are not, however, confined to that level but may occur at any point in the hierarchy. In some cases, foremen group themselves with the workers in opposition to higher levels. A striking instance of this was observed in the following case:

Department chief A was new to the organization, having replaced a man who had been very popular with both the foremen and the workers. A was very hardboiled in his manner, critical of the way the department was running and wanted to make a lot of changes. Foremen B and C had had long experience in the department, worked together well, and were popular with the men. The department had been running very smoothly; they objected to A's criticisms and rebelled at the changes. There soon developed open friction, with A in opposition to B and C.

D was a production control man reporting to the production control organization, but handling the planning and scheduling of work for this department. He was not of supervisory rank, but his particular job gave him status well above the ordinary office worker. Because of his job, he was well informed as to how work was progressing in the department. Also, he had once reported to A when A had been in charge of a production control department.

As friction developed between A and his foremen, interaction and communication diminished. The foremen admitted that they were always afraid of A's criticism and avoided him whenever possible. One of them said: "If he comes around, we find some excuse to be busy somewhere else. If he is at his desk, we stay out on the floor; if he is in one end of the department, we go to the other end. We never tell him anything unless he asks us and try never to discuss the work with him. We all went to a department party the other night, and if we were at the bar and he would come up, we would walk away."

As this blockage developed, A turned more and more to D as a source of information about the department. The foremen in turn reacted against D who, they felt, was carrying tales to A about the department and was, therefore, not to be trusted. They also felt that D was trying to gain favor in the hopes of being promoted to C's job, since A had threatened to get rid of C if he failed to do a satisfactory job. As a result they would have nothing to do with D beyond what was necessary for the job. Thus the department was split into two antagonistic groups, A and D who were friendly and working together, and B and C who worked together and were friendly with each other but would have nothing to do with A and D. The workers were not directly involved, but they shared the antagonism toward A and were therefore loosely grouped with B and C whom they liked and trusted [Fig. 7–8].

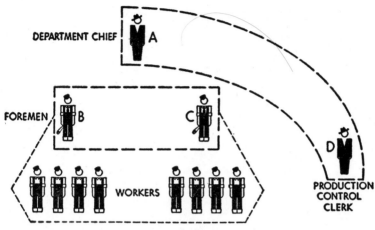

FIGURE 7–8.—An Example of Horizontal Cleavage

SUMMARY

It can be seen from this chapter covering the division of labor of the typical business that the work-a-day world is characterized by differences in values and interests. For the most part, these are honest differences arising out of the diverse points of view and aims created by the various jobs which men perform. Men strive to realize their aims and, as a consequence, make demands on others. Management makes demands on employees and employees make demands on each other. This is the natural condition of organizational life. Clearly the differences in values have to be reconciled in order that mutually useful exchanges can take place. Men try to achieve such reconciliation through conflict, adjustment, and compromise, and even by assimilation. Management's task is not one of eliminating differences but one rather of creating an atmosphere in which men can negotiate their differences in creative and positive ways. Instead of viewing differences in interests as evidence of the unco-operative, dog-eat-dog behavior of man, they should be accepted as natural and as real and acceptable differences in interests. With a positive, accepting attitude toward difference, management and employees alike can get on with the task of accommodating diverse interests and developing mutually useful exchange relationships.

8. AUTHORITY SYSTEM AND CHAIN OF COMMAND

THE man-boss relationship is one of the basic elements in an organization. The concept of supervision in which one person directs others is fundamental to the system of division of duties and responsibilities. Basic, also, are the different roles and expectations for supervisor and supervised. Thus the supervisor has a primary responsibility for getting a job done. And he is expected to get it done according to the standards and requirements set by himself or set by the organization.

In addition, he has *secondary responsibilities* which control or restrict the way he must function in getting the job done. He may have to keep within certain costs, see that safety requirements are met, abide by union contracts or personnel policies, etc.

As a supervisor, he does these things by influencing those under him. He must direct them, judge them and motivate them. And unless he can do these effectively, the job does not get done. However, the supervisor expects certain things of his subordinates:

1. They will accept his right to give orders, to judge, to direct
2. They will obey the orders, or at least try

In turn, the *supervised* have certain responsibilities and expectations. They have the *responsibility* for trying to carry out the orders. They expect that the orders will be:

1. Understandable
2. Possible
3. Reasonable
4. Related to their job and the work situation

They also expect that they will not be held accountable for failure if the job is not understood, is impossible or unreasonable, or is beyond their ability.

Now these expectations are basically part of our culture—we all grow up in a society which teaches us what these roles are and what we can expect of either supervisors or subordinates. Thus the idea that the boss has the "right to give orders" is merely an expression of an established social code of behavior. Furthermore, the obedience of subordinates is also part of the social code.

In terms of the exchange system when the employee accepts the job he accepts this relationship. In effect he says, "In return for the money and other benefits I receive I will work certain hours and so many hours each day, I will do the work for which I've been hired, and I will take orders from the boss within the limits to which it is customary and morally right for him to give me orders." If the boss exceeds these limits the worker may openly defy him, in effect saying, "I'm not being paid to do that," or "You can't pay me enough to take that guff." Or in many cases the worker obeys grudgingly or evades the issue and later evens out the transaction by doing poor work, cutting his output, or by other nonsanctioned actions.

We have, then, the situation in which the boss gives orders because his role, or his job, requires that he give them; and the subordinate obeys because his role requires acceptance of the boss's right to give orders.

One thing is clear—the obedience to the boss is not solely a matter of giving in to a superior force. While the boss has at his control certain power of rewards and punishments, he has far from absolute power. He can hardly "make" anyone do anything, and the extent to which he can try to force obedience is controlled by custom, by rules of the organization, and by the climate of opinion within the work group itself. Thus, in reality, his authority over others rests not in the power which is placed in the position, but in the acceptance of that authority by subordinates.

In spite of the general acceptance of the authority relationship, it is clear that not any order nor any act of the boss is accepted. In fact, the problem of how to get subordinates to do what you want them to do is a constant problem with any supervisor. How do you get them to come to work on time? How do you get them to do more work? How do you get them to obey the rules? How do you get them to talk less and work more? The supervisor's primary preoccupation is with how to get people to do things. Nevertheless, careful observation in almost any work situation will show that there is a vast body of acceptance of orders and of general obedience to the rules and directives set by management and imposed or enforced by the supervisors.

Turning now to the chain of command, we see that it is through the linkages of this man-boss relationship that the top man is linked with the bottom. Every person except one within the structure has a boss;

and every boss, in turn, has his boss, until finally at the top of the heap we find that rare and practically sacred individual, the president, the owner, the big-shot-who-has-no-boss. (Of course, even presidents have their boards of directors; but a director is a different sort from your personal boss, who seems to be ever present, asking questions and "breathing down your neck.") In most companies or factories there is one Big Boss and below him rank after rank of smaller bosses down to the very bottom, where we find those unfortunates who have no one to boss, those who are so numerous and so unimportant that their names never appear on the organization's charts—the workers.

The Supervisory Hierarchy

The whole structure forms a neat pyramid, with the Big Boss at the top and each rank of lesser bosses increasing in numbers as they decrease in importance, until at the bottom of the supervisory structure there is the largest and perhaps the most misunderstood group, the foremen or first-line supervisors. The whole forms a status system with all foremen having a rank superior to the workers, all the next level outranking the foremen, and so on.

Although each department chief outranks every foreman, it does not follow that a foreman will take orders from any department chief or even from any superintendent. (At least in theory they do not, but it is pretty hard to say "no" to a superintendent.) Instead, each person has his own personal boss to whom he looks for orders and instructions, for praise and criticism, for rewards and punishments. This extends on up to the top, so that each person is linked up to the Big Boss through a series of these man-boss relationships. This forms what is known as "the line of authority," or "chain of command" in the army. Since each level has more persons in it than the level above, each boss, as a rule, has more than one person reporting to him. This gives the fan-shaped pattern so well known on the formal organization charts, with a number of lines of authority merging at each level until finally they all merge into the supreme command of the Big Boss.

Just as the lines of authority converge toward the top of the structure, the lines of interest and attention converge also. In fact, everyone seems to be looking upward with his attention focused upon the people above him and especially upon his boss. His boss is the man who hands out the orders, assigns him to his work, gives him a pat on the back for a good job, and passes on a good word for him to the "higher-ups." And his boss is the man who can give him a dirty job to do, criticize him for doing it poorly, and give him a bad name up the line. His boss is his link with those above him in the structure. Thus the likes and dislikes of the boss, his moods and opinions, his comings and goings, his least comment and gesture, or the way he is distracted by that cute little redhead from the next department, all these are subjects of interest to his subordinates. Each subordinate is concerned over just how his boss feels about him. He wonders if his work is satisfactory, if he makes a good appearance, if his boss thinks he talks too much or not enough, or if he knows just what his boss does expect.

While each boss is thus the center of attention from his subordinates, he in turn is busy watching his own boss and wondering about him. As a result, he tends to look upon his subordinates in quite a different way. He rarely worries about their opinions of him; he does not lie awake at night wondering if he acted like a fool in front of them; he does not treasure their words of wisdom or of praise to be retold at the dinner table. He does not even remember that he is the center of their attention, and he is likely to be annoyed with them if they are upset by his indifference or demand a lot of his time.

Thus we have a series of man-boss relationships in which each person is intensely concerned with how his boss judges him and at the same time is busy judging his subordinates. Each is constantly looking at his subordinates, trying to determine how well they are doing their jobs and how they might do better work; and each is constantly being irritated and disturbed when they fall short of what he thinks they should be doing. At the same time, his concept of the job is often being mixed up with what his boss will think and what *he* expects, until "doing a job" often becomes a matter of "doing what the boss thinks is good." This concern is not merely with what the boss expects in terms of the work itself but also with what he thinks is "proper" behavior. As a result, the boss at each level judges his subordinates not merely in terms of the work accomplished but in terms of "what would my boss think if he saw them?"

Now one fundamental concept of formal organization is that responsibility is drawn together into fewer and fewer hands as we progress from bottom to top of the organization. Thus, each supervisor has responsibility for the work of, and supervision of, several subordinates but has only one boss. As a result, the man at the top has only a few whom he holds responsible and through whom his influence and authority reaches down into the depth of the organization.

Fundamental to this supervisory-subordinate relationship is the belief that superior status attaches to the one who gives orders. Thus the supervisor outranks his subordinates—in fact, he is referred to as the "superior." "Who is your superior?" is understood to mean "Who is your boss?" This basic relationship establishes the fundamental status system of the organization, with each link in the chain of command seen as a unit of status. This is best seen in military organizations, where each position, or "rank," is clearly described along with all the appurtenances of title, insignia, uniform, etc. In such situations, each individual clearly understands where he fits, both in terms of status and in terms of giving and receiving orders.

The chain of command also forms the primary channel of communication for the organization. It provides the series of relationships through which the commands of the Big Boss are carried downward through the structure to its most distant points. And it is also up this line that information is carried back to the Big Boss, so that he is kept informed as to the progress of the work or of significant occurrences. Thus, one of the major functions of the line is that of providing channels of communication extending from top to bottom throughout the structure.

The Limitations

It is not, however, the simple, direct channel of communication that it is often thought to be. By its very nature as a linkage of man-boss relationships, it has a number of peculiarities which affect the quality, accuracy, and speed of its transmission. In fact, much of the transmission is so difficult that it is rare for a superior who is several steps removed from the work level to have a comprehensive knowledge of what goes on in the shop. Such a statement may offend the many top executives who speak with glowing pride of how close they are to the work level, of how their subordinates trust them and tell them all. In any sizable plant, however, where there are hundreds or even thousands of workers at the bottom, it is obvious that the man at the top cannot possibly be kept informed of every detail. His knowledge of the work situation must be limited to only certain kinds of details or general information. The movement of information from the bottom to the top must be limited, and what goes up must be carefully selected. Ideally, only those things are communicated to the Big Boss which are necessary for his decisions or which will help him to perform his special functions. Actually, this ideal is rarely achieved, and often important information never arrives at the top, or a lot of small details clutter up the channels.

Although this is a two-way channel with information moving both up and down, there is a striking difference between the kinds of information which go each way. From above comes, "The boss wants to know . . . ," and "The orders are . . ."; while from below comes, "This is what happened . . . ," "These are the difficulties . . ." and "Here are our successes or our alibis. . . ." Rare are the occasions when direct demands move up the line from the bottom or explanations for failures move down from the top. (Remember that we are talking about the flow through the line of authority. Other systems of communication will be discussed later.)

The line as a channel of communication has an important function in two kinds of relationships: first, between each person in the structure and his job; and second, between each one and his boss. Probably everyone is aware of the first function and each one does communicate to adjacent levels the obvious things they need to know to do their jobs. Because this function of communication through the line is more or less effective, the system works, people do their jobs, and goods are produced. The second function of line communication is often ignored or misunderstood, however; and because it is overlooked, the man-boss relationship is often so unsatisfactory as to seriously impair efficiency and co-operation.

Communication Down

Because of the nature of the man-boss relationship, because each person is so dependent on his boss for recognition and communication up the line, because each person is so sensitive to his boss's moods, opinions, like, and dislikes, there is often much confusion and misunderstanding in communication down the line. Since everyone below him is constantly trying to anticipate his wishes, trying to read his every word and gesture, the boss does not always have to put into words his ideas and what he expects of the job. But as a result of this extreme sensitivity to the boss, there are, in any work situation, frequent misinterpretations, and the problem of impressing the boss sometimes becomes more important than getting the work done.

For example, we see the superintendent passing through the shop convoyed by the foreman. Being in a jovial mood, he makes a conversational comment that "the girls seem happy this morning, the way they are talking and laughing." The foreman thinks, "Is he hinting that I shouldn't allow them to talk? Does he think I don't keep proper discipline? Those girls ought to have sense enough to stop talking and act busy when he's around. Maybe I better move Mary off by herself because she always gets the others started talking." The boss leaves, quite unaware that his comments have been interpreted as criticism. As soon as he is gone, the foreman bawls out the girls for talking and not paying attention to their work; he moves the Marys around, and it is weeks or even months before the final ripples of disturbance have died down.

Or, again, the foreman may come in some morning with a slight indisposition or with family matters on his mind, and he does not notice Joe, who is standing near the aisle. Joe, of course, was all set for the usual, "Good morning, Joe. How's everything?" Now he's all upset, and he thinks, "What's wrong? Wonder if he's sore about something. Did I do something wrong? Wonder if he saw me kidding with that new girl yesterday and got sore about that." For the rest of the day Joe is so busy trying to figure out what might be wrong that his mind is only half on the job. Finally the boss speaks to Joe about something in a very matter-of-fact way. Joe heaves a sigh of relief and says, "Boss, when you didn't speak to me yesterday, I thought you was sore about something." And the foreman thinks, "These guys are just like a bunch of kids. Just because you don't go around waving and smiling all the time, they think you're sore at them. I wish they would grow up and pay as much attention to their jobs as they do to those little things."

Distortion up the Line

At the same time, and also because of their sensitivity to the boss and their dependence on him, there is a good deal of distortion of the facts in communicating up the line. Along with a great concern for "giving the boss what he wants," there is a constant tendency to "cover up," to keep the boss from knowing about the things that go wrong or the things that do not get done. No one wants to pass bad news up the line, because he feels that it reflects on him. He is supposed to handle his job so that there is no bad news; he has to give his superiors the impression that he is handling his job efficiently. As a result, he does not go running in to tell the boss what a poor job he did or how stupid he was. That is, he does not unless he thinks someone else will get to the boss first with the story. And when he does have to break some bad news to the boss, he will probably have gotten everything fixed up or developed a good alibi for his failure. In this way, people at each level develop methods of defense, often complicated and ingenious, by means of which they protect themselves from criticism from those above. For example, we may have the following interchange between a department chief and one of his foremen:

DEPT. CHIEF: "How are things going in your place, Joe?"

FOREMAN: "About as usual." (*Thinking*, I wonder what's on his mind. Maybe he would like to know about our output.) "Looks like we will finish that last order for the Model X gadgets this week. If we do, we will beat our promise by about three days." (*Thinking*, He ought to be pleased to hear that, especially after our slow start on that job. Guess I won't mention the trouble we've been having with the Model B, where the inspectors threw out half that first lot. Think we have it licked, but I would rather not worry him with it until we are sure.)

DEPT. CHIEF: "That's fine. Glad to see that job out on time. How's the new Model B order coming?"

FOREMAN: (*Thinking*, Oh, oh! What brought that up? Maybe he's been talking to inspection. Thought Jim would keep his mouth shut. He knew I was getting that fixed up.) "Had a little trouble on the first lot. Final inspection found some of them out of adjustment. We had to make some changes." (*He explains the details of the change at length.*) "Think we have it licked now but won't know until tomorrow."

(*Thinking*, That ought to show him that I'm on top of my job. Maybe I ought to tell him about my argument with the foreman of the machine department yesterday, just in case Bob takes it up with his boss. Then my boss will want to know all the answers, and I don't want him coming back asking why I don't tell him about these things. And I don't want him to think I'm not trying to co-operate with the other departments.)

"Say, here's something that came up yesterday. You know Bob in the machine department furnishes us with the base plate for Model N gadget. Now that's a tricky job and he wanted to make a few small changes that would make it easier for him. I tried to show him why we couldn't use them that way." (*He gives a technical explanation.*) "I would have liked to help him out because he's been having a lot of trouble on that job, but I just didn't see how I could do it. Maybe the engineers ought to take a look at that model."

DEPT. CHIEF: "Yeah, you're right. You couldn't do anything. If Bob's boss comes to me, I'll suggest that we get the engineers to try to straighten out the job. Well, glad everything is going along all right. So long."

FOREMAN: "So long." (*Thinking*, Guess he really didn't have much on his mind.)

In such contacts we see the subordinate selecting what to tell the superior, trying to anticipate what the boss wants to know or what he may want to know later, trying to present things in such a way that his boss will feel that things are not too bad, or, if they were, that they are now under control, and trying to give him good news and take the sting out of bad. And the boss goes away from such contacts feeling that he knows what is going on, that he has his finger firmly on the pulse of the shop.

Filtered Information

Thus we see each individual in the line acting as a filter who sorts over the information coming to him and carefully selects what he will pass on to his boss. Since the boss responds most favorably to good news, there is a tendency for good news to go up the line quite easily and rapidly. Information as to improvements in output, quality, costs, and so on are transmitted readily from level to level; and as it goes, it leaves everyone with that self-satisfied feeling, the I-gave-the-boss-some-good-news-and-he-was-very-pleased-and-thinks-I'm-fine-and-maybe-he-will-tell-the-big-boss-what-a-good-job-I-did feeling. On the other hand, bad news meets certain barriers; everyone is reluctant to communicate his mistakes or failures. The what-will-the-boss-think-of-me feeling acts as a brake upon full and rapid reporting of things which go wrong. It encourages delays; it fosters alibis; it develops skill in the tactful presentation of bad news.

Take the case of Bob, foreman in the machine department, when he suddenly discovers that he does not have enough bronze rod on hand to complete the order of part number X37A22 for the end of the week and that it will keep two hand screw machines going steadily to make delivery on time. So he talks to Charley, the machine operator who came to him asking for the rod:

Bob: "Are you sure there isn't any of that rod over in the rack? When we started on this job, I checked the storeroom records and there was plenty on hand."

Charley: "There sure isn't now. You remember when we first started on this order somebody gave us the wrong specifications and we turned out a lot that had to be junked."

Bob: "That's right. Well, I'll call the stockroom and get some more over right away." (*Thinking*, I sure did slip up on that. I completely forgot to order more rod.)

(*He calls the stockroom.*) "I'll need two hundred pounds of that ⅜ths bronze rod for part number X37A22. We're in a rush for it, got to get the order out right away and a couple of machines are waiting. Can you get it right over?"

Stockman: "Sorry, we are out of that rod. Won't be able to get it in before Friday. Why didn't you call last week?"

Bob: "Can't you get hold of any before that? If I don't deliver those parts before Monday, the gadget assembly department will be tied up."

Stockman: "We'll do the best we can, but don't expect it before Friday.

Why don't you guys give us a little more notice instead of waiting until your machines shut down and then expecting us to do miracles?"

Bob: (*Thinking*, This is a terrible note! I slip up on ordering that rod at the one time the stockroom is out of it. Why can't they keep some stock on hand instead of trying to work from hand to mouth. Just trying to make a good showing by keeping down inventory and they tie up production. They ought to realize that they are there to help the shop, not to give us all this trouble. Wonder what I can do now. The boss sure will give me hell when he hears this. Maybe I ought to check with Joe in gadget assembly to see how many parts they have on hand and how long before he will need more. Maybe I better let him know what's happened so he will know what to expect. Maybe he can plan his work so the people on that assembly job can do something else for a few days.

But if I tell him what's happened, he will tell his boss, and his boss will jump on my boss, and my boss will jump on me for letting this happen and not letting him know. So before I tell Joe anything I better tell my boss. Maybe if I tell him, he can tell Joe's boss, and I won't have to say anything to Joe. Joe's going to be plenty sore anyway. He got kind of hot the other day when I tried to get him to let me make some changes in the base plate for that Model N job. Seemed like he was just being stubborn. Wonder if he might have enough parts on hand so he could just go along and say nothing about this affair. If I knew he had enough, I just wouldn't say anything and take a chance on getting some to him before he runs out. I'm afraid to risk it, though, without being pretty sure, because if he did have to shut down, my boss sure would raise cain. Yeah, and Joe called the other day to know how we were coming on that lot we delivered yesterday, said he didn't want to get caught short. But Joe always does that. He starts crowding you for things long before he actually needs them. He seems to think no one will keep their promises unless he rides them. If I ask Joe how much he has on hand, he will suspect something and I will have to tell him.

Guess I better not take a chance on Joe. I will have to tell my boss first. But gee, how I hate to tell him! I know just what he will think. I know I should have remembered to order more when we spoiled that first run, but I was so busy getting caught up that I forgot. Anyway, you never would expect the stockroom to be out of a standard item like that. And if they ran this place right, they never would be. But my boss won't care about that. All he'll think is that I must be asleep on the job. He expects me to keep track of everything; and if I have to do the stockroom's job for them to keep my job going, he expects me to do that. What will I tell him, anyway, that won't make me look like a fool who doesn't know his job? Maybe I better not tell him now. It won't hurt to wait till tomorrow, and maybe then the stockroom will know when I can expect the rod. Maybe they will do better than Friday, and I might squeeze by. When I do tell the boss, I want to be able to tell him just when we will be able to start on the job again, and maybe I can plan it so we won't hold up the assembly. Guess I will wait till tomorrow and see what I can figure out.)

And Bob spends the rest of the day in a state of jitters trying to figure a way out of the predicament, or at least a partial solution which he can present to his boss when he finally is forced to tell him. He goes home that night with a terrible grouch, is cross to the children because they are so noisy, gets annoyed with his wife because she seems so cheerful, can hardly eat his supper, sleeps poorly, and hates to go to work the next morning. Such is the human element of communication up the line.

The Boss's Interests

Since the subordinates are interested in giving the boss what he wants to hear, any signs of interest in certain aspects of the work tend to stimulate the flow of information concerning them. If the general foreman expresses interest, or merely curiosity, concerning a new machine or process, or concern over some problem, or interest in some worker, then in every contact with the foreman the boss is likely to hear something about the object of his interest. If he has looked on some new worker with favor, the foreman is likely to find some complimentary things to say about the worker; if the worker is learning the job rapidly, the foreman reports that he is a whizz; if he is slow but friendly with the others, he gets along well; if he is just average, he is coming along well; and so on. If the general foreman did not think so much of a new machine the engineers wanted them to try out, the boss hears critical remarks. If the machine does the work, the operators find it hard to operate, or they cannot seem to get the hang of it, or the controls are wrong and it is tiring. If it does a poor job, then it is just a piece of junk and never will be worth anything. Furthermore, the minute the boss shows a loss of interest in such details, he stops hearing about them. The moment he responds with obvious boredom or lack of interest his subordinate is likely to sense it and to drop the topic and hunt around for something else to take its place.

As a result of this tendency, the boss may receive a considerable amount of minor and unimportant details about a few aspects of the job. Besides, since such information is usually conveyed merely for the purpose of interesting the boss, it is selected and faintly colored to fit that purpose. Thus he gets snatches of slightly distorted information which makes him feel that he is keeping well informed about what is going on. (Many executives may feel that such a statement does them a gross injustice and that *they* really do know all about their organizations. If they are at the intermediate levels in the structure, however, they will probably tell you confidentially that the Big Boss really is not in close touch with the job and its details.)

Since these selective processes are working in all communication from each subordinate to his superior, the taller the supervisory structure, the more filter stations the information must pass through before it reaches the top. Thus, for a small concern with only two or three levels, there is much less selection than for a large concern with five or six levels. Then, too, the larger the concern, the larger the mass of details at the bottom, a mass which is beyond the powers of any one individual to comprehend in its entirety. Between the sheer volume of detail to be selected from and the successive stages of selection at each level, the man at the top ends up with only a vague and highly generalized picture of what is going on.

Keeping the Boss Informed

Everyone in the supervisory structure expects certain kinds of information from his subordinates; and while the precise details vary with the nature of the job and of the individual, there are certain general types of information which all desire. For one thing, almost everyone in the structure wants to be informed concerning those things about which his boss will inquire. Nothing is more disturbing than to be forced to admit ignorance to your boss regarding events in your organization. When he calls you in and asks, "What about the trouble on X job yesterday?" and you have to reply that you did not know of any trouble there, you immediately feel that you have failed, that the boss is annoyed, and that he thinks you are not on top of your job. On the other hand, when you can reply to his question with a detailed statement of the trouble, you feel that you have impressed him with your alertness and ability, have relieved him of any concern about the way you are handling the job, and have generally been a success. There is nothing quite so satisfying as having the right answers for the boss, and having them on the spot without having to say, "I'll look into it and let you know."

Because of this, every subordinate is expected to be on the alert for those things which his boss should know in order to be able to give *his* boss an answer. If the foreman hears that the union is going up to the president on that case which has been kicked around in the department for the last two months, he warns the department chief. If there has been friction with some other department which is likely to be carried up the line, he warns his boss. If the monthly cost report will show some item out of line, the foreman warns his boss. Whatever happens that may get up the line without passing through the successive levels must be anticipated and each level warned.

The line of authority is, then, a channel through which information moves by fits and starts, is sifted over at each level, and is, to a large extent, dependent upon face-to-face communication. This means that the larger the organization and the more levels in the supervisory structure, the slower the flow of information either up or down the line. (I tell my boss something and he sits on it a day or so before he tells his boss, and so on until it may be weeks before something gets through from bottom to top, that is, if it does not get completely lost on the way.) To be sure, there are types of information or certain conditions when items may go bounding up to the top with very little delay. In any case, it is the type of channel which tends to limit the flow of information, slow it down, or censor it; and the longer the channel the greater these effects.

SUMMARY

The authority system is an important element in management's transactions with employees. It is through this system that management communicates its demands to employees and attempts to learn about the needs and performance of employees. The authority system is also a power and status structure. It serves as an important resource in management's efforts to secure employee compliance with its demands. The fact that employees accept the authority of management within certain broad limits makes management's task easier. As a result, however, there is a tendency for some managers to rely solely on the power and status of their positions to secure the support of employees.

9. SYSTEMS OF COMMUNICATION

Communication between people is essential to any group activity. In a sense, we might consider communication as the element which makes any form of organization possible. Without it, there could be no common understanding, no co-ordination of efforts, no direction or control. Communication, in this sense, is more than the written documents or the verbal commands. It is the whole complex system by which information of all sorts is passed back and forth throughout the organization. Part of this system are the formal orders, both written and verbal; part are the records and reports from various sources; part are the idle conversations and gossip; part are the queries and responses from one part of the organization to another.

Just as with the organization, we see the patterns of formal communications which have been established to serve the needs of the organization. In addition, there is the vast system of informal communication which arises spontaneously and is not subject to control. It can be understood and used, but it cannot be abolished. At the same time, it often fills a gap not provided for in the formal system; it takes care of unexpected situations; and without it, the organization could scarcely function.

If we examine the communication activities within an organization, we see that much effort is devoted to vertical communication, both up and down and through several channels. First there is the communication (discussed in Chapter 8) up and down the chain of command. This provides the primary channel for communication downward, for purposes of direction and control, and upward, for information as to what is happening in the organization. Some of this is highly formalized in the form of written orders and reports, but much of it is informal and verbal.

While the chain of command can provide top management with information of many sorts, it is not usually expected to be the source of many types of routine reports. For example, management desires regular information on costs, quality, production, sales, etc. For such information, it usually does not look to the chain of command nor expect each supervisory level to collect the data from its subordinates and pass it on to its superiors. Instead, there will be a system established which collects the data, organizes it into the proper form, and passes it directly to management. Thus, a report on the number of units produced may be compiled from the records and passed on to management without going through the hands of the supervisors. Or a report of number of units failing to pass inspection will be taken from the inspection records. In the same way, the accounting, or cost control, system keeps elaborate records from which they can report to management such items as costs on direct and indirect labor, overtime, material, repairs, etc. Often these can be shown for specific jobs, individual departments, or various time periods.

This kind of information can be considered as control information, since from it management can watch the functioning of the information and can judge its performance. In effect, it is the score board on which the hits, runs, and errors are reported. From it, management knows when and where it should dig into certain problems or situations. And without it, management would not know how the game goes, or who performs well or poorly.

This control information may be originated in many ways and handled through several organization channels. It is largely compiled from data existing at a low level in the organization. If, for example, it is a report on man-hours worked on certain jobs, it will be compiled from work records filled out at the work level by the workers, supervisor, timekeeper or clerk. If it is a report on purchases, it may be compiled from records of purchases in the payroll department.

Generally the cost records and reports are the most important and widely used of this control information. However, the basic data is accumulated, is collected according to systems established by the accounting department, and is passed into its hands for processing into the appropriate reports. Thus labor costs may start with records filled out by the worker and approved by his foreman. The form of the record has been established by the accounting or cost control department, which seeks to standardize records for the whole organization. Once the record leaves the foreman, the future processing is beyond his control, and he may never see the final reports compiled from it.

Here we have a flow of information which bypasses, or "short-circuits," the line. Instead of each link in the chain having the opportunity to see and interpret the information, it moves directly to management. This by-passing is not confined to control reports, however, but may occur both informally and through certain other formal systems. For example, it occurs when a worker with a complaint goes in to see a superintendent instead of his foreman or department chief, or when an engineer takes up some problem with a higher level before consulting the foreman on the job. In all such cases the line supervisors may feel very insecure, since their superiors will learn things about the work which have not first passed through the line and of which the line may know nothing. This information may give rise to criticisms or questions which the lower levels are not prepared to answer. There is nothing better for producing insomnia than to think the boss knows something about the job that you do not know and is going to ask questions that you cannot anticipate.

So we see that the accounting or cost control systems provide a one-way channel for communication, but the information leads tc action on the part of management. This action usually flows back down through the chain of command. Thus, a cost report showing excessive costs in a certain manufacturing department will stimulate the vice-president in charge of manufacturing to ask questions or give orders which move, step by step, down to the guilty department, until action is taken within the department either to justify the costs or to take corrective measures. Therefore it becomes important to each foreman and department head to anticipate such occurrences and to be prepared for the repercussions. Some of the techniques of such defenses will be discussed later.

Another channel of communication leads directly from management to workers, foremen, or other specific groups. Such communications may be through letters, memoranda, bulletin boards, or verbal expression at meetings, or, in some cases, over a loud-speaker system. In these instances, management—often top management—is seeking to communicate information, to give statements of policy, or to express management attitudes. Through such direct communication, management seeks to reach and influence the rank and file. Thus, when business is slow and orders are off, they may want to keep the workers informed of any change in the situation, and of what management is doing to get more business. Or when new policies are put into effect, they may want to be sure that all have been informed. Also, in case of conflict with the union, they may want to present management's side of the case.

The union provides a special channel for communication from workers to management and, to some extent, from management down to the workers. As we will see in Chapter 17, this is an especially important channel for certain types of information and often bypasses the chain of command. It is not, therefore, a channel controlled or directed by management or supervisors.

It is clear that the bulk of the formal communications serves to keep management informed. Also, most of the regular communications in a large organization deal with general information rather than specific details. For example, accounting reports generally present information from many sources, combined and condensed into certain patterns; and a report showing the ratio of sales expense to total sales is a highly condensed summary of many transactions. Thus management is constantly interpreting this generalized information and making decisions which may not be appropriate to many specific situations concealed within the general pattern.

When management wants information on specific situations, it relies on requests either through the chain of command or through the special information-gathering groups, such as cost control or accounting. However, these details are not called for unless attention has been drawn to them for some reason. In general, management relies on its subordinates to spot these situations requiring detailed attention. Thus management often requests special details when subordinates have drawn its attention to a problem situation.

These communications work to serve what management sees as its needs in running the organization. There is little provision for communication to management from the individual. For example, the plant manager may see his department heads daily, and they have opportunities to discuss their ideas and problems. The foreman, however, may only rarely see the manager and has little chance to express his ideas. If he wants to communicate something directly, he can only do it by taking extraordinary steps and by passing his general foreman and department head. The worker is even more remote and finds it even more difficult to communicate directly.

Communication between Organizations

Much of the communication between organizations is through the "channels," that is, up the line of one organization until it reaches the individual who is at the top and then back down the line of the other organization (Fig. 9–1). This is the formal, correct, and "safe" procedure. When followed, each level is informed and can control what is passed on to the next, and there is no danger of "short-circuits." There is also, however, some direct communication between the lower levels of the various organizations which does not go up the line.

Each type of communication between organizations has certain characteristics and certain difficulties. In a large organization, for instance, communication is often so slow that it seriously slows down the job. For example, take the following not too hypothetical case:

Joe, foreman of the Assembly Department, thinks it might help him to plan his work if he could have a little advance information on the progress of the work in the Machine Department on some of his piece parts. He would like to have regular weekly reports from the Machine Department, and he decides to ask his boss about it. His department chief thinks that it is a good idea and says he will take it up the line. The department chief waits a couple of days until he has a chance for a long talk with the division chief, when he presents the idea. The division chief says it sounds good to him, and why not bring it up in the weekly meeting of his department chiefs next Monday to

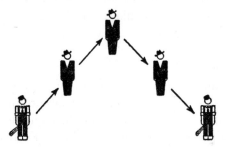

FIGURE 9-1.—Communication through Channels

see if something can be worked out. Next Monday the idea is discussed, and the department chief of the Machine Department says it sounds as if there might be possibilities. But, he says, it will put additional work on his foremen; so he would like to talk it over with them first. The division chief thinks this sounds reasonable, and so the next day the idea is presented to the Machine Department foremen by their department chief. They complain that the idea sounds good but is not so simple as it might be, since they do not ordinarily keep just the proper records to give that particular information. To do it accurately, they say, there will have to be additional records, which will mean additional clerical help—say about ten man-hours a week. The department chief then goes back to his boss and says it cannot be done unless they can arrange for this additional help. The division chief agrees to this, and the next day he tells the Assembly Department chief that the plans are being worked out to get the information. Finally, several weeks after he originated the idea, Joe is told that it will be carried out.

While communication directly across from one foreman to another is much quicker and simpler, it is likely to be limited because of each foreman's concern over his relations with his superior. If Joe talks to Jim about difficulties he is having, and if Jim repeats it to his department chief, and if the department chief mentions it to Joe's boss, who has not yet heard of the difficulty, then the boss questions Joe, and both of them are apt to be disturbed. One of the important principles of communication up the line, as already pointed out, is to be sure that you keep your boss informed about anything which he may hear of from other sources, so that, when these things are mentioned by others, he is able to talk about them intelligently. Since the movement of information out from the work situation through any other channel than the line is likely to place the higher levels in an uncomfortable position, all such flow is limited.

Written Communication

Written communication in the form of letters, memos, reports, records, instructions, and so on, plays an important part in the total process. Practically all communication through the accounting system is in some written form which can be retained for future reference. Also, anything from the top which becomes part of the formal instructions, rules, or policies is almost always in written form. As a rule, such written material has a permanence lacking in the strictly verbal communications. Thus, everyone keeps a file of correspondence, reports, memoranda, and so on, in which he keeps everything he receives and everything he sends out.

Written communication, however, is slow and time-consuming, compared to verbal communication. You want to get some information from someone in another department; so you dictate a memo and then wait for a reply. Your correspondent receives the memo and sooner or later dictates a reply. Or if you are at one of the lower levels without a secretary, you scribble out a note and try to get some typist or secretary in the department to type it for you. Or if you are one of those who came up the hard way, without benefit of formal education, and feel somewhat sensitive about your use of English, you just do not write anything you can avoid and trust to verbal communication. In any event, five minutes' conversation is more effective for the interchange of ideas or information than six weeks of correspondence, and it is only when there is serious antagonism or conflict between two individuals that they depend upon writing for much of their communication.

"The Grapevine"

Within any factory, too, there is also a large amount of what may be called "informal communication" which is not following the channels or any formally designated patterns and which is concerned primarily with the human relations of the work situation and serves the needs of the people rather than the needs of the job. This is what is commonly referred to as the "grapevine," and in most places comes to be an accepted feature of the system. Usually it is nothing more than the passing-on of information from one friend to another without regard to any formal organizational lines. Often there is a clique of secretaries to the top executives who keep each other informed as to what is going on. Sometimes there are luncheon groups of supervisors from various departments which enable them to trade news of changes and developments, and of rumors or gossip about what is going on throughout the company. Individuals have friends in various organizations, from whom they can get off-the-record information and keep in touch with those organizations, and to whom they are careful to give similar information and informal reports.

The successful operation of the grapevine, however, is dependent upon the discretion with which each person uses the information it brings him. If Jim tells Joe at lunch that his department is having trouble on a certain job, and Joe goes around talking about the trouble that Jim is having, it usually ends up with Jim being mad at Joe and feeling that he cannot trust him. And from then on, Jim either avoids Joe or is careful not to tell him anything that should be treated confidentially.

SUMMARY

Such a description of the complications and limitations of communication, especially through the line of authority, might give the impression that communication between levels in the industrial status system is completely ineffectual. Actually, of course, this is not true.

People at the bottom of the structure do produce the goods, and those at the top do control that production and maintain their authority over those below. The point to be made here is that, because of the nature of the man-boss relationship, because it and other status relationships in the system are not clearly recognized and understood, communication sometimes actually interferes with satisfactory work relations and effective production, even though it is thought of as facilitating these things.

10. STATUS AND STATUS HIERARCHIES

THE IDEA of relative status, of who outranks whom, is a basic ingredient in our society. Furthermore, it is not a concept which can be readily eliminated or ignored, even though it seems counter to our basic tenet that "all men are equal." We see it in the home, where parents are the superiors of the children, and the older child is superior to or "ahead of" the younger. And the child looks forward to being an adult, the youngest wants to catch up with the eldest, etc. We see it in every organization; and in every community there are those who, by virtue of formal position, ability, birth, possessions, or luck, are looked on as being in some way above or superior to others. We hear it expressed in a myriad of phrases, such as "leading citizens," "no-accounts," "upper crust," "ordinary folks." All this tells us that even in America we have, not a system of pure equality, but one in which there are great differences in social status.

Now there are two kinds of status relations. One is that of the subordinate to his boss, or the enlisted man to his commanding officer. This status relationship involves not only a general difference in rank—the officer is always thought of as superior to his subordinates —but also the right to give orders. It is always connected with specific positions in organizations in which superiors give orders to subordinates. This relationship comprises the chain of command.

The other type of status relation does not involve the right to command. It merely expresses a concept of relative positions, of who outranks whom. For example, an upper-class executive is felt by the community to be somehow superior to the "po-white" fisherman; he will be deferred to in many ways, while the fisherman will be ignored; yet the executive, merely because of his high status, has no "right" to give the other orders.

Any organization chart is a diagram of positions occupied by individuals, and each person is identified by his position. Thus John Jones, a machinist, becomes a different person in the organization when he becomes John Jones, a foreman. Furthermore, these different positions fit into systems of ranks, or status hierarchies, in which one is seen as superior to another. These systems are most clearly seen in military organizations, where differences in rank are carefully spelled out so everyone can know who outranks whom.

The supervisory structure is, then, a status system in which it is accepted as a matter of course that each level has more status and prestige than the ones below it. In fact, the words used in discussing it show this status factor. We speak of superiors and subordinates, of higher and lower levels, of up and down, of above and below—all of which imply differences in rank in such a structure. The problem of status or prestige does not end with this simple supervisory hierarchy, however, but intrudes itself into all sorts of situations and in innumerable guises. In fact, the matters of relative status, of where each person fits in terms of it, of how each compares with others, present some of the most interesting and, to those involved, some of the most annoying and painful problems of people at work. Certainly, if no one was ever bothered by the status of himself or others, life would be much simpler for everyone.

As we have seen, the chain of command establishes the most clearly defined hierarchy, with the supervisor outranking the supervised. Now differences in rank extend beyond the command, or supervisory relationship, so that all foremen are considered superior to all workers just as all officers outrank all privates. Thus we have rank hierarchies based on ideas of relative position rather than on face-to-face relationships. And these types of status systems, which are very widespread both within industry and in society generally, have great influence on human behavior. In this chapter, we will examine some of the common types of status hierarchies and their significance in the work situation.

Shop-Office Distinctions

In the first place, we find the important status distinction between shop and office or "white-collar" jobs. Despite the talk about the "dignity of labor" and the pleasures of working with your hands, there is an almost universal feeling that the office jobs are in some sense "superior" to the shop jobs and that the person who runs a typewriter or adding machine has a higher status than the person who runs a drill press. This feeling was well expressed by a girl working on a shop job, who said:

I'd really like to work in the office. Isn't it funny the way office people treat factory people? I don't see any difference between them myself, but the office people think they are so much better than the girls who work in the factory.

Lots of them have the same education as the office girls, and we are just as refined as they are. They seem to think that factory girls are loud and rough, but there are just as many girls in the office who drink and smoke and are immoral as the girls in the shop. It just seems that having an office job makes them feel that they're better than we are. I've seen the difference in some people I know. One who came from a farm in Missouri went to school and got an office job. Well, she talks about her office job as much as she can and isn't near as friendly as she used to be. We don't have anything to do with each other any more.

I've noticed it with other girls too. I'll meet them at church and they ask me where I work. I tell them. They ask if I work in factory or office. When I say factory, they say, "Oh," and then ask me if I don't get tired of it, and ask me if it's dirty. Then they take every chance to talk about their office jobs.

My mother feels the same way as these people do. She says that since I've worked in the factory I've gotten more boisterous. I talk in a louder voice, not as refined as I used to be. Well, you don't like to hear those things. You don't like to feel that something's happening to you.

In this interview, an important characteristic of the status system was expressed, that is, the fact that the person who occupies the higher status position tends to identify himself with the status of his position until it becomes a part of him which he carries into all his contacts with those of lesser status. Thus the girl who had obtained an office job began to draw apart from her former factory friends, and the factory girl was looked down upon by the office girls whom she met in church. And so the status of one's position is not something which is shed when he leaves his job; it is carried with him into all kinds of situations.

This interview also shows the general feeling of superiority which the higher-status group has toward the lower. Not only is their work felt to be of a higher order of importance or value, but they are superior beings. The office group tends to look down upon the shop-workers as inferiors in mind, manner, and morals. The shopworkers have grimy hands and poor taste, they say; they are loudmouthed and use coarse language; they are less educated, or at least less intellectual. Although these attitudes of office workers may seem to be extreme expressions of feelings of superiority, similar feelings are expressed by every high-status group toward their "inferiors." Executives have something of the same attitude toward foremen, foremen toward workers, the old-timers toward the newcomers, the skilled workers toward the semiskilled. In fact, we can safely say that everyone in a factory busies himself from time to time with looking down on someone, looking up to someone, or assuring himself that, in spite of what certain others think, he is just as good as they are. As the girl in the interview said, "We are just as good as they are," and in the next breath voiced her doubts.

Status and Wages

The rate of pay or earnings is, of course, another important source of status differences. This is quite in keeping with a business or factory as an economic enterprise in which everything is supposedly evaluated in terms of money. Thus the higher the pay, the higher the status of the job or the individual. The ten-thousand-dollar-a-year man is far superior to the five-thousand-dollar man, or the dollar-forty-an-hour shopworker is superior to the eighty-five-cent man. In the same way, the job that pays a dollar-forty an hour is superior to the eighty-five-cent-an-hour job. ("Superior" in this sense does not always mean more desirable, since individual tastes in jobs vary considerably.) As a result, every work situation in which there is a gradation of wages has a status hierarchy revolving around these wages and one which is readily upset by any changes in the wage structure.

There is also a status system based upon the different kinds of jobs found in any work group. As a rule, the jobs requiring the most skill are at the top and those requiring the least are at the bottom, although other factors may enter in to disturb such a simple arrangement. For example, a job which receives a great deal of attention and recognition from the boss may become the superior job even though other jobs in the group require more skill. Sometimes, too, jobs acquire status because they are always held by long-service people who receive recognition because of their service.

Seniority and Status

Seniority forms the basis for other status differences, with the old-timers feeling that they are somehow superior to the young people and newcomers. In most stable companies there is a feeling toward long-service people something like the attitude toward age which we find in our society generally. The youngsters are thought of as lacking in knowledge and understanding and are expected to give recognition and deference to their elders, while the very old have a place with certain rights and privileges because of their age. The special privileges of old-timers were demonstrated by the nurse in one factory. We quote from an observer's notes:

In a plant which had, before the war, found it necessary to employ only one nurse, the expansion due to the war brought the need for more nurses.

The original nurse had been with the company thirteen years. Then a male nurse was hired for the 4–12 shift. And when a 12–8 shift started, he was transferred to it. Two more nurses were hired, and since none of them wanted to work 4–12 all the time, it was agreed that they should alternate.

The nurse who had seniority took one turn at the afternoon shift and then refused to work it again. The doctor and the personnel manager agreed that she need not take her turn; and the other nurses, although they resented this evident favoritism, seemed to feel that it was done because she had been with the company so long.

Organizational Differences

There are also status differences among organizations, and in any plant there are usually certain organizations which are generally thought of as superior to others. The shop-office distinction accounts for some of this, as the strictly office organizations are usually superior to the shop organizations. As a result, a typist or file clerk with the shop department is usually thought to have a "poorer," that is lower-status, job than the typist or file clerk in an accounting department. Also, organizations such as engineering or sales, where much of the work requires technical skills or special training, are usually of status superior to shop or accounting organizations. In all such cases the feeling of superiority does not remain merely the prerogative of the salesmen or engineers but carries over even to the most routine jobs in the organization. The office boy in the engineering department, for example, is likely to feel superior to the office boy in the accounting organization.

Occupational Hierarchies

We have seen how certain types of jobs carry differences of status. However, this extends often to very elaborate rankings in which there may be recognized differences between many jobs. Thus in many of the skilled trades, we find the hierarchy of apprentice, journeyman, master. In these, a man's position is based upon his progress through a clearly defined system of training and experience.

In addition, we see differences in rank between jobs based on the levels of skill required, such as the semiskilled versus skilled worker. Or the simpler machines are lower than the complicated machines. Or the job that requires long training outranks the one that requires little training. In general, all jobs in a plant can be placed on a scale which expresses the general beliefs as to where each fits in relation to the others.

As we have seen, many of the status systems are based on the characteristics inherent in the work organization. Supervisory rank, levels of skill, wage differences, etc., are largely defined within the organization. However, there are other types of status which are general to the society and are carried over into the work situation. In communities where the particular hierarchies do not already exist, they do not appear in the local industries.

Men versus Women

In our society, women are traditionally defined as the "weaker sex," subordinate to the male. This traditional role of subordination and inferiority is carried over into the work situation. Women's jobs are thought of as simpler, requiring less skill, or in some way unsuitable for men. And attempts to place women in jobs habitually defined as men's work meet with considerable resistance from men. Also, the man who is placed alongside of women, doing the same work, feels that he is degraded.

Negro versus White

Here again we find status differences between the Negro and the white existing in our society. This is expressed in the most extreme form in the deep South, where the Negro is thought of as socially separate and inferior. There he is generally restricted to the lowest status and lowest paid jobs and is rarely permitted to occupy a supervisory position over whites. And while the system is less rigorous in the North, many of the same attitudes and restrictions still exist.

Complicating Factors

These status systems are not nicely co-ordinated, however, so that the older person always gets more money, has the better job, or is higher in the supervisory structure. We see old-timers in some of the poorest jobs at the lowest pay. We see bright young executives who, with only short service, have climbed high in the supervisory ranks. We see office jobs paying less than shop jobs, or skilled workers earning more than their foremen. We see innumerable complicating factors, so that it seems impossible to present a simple picture of the status relationships between individuals within any plant or even in any one department.

We do find, however, that there is a feeling that these various status systems *should* be co-ordinated. This is most strongly expressed in the idea that superiors should earn more than their subordinates. Generally in the supervisory structure wages rise rapidly as you go up in the structure, and it is usually felt to be wrong for a foreman to get less pay than his subordinates. There is also some tendency for wages to increase with age, and a feeling that this should be so, especially when the rate of pay is not rigidly tied to the kind of job. Also, the more highly skilled jobs are often held by the long-service people who have worked themselves up. Interestingly enough, the status difference between office and shop is usually not recognized in pay, especially at the lower levels. Apparently the office jobs are sufficiently attractive, especially to girls, that they are preferred even if the wages are lower, so that in many organizations we find these "better" jobs being paid considerably less than the others.

"Placing" People

A matter of common interest and concern to everyone in the factory is the problem of "place" in the social organization. Everyone wants to know where other people "fit" in terms of the functional relations of the work and, what is to many even more important, in terms of the status systems. The newcomer is always faced by the questions, "Who are you?" and "Where do you fit?" In fact, one of the important aspects of getting acquainted on a new job is the process by which the newcomer finds out just where he belongs. He learns with whom he will work and what their relationship is to him and to each other; he learns who are his superiors in the line of authority, who can give him orders and who cannot, to whom he should defer and whom he can ignore. All this is the real function of much of the introduction and conversation which often takes place when a new worker comes into a group. For example, the foreman brings a new man over to Joe Blow on the dinkus assembly line, and the conversation goes like this:

FOREMAN: "Joe, this is Jim Blank, who is going to work on this assembly. I wish you would show him how to do the job." (Telling Joe that Jim is new and inexperienced on the job.)

JOE: "Howdy, Jim. You ever had any experience with dinkus assembly?" (Trying to place Jim a little more accurately.)

JIM: "No. I been on a drill press in the gadget department for a couple of years." (Letting Joe know that he is not entirely a greenhorn and has had experience on machines, as well as service with the company.)

Joe: "You did? Why I worked over there when I first started eight years ago. Is old Jake, the foreman, still as 'sour-puss' as ever?" (Telling Jim that he need not feel that two years of service amounts to much and that he knows about the gadget department also.)

Jim: "Well, Jake's a pretty decent guy after all, even if he does act sour at times. I kinda hate to leave the department, but work was getting slack on the drill presses." (Showing a little annoyance at Joe's implied criticism of the gadget department, and also telling Joe that he had not left to get out of the place or because they did not want him.)

Joe: "Yeah, I used to like Jake and hated to leave there myself." (Sensing Jim's irritation and trying to express a common attitude.)

Scenes such as this occur constantly; and in every one the individuals are consciously or unconsciously telling each other just where they fit and how they feel about it, and at the same time finding out about each other. When making introductions or when talking about newcomers, there is this same emphasis on "placing" people. Once the individual's place has been established, however, interest in him and gossip about him shifts to other topics.

Symbols of Status

Because of the importance of status, the individual himself is greatly concerned that he be placed properly, at least not in a position inferior to what he actually occupies. The private may be amused to be mistaken for a lieutenant, but the lieutenant who is mistaken for a private is really burned up. Undoubtedly, that is one of the important functions of military insignia. In industry people feel much the same way, with the result that almost every large plant has developed its own insignia, its own set of symbols by means of which everyone can be placed properly in the status system. In general, these symbols are not the simple and obvious types evolved by the Armed Forces but are much more subtle and indirect. The sort of clothes you wear, the desk you sit at, the position of your desk or workbench, the machine you operate, and many other things may indicate status. In fact, these things are often so indirect that the outsider is not aware that such a symbol system exists at all. Many executives, too, deny that there are such systems; but usually these denials are coupled with an assertion that, even if they do exist, they are wrong and should be abolished. Unfortunately for such a point of view, there is no way to stop people from trying to place one another or to keep them from being concerned about their own status.

Because of the importance of the distinction between shop and office, there is a strong tendency to differentiate between them in many ways, each of which becomes a symbol to indicate the position of the individual. While the nature of the work usually leads to a separation between office and shop groups, the separation itself becomes an important symbol of the difference in status. As a result, most office workers are upset and feel that they have lost status if they are moved from an office location to a shop location even though there is no change in the job. In most large plants where there is a separation of the office and shop organizations, there are usually separate washrooms for the office people; and any attempt to have the office people use the shop washrooms, or to bring shop people into the office washrooms, meets with strong resistance from the office people. To be forced to share lockers or washrooms with these "uncouth and inferior" people is a bitter pill to the office people. In such instances, all sorts of complaints are voiced about the crowded washrooms, about how untidy the shop people are, about how they throw paper towels or cigarettes on the floor or leave the washbasins grimy from their dirty hands, or about their bad manners and unrefined language. This whole attitude was well expressed in the behavior of a typist who had been transferred from an office location to the same work in a shop: rather than use the shop washrooms which were adjacent to her new location, she would walk across a building and up a flight of stairs to a washroom used by an office group.

In many companies there is a payroll distinction, too, between shop and office, the shopworkers being paid by the hour and the office by the week. Since both groups are actually paid every week, there is no obvious difference; yet the different payrolls assume the status differences of the two groups. And to move from the hourly to the weekly or salaried payroll is a step up in the world. In some cases this difference may be accentuated by having different time clocks or a different payday for each group, so that there remains no doubt as to where a person fits. Separate time clocks or paydays are, of course, usually thought of as devices to assist the payroll department in preparing the pay checks, or to spread the work load a bit; but it is surprising how often such devices get mixed up in the status system and become status symbols in themselves. And once they become status symbols, any attempt to change them meets with strong resistance from the people.

An almost universal characteristic of all types of status hierarchies is that certain prerogatives accompany high status; and as one ascends in the structure, he acquires certain rights and privileges which are denied to those below him. Some of these rights have to do with the symbols of status themselves. As one is promoted, he acquires the right to display the insignia of his new place. Others are much more tangible rewards, such as increased freedom from restraints, special rights, additional pay, and so on. For example, the following situation was observed in one small plant:

As more machines were added to the departments, the girls who had the best records in attendance and production or showed aptitude for mechanics were made adjusters. This was considered a promotion, although there was no increase in pay. They had a small measure of authority in that they were responsible for seeing that the operators turned out perfect work and for adjusting the machines to make this possible. Since the adjusters operated the machines during the regular lunch period, they ate alone. There were no bells to ring to signify the beginning and end of their lunch period; so they took a few minutes extra. Although everyone knew about this, nothing was said, so the adjusters felt that they were a little above the ordinary workers.

These symbolic distinctions are well shown, too, in the shop-office division, with the office usually having definite privileges denied to the shop. For example, office workers frequently have a longer lunch hour than shop; they may be free to leave their desks to go to the washroom whenever they please, while the shop is limited to fixed rest pauses. Through the device of the weekly pay, the office workers may take time off or come in late without penalty, while the hourly paid shopworkers are usually paid only for the time they are actually on the job.

It is interesting that foremen are generally on the weekly payroll and so are grouped with the office people. It appears, then, that the ordinary factory is split into two groups, one of which is composed of the hourly paid shopworkers, the other of the weekly paid office workers and the entire supervisory staff. The nonsupervisory office workers, furthermore, tend to think of themselves as akin to the supervisory and executive group rather than to the shopworkers.

Within the office group itself, there is usually a high development of status symbols. Almost anything in the work situation seems to have potentialities for becoming such a symbol, whether it be a desk, chair, telephone, location, arrangement of furniture, or whatnot. For example, a telephone directory usually becomes a sort of *Who's Who* which reflects status more than phone calls. Whether you have a telephone on your desk, or share one with the next desk, or have none

at all may be a direct reflection of your status and is usually interpreted that way. In one large organization, desks were an important
symbol: the lowest clerical workers worked at tables, the next level
had single-pedestal desks with one bank of drawers, the supervisors
had larger, double-pedestal desks wth two banks of drawers, and so
on, up to the plant manager, who had a great big desk of fancy woods.
In such a system, to give a man a promotion without the proper desk
would have given rise to elaborate speculations as to whether he really
rated the title or just what was wrong. It would be like promoting
a lieutenant but telling him that he would have to still wear his
lieutenant's bars, that he was not really a captain yet. The emphasis
on these status symbols in one small factory was described by an office
worker, as follows:

> This same vice-president has three assistant vice-presidents in his depart-
> ment besides his department manager. He gets them increasingly large bonuses
> each year. He can't give them all private offices, so he gathers them all into
> one special corner of the office away from their secretaries, gives them each a
> desk *and* a table and more space for visitors. Their desks have leather desk
> pads with green blotters instead of the usual rubber mat, and, on the whole, he
> keeps them happy. But if one of them were to get a bronze wastebasket, they
> would each have to have one.

In the same way, offices for executives become important symbols
of status. In most large organizations there are certain superior offices
which, because of size or location, are preferred. Usually these better
offices are occupied by the top-ranking men in the organization and
reflect their status. Other offices may fit into the status pattern on the
basis of their proximity to the "brass hats." Thus the office next to the
president is superior to the one down the hall. Where offices occupy several floors of a tall building, the higher offices usually have
the most status. The manager or president usually occupies the top
floor, and the lesser officials are found somewhere below. In such
cases, moving to a higher floor is getting up in the world in more ways
than one. The importance of location as a status symbol affects
the people who work for executives, too, so that their secretaries,
stenographers, and even their office boys, feel very strongly the status
significance of working on the top floor or in the office next to the
president's suite. This was described by a girl in the personnel department of one organization, thus:

> Then there is the social problem caused by the physical layout which com-
> prises three floors. The executives' offices are on the tenth. (This is special!)

Several departments, including accounting and payroll, are on the ninth. (This is O.K.) There is the eighth floor, with dictaphones, typing, filing. (This is Bargain Basement!) The girls on the eighth feel that the girls on the ninth and tenth look down on them. The secretaries on the tenth floor are supposed to be pretty high-hat. Girls on the ninth beg to be transferred "upstairs."

Among shopworkers, on the other hand, there is not quite so much emphasis upon status symbols. In general, a person's position in the shop is pretty clearly shown by the work he is doing. The man operating an automatic screw machine is obviously different from the sweeper or material handler, the machinist is superior to his helper, and anyone familiar with shopwork can place people easily in the general status system. This does not mean that shopworkers are not concerned about status, but merely that the work itself provides fairly obvious status insignia.

With office people, however, as pointed out, the symbols of status are often a major concern, and changes in them are sure to create disturbances. To account for such emphasis is difficult, but we may present two possible hypotheses. In the first place, the office and supervisory groups probably contain more people who want to improve their status. And these people naturally want to display evidence of any gains; they want people to know where they belong. At the same time, the nature of office work is such that all jobs look alike from a distance; people sitting at desks writing and shuffling papers may be either important executives or the most unimportant clerks. For that reason, it becomes important that the superior people acquire symbols to distinguish them from the rest. (And everyone gets upset if the new clerk gets the desk by the boss or one by the window.)

These status symbols are a constant source of conflict and anxiety. Each watches his equals lest they acquire symbols which he lacks; each longs to have the choice office or the large desk and schemes to get it; each judges the importance of his job by symbols which go with it. As a result, every change in arrangement, every movement of people or organizations, may upset the status systems and cause trouble.

An Example of Status Problems

A situation involving status problems, changes, and disturbances in one small factory was described by a personnel officer, as follows:

Fred J., aged 45, was one of the most capable all round machinists in a tool industry of about 350 employees. A year and a half ago he was placed in charge of a night shift in the approximate capacity of superintendent. The night shift had just been started, and none of the day foremen who might have been eligible for the job seemed to want it.

The initial night force was small, but it grew rapidly to a total of 125 employees. The top management never made a clear announcement of Fred's position as superintendent. He had the duties of a superintendent except that one department operated at night as an independent unit. No clear directive was given to the effect that Fred was in complete charge, although it was intended that this should be generally understood up to the point of his being responsible for all night activities except in the one independent department.

A great deal of antagonism having the appearance of jealousy immediately developed among the foremen of the day shift. The day superintendent likewise seemed to resent the fact of there being another superintendent in the plant. He would often challenge Fred's right to deal with operational matters that extended through both shifts. In a showdown between these two, Fred answered the challenge by saying, "All right, let's go up to George's (the general manager's) office right now, and I'll apologize to you in his presence." The offer was declined.

Characteristic expressions of the day foreman in referring to Fred would run somewhat along the lines of "that fellow that's on nights. . . . I don't know what you'd call him. . . . He ain't a superintendent, and I wouldn't even call him a foreman."

The management says that, had they clearly designated Fred as a superintendent, they would have had a blowup. They had to place him where they did because the job had to be done and there was no one else in the place who would take it and would have their confidence to the same extent.

Over a period of sixteen months Fred seems to have been winning his battle slowly. But the whole thing has been marked by a good deal of antagonism, frequent ignoring of notes left by Fred for the day supervision, and quite obvious buck-passing, such as the charging of scrap against the night shift when portions of it belonged unmistakably to the day shift.

In one instance Fred had one of his night operators mark each piece he turned out, a piece which was being produced by both shifts. In the inspector's reports on rejects, all the scrap was charged against the night shift. Fred examined the rejected pieces, found that his man's symbol was not on them, and demanded of the inspector, "How come?" The inspector explained: "The day superintendent told me to charge them that way."

11. THE FUNCTIONS AND PROBLEMS AT EACH LEVEL

So far we have been looking at supervisors as a uniform group, all part of a status system and part of a communication system, all links in the line of authority, and all having the same kind of role in an intricate linkage of man-boss relationships. When, however, we examine the kinds of work they actually do at each level of supervision, and the kinds of relationships they have with others, we see that there is a shift in activities and job functions from one supervisory level to another up the line. A superintendent does not have the same function as a foreman. He doesn't have the same job, or the same contact with the work situation, or the same relationship with the workers. His attention, power of authority, and feelings of identification are different from those of a foreman.

Suppose we consider again a representative hierarchy for a concern in which we have a president, superintendents, division chiefs, department chiefs, and foremen, as five levels of supervision. In such a factory the foremen and department chiefs are usually located at desks in small office spaces in the work location in plain sight of the workers. The division chiefs, superintendents, and president are located in private offices on the top floor of the building, away from the noise and dirt of the work location.

THE FOREMAN

Daily Activities

Most of the daily activities of the first-line supervisor are related directly to the work and the workers. He is on the floor, actually seeing that work gets done, a good part of the day. Usually he spends a few minutes at his desk looking over the work schedules or orders for the day and the records of deliveries for the day before. Maybe he consults with other foremen, or with his department chief, about plans for the day. He then goes out on the floor for the rest of the day. Or he may start the day by walking around the shop, seeing that everyone is getting started on his work, perhaps answering questions, giving instructions, and then go back to spend some time at his desk. Throughout the day he usually spends most of his time on his feet, moving about the floor, keeping in contact with the workers and the work, listening to problems, making decisions, and directing the workers. He does not wait for his group to come to him with problems, but tries to keep in touch with them and available at all times. He also spends some time with other foremen in the department and may join them at rest periods for a smoke and a cup of coffee or have lunch with them. He may spend a little time with his department chief whenever he is available, and may show him various jobs or discuss problems with him.

From this we see that the foreman, who is usually considered the first level of management, is the one who has the most direct and detailed knowledge of the job and the workers. He is the one who has the most frequent contact with the workers. He plans and directs their work; he checks and judges their work; he maintains discipline and enforces the rules. To the workers he is the one who gives orders, who rewards and punishes. And it is through him that all the pressures downward through the structure, all the demands and orders moving down the line, are transmitted directly to the work group.

Orientation and Perspective

Out of his intimate relationship with the work the foreman develops an orientation toward it which is different from that of the rest of the hierarchy. In the first place, his attention is focused on the everyday details; he sees all the immediate difficulties and the complexities of getting the work out; and he usually knows a lot about the workers and their attitudes. As a result, he tends to be impatient with higher levels or with staff people who try to generalize on the basis of partial knowledge and make decisions which affect his job. He frequently feels that his superiors impose tasks on him and on his group without trying to understand the difficulties of his job. He feels that it is easy for them to say "do this" or "give us this information," but that he is the one who has to carry out the orders and still keep the job going.

Since he controls his job primarily through direct knowledge of the details, he feels little need for records or reports. He tries to know what is going on when it happens rather than learn about it later through reports. In many cases he is expected to collect data and prepare reports which his superiors then use to put pressure on him. He is impatient, therefore, of elaborate reports or paper controls, since they tend to keep him at his desk away from contacts with the job and since they mean extra work and may mean more pressure from above. Also, he knows the inadequacies of such records and is critical of decisions based upon them. Thus he always prefers the job on which records and reports are kept to a minimum and can be taken care of by some clerk so that he does not have to do paper work himself.

Attitudes and Identification

When we talk to foremen about their jobs, their superiors, and their subordinates, we see a variety of attitudes. In some cases they have strong feelings of sympathy with the work group, a sort of identification with the workers in which the foreman acts as though he were one of them and is constantly defending them both from his superiors and from outside organizations. In such cases, there is usually a very friendly and informal relationship between the foreman and his group. They may joke together, and the workers feel free to discuss their personal and work problems and to voice their complaints. Generally, in this situation there seems to be very little barrier between them because of difference in rank, and the foreman maintains little social distance or distinction between himself and the group. Many of these situations are characterized by a much greater distinction between the foreman and his department chief, and sometimes there is a very strong barrier between these two levels. In such cases there is little interaction between the two, and the foreman may actually avoid contacts and force the department chief to come to him. Also, the foreman will try to keep the department chief away from his group, try to be present when he is around the work situation, try to cover up mistakes, protect individual workers from his criticism, and otherwise try to build strong barriers between them. He will resist demands for changes from above, always finding reasons for not accepting them or for their failure if they are forced upon him. Such situations are diagrammed in Figure 11–1.

The opposite of this situation is the foreman who has a strong identification with management and his superiors and holds his subordinates at a distance. He tends to be critical of the workers, feels that they are not dependable or are not trying to do a good job, and

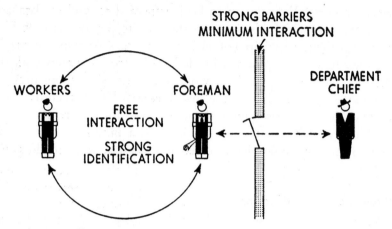

FIGURE 11–1.—Foreman Identified with Workers

is not interested in them as individuals. They feel that he is aloof and disinterested, and they hesitate to talk freely to him or to discuss problems with him. When together at department parties, neither he nor the workers feel comfortable, and they tend to stay apart. He is likely to seek out contacts with his superiors, both on the job or outside. He is often concerned about his relationship with his department chief and always tries to make a good impression. Thus there is a situation of close relationship between foreman and department chief and considerable distance between foreman and worker (Fig. 11–2).

In this type of situation the workers feel forced to be on their guard against their foreman and think of him as someone who is

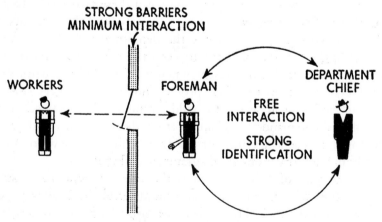

FIGURE 11–2.—Foreman Identified with Department Chief

against them rather than for them. They develop various defenses; they watch their behavior whenever he is in sight; they may restrict output without his knowledge; and they may complain about him to the union. Sometimes the tension makes contacts so uncomfortable that even he is aware of it and may withdraw to some extent from the work situation. In such extreme cases, he spends most of his time at his desk, talking to his superiors, or entirely out of the department.

Sometimes, on the other hand, we find a situation in which there is very strong identification and integration between all three—the workers, the foreman, and the department chief. In such cases we see very easy interaction between workers and department chief, and the department chief is usually in close touch with the details of the job and with the individuals. The foreman feels very comfortable under these conditions, does not worry about the presence of the department chief, and does not need to cover up mistakes or try to protect the group, since the boss can be trusted. In many instances of this kind, the whole department stands as a unit against outside pressures or against demands from above. Probably these are the most comfortable and satisfactory work situations for the foreman and for the workers.

Sometimes we see a foreman who is isolated from both his department chief and the work group. In these cases, there is considerable avoidance on the part of all concerned. If the job will run with a minimum of direct supervision and interaction with the workers, the foreman may stay out of the group most of the time and stay away from his department chief, too. As long as the work goes all right, the department chief also avoids the foreman and the group, and all contacts are very formal and uncomfortable. If the job does not go well, the foreman is in a difficult spot, since his boss will be quite critical of him and often make arbitrary demands. At the same time, the group is defensive and does not respond to the foreman's demands. He tries to pass the buck to them for any failures and is generally critical of them; just as his boss is critical of him. Under these conditions, both the foreman and the workers are uncomfortable; and whenever there is pressure on the foreman from above, he feels extremely isolated and defenseless and takes it out on his subordinates. In other words, such situations may be fairly stable so long as the work is running well; but under pressure, a great deal of friction between foreman and workers develops.

The Forgotten Man

Because of his position at the bottom of the management hierarchy, the foreman often feels that he is the forgotten man. He rarely participates in the making of decisions or the determination of policy, and often he is not well informed as to the why and wherefore of such decisions. All too frequently he knows only that management has decided to do thus and so and, in many cases, expects him to put the decision into action. While theoretically his ideas or sentiments are communicated up the line and are taken into account when management makes decisions, he knows that, actually, they only get through to the top in a very hit-or-miss manner and rarely influence decisions or policy. Certainly he almost never has the satisfaction of communicating them directly and seeing that they are actually considered. Of course, management occasionally makes the gesture of consulting the foremen, but usually all it amounts to is to call them together after a decision has already been made and to go through the motions of talking it over with no real idea of changing if the foremen object. Such meetings are often thought of as an attempt to "sell" the foremen on management's decisions rather than as an honest attempt to let them join in making the decisions.

All this does not mean that foremen necessarily think that they are qualified to make the decisions which top management must make. While top management often talks of them as being part of management and expects them to identify themselves with the interests of the company and of top management, they do not feel that they really "belong." They feel that they are expected to take whatever is handed down to them from above, no matter how arbitrary it may seem to them or how difficult it may make their jobs.

Management's Ideal

Nevertheless, top management is frequently concerned about the attitudes of the foremen. Management often feels that the foremen are incompetent and need more training, that they do not identify themselves with management, do not understand and accept the aims of management, and do not carry out decisions. Top management's ideal of a foreman is one who thinks much as they do, who understands their problems sufficiently to accept their decisions without question, and is a "good soldier"—that is, one who accepts orders and carries them out without question or reservation. Yet, often it is the actions and pressures originating at the top which create doubt and uncertainty on the part of the foreman, prevent him from becoming identified completely with management, and make him feel insecure.

Foreman and Morale

As we have seen, a foreman is in constant contact with the workers and has the responsibility of putting into action many of management's policies and decisions. Thus he is, to a considerable extent, the one who interprets management to the workers; he is, to a large degree, the only representative of management with whom the workers have much contact; he is the one who imposes management's controls upon them. For this reason he has an important influence upon their attitudes toward the job, the management, and the company generally. He is the one who can most directly affect their morale and loyalty. While his importance to employee morale has long been recognized, studies have shown that in many respects he is the most important factor in the work situation. For example, in a preliminary report on extensive research conducted by the Committee on Human Relations in Industry of the University of Chicago, the author reported as follows:

Some of the things which stand out quite clearly are the factors which are especially significant in determining the attitudes of people toward their jobs. In general, it appears that a few factors in the work situation are generally responsible for active enthusiasm or dislike, while other factors play a much more passive role.

It is important to note that these active elements are those things involving the individual's relations with others on the job. The things that really "burn 'em up" are the things the boss says or does, or the things that go on in the gang, or the way other employees act toward them. And they respond with enthusiasm to the congenial group and friendly boss. This was well shown by the statement of an industrial truck driver:

"I've had a lot of different jobs; I've worked in lots of factories, but I've never seemed to feel quite right about them somehow. I mean that I never cared much about the job; it was just something I had to do. But this is different. I've never been on a job before where the men help one another the way they do out there. Why, if one man is done with his work, he doesn't sit down and wait for something to turn up like they do on most jobs. He goes and helps somebody else. And the men will ask someone to help them, and I never seen one of them get turned down. Everybody always seems to want to help everybody else. And sometimes when I don't have anything to do for a minute or two I go over and watch one of the machines and the fellow who runs it, he'll explain it to me and tell me how it works. That's something I never seen them do any place else."

It is quite clear, furthermore, that of all the relationships within the work situation, the relation with the foreman or immediate supervisor is the most critical of them all. This is nothing new and is often expressed in the statement that "the foreman is the front-line personnel man." It is interesting, however, to see the strong emotional significance of this relationship as it is expressed in interviews. For example, a former machine setter with ten years' service left his job to take one for less pay and said:

"On that job there wasn't a day went by without the foreman would have some crack to make just to get your goat or just to be mean to you. He's supposed to be the foreman, but as far as I can figure he didn't do nothing but go around making everybody sore. If you'd ask him some question about the work, something about one of the machines or something like that you wanted to know, he'd look real nasty and he'd say, 'You're the operator. What d'ja want me to do about it?' And then he'd walk off; he'd never give you any help. 'You're the operator,' he'd say. 'What d'ja want me to do about it?' And that's all he would ever do for you.

"But if you'd argue with him about something or make some suggestion or something, he'd tell you to just mind your own business and do your own job. 'I do the thinking around here,' he'd say. 'You just tend to your work and I'll do the thinking for all of us.' *He* does the thinking! Huh! Yeah, the heck he does. All I can see that he ever does is to go around pickin' on everybody.

"And when you go over to ask him a question, any kind of question—Well, maybe it does sound a little dumb or something, but you're sincere when you ask it and it's something you want to know—but he'll just make fun of you for asking it and say the question again, mocking you, and not give you any answer to it. He could never give you a polite answer, always got to be something sarcastic, so that you get so you don't want to have to talk to him about anything if you can help it. And you get so when you see him coming you get all nervous and wonder what's coming now. What kind of a nasty crack he's going to make this time.

"When you get someone like that around you all the time it makes you get so you don't want to go to work at all. Some jobs you get up in the morning, and you feel like going to work; you feel good about it and you're glad you got a job and that you're going to it. But this job, I got so I'd lie in bed in the morning and think, 'If I just didn't have to go to work, if there was something the matter with me so I wouldn't have to go, if I could only think of some reason for staying home today!' I'd just wonder to myself, 'Now, what's he going to think of today? What's he going to find that he can pick on?' And then I'd start worrying. And by the time I'd get to my breakfast I didn't even want to eat. And I'd just sit there trying to figure out some way I could get out of having to go down there; but there never was. You gotta work; if you have a job you gotta go to it."

When we seek to determine the effects of such things as employee benefits, vacations, good working conditions and all the morale building devices, we immediately find ourselves in a region of vagueness and contradictions. While the interviews were with all kinds of people from a wide variety of companies, there was little spontaneous talk about such factors in work situations. Even with workers from companies which were well known for their advanced personnel systems, it was rare to have enthusiastic talk about these matters. What people seemed most concerned about, what they really wanted to talk about, were the matters of their daily relationships with their boss and fellow-workers. Furthermore, where there was some show of enthusiasm for company policies or benefits, it was always coupled with statements about it being a friendly place to work or having a swell boss. In fact, if the supervisors were fine and fellow-workers friendly, almost anything might be referred to as showing what a fine place it was. For example, in some cases, after praising the boss, the individual would make some such statement as, "The company is really interested in the workers. Why, you know they give us a ten minute rest period every morning and afternoon, and recently they put in a vending machine so we could buy a coke during rest period."

Closely related to this problem of the attitude of workers towards their jobs is the problem of turnover. In considering this we found it useful to think of the work group as being subject to a number of forces, some of which tend to hold it together and others of which tend to force it apart. Furthermore, it is clear some of the forces operating arise from the outside society and are not readily controllable by management. On the other hand, many of the forces arise within the work situation itself and can be influenced or controlled by the management of the individual concern.

When we examine present conditions we see that the war has set in motion a variety of disrupting forces which increase the rate of turnover. Obviously, unless such disruptive forces are compensated for by the cohesive forces within the work situation, there is bound to be a sharp increase in turnover. Unfortunately, the effects of wartime expansion and conversion have also increased the disruptive forces within the work situations, with the result that turnover has increased excessively.

Discussion with people concerning why they do or do not change jobs has shown several things. Just as their attitudes towards their job is strongly influenced by their relations with their superiors and with fellow-workers, also their decisions as to whether to stay or leave often hinge on these relations. As in the interview quoted, it is apparent that unsatisfactory relations with the boss constitute a powerful disruptive force, while the foreman who is liked is an equally powerful stabilizing force. To quote a worker who had made several changes in the last few years:

"You know why people are changing jobs? It's simply because jobs are plentiful and people don't have to take a pushing around by these dumb grafters who call themselves supervisors. Sure, when times are tough a man has to work at his job whether he likes it or not; he has to take it. But why should he today. You know, it's a funny thing, but when you work around here and there and see how people are treated, you get so you enjoy telling a foreman to go to— it's fun.

"My present boss I would do anything for simply because he is the only man who has ever shown any confidence in me. It's the one company I worked for where a man in supervision shows some consideration for the people under him. I think the entire management shows that attitude. These companies are always talking about backing up the foreman, yet the only backing that really means anything to a foreman is the backing of the men under him. What good does it do the company to be constantly backing up the foreman if that foreman has a big turnover or can't get the cooperation of his men? My boss never has to ask the company to back him up, because he has the backing of the men. I would do anything for him and so would the other guys."[1]

THE DEPARTMENT CHIEF

The activities, attitudes, relationships, and functions of a department chief are usually quite different from those of a foreman. As we have seen, he is not so close to the actual work even though he sits nearby. He usually spends more time at his desk, reading reports, going over and signing various papers, preparing memoranda to his boss. He spends much more time out of the work location, in the division chief's office, in conference with other department heads, or with engineers, inspectors, or other staff people. He deals with many of the relationships with other departments, and he may be active in co-ordinating the work of his department with that of others.

Since he is not directly in control of the job, he relies to a considerable extent upon reports from his foreman for his knowledge of what is going on. He usually expects his foremen to keep him informed daily as to the progress of the work and as to any significant occurrences, especially anything about which he may be questioned by his division chief. Thus he is constantly gathering information from his foremen which he uses in his contacts with superiors or with others. The foremen may report to him any failures of delivery or faulty materials from other departments, and he can then use this information either in contacting the other departments or for communication to his boss. He pays more attention to formal reports, too, such as cost, quality, or earnings, than does the foreman. On the whole, he relies on his foremen's verbal reports to keep him in touch with the job, and thereby expects to have a general idea of how the department is getting along before the formal control reports appear.

Perspective and Participation

Department chiefs generally identify themselves with management much more than foremen do. They seem to be much more "manage-

---

[1] Burleigh B. Gardner, "A Program of Research in Human Problems in Industry," *American Management Association, Personnel Series Number 80* (1944), pp. 35–38.

ment minded"; they show more interest in costs and efficiency; and they accept the rules more completely. This may be the result of their separation from the work itself, plus their increased participation in planning, co-ordinating, and contacts up the line. In general, the broadening of participation, so that the individual has to become familiar with problems of co-ordination beyond those of his immediate organization, seems to shift his orientation so that he thinks more like management and sees the more general problems. Furthermore, the department chief is likely to participate in discussions with both division chiefs and superintendents. He may be called in to discuss proposed policies, changes in practices, technological developments, and so on. He has more opportunity than the foreman does to voice his opinions, to see the processes of decision-making, and possibly to influence them; and he generally has more of a feeling of being a part of management.

Relations with Workers

To the workers the department chief is the highest level of authority readily available with whom they may have fairly frequent contact and to whom the foreman must turn for decisions. He is the highest level of "visible" authority, and to many he is the "boss." While they recognize that he is subordinated to the higher levels, he is still the one who transmits the demands from above the department. He has the final say on most matters concerning them and may overrule the foreman. Because of his location in the shop, the barriers to approaching and contacting him are much less than with higher levels of supervision. He is someone they can get to. But, at the same time, actual interaction with him is considerably less frequent than with the foreman. He is not the one who constantly watches over their work; he is not ever present, "breathing down their necks" all day long as the foreman is. As a result, if he is friendly and has an approachable manner, they may often feel that he is more understanding and sympathetic than their foreman and that he can be trusted to be fair with them even if their foreman cannot. On the other hand, if he is forbidding and critical, he may be the focus of their complaints and may be thought of as the source of everything that goes wrong on the job. If he is friendly, they feel that they can speak to him if their foreman is too disagreeable and that he will fix things up. If he is unfriendly, there is no escape from an unpleasant foreman; there is no one in authority to whom they can turn for help.

On his part, the department chief usually has quite a different attitude toward the workers than that of the foreman. The foreman has to deal directly with the workers in his efforts to get the job done; he must deal with them each individually; he sees their faults and errors; and, when things are going badly, he is apt to be irritated and critical of them. The department chief, however, usually thinks of the foremen as being the ones responsible for the work and even for the behavior of the workers. When things go poorly, he blames the foremen rather than the individual workers. Even when the workers break the rules, he is likely to blame the foremen for not maintaining discipline. Thus each level wields authority over the one below; and, under this direct pressure, friction is likely to be generated. At the same time, the department chief can remain aloof and friendly to the workers without becoming involved in frictions between them and the foreman.

THE DIVISION CHIEF

At the division chief level, we move into the area of invisible authority. The division chief sits in an office away from the shop. He has little firsthand contact with the job and may appear among the workers only infrequently. He really is in the realm of the "big shots" and the "brass hats." And not only is he far from the work, but the gap between him and the department chief, or what has been called "social distance,"[2] is likely to be greater than between any other two levels. The marked cleavage between these two levels was noted by Roethlisberger and Dickson in the Western Electric study.[3] As they point out, however, this does not mean that there is more conflict and hostility between these two levels. It does mean that there is a greater difference in sentiments and interests with the change from visible to invisible authority.

---

[2] a) "The concept of 'distance' as applied to human, as distinguished from spatial, relations, has come into use among sociologists, in an attempt to reduce to something like measurable terms the grades and degree of understanding and intimacy which characterize personal and social relations generally" (Robert E. Park, "The Concept of Social Distance," *Journal of Applied Sociology*, VIII [1924], p. 339).

b) "If, as we shall assume, grades of understanding and intimacy between persons or groups, or between a person and a group, are dependent upon the degree to which they share the same sentiments and interests, 'social distance' measures differences in sentiment and interest which separate individuals or groups from one another or an individual from a group" (F. J. Roethlisberger and W. J. Dickson, *Management and the Worker* [Cambridge, Mass.: Harvard University Press, 1939], p. 359 n.).

[3] *Ibid.*, pp. 359–60.

At the division chief level we really come to the management group. Division chiefs are away from direct contact with the work level; they cannot just step out into the shop to see how things are getting along, the way a department chief can; and they are not generally concerned with the details of one small part of the job or with the work of one group. They sit at their desks and gather their information through reports, memos, and conferences with their department chiefs. They concern themselves with problems of coordination and planning for their divisions and with liaison with other divisions. They rely to a great extent upon cost and performance reports and usually have charts showing various measures of performance so that they can keep a close watch on any changes. They are likely to be very cost-minded and to be constantly after their departments to keep costs down or to keep within the budget.

While the division chief level is getting into management, this is not really top management. The primary concern of a division chief is with running the job, keeping the pressure on the shop departments, and keeping a close watch on the controls. He does not spend his time with future planning, with policy-making, or with major decisions. We might say that the focus of his attention is downward upon the job; and he often resents too much change or interference coming from above, since these things always disturb the equilibrium which he is attempting to maintain in the job.

THE SUPERINTENDENT

At the superintendent level, we really reach top management. Supervisors at this level usually constitute the "staff" of the president. They sit in on decisions of policy; they participate in the planning; they must concern themselves with the future. In dealing with the job they are even less concerned with details, and even more concerned with the over-all situation, than the division chief is. They do not feel that they must keep up with a mass of everyday details, but rely on their subordinates for that. And when, as often, they have to make decisions about specific situations, they expect their subordinates to bring them such details as are pertinent and must be considered.

Diverging Points of View

In many companies a sharp cleavage can be found at about this level. The striking thing about such a cleavage is the sharp divergence in point of view and attitudes between the executive, whose attention seems to be directed downward and who is always thinking in terms of his organization and is engrossed in the problems of its operation, and the higher-level executive, who thinks more in terms of the company as a whole and all its extended activities and relationships. In some cases this cleavage appears just above the superintendent level, between president and superintendent; often it is particularly striking between the president and the superintendent who is in charge of the manufacturing organization. In other cases the greatest divergence is found just below the superintendent, between superintendent and division chief; this is particularly true in large companies with an extended supervisory hierarchy. Because this cleavage seems to appear with equal frequency at either level, either just above or just below the superintendent, it is difficult to talk about superintendents as a uniform or general group.

Identification with Work Group

On the one hand, we find the superintendent who is looking downward, identifying himself with the work group, sympathetic with his division chief, and impatient with the Big Boss, who seems to be more concerned with his luncheons and clubs than with running the business. These attitudes seem to be especially marked when there is a great difference in background or industrial experience between a superintendent and the man at the top. A manufacturing superintendent, for example, is often an old-timer who has risen gradually through the ranks of the manufacturing organization and has spent his whole life in that setting. Higher executives, on the other hand, have frequently risen through other channels, such as engineering, sales, or accounting organizations, or may have been brought in from other positions or locations. Such divergence in background seems to sharpen the differences which arise out of their positions and functions in the structure, and frequently results in mutual feelings of irritation and exasperation. The superior thinks that his subordinate is hardheaded and "sot in his ways" and that it is impossible to get him to accept new ideas or see changing conditions and adapt himself to them. He has an excessive tendency to cling to the old ways and to stay in the same old grooves, thinks the top executive. At the same time, the superintendent feels that his superior is trying to change things just for the sake of change, that he does not see the difficulties or the effects of these changes upon the work. His superior seems to be always critical, when the superintendent wants merely to be left alone to run the job and see that the work gets done. As a result, we often find this type of superintendent on the defensive, trying to protect his organization from the demands of the Big Boss, reducing interaction to a minimum, and generally trying to erect a protective wall around himself and his group, much as division chiefs and department chiefs do. And how this annoys the Big Boss! As one top executive said:

> For all the influence I have, you would never know that the plant is part of the company. Why, if I go into the plant for anything, I hardly get in the door before the superintendent is standing by my side, and he stays with me until I leave. And I know that I only get to see the things that he wants me to see. And trying to introduce any changes seems a hopeless task; it's like pushing against a stone wall. Even when he seems to agree to something, it goes only slowly and halfheartedly, and there are a dozen things wrong with it.
>
> And yet the plant runs well in terms of getting production and making money. There isn't any major thing to complain about. But we feel that it isn't going ahead. Instead of constantly improving the plant, the processes, or their organization, they are just marking time. While it seems to be going along all right now, we are afraid of what it will be in a few years, and we want to see it improving so it can meet whatever comes.
>
> We have just been sitting tight and trying to make a few changes gradually, and I think we are making some progress, but it is awfully slow. I suppose the only way to do anything with it very rapidly is to go in and tear it limb from limb and put it back together the way we want it. But the situation isn't bad enough to justify that, and that would mean the end of the superintendent; he would just have to quit along with a few others. We would much rather handle it without taking such drastic steps.

Orientation

On the other hand, there are many superintendents who are oriented like the president, who look outward to problems of public relations, governmental regulations, and all the various external things which affect the functioning of a business. They are often active in outside affairs, attend meetings and luncheons, belong to business organizations, take part in community affairs, and in various ways extend themselves beyond the walls of the plant. In such cases, there is likely to be the same antagonism, the same social distance, the same mutual feelings of annoyance between superintendent and division chief as that described between president and superintendent above. And, as at the higher level, these feelings are intensified when there is a marked difference in their backgrounds—when the division chief is the one who came up the hard way and the superintendent the one who came in through staff organizations or from outside.

THE BIG BOSS

Outside Activities

Top management, and especially the very top (the president or in larger companies the works manager or the plant manager), faces certain problems which are of little concern to those lower in the structure. In the first place, the top executive is concerned with the position of the company in the entire industrial and economic system and with co-ordinating its activities so that it will meet competition, survive social, economic, and political changes, and generally maintain itself as a going concern. This means that he must keep informed on a whole range of matters in the outside world, must be evaluating them in terms of their effect upon his concern, and laying plans or making changes in the internal activities to meet these conditions. As a result, he is constantly seeking information through various sources. He reads newsletters, market reports, and technical journals, and follows the financial pages carefully. But, often, even more important to him is a knowledge of what other businessmen are doing and how they are interpreting the course of events. So he belongs to businessmen's clubs and attends dinners and meetings where he will be able to exchange ideas and information with others on his own level. These contacts often make it possible for him to act in harmony with other top executives as a group, either through conscious effort or, more often, unconsciously, merely by following the example of a few leaders. These groups in which he moves are, furthermore, an important part of his social environment; they become the groups he feels identified with; they are his kind; and inevitably he tries to maintain his position among them. This means that he often acts and talks in ways which he thinks will be acceptable to the group, or tries to gain their respect for his judgment and abilities, or tries to increase the standing of his company in terms of size or prestige in its field.

These activities of the top executive are very important to the concern as a whole, since they provide the basis for many new decisions which affect the future adaptation of the organization to the total society, and which may even determine its future existence. Similar contacts or information at levels below the president and sometimes his immediate staff have much less significance, since the fundamental decisions flow from the top down. Thus, while it may be of vital importance for those at the top to be well informed on national and world affairs and well integrated into groups at their own level, it is not especially important for those at lower levels; and, as a rule, their attention is directed inward toward the details of the company rather than outward to the external world.

Maintaining Equilibrium

Another major concern of the top executive is that of maintaining an effective equilibrium and balance within the company. One of his aims is to develop an organization which functions smoothly with little friction, which has an adequate equilibrium so that the company can sell its products at a profit, and which is sufficiently stable to function with a minimum of attention from him. When he has such a situation, he can devote his energies to other things, and especially to relations with the outside world without worrying over the details within the walls. Probably almost every president longs to have just such an organization, and probably few of them attain it.

The Big Boss must continually concern himself, too, with keeping what he considers a proper balance of all the parts of the structure. Since every organization within the company is concerned primarily with its own function, each constantly acts as a pressure group demanding that its point of view and ideas be given more consideration, that things which hamper its activities be changed, that other organizations give way to it, and that it be expanded or improved so that it can do a better job. Thus the accounting organization will be in love with its own theories and systems; it will want to have better methods, more records, closer controls, and will frequently feel that all other activities should be subordinated to its routines. To other organizations it may appear that the accountants think the business is being run for their own exclusive benefit. In the same way, however, the engineers seek to improve and expand their activities, seek more authority and control, and try to subordinate the shop to their ideas. The personnel organization struggles to build up its functions too, and so do all the other organizations and every segment of them. The man on top has to be judging the total situation constantly. He must decide just where to limit the functions; he must decide on size and cost for each, balance the demands for control and authority, and not let one take over the place to the detriment of the company as a whole.

As part of the pressures from the different segments, there are also frequent frictions and conflicts between them, many of which are carried up to the top executive for settlement. Thus, he must not only try to decide on and maintain the proper balance among the segments, but he must also preserve harmony and co-operation among them. All too often these conflicts between superintendents are communicated to lower levels and thus increase the friction and instability of the organization as a whole. For this reason it is extremely important that the president pull his top executives together into a smooth-working, co-operative group.

Keeping in Touch with the Company

Although much of the top executive's attention is focused outward, it is still important for him to keep well informed about how things are going in the concern. For one thing, it is important for his own sense of security, since, if he feels any doubt about the way the organization is functioning, he develops anxieties which harm his relations with his subordinates. Also, if he is to be able to make proper decisions, to settle conflicts, and generally to function properly, it is necessary for him to have adequate information. For this he relies on both formal reports, such as costs reports, and on verbal communication from his staff. All reports, especially the highly formalized cost reports and production records, present quite a problem in interpretation, since they are extremely oversimplified condensations of very complex data; and to know what they mean requires a detailed knowledge of the work and all conditions which might affect it. In fact, a great deal of the verbal communication of subordinates usually has to do with the interpretation of these formal, written communications. In their efforts to be informed, therefore, the top executives are constantly asking their subordinates for reports covering many types of activities.

Top management in general is always interested in raising the organization to new levels of performance. The top executive likes to see new records set for output, quality, cost reduction, and so on, and is frequently trying to work out new methods for producing such improvements. He is interested in learning of new incentive systems, or new technical developments, or better control methods which can be used to produce these results. Also he is constantly using the various reports as a basis for stimulating performance. Thus, nearly every plant has certain reports which lower levels think of as "batting averages" or "score cards," since top management uses these figures as a method of comparison between organizations. By such comparisons, the president often attempts to develop competition between units and to keep them all trying to improve.

Besides trying to improve performance by putting pressure on the organizations, management also seeks improvement through changes in organization, personnel, control methods, and so on. Many internal changes, too, grow out of the need to adapt the organization to changes in the outside world. In many cases management faces the problem both of deciding what changes will make a more effective organization and of handling the change in such a way that it will not cause serious disturbance in the organization. For example, a certain change in organization which appeared to be an improvement might so disturb the supervisors as to ruin the morale and efficiency of the entire group. For that reason, top management must try to anticipate the results of even the simplest changes and must take whatever actions may be necessary in order to make the changes successful.

Top Management and the Workers

It is clear that, as you move upward in the structure, the frequency of interaction with the workers decreases. In fact, it drops off sharply above the department chief level simply because there is little opportunity for those located away from the shop to have casual contact with the workers. Of course, many executives make a point of chatting with some of the workers whenever they visit the shops, but actually such contacts are likely to be infrequent and limited to only a small portion of the workers. The president who walks through the shop every day and speaks to a few of the old-timers may feel that he is "keeping in touch." Actually, such contacts are usually somewhat artificial and rarely are extended to new workers. Certainly in any plant with several hundred workers, it becomes impossible for the president to spend the time necessary to really maintain contact with all the workers. This means that his knowledge of the attitude of the workers is based principally upon what other people say it is.

In spite of the little interaction, or perhaps because of it, the workers often look to top management as being fair-minded and sympathetic. In part, this seems to arise out of the fact that a worker often receives a sympathetic hearing and gets action when he does approach the man at the top with a request or complaint. If Joe, with twenty years of service, works up enough courage to go to the Big Boss and complain that he thinks it is not fair to give all the better jobs to new men without giving him a chance, the Big Boss is likely to think only of Joe and the way Joe feels without knowing the factors in the situation which made the foreman decide not to put Joe on the job he wants. Even if he realizes that there may be more than meets the eye, he can be friendly and soothing and say that he will talk to Joe's foreman about it. And Joe goes away feeling that the Big Boss is certainly a fine man. Furthermore, when the executive asks about the case, the foreman may either give Joe the chance he wants, in which case the Big Boss gets the credit; or the foreman may show why it cannot be done, in which case the foreman gets the blame from Joe. This sort of thing does not happen often, of course; individual workers only rarely step out of bounds to take their troubles to the president, or to the plant manager, or even to the superintendent or division chief. If many such things were placed in the Big Boss's lap, he would probably be forced into the position of backing up his foremen and would no longer be thought of as such a fine man.

In order to retain some contact with the worker, and especially to provide a channel for complaints, many top executives maintain what is referred to as an "open-door policy." This merely means that they announce that they will talk to anyone in the organization at any time, that any worker can come up and see them about anything without asking permission to do it. While the executives are sincere in their attitude of wanting workers to come to them with complaints, unfortunately such a device does not work. In the first place, the fact that the worker has to take the initiative, that he has to go out of his accustomed environment into the office and approach the Big Boss, blocks such action except under very exceptional circumstances. Usually a worker has to be really "burnt up" about something and has to have reached the point where he feels he is ready to risk anything to get a hearing before he will take such a step. And with the men at the very top, who have secretaries to protect them from informal contacts, the barriers are even greater. Of course, under such a policy a few workers may get through to see an executive, giving him a feeling of being available to the workers and of being in touch with what is going on. If he would only note how few such contacts he has in any given month, however, and consider how many workers there are, he will realize that any belief that the open-door policy really works is more wishful thinking than actual fact.

12. EXECUTIVE BEHAVIOR AND VALUES

BUSINESS EXECUTIVES, especially those that occupy positions in top management, can be divided roughly into two groups: those who develop and head a new business, often their own, and those who rise in an established enterprise. It is convenient to think of one as an entrepreneur and the other as the "organization man."*

Enterprise Management and the Influence of the Organization

Enterprise management—or to use Peter Drucker's phrase "managing a business"—is essentially the same whether we are discussing new enterprises or old. Certain kinds of problems and challenges must be met regardless of the size of the enterprise or its age. Entrepreneurial tasks typically involve building or generating new exchange relationships where none existed before and maintaining or consolidating existing relationships. The same round of activity characterizes executive behavior in large-scale, established companies. Their efforts to develop new products, conceive of new market structures, finance expanded activities, and develop organizations of people, tools, and machines in the pursuit of new entrepreneurial objectives are all part of the same picture. Big businesses do the same things that little businesses do; to survive, they must be just as entrepreneurial, perhaps even more so because of the immense resources which must be continuously revitalized through new activities.

There are, however, differences between the executives of large-scale, established companies and the entrepreneurs, especially in the circumstances in which entrepreneurial tasks are performed. These are at first blush rather obvious. The established organizations have the resources of an existing and viable business on which to build. They have capital and credit upon which to draw; but, even more important, they have high-talent manpower organized around the key entrepreneurial activities. They have research and development laboratories, marketing

---

* Some of the following material also appears in Orvis Collins and David G. Moore. *The Enterprising Man*, to be published in 1964 by the Bureau of Business and Economic Research, College of Business, Michigan State University, East Lansing, Michigan.

organizations for launching new products, and existing production facilities which considerably reduce the expense of developing new product lines. Moreover, they have well-trained management personnel who can move in and take over new developments. It is quite different with entrepreneurs starting from scratch. Many of them enter business without much more than a yearning for a place of their own and an overwhelming compulsion to be on their own. Typically, they have a craft, some tools, perhaps a few thousand dollars saved, and that is about all. The fact that some succeed is perhaps one of the most important aspects of our economy. The circumstances of their beginnings are such that considerably greater emphasis must be placed on their motivation and persistence than on their capital and personal resources. Their greatest limitation is that they lack financial resources to survive mistakes or to ride through economic recessions.

More than resources, however, differentiate executive behavior in established companies from entrepreneurial behavior in new companies. Established companies by definition are characterized by existing organizations involving a complex division of labor and especially a hierarchy of authority and control. As has been discussed earlier, this structure represents not only a functional division of labor but is also inevitably a social structure. The various functional and hierarchical positions in the organization take on social significance and meaning to the participants. Employees and executives alike become identified with the various functional interests and frequently internalize the values of their occupations. In addition, the hierarchy of control in the established business is viewed as a status ranking involving power, prestige, and expectations of deference. Finally, there are strong tendencies to view the entire organization as a self-contained entity in which the individual plays a greater or lesser part.

While the key entrepreneurial activities of the established company must still be successfully performed, these become an organizational undertaking which are not necessarily clearly perceived by the individual participant, in some cases even at the executive level. Rather we find a focus on specialized job activities and career interests—a narrowing of interests which sometimes obscures the ultimate entrepreneurial goals of the business. In other words, the entrepreneurial activities are built into the organization and the actual interests of employees are primarily those of successful job performance within the structure.

The significance of this transmutation of entrepreneurial interests to organizational and job interests can be observed by examining the career line of the typical big business executive. Interestingly enough, when he first enters a company, he is not concerned with running a business as much as he is with occupying a job. His interest lies in finding a niche where there is a potential for advancement. To him, ultimate success is the top of the ladder, which is to be climbed rung by rung. Each step up the ladder represents not only effort on his part but the willingness of those higher on the ladder to allow him and even help him to move up. He quickly becomes aware that he is operating within a system where job performance, to be sure, pays off but also where acceptance by those above him is of crucial importance. More than this, he learns that the climb is not just a matter of acquiring new job skills but also of developing social skills associated with higher status and organizational power.

During most of the typical executive's career, his climb is confined to one occupational area. He moves up, for example as a manufacturing executive, or sales executive, or personnel officer. Within this activity, he typically becomes, at least by ordinary standards, an expert. There is in established companies a continuous trend toward increasing complexity in the various functional areas. What could be done a generation ago by high school graduates now requires college-trained personnel or even those with graduate training beyond the college level. This grading up of educational and personal requirements is in part a reflection of the real and growing complexities of modern business, but it also results from job competition, trends towards the professionalization of key occupations, and the outright status exclusion which frequently develops within hierarchical structures.

Characteristics of Established, Bureaucratic Organizations

1. *Prior existence.* An obvious fact about established organizations is that they existed prior to the individual executive. Some are currently being managed by the third or fourth generation of executives. Coming into a business after its establishment gives one the feeling that the organization has an existence of its own. Executives come and go, but the organization goes on forever. In this connection, the demise of a well-known, established business is, for those who know it, very much akin to the death of a great and often noble figure.

The fact of prior establishment and historic continuity gives the individual executive a "generational" view of managerial succession. He develops a sense of son succeeding father. The world of work and of personal success to him is one of occupying a position in an established structure and hopefully climbing an existing hierarchy. It is seldom, if ever, one of creating an organization; indeed, for more business executives in our society, this would hardly be a challenge. The challenge rather lies in becoming a management representative or top official in an established structure.

2. *Hierarchical organization and division of the entrepreneurial function.* A second characteristic of established businesses, which we already pointed out or alluded to in several places, is that they are hierarchically organized. In addition, the over-all entrepreneurial function is divided into several major functional areas and into a great variety of subordinate tasks. The hierarchical structure and functional division results in a complex of occupational circles within circles of ever-widening scope. At each higher level of the administrative hierarchy, the circle expands to include a broader segment of the business.

The young junior executive usually begins his career within a narrowly circumscribed functional activity. He sees himself as holding a job, occupying a niche, rather than running a business. Until he reaches the very top, in most organizations, his success depends on his occupational and professional competence. As a consequence, the demands in most established organizations for occupational or functional competence are very high indeed. A man simply cannot achieve success in large-scale, established organizations without extensive formal education and long years of experience in a particular field. Yet, he can, with all of his experience and education, often climb to the upper echelon of management knowing less about running a total business than many pushcart merchants.

The hierarchical structure of power and control in the established business automatically makes climbing the hierarchy the main route to success. There are, to be sure, "blind alleys" and "cul de (sad) sacs" which may represent positions of moderate success. A man can become, for example, a great scientist or technologist in his organization and may even enjoy considerable respect and recognition for his sense of duty and his persistent pursuit of occupational competence. These are always respected virtues in our occupationally oriented society. But the main line is straight up the administrative hierarchy. Vertical mobility accordingly means climbing a ladder of positions of increasing administrative power over larger and larger segments of the functional activities of the business.

3. *Social organization.* To understand fully the significance of ver-

tical mobility in a hierarchical structure, we must call the reader's attention to still a third characteristic of established businesses. We are referring to the social organization which typically develops whenever there are continuous relations among people over long periods of time. Under these conditions, the administrative hierarchy becomes a structure of status levels. Expectations develop both from topside and from below regarding the behavior and demeanor of persons occupying the various levels. These expectations not only include notions regarding a man's occupational competence but also encompass various beliefs about his appearance, use of language, expressive skills, mode of dress, life style outside the organization, and so on. In other words, he must "make sense" socially as well as occupationally. Indeed, the truly social expectations become so intricately intertwined with the occupational and functional demands that it is impossible really to separate them. It is very possible that the demands, especially in big business, for more and more education among those in the top ranks arise out of social considerations rather than the increasing complexity of the executive role. Or perhaps a more accurate way of viewing it is that the increasing need for education and the growing complexity of the executive role in big business go hand in hand, one giving rise to the other.

The social organization developing in the established business has other important implications. It gives rise to a sense of unity and overall purpose not only at the executive level but down the line among employees, supervisors, and middle management. Thus, management and employees alike develop the feeling that they are part of a unified structure of action, working together to achieve broad goals and purposes. This impression is enhanced by the co-operative work systems developing around the productive efforts of the organization, for technological activities are goal-directed and purposeful with individual efforts organized around a common objective.

The sense of unity and purpose arising within established businesses transforms the executive function from the strictly entrepreneurial function of developing exchange relationships and negotiating differences in interests and values to a leadership function. This alteration in the entrepreneurial function cannot be too strongly stressed, since it is a key factor in shaping the role of the modern business executive. A leader weighs the unfolding reality against the needs of his group; his interpretations and the decisions which he reaches are effective if the group's needs are successfully met. In established organizations, the leadership function follows similar patterns. The needs of the group, however, are viewed in terms of the occupational specialty. The executive within each functional specialty attempts to develop action programs which will enhance the relative position of the function in the larger organization. Typically, these programs are aimed at making the entire organization more effective and successful. Thus, what begins as an expression of narrow functional interests is broadened to include the common interests of the entire organization.

The "leadership" concept places great demands on the executive in the established organization to develop an action program, posture, or stance which will serve as the basis of his decisions and actions in the organization. He is expected to have a sense of direction—to know what it is all about and to be on top of the situation. His decision function is accordingly conceived as one of developing and launching programs —programs which will excite the interests of those whom he leads and which can at the same time be "sold" to higher levels of management. Success can often be measured by the ability of the executive to gain an allocation of resources which is favorable to the interests of his department or division. Not only does he as an individual gain power, status, and prestige by securing such resources, but the morale of the entire group is typically enhanced by the heightened sense of status and recognition.

The demands on the executive in the established organization for leadership and direction place a premium on personal courage, conviction, and ego strength. No matter what a business looks like as a result of the social organization that develops and the sense of unity and purpose that accompanies its development, it is still an entrepreneurial system of exchange and transaction—a complex structure of interaction in a continuously changing and often conflicting world. Its unity and purposefulness are illusory and its directions, circular and self-fulfilling. The sense of direction developing among executives accordingly is largely a subjective phenomenon; it is, to put it another way, a projection of the individual's own sense of purpose and his own interests. Ego strength, therefore, becomes a very important consideration in the choice of executives for established organizations.

4. *Management by an executive team.* Another characteristic of established, large-scale organizations, which has been suggested in the foregoing comments but needs greater emphasis, is the pattern of team management. The executive team is essentially a competitive but interdependent structure of relationships. Each executive competes with the others for a greater allocation of resources; but, at the same time, each

recognizes that he controls and directs only one segment of the total business. Successful performance of one function accordingly requires the support of other key executives. This leads to a variety of activities in mahogany row which may seem like unnecessary political shenanigans but which are really very much a part of getting a job done in a large-scale business. Executives in some instances attempt to form coalitions in order to dominate the management organization. There is often a good deal of mutual good fellowship to avoid making enemies who can sabotage programs at crucial points. In some cases, there is an almost conscious trading of favors. Some of the emphasis on good human relations at the executive level is little more than sophisticated bargaining. We have known executives who kept lists of the mistakes of others in the organization to have them ready at hand if they were accused of errors and inadequacies.

Rather typically there are various bids for leadership in the executive team. Some executives strive to give the impression that they have top-side support from high-level executive officers or even from the board of directors. Sometimes they truly have this support. Others strive for leadership on the basis of the strength of their programs. Still others strive on the basis of their personal qualities of leadership.

In the struggle for domination of the executive team, executives typically assume the various strategic roles possible for them. Thus, we will almost always find at least one executive who places heavy emphasis on "tight" administration; he is the "t-crosser," "i-dotter" par excellence. Another will stake his claim to leadership on innovation and new ideas. Still another will emphasize expansion and increased sales, while yet another talks consolidation and increased profits. Like any political arena, the potential roles are limited; but, as in politics, each possible role is occupied by an ardent proponent of the strategic position which it represents. If the role is emptied by death, retirement, or other turnover, someone typically moves in to pick it up.

Part of the creativity of executive behavior is conceiving and promoting new strategic positions in the organization. Interestingly enough, the proliferation of new executive positions at the top of established businesses represent the successful efforts of men to conceive and develop new executive roles. The way that this is done is a story in itself involving the whole process through which a particular occupational specialty is validated. However, we do not have the space here to develop this notion to its fullest.

The competition within the executive team considerably narrows the innovative possibilities. Ideas are supposed to be practical and plausible, which often means simply conventional and safe. Too much of a deviation from the perceived reality is likely to be criticized. Any idea which threatens to restructure the executive organization and the existing pattern of occupational and strategic positions will be openly fought, for the success of such an idea will diminish and even eliminate current centers of power. Yet, great, new advances are made precisely in this manner.

Psychodynamics of the Executive Role

With this somewhat sketchy outline of the characteristics of large-scale, established businesses and their demands on the executive role, we can turn now to a consideration of the psychodynamics of the executive role. What is the personality configuration of those who are successful in this role? We shall refer first, to the research conducted by Professor William E. Henry of the University of Chicago[1] in collaboration with Social Research Inc.[2] Professor Henry studied a group of more than 100 business executives using the Thematic Apperception Test (TAT). The interpretations of the TAT data were done "blind," that is, without any prior knowledge of the individuals who were being assessed. Surveys of past job performance, summaries of current job behavior provided by others, and certain existing test information were used to distinguish a group of "successful" versus "unsuccessful" executives. "Successful" executives typically had a history of continuous promotion, were still regarded as promotable, and at the time of the study held major administrative posts. Dr. Henry, in collaboration with the social scientists at Social Research Inc., has developed an adaptation of the Thematic Apperception Test as a standard instrument which has proved an effective tool for the evaluation of executive and professional people for its clients. SRI pioneered in this area and has employed this adaptation since 1948.

Professor Henry identified a personality pattern which seemed almost specific for those individuals who achieve success in the executive role in established businesses. This unique configuration, according to Dr. Henry, is not found among "men in lower level supervisory posi-

[1] William E. Henry, "The Business Executive: Psychodynamics of a Social Role," *American Journal of Sociology*, Vol. LIV (January, 1949), pp. 286–91.

[2] Burleigh B. Gardner, "What Makes Successful and Unsuccessful Executives?" *Advanced Management*, Vol. XIII, No. 3 (September, 1948).

tions, men who are considered 'failures' in executive positions, and men in clerical and laboring jobs." Professor Henry states: [3]

From the research it became clear that the "successful" business executives studied had many personality characteristics in common. It was equally clear that an absence of these characteristics was coincident with "failure" within the organization. This personality constellation might be thought of as the minimal requirement for "success" within our present business system and as the psychodynamic motivation of persons in this occupation. Individual uniqueness in personality was clearly present but despite these unique aspects, each executive had in common this personality pattern.

What are some of the characteristics of "successful" executives which Professor Henry identified? We shall discuss these in relation to our previous discussion of the demands made on the executive role in established bureaucracies.

1. *Mobility drive.* We have already described the hierarchical structure of the established business organization. Success in a hierarchy means climbing a status ladder. A man isn't likely to climb unless he has the desire—not just the inclination but real desire. It is, therefore, not surprising that Professor Henry found that his "successful" executives were all mobile, feeling "the necessity to move continually upward and to accumulate the rewards of increased accomplishment." By "mobile," we interpret Professor Henry to mean "desirous of getting ahead in the organizational hierarchy." The term "mobility" usually refers to "social class mobility," that is, movement from one class level to another. A number of these executives are no doubt also "socially mobile" in this sense, but certainly not all of them.

Mobility in the hierarchy can take two forms. First, there are those who desire mobility as evidence of increasing competence on the job. Second, there are those who are motivated by a desire for increased status and prestige. Whatever the source, the motivation is strong. No one gets up there who isn't willing to make a strong effort.

2. *Positive attitude toward the boss.* The climb up the hierarchy depends on acceptance by those at higher levels in the organization. Without a nod from the boss, a man doesn't move. More than this, movement upward ultimately means taking the place of those in higher authority. Both of these considerations indicate the advantage of liking the boss and the boss's style rather than hating him. Professor Henry says that the "successful" executive looks to his superiors as persons of more advanced training and experience whom he can consult in special

---

[3] Henry, *op. cit.*, p. 287.

problems and who issue certain guiding directives. He does not see the authority figures in his environment as destructive or prohibiting.

Obviously, such men are going to have real advantages in building effective relations with superiors particularly over those associates who believe that their superiors are "jerks" and who view authority as essentially prohibiting and destructive. The latter are apt to have very inadequate relations with their superiors: they won't like the boss; and, what's more important, the boss won't like them.

3. *Work and activity.* Hard work never hurt anyone's chances. The man who can channel his energies effectively and can turn out more than the next man is likely to be spotted by his superiors. The "successful" executive is an "eager beaver" who really likes to work and keep moving. In other words, it isn't just show for the boss. According to Professor Henry, these are men "who must accomplish in order to be happy." They gain their satisfaction from the actual doing of the work rather than "merely from contemplating the completed product."

The advantage of being able to work on a piece of a total task and gain satisfaction just from the doing goes without saying. The young junior executive starts his career on a small segment of the total job of the organization. If he can find motivation in these limited tasks, he is more likely to do a good job and gain the support of higher authority. If he can go on to other tasks with equal drive and energy, he is more likely to gain new and broader assignments.

According to Professor Henry, the "successful" hierarch is basically an aggressive individual who channels his energies "into work or struggles for status and prestige." In other words, his motor is always running; it is only a question of gearing it into the work or other activities at hand. He doesn't have the problem of motivating himself and striving continuously to find work inspiration and new sources of energy.

4. *Decision-making ability.* Previously we discussed the heavy demands placed in the executive role for direction and action programs. The executive is supposed to know what it's all about; he is supposed to be a stalwart source of stability and structure in what could be a chaotic, ill-defined situation. The "successful" executive has the ability to "organize unstructured situations and to see the implications of their organizations." According to Professor Henry, "They have the ability to take several seemingly isolated events or facts and to see the relationships that exist between them." More than this, they are future-oriented and are "concerned with predicting the outcome of their decisions and actions."

We can testify from our own experience and research that the conceptual ability of executives exists at various levels. Some structure events in very conventional, mundane, and uneventful ways. Others are capable of integrating many considerations into plausible pictures of reality. Some force familiar patterns on new and unfamiliar events. If they don't quite fit, they "bang" the facts around until they do. Others are more flexible and capable of altering existing structures in order to adapt to change. But, however they do it, the "successful" executives at least think they know what's going on and are never at a total loss for an answer, even though it may take the more deliberate ones some time before they find one.

Closely related to the ability to structure events and come up with a picture of what is going on and what is likely to occur is the ability to make decisions. Decision involves choice among alternatives. There are inevitably more ways than one of structuring a situation and certainly more ways than one of acting on it. The choice is seldom between good and bad, since the various alternatives typically will have both good and bad consequences. It is here that courage and conviction are clearly required. Professor Henry indicates that the "successful" executive has the ability to act effectively in decision situations. He is quite capable of pushing through to conclusions even in very trying circumstances. If he loses the sense of certainty and decisiveness and becomes confused and distraught, others lose confidence in him.

5. *Deeper psychological considerations.* The foregoing constellation of factors in the personality of the "successful" executive are fairly obvious and directly related to the requirements of the executive role. Professor Henry, however, based his observations on a deeper, clinical analysis of the personality of the respondent. Rather typically, the psychologist analyzes current behavior in terms of the subject's earlier adjustment to childhood experiences. The established organization is a hierarchical social system not unlike the family structure, at least in general form, in that there are authority figures (parents), colleagues and associates (siblings), and subordinates (the children in relation to the parents). Almost always, higher levels of authority are identified with masculine figures. The organization is sometimes viewed as essentially feminine. In any event, the relationship with authority—the direct authority of higher levels of management and the idealized authority of the organization—is determined by prior patterns of adjustment with one's parents.

Professor Henry describes the "successful" executive as a "man who has left home." He has broken his emotional feelings of dependency on his parents. Most important, he has severed these ties without any strong feelings of resentment. To put it another way, the "successful" executive is independent and capable of handling his relationships with authority figures and with the organization without emotional involvement, feelings of hostility or antagonism, or overriding feelings of dependency.

Narrowing his analysis down, Professor Henry points out that the tie is most clearly cut with reference to the mother. These are not men who are "tied to their mother's apron strings" as the saying goes. There is, however, a residual tie to the father, but this remains positive. The "successful" executive is positively oriented toward an "admired and more successful male figure."

Pursuing this consideration further, Professor Henry suggests that the "successful" executive really is not totally independent of the father. Indeed, "there must remain feelings of dependency upon the father-image and a need to operate within an established framework." Thus, we gain a picture of man who in fact does not set his own ultimate goals but prefers to work within an already established framework where over-all goals at least are provided. Professor Henry points out that those executives who were truly independent and more narcissistic in their views would probably feel loyalty only to themselves and find themselves "unable to work within a framework established by somebody else." This observation obviously has some bearing on our analysis of entrepreneurs.

6. *Middle-class beliefs and values.* The deeper psychological influences on the personalities of "successful" executives also must be related to cultural beliefs and values. As we shall presently see, a great percentage of "successful" executives come out of the middle class. In this segment of our society, child rearing and early family relationships are such that a larger percentage of personalities of the "successful" type may be produced. If nothing else, the father of the upper-middle-class family is likely himself to be successful and therefore a powerful source of inspiration and emulation. But, in addition, certain values are inculcated into the children which become a major part of system of beliefs characterizing the executive. Professor Henry says:

The successful executive represents a crystallization of many of the attitudes and values generally accepted by middle class American society. The value of accumulation and achievement, of self-directedness and independent thought and their rewards in prestige and status and property are found in this group. But they also pay the price of holding these values and of profiting from them. Uncertainty, constant activity, the continual fear of losing ground, the inability to be introspectively leisurely, the ever present fear of failure, and the artificial limitations put upon their emotionalized interpersonal relations—these are some of the costs of this role.

Personalities of Elite and Mobile Executives

We have another source of information which sheds additional light on Professor Henry's pioneering study. This is the research of W. Lloyd Warner and James Abegglen.[4] The primary purpose of their study was to analyze the career histories and social origins of top business executives in our society. Altogether 8,562 executives were studied through a questionnaire. In addition, a number were personally interviewed, and some were given the Thematic Apperception Test.

For purposes of analysis, the top executives can be divided into two main groups: those who were in a sense born to the managerial class; and those who rose from more humble beginnings to attain this position. The first group can be referred to as the *elite;* the second, as the *mobile,* meaning, of course, the upwardly mobile.

Our interpretation of Warner and Abegglen's study suggests that the unique personality constellation described by Professor Henry may be truer of the elite executive than of the socially mobile executive. Professors Warner and Abegglen state about the elite executive:[5]

. . . the central and overriding fact in the life of the man who is trained and expected to take his father's place is the figure of the father—often energetic, ambitious, successful, dominant, demanding. To succeed easily to the father's position, this man must be able, ambitious, and energetic. He must be on the whole an independent person who can function in a position of major responsibility. At the same time, he must be willing to subordinate himself to his father as an adult and limit his personal drive to the role his family and its social status assign to him.

To give us more understanding of what this relationship means to the individual, Warner and Abegglen quote a TAT analysis of an individual whom we can assume is typical of the elite group.[6]

Curtis' relations with his father are marked by reserve and caution. At no point does he give any indication of close or warm relations with, or feelings toward, his father. Rather he portrays the father as a basically helpful figure, not at all punishing, but someone who is approached on a rather impersonal basis. He is willing to listen to the father and recognizes the abilities of the father, but very

---

[4] W. Lloyd Warner and James Abegglen, *Big Business Leaders in America* (New York: Harper & Bros., 1955).
[5] *Ibid.,* p. 157.
[6] *Ibid.,* p. 169.

strongly emphasizes his own need to reach conclusions and take action as a separate person. The manner of reaching these conclusions is curious, and is repeated, probably representing a deep-seated pattern in the father-son relationship. The son is shown as impetuous and emotional. The father is a controlling and advising figure, but the advice serves as a brake on the son's behavior, and is not accepted immediately. Only on reflection, and after action, is the father seen to be right.

With the socially mobile executive, the pattern seems different. However, the interesting fact is that the examples given by Warner and Abegglen are all entrepreneurs very much like the ones whom we will meet later in this report. For example, Donald Hayes became a major executive by starting his own business, which was later bought out by a larger company. The story of Donald Hayes is very similar to those of many entrepreneurs and accordingly is worth presenting here, partly as a preview and partly to complete this section covering the personalities of successful big business executives. Quoting now here and there from Warner and Abegglen, we find the following of interest in the story and personality of Donald Hayes: [7]

His father was a machinist and the family lived in Cleveland. "My father used to like to drink, and spent little time at home. I can't remember my father ever doing anything for us. Yes, my mother had to work. She took in washing, and we were still delivering it until after we were married. Mother was always even-tempered, hard-working. She made a good home with what she had to do with. She was always serious but she was a good mother. She had to make all of our clothes and there were five boys to take care of."

Mr. Hayes' parents disagreed about money often. "We were afraid of my father, and so was my mother. I never saw my father comb his hair or tie his shoelaces; my mother did it for him. Of course we didn't see my father much as he just wasn't around."

* * * *

"My first job was when I was twelve, pulling weeds in a factory farm. During the first three years of high school I worked after school and in the summers at a store in town."

* * * *

"I liked school a lot. Did well in it. I finished high school in mid-year and had an idea that I would like to go on to college. I looked around for a temporary job, and got one with a floating repair gang on the railroad. I found out that I wouldn't have enough left to pay for college, and I didn't like the repair gang work, so I left after a couple of months and got a job with an advertising agent in Seattle. I liked to travel a lot—I guess all kids that age do. So I went back to the railroad in their freight office in San Francisco. But the idea of college and

---

[7] *Ibid.*, pp. 64–75.

more education kept gnawing at me so I left the railroad and enrolled in Ohio College, in the law school. I wasn't interested in becoming a lawyer but I thought I could get some business law which would help me. After a year, I ran out of money and the only thing to do was to go back to business. In 1920 I got a job in a machine shop—it required no training and the boom was still on and I got $75 to $80 per week."

Hayes stayed on this last job only a half year because "the bottom dropped out of the boom and the department was laid off." He found machine work of various kinds after that, but "knew the bitterness of unemployment." He tried selling door to door and shop to shop.

*   *   *   *

"I finally got a job at Universal Steel in their plant." Hayes said in five months he was offered the job of assistant foreman. When I asked if he was surprised by the rapid promotion, he replied, "No, I expected it. I still want and expect better things."

In 1934, Hayes said, he got "ambitious." "Three of us with the company decided to start our own fabricating plant in Detroit. This was the Midwest Pipe and Wire Company. One of the others was president. I was vice president, and the third man was secretary. They were not active though. One was too old and the other had too much money. We hardly made out for the first few years and then received federal war contracts in 1941 which really boomed the business. By 1948 I was made chairman of the board and when the company was bought out by Allied Products I was made a director and vice president of the company."

*   *   *   *

Hayes is the son of an unreliable, apparently rather dangerous, certainly unsatisfying father. Neither from mother nor father did he get the kind of emotional satisfactions that might make him an easy or comfortable person. On the contrary, he learned that his home was inadequate and that he must "escape" it to achieve the goals his mother perhaps, among others, helped set for him. From this background Hayes merged an independent and solitary figure.

*   *   *   *

Hayes is a man who is involved in repeatedly demonstrating to himself and to others that he does not need them, that he is able to conduct his own life successfully through his own abilities.

The similarity between Hayes' early experiences with his parents, subsequent work history, and ultimate solutions and the pattern of development of many of our entrepreneurs is very great. There is the same inadequate father, the same inconsequential, scattered work experience, the same early reliance on self, the same suspicion of others, the same rejection of partners and associates, and the same compulsion to start one's own business. If Hayes is typical of the truly mobile business executive, then many entrepreneurs, it will be seen, clearly fit into this pattern. This observation is supported by further data presented by Warner and Abegglen. They say:[8]

> This set of attitudes toward the home and parents is not true of Hayes alone. The remarks of some of the other mobile men interviewed concerning their parents may serve to make this area clear.

There follows a whole series of excerpts illustrating inadequate relationships particularly with the father which we will not quote here. However, we will quote some of the conclusions which Warner and Abegglen reached, as follows:[9]

> Generally the focus of energy on mobility derives from the mother. At the same time, the TAT indicates some negative feeling toward the mother as the figure who attempts to hold and control the son. The fathers seem in most cases to have been distant from the sons, and not at all supporting or reinforcing. The father is an unreliable figure. At the same time, there is this feeling of loss and deprivation, that the father is withholding something from the son that he might provide, and some of the process of mobility may be seen as an effort to gain this withheld support, and to prove oneself a worthy and able figure in the eyes of the father.

> *   *   *   *

> A problem in understanding many of the mobile men involves the fact that a troubled or unsatisfactory home, such as they describe, is held to be a fundamental factor in the widest range of special groups, and especially to be a factor in maladjustment and behavior disorders. What then makes it possible for these men to make the kind of social adjustment they do—almost to exploit to their advantage a situation that wrecks the lives of others? Certainly the nature of the mother is important, for apparently it is through her that these men learn to strive, to work hard today for rewards that may possibly be forthcoming at some future time, and deeply believe in this. Also, and unlike the typical history of social maladjustment, these men seem to have during their adolescent years positive experiences with male figures, and to have experiences that reinforce the training and life-view implanted by the mother.

Our study of entrepreneurs will shed further light on the behavioral dynamics of the truly mobile individual in our society.

Origins of the Big Business Executive

We shall turn now from an analysis of the psychodynamics of the executive role to the purely demographic facts of their origins. Again, we shall draw heavily from Warner and Abegglen—this time from their more detailed analysis of occupational mobility.[10] We shall be

[8] *Ibid.*, p. 76.
[9] *Ibid.*, p. 77.
[10] W. Lloyd Warner and James C. Abegglen, *Occupational Mobility in American Business and Industry* (Minneapolis: University of Minnesota Press, 1955).

concerned with three main considerations in our presentation: first, the occupational origins of big business executives; second, educational factors in mobility in established businesses; and, finally, career patterns.

The occupational origins of big business executives can be assessed by analyzing the occupation of the fathers of the approximately 8,000 top executives included in the study. Each executive was asked to indicate the principal occupation of his father. This information gave some indication of the social class origins of the respondents. Table 12–1, adapted from the Warner and Abegglen study, shows the occupations of the fathers of top business leaders in 1952:[11]

TABLE 12–1

The Occupations of the Fathers of 1952 Business Leaders

Occupation of Father	Percentage of 1952 Business Leaders
Unskilled or semiskilled laborer	5
Skilled laborer	10
Farmer	9
Clerk or salesman	8
Minor executive (including foremen)	11
Owner of small business	17
Major executive	15
Owner of large business	9
Professional man	14
Other	2
Total	100

The "blue-collar class" as such produced only 15 per cent of top executives in the country. The upper levels of the "white-collar" group, that is, major executives, owners of large businesses, and professional men, produced 38 per cent of the top business leaders. The rest for the most part were produced by farm families and especially the lower levels of the "white-collar class." This is, of course, very significant and becomes even more so when we examine, as Warner and Abegglen did, the proportion of these various occupational groups represented in the general population at the time these executives were first starting out. Warner and Abegglen say:[12]

In 1920, 47 per cent of the U.S. adult male population belonged to the laboring group. In 1952, 15 per cent of the business leaders were sons of laborers. If the sons of laborers had been represented fully in the business elite, about 47 per

---

[11] *Ibid.*, p. 45.
[12] *Ibid.*, p. 47.

cent of the 1952 business leaders would have had fathers who were laborers. Instead of this ration of 47:47 (1.00), we find a ration of 47:15 or 0.32.

While Warner and Abegglen are primarily concerned with changes in occupational mobility between 1928 and 1952 and demonstrate that more sons of laborers are becoming top executives than in 1928, we are primarily concerned here with the essential fact that those who climb in the organizational hierarchies of established businesses typically enjoy at least a "white-collar" background. Moreover, a very large number, perhaps even a majority, come from a fairly substantial background.

This observation is partially confirmed by the number of college-educated leaders in the Warner and Abegglen sample. College education usually requires resources and the opportunity to substract at least four years from one's life to devote to educational pursuits. Of the total group of 1952 business leaders, 57 per cent were college graduates and 19 per cent had some college.[13] This means that more than three quarters of the top leaders had some college work or had actually graduated from college.

With reference to career histories, an important finding in the study was that "no more than 14 per cent of the businessmen studied began their careers in the 'laborer' or 'foreman' categories. The office, rather than the shop, provides the background for most of these executives."[14] If they did start in the shop, they were out of it rather quickly.

In 1960, Professor Thomas R. O'Donovan made a study of executives in four major "multiplant corporations" in the Michigan area, following the Warner approach.[15] Dr. O'Donovan was interested in comparing top executives with lower-level executives on a number of social, career, and educational factors. His sample consisted of 178 top executives and 148 from the lower levels. The ages of both groups of respondents were the same. The top executives in O'Donovan's sample included those management representatives at the upper three or four levels in the corporation. For the size of company in which the study was made, these would certainly be regarded as top executives. The lower managers were first- and second-level supervisors, that is, foremen and those just above foremen.

---

[13] Ibid., p. 96.

[14] Ibid., p. 116.

[15] Thomas R. O'Donovan, Contrasting Orientations and Career Patterns of Executives and Lower Managers (Michigan State University, unpublished Ph.D. dissertation, 1961).

With regard to the so-called occupational origins of the top executives, O'Donovan found little difference between his sample and that of the Warner and Abegglen study. Because of differences in the way the data are analyzed and presented in the two studies, we will not present figures confirming this similarity.[16]

The educational level of O'Donovan's sample was somewhat higher than the Warner and Abegglen sample. O'Donovan found that 69 per cent of his executives as opposed to Warner's 57 per cent had undergraduate degrees or better. There were many more with advanced degrees in O'Donovan's group—20 per cent of the total as compared with only 3 per cent in Warner's group. Whereas Warner and Abegglen found 76 per cent of the top executives in 1952 had some college or better, O'Donovan in his more recent but considerably more limited study found that practically all top executives in four of the major corporations in the Michigan area had some college work or better—all but 10 per cent as a matter of fact.[17]

It is interesting to note also the similarities in career histories between the O'Donovan group and the Warner and Abegglen group. Once again we find top executives starting primarily in white-collar and administrative jobs.[18]

Turning now to the lower managers in the O'Donovan study, we find that this is quite a different group from the top executives. Almost 50 per cent of the lower managers originate in families where the father was a blue-collar worker. Only about 15 per cent came from backgrounds more typical of top executives.[19] The educational achievements of the lower managers were even more significant. Only 30 per cent had graduated from college or had had academic work beyond this.[20] Furthermore, as might be expected, they started their careers at lower levels, almost half of them beginning as hourly laborers.[21]

The O'Donovan study confirms the picture presented in the Warner and Abegglen research. Mobility in the large-scale organization is strongly influenced by social class background and above all by education. The study, however, does a good deal more than confirming this theme. It provides us with direct information on a number of salient points about those who do not rise in the hierarchy.

---

16 *Ibid.,* p. 48.
17 *Ibid.,* p. 49.
18 *Ibid.,* p. 102.
19 *Ibid.,* p. 47.
20 *Ibid.,* p. 59.
21 *Ibid.,* p. 102.

SUMMARY

In this chapter, we have examined the business hierarch, that is, the man who rises in established businesses. We looked first at the entre-preneurial environment of business and concluded that there was little difference in enterprise management from one company to the next. It was apparent, however, that established businesses altered the role of the executive in a number of ways. An important consideration was that the executive in the established organization climbed to a position of power through a hierarchy and within a social organization. We found it important, therefore, to examine some of the characteristics of established organizations, and their influence on the executive role.

The studies of the psychodynamics of the executive role demon-strated the influence of the hierarchical and social structure of estab-lished businesses on executive behavior and especially on executive mobility. It was interesting to note in this connection the rather consid-erable importance of a man's relationship to authority to his success or failure in the established organization. The relationship to authority at a deep level of analysis appeared to revolve around the man's earlier experiences with his father and mother.

The studies of business leaders highlighted the significance of the hierarchical and social structure of modern business to mobility in the executive ranks. If it is true, as these studies suggest, that a man's chances are considerably reduced by his social origins, educational achievement, and early career, one cannot help wondering what happens to those who do not have social and academic advantages. O'Donovan shows what happens to one group of them; they stay at the lower management level if they rise at all.

13. THE PROFESSIONAL
EMPLOYEE IN INDUSTRY

A MAN's occupation and his sense of identification with his job are
strongly influential in determining his beliefs and interests, his relations with others, and his daily round of activities. His occupation gives
him a sense of direction and of structure in a complex world. More
than this, it provides him with a feeling of security and it gives him a
recognizable position in our society. Altogether then, a job is more
than an impersonal function to be performed routinely and without involvement; it is literally a place in our occupational, career-oriented
society.

Jobs can be classified in terms of their relationship to organized activities. Most jobs are specific to particular industries and technologies. In
other words, these are the many occupations which owe their existence
to a given technological process. Literally thousands of such jobs have
been generated by the myriad of subtechnologies that characterize the
modern industrial nation. There are, however, jobs which involve special talents, know-how, and skills which are more broadly applicable.
These are mainly in the skilled trades. We can also include in this category the semiprofessional jobs such as accounting, engineering, and
other near-professions. All of these occupations are in an intermediate
position in terms of their relation to organized activities. They allow
a certain degree of freedom in that the employee in these occupations
can, so to speak, "pick up his tools" and take his broadly applicable
talents elsewhere. Furthermore, some in the near-professions have become completely professionalized, separating entirely from organized
activities and setting up their own public accounting firms, engineering
firms, or management consulting firms of all varieties.

Very few occupations, however, are completely "free"—in the
sense of *die freien Berufe* as Professor Everett C. Hughes defines the
term.[1] In short, very few independents work for a clientele directly and
charge fees. The reason for this is not hard to find. In the modern world,
almost every occupation requires expensive facilities; these can only be

---

[1] See Everett C. Hughes, *Men and Their Work* (Glencoe, Illinois: Free Press, 1958).

obtained through the pooling of resources which rather typically means setting up an organization of some kind. Even the medical profession, which is among the last of the "free occupations," could not function without the organized hospital. However, the doctor maintains his independence, even though he has all of the facilities of the hospital at his disposal. Professor Hughes points up the trend toward organizational affiliation among most professionals, as more and more of them in recent years have become salaried employees of industry or government.

Nonetheless, the pull toward occupational freedom and independence is exceedingly strong in our society. In a way, this is one of those countervailing adjustments characteristic of human relations. The strength of the occupation provides some protection against the overwhelming power of the organization and its facilities. Occupational identification thus can be thought of in part as a compensatory mechanism—an effort to equalize the transactional relationship that the individual in the occupation has with the organization and its management. Whatever the nature of the adjustment, however, there is a strong trend toward "professionalization" among all occupational groups requiring advanced training. Thus, we find personnel managers, purchasing agents, accountants, engineers, and many others forming professional societies and referring to their occupations as professional activities. Because of this trend and because of the increasing number of highly trained individuals employed by industry, it is important for us to understand the nature of a profession and the appeal which it offers.

The Nature of a Profession

The occupational pattern which we refer to as professional is fairly well defined and has been described by a number of scholars in the field.[2]

1. *Professional association.* All professions have an established professional association made up of qualified members which defines the profession, regulates its activities, and in general strives to validate the occupation as a profession. The professional association typically holds meetings periodically at which learned papers in the field are presented, publishes learned journals, and provides a social organization through

---

[2] Theodore Caplow, *The Sociology of Work* (Minneapolis: University of Minnesota Press, 1954).

which members can gain a sense of occupational identity, status and prestige, and differentiation from other occupational groups. In addition to these functions, the association can also represent the profession to the public and to the government which may support it through granting of licenses. In other words, the professional association can and frequently does serve the same function as other trade associations in our society in representing, supporting, and giving credence to the particular activity.

The importance of professional associations is born out by the fact that all occupational groups seeking the professional posture typically begin by organizing a professional association.

2. *Specification of qualifications for entry into the profession.* The second phase in the development of a profession is the specification of the educational qualifications necessary for entry into the profession. A profession assumes a unique body of knowledge—special understandings, techniques, and judgment—which are not possessed by the so-called "layman." This raises certain problems in the development of a profession. To become a true profession, an occupation must literally capture the educational facilities through which men are trained.

The "capturing of educational facilities" moves through several stages. The first stage is merely that of gaining academic recognition. In other words, you try to get key professors in major universities interested in your occupation and its association. As time goes on, a second phase is reached in which the association grants scholarships and other financial aids to the university to support educational programs and curricula which presumably train the individual for a career in the particular occupation. If the association can grant substantial financial aid, these highly specialized programs can become an important part of the educational efforts of universities. The third stage is the development of a school which specializes in the training of students for particular occupations, such as, a school of medicine, a school of law, a school of theology, a school of education, a school of engineering, a school of hotel, restaurant, and institutional management, and so on.

If an educational facility has been completely "captured," access to the specialized knowledge of the profession can be limited and controlled. Nonetheless, something else is needed; the educational requirements must be arduous, lengthy, and in general discouraging except to those who have a genuine interest in, and desire for, a career in the profession. There is a tendency in all professions for the educational barrier to be raised higher and higher. This tends to raise the status of the profession, of course, but in addition limits entry into the field. The arduous and lengthy educational experience required of the budding professional is a kind of purgatory of hard work, low income, and increasing commitment to the profession. Various ceremonial occasions mark the progress of the individual. These ceremonials appear in the form of examinations, the ultimate of which is an oral examination by one's peers.

Complete control over educational requirements and entry into a profession cannot be achieved without the support of government. As a consequence, professional groups as they become established seek to gain governmental support for their specialized occupations through laws and licensing.

3. *License to practice.* A profession has truly arrived when it is granted the license to practice by the state. Licensing typically involves a specification of the qualifications required for the profession. More than this, however, it excludes those who do not possess these qualifications. Licensing creates an occupational monopoly. A man can be arrested for practicing without a license.

The importance of license and the mandate to practice which the license grants is emphasized by Professor Everett Hughes in a brilliant article entitled "The Study of Occupations" which appears in *Sociology Today*.[3] Professor Hughes takes a somewhat broader view of license, as follows:

License, as an attribute of an occupation, is usually thought of as specific legal permission to pursue the occupation. I am thinking of something broader. Society, by its nature, consists in part of both allowing and expecting some people to do things which other people are not allowed or expected to do. Most occupations—especially those considered professions and those of the underworld—include as part of their being a license to deviate in some measure from some common modes of behavior. Professions, perhaps more than other kinds of occupations, also claim a broad legal, moral, and intellectual mandate. Not only do the practitioners, by virtue of gaining admission to the charmed circle of the profession, individually exercise a license to do things others do not do, but collectively they presume to tell society what is good and right for it in a broad and crucial aspect of life. Indeed, they set the very terms of thinking about it. When such a presumption is granted as legitimate, a profession in the full sense has come into being. The nature and extent of both license and mandate, their relations to each other, and the circumstances and conflicts in which they ex-

---

[3] Robert K. Merton, Leonard Broom, and Leonard S. Cottrell, Jr., *Sociology Today* (New York: Basic Books, Inc., 1959), p. 447.

pand or contract are crucial areas of study, not merely for occupations, but for society itself. Such licenses and mandates are the prime manifestations of the *moral* division of labor—that is, of the processes by which differing moral functions are distributed among the members of society, as individuals and as categories of individuals.

In these terms, the license to practice is a mandate granted by the sovereign power of the state to perform specific functions but, more than this, to exercise more functions as well. The profession, in other words, is granted the privilege of policing itself and controlling the behavior of its members. The process of self-policing is a story in itself inasmuch as it goes on behind "closed doors," at least as far as the lay public is concerned. The assumption here is, of course, that a professional can only be judged by another professional. The moral latitude and self-policing characteristic of a profession make it extremely important that a profession sets forth a code of ethics.

4. *Code of ethics.* The code of ethics of an established profession is frequently a written document, but it may be unwritten. In either case the code constitutes a set of beliefs and values, usually concerning the relationship of the professional to the client. In general the code deals with the problem of the relationship of professional norms to the demands of the clientele. Thus, the code of ethics can be regarded as generalized rules of conduct in the transactional relationship that develops between the professional and his client.

5. *Payment through fees.* The "free occupations" demonstrate their freedom from organizational affiliation by charging fees. Fees as a source of income carry a higher status ranking in our society than salaries and wages. The notion of a retainer is a common one in some professional circles. Here we have a method of payment which carries all of the status implications of a fee but the steadiness of income of a salary. However it is done, the method of payment is symbolic of the free and independent role of the professional in his relationship to the client.

6. *Specialized language.* Finally, mention should be made of the specialized language or argot which develops in professional groups. Specialized language has several functions: First, where a specialized body of knowledge has developed, the language describing various complex phenomena within the professional field serves to facilitate communication within the profession; second, the specialized language with its polysyllabic tendencies enhances the status and authority of

the profession; and last but not least, the specialized language serves the function of excluding the outsider, that is, the lay public.

These, then, are the major characteristics of a true profession. Obviously, very few professional groups have achieved all of these characteristics with the exception of medicine, law, and a few other groups. As indicated previously, most professionals have organizational affiliations. This trend should not be attributed to the diminishing significance of the "free occupations" in our society. It is rather a reflection of the increasing complexity of modern large-scale organizations, particularly in the technological areas.

The Employment of Professionals in Industry

Practically all types of professionals and near-professionals are employed in industry. There are industrial physicians, psychiatrists, nurses, lawyers, even ministers affiliated with industrial organizations. However, by far the largest group of professionally trained employees in industry are the physical scientists and the engineers. These employees are concerned primarily with research and development activities and with technological developments.

Some indication of the importance of the engineer to modern industry can be gleaned by the data provided by the National Science Foundation on the number of workers on the labor force per engineer. The evidence shows that "since 1930, the number of employed civilian workers per engineer has decreased from 226 to 102."[4] This means that the proportion of engineers has more than doubled in the past thirty years. Between 1920 and 1956, the actual number of engineers employed in the United States increased from approximately 125,000 to 700,000.

Indications of the increasing importance of scientists to industry can be found in the analysis of research and development expenditures since 1941. In 1941, these expenditures from all sources amounted to $900 million. By 1955, these had increased to over $10 billion of which 55 per cent was contributed by industry.[5] The amount contributed by industry over the past decade and a half has been a generally increasing one. Professor Simon Marcson has the following to say:[6]

---

[4] Alfred Iddles, "Effective Utilization of Engineering Personnel: A Challenge to Management," in *Effective Utilization of Engineering Personnel* (East Lansing, Michigan: Labor and Industrial Relations Center, Michigan State University, 1957), p. 5.

[5] *1959 Statistical Abstract of the United States*, p. 539.

[6] Simon Marcson, *The Scientist in American Industries* (Princeton: Industrial Relations Section, Princeton University, 1960), p. 3.

Expenditures on industrial research and development laboratories have more than doubled in the past decade, and it is more than likely that such expenditures will again double in the next five years. In a very real sense, competition in American industry is becoming a race in innovation. For example, companies in the electronics industry estimate that more than three-quarters of their current sales are of products that were unknown ten years ago. At the same time chemical companies forecast that more than half of their 1975 sales revenue will be based on products now in their introductory stages or still to be invented. The spectacular expansion of drug firms in recent years is due largely to their intensive investment in the development of new products. In terms of the future growth of the United States, the research is a critical activity.

The Domination of the Scientist-Engineer in the Technological Order

The foregoing figures indicate the increasing importance of science in industry, but they do not necessarily reveal the domination of industrial technology by the scientist. Since World War II, the physical scientist has become a dominant figure in the industrial technological order; for he has not only social prestige within the system but often superior and, therefore, more powerful knowledge. The engineer is an applied scientist, translating science into action designs. Skilled tradesmen working from the designs, blueprints, and orders of engineers create the tools, machines, and setups for production. Finally, the semiskilled and unskilled production workers tend and feed the machines. This is an oversimplified view of the social and functional arrangement of the technological order, but it will serve our purposes of the moment.

The dominance of the scientist-engineer in the technological order has not always been so. In the past, men of practical knowledge and skill controlled the industrial technology. These were men trained through the apprentice system; many of them attained high scientific knowledge without benefit of formal education. Some of the greatest inventors of recent times were not trained scientists or engineers but men who attained deep insights, knowledge, and understanding through practical experience. However, since World War I and particularly since World War II, there has been a sometimes gradual and sometimes accelerated replacement of the "practical man" with the "scientific man." At the present time, the "scientific man" has moved into a position of clear dominance.

This transition has not taken place without contention and conflict. Indeed, some of the major human relations problems in industry grow out of conflict between those with "book learning" and those with "practical experience." Nothing delights the "practical man" more than to prove that "those smart engineers" weren't so bright after all. Cases have been reported to the authors in which tool- and diemakers have gone ahead and followed the blueprint, spending thousands of dollars to produce a tool or die, when they knew ahead of time that the die was unworkable. All of this to show up the "smart aleck" engineer who knew so much. There are many instances reported of production foremen and production workers who have literally sabotaged new production methods introduced by engineers who forgot the conflict in interest between the "practical" and educated technologist. Indeed, the really smart engineer who wants to accomplish something quickly learns the importance of effective interaction in the workplace in getting a job done.

Given present trends, however, it seems evident that the "practical man" will within the near future succumb to the superior knowledge of science. In fact, as scientists and engineers gain strength within the technological order, the entire system will be changed and altered to accommodate their interests, and these will tend to exclude those without the necessary educational qualifications. The production worker who is the lowest man on the technological totem pole doesn't have a chance.

The Beliefs and Values of the Scientific Order

Because of the combination of science in the technological order, it is important to understand the beliefs and values of scientists. In its purest form, the scientific posture is one of "intellectual honesty, integrity, organized skepticism, disinterestedness, impersonality" to use the words of Robert K. Merton.[7] The scientist is seen as an objective observer; and the greatest threat to his objectivity is the "human equation," that is, human failures not only at the physiological level but even more at the personal and emotional level. Science sets up all kinds of safeguards to eliminate human failures. The scientific method itself, in which the scientist sets up hypotheses and then proceeds to prove them *wrong*, is one kind of safeguard. The concern of the scientist with pure research, that is, research that is not directly related to practical ends, is another. There are all kinds of institutional norms which encourage impersonality and detachment. For example, the greatest prestige in scientific circles is granted to those who make discoveries in the realm of pure science. The scientist in the university is the ultimate

---

[7] Robert K. Merton, *Social Theory and Social Structures* (rev. ed.; Glencoe, Ill.: Free Press, 1957).

model. In fact, the university is a key factor in the scientific belief system. Herbert A. Shepard states the following about the core of the value system of pure science:[8]

The core of the value system of pure science consists of two related beliefs: first, that new knowledge should be evaluated according to its significance for existing theory, and second, that scientists should be evaluated according to their contributions of new knowledge. Highest honors go to those whose work involves radical reformulations or extensions of theory or conceptualization. Next come those who do the pioneer experimental work required by theoretical reformulation. Next come those who carry out the work logically required to round out the conceptual structure. Next come those who carry out redundant experimental work of a confirmatory nature, or concern themselves largely with relevant data accumulation. Last are the doers of sloppy or dull work.

Professor Shepard goes on to say:

Metaphorically, to be a scientist is to be a worker engaged in the construction of a great cathedral of knowledge, eternally incomplete, but slowly taking form over the centuries. . . . For the conduct in this task of building the cathedral of scientific knowledge, standards of method and ethic are prescribed, criteria of beauty, workmanship, morality and social worth are elaborated. The scientist learns to esteem himself for honesty, humility, objectivity, self-discipline, curiosity, creativity, skepticism, rigor and industriousness.

Because objectivity and impersonality are important scientific norms, the physical sciences have inevitably become the center of the scientific belief system. Here the possibilities of objectivity and impersonality are at their very highest and serve as a model for other sciences, even the social sciences. Moreover, science in its purest forms tends to attract those who by nature are more impersonal and find comfort and satisfaction in the object quality of physical reality. Natural tendencies are reinforced by education and university norms so that the budding scientist begins to view the physical world as tangible and the world of people as intangible, even unreal and "phony." As one young engineer told us in an interview when asked what he thought of business administration, "When I think of business administration, I think of salesmen; and when I think of salesmen, I have a feeling of revulsion." Sometimes, a moral view of human foibles is taken such that any failures to be objective or any tendencies to personalize one's judgments and behavior are regarded as "sinful." This carries over to the notion that

---

[8] Herbert A. Shepard, "Basic Research and the Social System of Pure Science," in Robert T. Livingston and Stanley H. Milberg (eds.) *Human Relations in Industrial Research Management* (New York: Columbia University Press, 1957), p. 117.

the influencing of people other than on the basis of "rational, scientific" considerations is "sinful." Recently, we had the experience of asking a group of business executives in a company employing a large number of scientists particularly in the field of chemistry to set up an organizational model in keeping with the belief system and values of scientists. They came back after their discussion sessions scratching their heads. One said, "My Gawd, their beliefs are so objective and depersonalized, the organization would look like a communist state." Another said, "Well, the marketing function would go to hell, but it sure would be honest."

Another belief which characterizes science is the idea that there is only one explanation of the physical universe, one science, so to speak. There may be different theories at any one time, but less efficient theories will give way to superior conceptual explanations as the evidence comes in. Closely akin to this belief is the notion that the scientist's role is one of revealing the essential logic inherent in nature itself. This view has a religious base in the Protestant Ethic or the Puritan Ethos as Robert K. Merton translates it. He states in writing about early scientific beliefs: "The deep-rooted religious *interests* of the day demanded in their forceful implications the systematic, rational and empirical study of Nature for the glorification of God and His works and for the control of the corrupt world."[9] While science has become secularized through the centuries, scientists still are striving to reveal God's will in the physical universe—God's will being order, regularity, and causally related events.

The beliefs of the modern scientist tend to follow along the historical lines. Gerald De Gré lists eight major values which he believes characterizes modern science:

1. Rationalism
2. Empiricism
3. Logical experimental method
4. Belief in the rule of law
5. Pragmatism
6. Worldly asceticism
7. Skepticism
8. Individualism

Robert K. Merton identifies four sets of institutional imperatives which "comprise the ethos of modern science":[10]

---

[9] Merton, *op. cit.*
[10] *Ibid.*

1. *Universalism.* The concept of universalism refers to the essential objectivity and universal application of scientific findings. It is the opposite of particularism.
2. *Communism.* The findings of science belong to the community. "They constitute a common heritage in which the equity of the individual producer is severely limited." Closely allied to this concept of property rights in science is the imperative for communication of findings. "Secrecy is the antithesis of this norm; full and open communication its enactment." "The communism of the scientific ethos is incompatible with the definition of technology as 'private property' in the capitalistic economy."
3. *Disinterestedness.* This institutional element refers to the ethical stance of the scientist. "The virtual absence of fraud in the annals of science, which appears exceptional when compared with the record of other spheres of activity, has at times been attributed to the personal qualities of scientists." However, institutional controls are perhaps more significant than personal integrity. "The activities of scientists are subject to rigorous policing, to a degree perhaps unparalleled in any other field of activity."
4. *Organized skepticism.* Organized skepticism refers to the "suspension of judgment until 'the facts are at hand' and the detached scrutiny of beliefs in terms of empirical and logical criteria."

In a study of the attitudes of professional employees in industry, Moore and Renck state the following:

It seems clear from the evidence available that the professional is job-oriented. He is concerned primarily with competent performance in his chosen field. He seeks status through specialization. In a sense, he takes a field which might appear to be extremely narrow to the layman and develops it to the nth degree.

Because of his job-orientation, the professional tends to work within the framework of his field and seeks to extend knowledge within its framework. He proceeds or at least would like to proceed in a systematic, often pedestrian, fashion to develop his field on a broad and complicated front. He is keenly aware of the many facets of his discipline and the total effort required to apply it to the technological and research problems of industry.

There are many other useful analyses of the attitudes and beliefs of the scientists. However, the preceding paragraphs should be sufficient to give us some understanding of the dominant belief system of the scientific order.

The belief system of the scientist coincides to a degree with the beliefs of the craftsman who also gains his status and livelihood by being able to grapple effectively with physical reality. The craftsman is a man who knows how to do things, how to reshape the material world. His behavior tends to be more traditional and ceremonial than the scientist's. Moreover, he naturally places a higher premium on practical experience, direct contact, and a personal, intimate "feel" for physical phenomena. But, nonetheless, he is in essence a "primitive" scientist, or, as one person described him, a Neanderthal engineer. As he moves from direct know-how to generalizations, he moves in the direction of science, recapitulating the development and history of science. If he does not generalize, he tends to view the world as a great amorphous block of wood or metal or other material of various degrees of hardness which can be cut, shaped, formed, and put together in diverse new forms.

The engineer links science with the craftsman and ultimately the production worker and the machines and tools that he tends and uses. In the professional schools in which the engineer is trained, the trend is more and more toward basic training in science and less and less in the direction of trade skill. For all intents and purposes, he can be regarded as a scientist or subscientist with the same basic belief system and with the same, ultimate models of successful performance. Remember we are speaking here of engineers as engineers not engineers who have gravitated toward other occupations such as sales or management. Furthermore, we are talking here about basic beliefs, those which serve as the essential guide lines within the technological order; individual scientists, engineers, and craftsmen may adjust in various ways to the basic norms and occupational expectations. The important point to keep in mind is that, no matter what the range of individual adjustments, the technological order is a social system and has a dominant pattern of beliefs which is largely shaped and controlled by a social organization, the influential center of which is made up of scientists and engineers. What they think and believe represents a powerful force within the business organization and the technological patterns which emerge.

The absorption of the professional scientist into industry creates a special set of problems. In the first place, the scientist is usually emotionally attached to the world of his science. He has spent long years winning his spurs as a physicist, chemist, or biologist and by training and inclination gets his greatest satisfactions from practice in his field. Furthermore, the acclaim of other scientists in his field is more important to him than is the respect of nonscientists in the company. He feels that his true worth can only be judged by his scientific colleagues, not by any "mere business executive."

Essentially such men, and this is especially true of top research scientists, identify primarily with their profession rather than with the organization. The company for which they work merely provides the setting in which they pursue their search for knowledge in their field.

The rules and limitations imposed by the organization are at best necessary evils and at worst intolerable restraints.

Inevitably it is believed (with some element of truth) that a research group can be supervised and administered only by a competent scientist who will be accepted by the professionals as a colleague who understands their field. To have a layman directing and evaluating them and their work is a desecration. (This is also seen in hospitals where a non-medical administrator must tread with caution in dealing with matters affecting the doctors.)

As a result, in developing their research departments, management must draw from the ranks of the scientists to fill the role of department head and administrator.

For the usual executive who is devoted to a business career rather dedicated to a professional career, this is as it should be. The scientist "should" want to be advanced to a higher-status level in the regular management hierarchy. To the professional man, however, this represents a serious and threatening change in his role and in his career line. The more he becomes an executive the less he is a scientist. He can no longer "dirty his hands" on the research, he no longer struggles with complex technical theories and problems, he no longer has the thrill of discovery. Also, how will he continue to merit the friendship and respect of colleagues? When they ask what he is up to now and he tells them he is running a department and not doing research, a chill descends. He feels they think he has sold his glorious birthright for a mess of pottage.

Furthermore, since the scientist feels that the work and skill of the administrator or executive is of a lower order than that of professional work, he is likely to be an inept leader. Maybe only the research scientist can understand the work of other researchers, but often he can understand only the work and not the human factors. And anyway, to him the human factors and feelings should not be allowed to intrude in the work situation. As a result, we have seen cases where the creative research man is promoted to head a department and the company loses his most valued talent and the department is wrecked besides.

As these important professional skills become more and more essential to modern industry, it will be necessary to develop methods for integrating the professional man. He must be able to maintain his value systems and yet become a loyal, integral member of the company.

This elite of the research scientist is not the only professional elite which moves into industry. The professional engineer has become increasingly essential to modern industry. He in a sense is a bridge between the growing body of knowledge emanating from the research laboratories and the practical applications to serve the needs of our society. Although professional in training, he usually does not have the strong professional identification of the "pure" scientist. To most engineers the application of knowledge is more exciting and satisfying than the search for knowledge, and the world of industry is a challenge to and test of their skills. In general, they readily make the transition from practicing engineer, to supervisor, to executive with less strain than does the scientist.

As they move away from their professional work into management roles, both engineer and scientist have a common shortcoming. They have been trained to deal with the rationality of the physical world, with neat cause-and-effect relationships, or highly logical theories. When they face the complexities of the human organization and the emotionalities of human reaction they are often lost. They feel that these irrational behaviors are morally wrong, that feelings should not intrude in work relationships. And until they learn to deal with man as he is and not as he ought to be, they have difficulties in any management role.

14. THE SALES

ORGANIZATION AND THE

SALESMAN

IT IS essential for any business enterprise that it maintain an adequate rate of transactions involving sale of its output. It can only grow if this rate of transaction increases, and it will decline and even die if it decreases. Thus, no matter how effective it may be in its internal operations, in its skill of management or efficiency of production, these can all be meaningless if it cannot maintain its sales.

The sales department is the organization unit directing and maintaining this transactional relationship. It has the responsibility for determining how the company's products or its representatives will be brought into contact with potential customers. Sometimes the process is simple, with the salesman for the company calling directly on the potential customer. Often it is more complicated, with the product moving through outside distributors whose salesmen call on retailers who in turn sell the product to the public. In the simpler case the movement from producer to consumer is one transaction handled completely by the company personnel. In the other the producer-consumer movement is broken into a series of steps and series of transactions of which only the first is in the hands of the company.

In addition to its primary function of maintaining the transactional activities, the sales organization has other roles in the company.

1. It serves as a channel of communication between customer and company. Information regarding the product, complaints about service, prices, and so on, are relayed back through the sales organization.
2. Its executives participate in determining prices. Pricing is usually influenced by what the sales executives think they can get for the product as well as by manufacturing costs.
3. Its executives participate in planning new products or product improvements. Their familiarity with what competitors are doing, with product deficiencies, and with what is acceptable enables them to advise management on product development.
4. Its executives play an important role in planning competitive strategy. The sales department is concerned not only with selling the product but with

selling it in competition with other products. Thus the executives are constantly concerned with adjusting their activities in the face of changing competitive actions.

The Salesman

The salesman functions in the face-to-face relationship with the customer. He must establish a personal relationship with the customer which facilitates the transactional relationship between customer and company. Traditionally the salesman is thought of as being skilled in interpersonal relations: he can make friends easily, he gets along with people, he establishes strong personal attachments. To a varying degree the customer buys because of him and not primarily because of the desirability of the product or company he represents.

In many types of selling the salesman feels that he is an intermediary between the customer and the company. In many cases he tends to think of them as "his customers" and feels that he must protect them and must see that the company "does right by" them. Thus, the salesman will identify with the customer and try to look out for his interests in dealing with the company.

However, there are many types of selling and of sales situations, and to some extent each makes different demands on the salesman. Also, each tends to attract a different type of person and often the successful salesman in one type of situation does poorly in another. Or often a person who performs well in one type of selling will fail in another.

Types of Sales Situations

The salesman in general does his selling in a situation where he is face to face with the customer, and can both respond to and influence the customer. In addition, this interaction is influenced by certain characteristics of the type of product and kind of selling. Some of the important characteristics are as follows:

1. Where the interaction takes place:
   a) In the salesman's place of business such as in retail stores, auto agencies, and gasoline service stations.
   b) In the customer's home as with Fuller Brush salesmen or Avon cosmetic saleswomen.
   c) In the customer's place of business as with industrial goods.

In the first location the customer comes to the sales location, brought there by the desire to purchase. The salesman has no responsibility for establishing the contact but merely deals with the customer when he appears. In many cases the salesman can be quite passive, merely showing the customer what he asks for.

In the second two locations the salesman must take the initiative in approaching the prospect. He must knock on the door or call for an appointment. This requires more aggressiveness and energy than the salesman in a store waiting for customers.

> 2. The frequency of the interaction with the customer. This varies from the one-shot sale to the frequent repeat sales to the same customer.
>
> *a*) The one-shot sale. This is seen where the salesman handles only one product which is not frequently replaced. The door-to-door encyclopedia salesman is an example of this.

This type of selling requires skill in establishing the relationship rapidly, arousing interest, and closing the sale. It requires considerable aggressiveness and lends itself to the "gyp" or "suede shoe boys" who exploit the customer. Many of them see the customer as a "sucker" to be "taken."

> *b*) The repeat sale. Here we have a continuing relationship in which the salesman must maintain a satisfactory rapport with the customer. In house-to-house selling, as is done by the Fuller Brush man or the Jewel Tea route man, the salesman returns at regular intervals and must find himself welcome. If he is too aggressive in his selling, pushes too hard, or gets the customer to buy too much, the door may not open the next time he appears.
>
> 3. The dependence of the customer on the technical knowledge of the salesman.

At one extreme, represented by the salesgirl at the notion counter in the department store, the customer knows what she wants and asks for it. The salesgirl is not considered expert at all and merely finds what the customer asks for.

At the other extreme are sales engineers who help the customer solve a problem. Often the customer has high regard for their technical knowledge and relies on them to show how the products they are selling can be used effectively.

For most people the insurance agent is an expert upon whom they rely for help with insurance problems. They will accept his advice on the kind of insurance to carry, the amount of insurance, etc. Furthermore, he usually attempts to maintain a continuing relationship by periodic visits, reminders that policies must be renewed, and so on.

4. The nature of the product.

Products vary from standardized items such as the packaged shelf items in the supermarket to the complex technical products such as computers. The buyer of the standardized can of peas knows the product and needs little or no product information. The buyer of a computer, or machine tool, usually needs a great deal of technical information in order to make his buying decision.

In the first case, the salesman tends to try to influence the customer through interpersonal relationships. He tends to try to build close friendships, entertain the customer, give presents, and so on. Since there is little to tell the customer about the product the salesman's talk is often devoted to jokes and anecdotes, discussion of sports and hobbies, anything but business. His entertainment of customers often exemplifies the extreme of "expense account living."

With the complex technical products, technical "know-how" is more important than sociability. The sales engineer wins customers because of his ability to help them with technical problems and not because he is a jovial raconteur. In these situations, the friendship between salesman and customer is based on mutual interest in technical problems and respect for technical ability.

The four factors we have discussed are found in various combinations in every sales situation. The combination affects many aspects of sales management and sales supervision and also the qualities of the effective salesman.

Characteristics of Salesmen

When we examine the personalities of good salesmen we see certain characteristics which are generally important.

We will not attempt to go into the complexities of the psychodynamics of the characteristics but will confine our description to a simple behavioral level.

1. They are active and energetic. Selling, especially where the salesman must seek out the customer, is no job for the passive, lethargic person. The salesman must be able to take the initiative, seek out the customer, find ways to make contact, and make an impression.
2. They respond to the sales encounter as a challenge. Each such encounter is a situation in which they must overcome the resistance of the customer. There is a strong element of competitiveness, of aggressive desire to dominate, desire to win over the customer. Without this response to the challenge, the salesman is too readily stopped by lack of interest or by counter-

arguments and is apt to be stopped prematurely by normal customer resistance.

3. They enjoy interacting with people. They enjoy meeting customers and potential customers and try to make a good impression. Unless they can enjoy interaction with new people, the emotional effort needed to keep seeking out and developing new customers is too great.

4. They like clear-cut measurements of their performance, and respond to rewards based on immediate performance. They like the feeling that their sales record shows how well they are doing. Good sales results reaffirm their worth to themselves and to their company. They tend to prefer compensation and other rewards based directly on their sales performance. Each sales situation is a challenge, and they want the fruits of winning. Also they are not willing to await rewards in the distant future but want them now.

Compensation and Motivation

Most salesmen are paid on some plan which directly relates compensation to sales performance. There are three basic types:

1. Direct commission in which the salesman receives only a percentage of his sales. If he doesn't sell anything for a period of time he has no income.

2. Draw against commission. In these plans he receives a weekly or monthly payment which is charged against any commissions he earns. This provides a basic income during periods when sales are slow. However, over a period of time he is expected to bring in enough sales to more than cover his draw.

3. Salary plus commission. Here he has a basic weekly or monthly salary not dependent on sales. In addition, he receives a small commission on any sale.

The direct commission plan puts the most pressure on the salesman to produce, since no sales, no pay. It also leads to a more erratic income to which he has to adjust his way of living. This means great economic insecurity, with the risk that sickness or other mischance can terminate the income.

The salary plus commission is often used in industrial selling where the sales are large and require long periods of calling on, or working with, potential customers. For example, a sales engineer for custom designed equipment may work with a prospect for months or even years before a sale is completed.

For management, the straight commission provides the tightest control over selling costs, or at least salesman costs. (There are other selling costs not directly tied to sales volume.) On the other extreme, with salary plus commission, management may make considerable investment in salesman salaries in anticipation of sales which may never come off.

The commission serves as a direct and clear-cut motivation for the salesman. He is directly rewarded for a clearly defined performance. His feeling of his own worth is often tied to his sales volume, and each day or week he reaffirms his worth to himself and others.

However, the commission system alone is not sufficient to keep the salesmen exerting themselves to the utmost. If left alone salesmen tend to establish a comfortable equilibrium in terms of earnings, self-value and effort, and this is often below their potential performance. One of the constant problems of sales management is how to stimulate the salesmen to work harder, see more customers, close more sales. The attempts to stimulate increased sales effort cover a wide variety of contests, sales meetings, and special rewards and recognition.

15. WAGES AND WAGE SYSTEMS

THE CONCEPT OF WAGES

WAGES are the center of the most important transactional relationship in business. One thing practically everyone in industry has in common is that they work for pay.[1] They give of their time and effort and receive money in return, and this exchange represents some agreed-upon equivalence of value and some reciprocal rights and responsibility between employer and employee.

Wages represent one of the most complicated forms of transactions. When money is exchanged for an object, as when a woman shops in the supermarket, little else is involved or implied beyond the possession of the money and the object. But when a person accepts a job he is committing himself to a daily routine, a pattern of activities, an organization, and a wide range of interpersonal relations, and for this he receives wages. If he leaves the job, he leaves all this behind along with the wages. Thus, in exchange for this symbolic and exchangeable thing called "money," a man commits an important slice of himself, his efforts, and his life.

Because of these complications wages can be viewed in many ways, and each way is part of the complex meanings. Three of the important meanings are:

1. Wages are payment for the commodity called "labor."
2. Wages are a measure of the worth of the individual.
3. Wages place people in a status hierarchy.

All of these are true and all are constantly present in any work situation.

Management Looks at Wages

To the owner or manager of a business, wages are a necessity; they

---

[1] We are using the word "pay" as synonymous with wages or salary, but it should be noted that there is actually a certain amount of prestige or status difference in the terms. Executives usually receive salaries, and wages or pay are usually reserved for those at lower levels.

are the price he must pay to get people to work for him. In a sense, labor is to him a commodity which must be purchased just as he purchases coal or copper or other materials. In this sense the payment of wages is a simple economic transaction which may be governed by the same reasoning or logics as any other purchase, in which one endeavors to obtain the greatest quantity and highest quality possible for his money. Out of this comes the idea of a "labor market" in which employer and employee bargain over the services, or in which there are established scales of prices for various grades and types of the commodity. Unfortunately for the potential employee, he is like the farmer with a truckload of ripe tomatoes; if he does not sell today, the tomatoes will not be worth anything tomorrow.

Actually, to the employer the labor he purchases is not a simple commodity such as a sheet of steel, which he can buy according to certain specifications as to size, weight, strength, and chemical composition—all of which can be tested beforehand and which can be expected to remain stable. Labor as a commodity is even more perishable than the load of tomatoes, since it is the ability of a person to do work, and since this ability may vary from day to day and may be affected by all sorts of things. Management generally recognizes this and thinks of wages, not just as a payment for a simple commodity, but as a means of stimulating the individual to be a better and more effective worker. It feels, too, that the wages should promote a feeling of loyalty toward the company and enthusiasm for the work. Labor is not, then, like the load of tomatoes, because the tomatoes do not care whether their price is high or low and they cannot be motivated to make more or better soup.

Management also believes that with their wages they buy something more than so many hours of time. It is felt that the individual in return should give an appropriate amount of effort, should accept and adjust to the regimen of the work situation, and should give some degree of loyalty to the organization. The payment is not merely payment for time but is payment for participating acceptably in the organization and contributing to its success. What constitutes an appropriate reciprocity in these more or less intangible matters is usually ill defined and is more a matter of custom than of rational plan.

The act of hiring a person and of accepting a job is in effect a kind of covert bargaining in which the employer is saying, "I'll pay so much to hire you to do this kind of work." In reality in modern business there is little actual bargaining—the employer states the wage offered and the job-seeker accepts or rejects. (This is part of the fixed-price concept which is applied to consumer products—we no longer haggle over the price to pay.) However, whether either the worker or employer feels it is a fair wage offer is largely a matter of current custom; that is, the "going wage," or what others are paying for the same effort or type of job, is important in determining the "fairness" of any specific offer. The individual often rejects a wage offer on the grounds that he doesn't want to do that kind of work, or he can get more at some other type of job, even when agreeing that it is a fair wage for the job offered.

In setting the pay scale for jobs, management generally wants to keep the wages "in line" with what others pay for similar work. If they are paying much above what seems to be the generally accepted rates for a job, they feel that they are being very generous and fear that they may be wasting money. Many companies, however, pride themselves on paying above the average and justify it on the grounds that to pay high wages gives them the pick of the available labor supply and promotes loyalty and efficiency among their employees. Others feel that if they are paying the going rate on the jobs, then their wages are "fair" and the workers should have no complaints. Still other companies make a practice of paying no more than they have to, and they feel that unless they keep wages down they will have difficulty in meeting price competition on their products.

Determining how much to pay for a job is often a very haphazard procedure, especially in companies which do not have a union contract. You need a drill-press operator; so you hang out the "Help Wanted" sign; and when a drill-press operator comes in, you offer him about what you have been paying others for similar work. Or else you call a friend in another plant and ask what they are paying drill press operators at present. Or, if you want to be really "scientific" about it, you conduct a wage survey and compare your wages for various jobs with the wages paid by other companies. Or perhaps you make use of similar surveys conducted by groups of companies, trade associations, and so on. In any case, you come out with some idea of what the market is and what you may expect to pay.

A great many wage surveys ignore efficiency and productivity in their determination of the proper wage for any job. They arrive at the supposed market value of a job, expressed solely in cents per hour or dollars per week or month, with no correction for the fast or slow worker. In general, the assumption is that their figures are based upon average performance, but they do not specify just how much output should be expected for the wage. It is almost as if they quoted a market value for a commodity without considering quality. You pay a lathe operator so much an hour, and it is up to you to determine what is a proper day's work and to see that you get it. This is in keeping with the way most people look on jobs and on wages. For example, almost everyone has certain ideas about the value of various jobs. They think of a job, such as typist, toolmaker, or office boy, as paying about so much; and the person who is paid more or less than these amounts is considered well paid or underpaid. Very rarely do they think of differences in pay for similar jobs as being a result of differences in individual ability or effort. They do not think that Mary is paid less than the "fair" rate because she is not worth it, but only because her employer is a cheat who is taking advantage of her.

Wage Differentials

For factory jobs or all jobs requiring the use of tools or manual skill, there is a rough relation between the skill and training required and the wage. Thus the skilled worker is paid more than the semiskilled worker, the machinist more than his helper, and the machine operator more than the laborer. This relationship is, of course, a rough one and may be affected by other factors, as, for example, in certain jobs which have carried prestige and corresponding high pay over a period of years even though technological changes have reduced the actual skill required by the job.

If we look at the wage structure of any factory, we see that the wages themselves form a hierarchy which conforms roughly to the general status hierarchy and which usually forms a similar pyramid, with the majority of the people at the lowest wage levels and the head of the concern and the top executives in the highest wage levels. Thus the wages of the individual tend to place him in the general status hierarchy in relation to others. There is, in fact, a strong feeling that an individual's wages *should* reflect his status in the structure and that it is therefore "wrong" for a supervisor to earn less than his subordinates or for a person to be promoted without being given a raise.

In most companies we find that the wage structure divides the people into two major groups, usually referred to as the hourly rated people and the salaried people. This usually conforms to the office and shop division, the factory workers being paid on the basis of the number of hours they work, and the office or white-collar workers being paid by the week or month. Thus, we see a separation between people who work for "wages" and those who work for a "salary." As a rule, foremen and supervisors are placed in the salaried group. In addition to this major division, many large concerns further divide the salaried group, placing the higher levels in a separate group from the ordinary clerks and stenographers. Usually this division is reflected in differences in payroll and accounting procedures, and it may follow along strict lines of amount of salary or upon differences in function. In one company the division is based upon amount of pay; all salaried people who earn above $400 a month are paid once a month and are referred to as "monthly rated people," and all others are "weekly rated people." The top group are thought of as executives and are not required to punch a time clock. In another company, all executives and foremen are paid on what is called the "main office payroll," and their checks are sent out from the headquarters of the company rather than being made up in the individual plants. Such divisions are themselves status groups; and to move from the hourly to weekly payroll, from weekly to monthly, from plant to main office, is felt to be an increase in status, something which merits congratulations from the group and something to tell the wife with pride.

One interesting aspect of the division between hourly rated and salaried employees is that the groups generally have sharply different functions in the structure and that, within each group, there is a wage hierarchy which is quite independent of the others. The hourly rated people are shopworkers who are directly engaged in the manufacturing processes. They are the skilled and unskilled workers who run machines, handle tools, wear overalls, and get their hands dirty. In contrast are the salaried people who work with papers, handle the mechanics of controls, and tell the other workers what to do. They are the typists, secretaries, accountants, supervisors, and executives; they wear the clean clothes and the white collars.

The rate of pay of salaried people is not necessarily higher than that of the hourly rated people, however, in spite of their being a higher status group. In fact, in the lower levels the office workers may earn no more or perhaps less than the lowest level of shopworkers. For example, office boys or file clerks may be paid at rates as low as, or sometimes lower than, the lowest shop wages; and a boy or girl just out of high school can often earn more by starting work in the shop than in the office. There are, then, two separate wage hierarchies, and the status of the individual is determined by his position in these hierarchies as well as by the actual level of his wages. Thus the young fellow in an accounting job may feel that he has advanced over his father, even though his father earns more money as a machine operator in the shop.

Maintaining the proper wage differences between jobs is one of the problems of management. Those jobs whose wages are "out of line" in the status hierarchy, in the thinking of either the operators on those jobs or other workers, will be a source of complaint and trouble. For example, if you pay a helper as much as the machinist he works with, the machinist thinks either that the helper is overpaid or that he himself is underpaid. In fact, examination of any work group shows a fairly definite hierarchy of jobs; and if the wages for different jobs vary greatly from this accepted scale, the workers feel that the wages are "wrong."

In order to maintain a wage structure in which different jobs maintain the proper wage relationship to each other, many companies use a system of "labor grading" or "job evaluation." In these systems, jobs are graded on the basis of such factors as skill, education, learning period, and responsibility, so that they can be arranged on a scale ranging from the job having the most requirements to that having the least. At the same time, a wage scale is established with the highest-rated jobs in the top pay grade and the lowest-rated jobs in the lowest pay grade. Then the pay for any job will be determined by its place, as established by its evaluation. Such systems provide a systematic means of comparing one job to another or of placing a new job in the established hierarchy.

From the point of view of management, such systems are expected to serve two purposes. In the first place, they are expected to prevent complaints from workers or from unions that certain jobs are not paid properly in comparison to others. Undoubtedly, the systematic grading of jobs, if used consistently, does prevent serious variations in pay between jobs. If, however, the particular system does not place jobs about where the workers think they belong, the system itself will be the source of friction. For example, in one case where a job evaluation system was introduced, the grading of jobs reversed the relationship between two jobs, so that the job which had always been thought superior and more desirable was placed below the other job on the wage scale. This gave rise to so much friction and dissatisfaction that the management was forced to restore these jobs to their accepted relationships.

Job evaluation serves a second purpose for management as a means of establishing proper control of labor costs. By careful analysis of the jobs and comparison with similar jobs through wage surveys, it is possible to set rates which presumably approximate the "market value" of the work. Thus, if other companies are paying one dollar and fifty cents an hour for jobs with such-and-such requirements, the company is able to show that one dollar and fifty cents an hour is a fair wage for all their jobs having these requirements. This, in effect, prevents individual bargaining on jobs, a practice which often tends to push jobs out of line. For example, in large concerns it is customary for the executives to ask for raises for their secretaries; and because some executives are more aggressive or cleverer at justifying such raises, a great discrepancy results in the pay of secretaries on comparable work. Eventually someone investigates the pay of secretaries; some cost-minded top executive is shocked by the high salaries paid to some; and the company puts in a form of job evaluation by means of which secretaries can be graded and their salaries kept within certain limits.

The Worker and His Pay Check

To the wage earner his pay check is something much more complicated than money in his pocket or payment for services; and his attitude toward the fairness and adequacy of his pay is affected by many factors both within the factory and in the larger society. To begin with, as we have pointed out, his wages tend to place him in relation to all others in the factory system and, so, to direct and limit his relations with them to some extent. His place in the wage structure affects his attitudes and relations to Joe and Jim who work beside him, to the new man who has just started on the next bench, and to the women who are learning to run certain machines. At the same time, his ideas of what constitutes a fair or an adequate wage are, in part, a reflection of both these attitudes and relations and of his place in the wage hierarchy. This is particularly apparent when he or another worker associated with him is given a raise. When a raise is given to one worker in the group, that one usually feels that he has been set apart and is somehow above the rest. The others feel slighted, think they should have raises too, and assure themselves that they are just as good as he is. They all feel vaguely that they have lost status in relation to this one, and the effect is much as if everyone had been given a cut in wages except him. Their idea of a fair wage changes immediately, and all feel that what is fair for him is fair for them all. Very rarely will they admit that the other is a better worker, and they may claim that they have not had an opportunity to show their ability or to develop it as he has. In any case, the supervisor has on his hands a very dissatisfied group who are likely to turn against the favored one.

Besides these personal attitudes, there are some general beliefs among workers about the fairness of wages and job differentials. As we have pointed out, it is not considered fair to pay a machinist less than his helper or a foreman less than his workers. Sentiments toward length of service—either on the job, in the department, or in the company—also affect attitudes toward pay. A new man, for example, can not be brought into a job at more pay than others already on that job without causing resentment and dissatisfaction. Old-timers and experienced workers believe firmly that they should be paid more than newcomers or beginners. And the man who spent years as an apprentice feels that he is worth more than the man who learned the job through some speeded-up training program.

Another important consideration for the wage earner is the effect of his pay upon his life outside the factory. The size of his pay check has a very real influence upon his place in the community. It may limit and determine the kind of home he has, the neighborhood he lives in, and the friends he may acquire; and it is frequently a symbol by which others place him in the status system of the community. For instance, rent is often thought of in terms of a week's pay for a month's rent, so that a man earning $100 a week is likely to live in a neighborhood where he pays $100 a month for rent. As he increases his earnings, he will probably move to higher rental areas, where he can live according to his income. The man who makes $75 a week and lives in a $100 neighborhood often feels that he cannot quite keep up with his neighbors and is likely to think that his wages are inadequate.

An individual's ideas of an adequate wage are, then, a reflection of what he expects in the way of living conditions and comforts, association with others, recreation, and social place. His concept of an adequate wage is actually more a part of the way he thinks about himself and his whole way of life than a part of the job he does. From his point of view, an adequate wage is one which enables him to live in the kind of neighborhood, among the kind of people, to which he feels that he belongs. He should be able to have a car if the others do, wear the same kind of clothes, eat as they do, entertain in the same way, and generally spend his money as his friends and neighbors do. If his earnings do not permit these things, he worries about his relationships and his place in the neighborhood or community, and he thinks that his wages are inadequate and unfair. For example, a college graduate, son of a professional man, living in an upper-middle-class neighborhood, would feel that the $90 a week earnings of a shipping clerk were completely inadequate, since they would not enable him to maintain his accustomed relationships and activities in his community. On the other hand, a high-school graduate from a tenement neighborhood, whose father is an unskilled worker, might feel that he was doing well to make $70 a week.

In evaluating the fairness of his job and his pay, a worker does not usually think of it in terms of what the work is worth on the labor market, or in terms of what is fair pay for that kind of work, but in terms of what is fair pay for himself. In other words, an individual thinks of himself as having a certain value, quite aside from any particular job. This same attitude is seen when, for example, a highly skilled man is put on a less skilled and lower-paid job for some reason. He invariably feels that, since he has the ability to do more skilled and more valuable work, he should be paid accordingly. This does not mean that he thinks the job is worth more; in fact, he may quite agree that the job is only worth so much. It does mean that he has certain ideas of his own worth and of what wage he must have to maintain his established relationships and feelings of status.

Sometimes a wage may be adequate and still not be considered fair. There is, as we have pointed out, a rough correlation between status in the work hierarchy and rate of pay. In the community outside the factory, both these things—the kind of job he does and the size of his pay check, as demonstrated by his spending—are indications of the individual's status and importance at work. Each group in our society has certain ideas about what is a fair income for "people like them"; and members who earn less than is "proper" for their group generally feel sensitive and insecure, try to conceal the fact from their friends, and think that their rate of pay is unfair. Even an individual who has other income than his pay check, who has no actual financial difficulty in meeting the economic standards of his friends, is usually ashamed and apologetic if his wages are much below theirs. If his rate of pay does not indicate a work status comparable to that of his friends and neighbors, he may feel that it is unfair, even though he does not "really need" the money.

MERIT-INCREASE SYSTEMS

Management's Point of View

Management is inclined to believe that money is the principal motivation of people in industry and that, by proper manipulation, wages can be the most effective incentive to better work and greater production. Many top executives even assume that all difficulties between people at work, all problems of co-operation, can be solved by the proper wage formula. They believe that the economic difficulties of paying high wages in the face of stiff price competition is all that stands in the way of their having a loyal, enthusiastic, and efficient force of workers. As a result of such beliefs, the matter of proper wage policies and systems is of great concern to management. Probably every factory or business is interested in obtaining maximum results from the money spent, and is, therefore, always interested in wage systems which will provide effective incentives to their employees. Out of such interest a wide variety of wage systems have arisen, each one usually based on a few simple assumptions concerning the way in which money can serve as a motivating factor. The simplest system is that which may be called the "merit-increase," or "merit-raise," system, in which wage increases are granted at the discretion of management or other supervisors on the basis of an individual's performance and his value to the company. In theory, management, or its representatives, is watching the performance of every worker; and as one improves and demonstrates his increased value to the company, he is rewarded by an increase in his wages. Also, as one backslides and decreases in efficiency or value, his wages are cut. Such a theory puts management in the role of the all-wise and all-just, weighing every act and meting out rewards and punishments accordingly.

The individual working under such a system, whether a shop-worker, supervisor, or executive, is expected to be earnest and enthusiastic because he knows that he will receive a wage increase if he improves his performance. He should be enthusiastic in co-operating with others for the good of the job and the company because such co-operation will be noted and rewarded. He should be constantly trying to increase his knowledge of his own job and of others; he should be interested in the success of the company. He should not be critical of the policies or decisions of management but should be a "good soldier" and do his best to carry out the orders. If he does all these things well, his superiors will know it and reward him accordingly.

The Limitations

Unfortunately most such merit-increase systems have certain "bugs" in them and do not seem to work quite according to theory. For one thing, there are usually limits to the amount management will pay for any one job, so that the job one is on sets the ceiling beyond which he cannot go, no matter how much he improves. A janitor, for example, is usually paid less than a machinist; and no matter how hard the janitor works or how he improves his efficiency, he will probably never rise to the wage level of the skilled machinist. This means that, to rise beyond the limits set by a given job, the individual must move on to a higher-rated job. Since this movement is limited by the openings available, and since the higher-rated jobs are usually fewer than the low-rated jobs, it is obvious that hard work and self-improvement are not an automatic passport to continued wage increases.

Economic conditions further affect the merit raises. When times are good, management may be very generous with raises; but when business is bad, raises may be few and far between, because management believes that raises are an increase in costs which cannot be permitted under such conditions. The result is that, when business is bad, the wage progress of an individual is usually very slow, regardless of how much he improves his efficiency; while in good times he may progress rapidly with comparatively little effort toward improvement. To the worker who progressed very slowly to the top level for his job during bad times, it usually seems very unfair that people coming in during good times rise to his level very quickly.

In companies which have periodic rate revision, the amount of raises at any one period is continually being adjusted to meet conditions at that time. Top executives look over their budgets, estimate how much increase in payroll can be allowed, and decide that increases can amount to only a certain percentage of the total payroll for this period. The foremen's recommendations, which are usually too high for these estimates, will then be trimmed to fit the required percentage. In this way, management maintains the necessary control and, at the same time, gives the impression to the lower levels that a raise is not something to which they have a right because they have earned it but is something which may be given or withheld at the discretion of management.

Evaluating the Workers

The problem of evaluating the individual workers presents one of the most difficult and complicated problems in any such system. In the first place, there is the problem of what the executives expect from the individual. For what are they paying? Do they judge the individual's value solely on the basis of quantity of work produced, or will they pay for willingness to co-operate, for conscientious endeavor, for loyalty, dependability, and so on? And then how do they measure these things on which they base their increases? If output is the chief criterion, what happens to the fellow who sacrifices output for the sake of good workmanship, or who co-operates with others in the interest of the job as a whole, even though it cuts down on his own output? And what happens to the fellow who increases his efficiency very rapidly until he reaches his maximum and then cannot show further improvement, although he works at that same level of efficiency year after year? And what do you do for the conscientious worker who goes along, year after year, taking whatever jobs are given him without complaint, doing them well if not brilliantly, accepting the judgment and decisions of his superiors without question or doubt, and generally doing the best he can? Every worker knows what happens to him: he goes just so far and then stops getting raises.

In theory, merit increases are an expression of the increased value of the individual to the company and should, therefore, have little relation to what others do. Actually, there is considerable confusion when deciding upon the merits of an individual; and he is not measured against any absolute yardstick of value or by any set standards to show degrees of improvement, probably because such standards of measurement are almost impossible to devise. As a rule, an individual is compared, not with any scale, but with his own past performance or with the performance of others. Thus the individual who has shown pretty clear-cut and obvious improvement in performance may be judged deserving of a raise, or the one who is the most efficient of a group may be thought to deserve a higher wage than the others. There are, then, two different merit-raise policies. In one case, a person is working against his own past record and will be given a raise if he beats his own performance. In the other, members of the work group are competing with each other, and the one who does the best work gets the raise.

To further complicate the evaluation of individual workers, in many or even most jobs there is no simple way in which performance can be measured. This is especially true of office work or jobs that are quite varied in nature, so that the worker does not repeat the same routine operations over and over. Even where output can be measured, such as on routine machine jobs, it is still necessary to set up routine procedures for measuring it before output can be used as an absolute basis for determining increases. As a result, decisions as to merit are very often based upon the judgment of the boss. He gives raises—or recommends them—where, in his best judgment, they are deserved; and if a worker does not deserve a raise, he does not get one. In large organizations there is the added difficulty in that the immediate supervisor, especially at the foreman level, cannot make the final decision but must get approval for raises somewhere up the line. And when, as sometimes happens, some of his recommendations are turned down by those higher up, the foreman is furious but helpless. Probably the only thing which can make him madder is to have his superior give out merit raises to people whom he has not recommended.

Generally, merit raises are not based on simple clear-cut criteria but are affected by a number of different considerations. In some cases they seem to be given in response to pressure from the individuals. Joe, for instance, goes to his boss and says that he is dissatisfied and discouraged, that he has been working for two years without a raise, and that he feels his work has improved a lot and he is sure that he is doing better work than some of the others who are making as much as he is. He adds that the cost of living has gone up and that he had an offer of a better job elsewhere. The foreman thinks that Joe is a good worker who is conscientious; he has shown improvement and really deserves to be making more than that loudmouthed "griper" Jim. It is hard to replace men now, anyway; so he gives Joe a raise on the basis of merit. (There is always some doubt that such raises should be called "merit" raises.) The next day Joe tells the group that he got a raise, and Jim and the rest all ask for raises within the next few weeks. The foreman may give out a few more, and then his boss begins to ask questions about the sudden burst of improvement in the work group, since he has noticed little change in the cost reports. At that point the foreman stops giving raises and tells the group that he cannot give any more until they show him that they are really improving, that he only gave raises to those who were the most deserving. After that, it is likely that two or three fellows who have not had raises for some time will go out and get other jobs; or they may complain to their union steward, who will start working on the foreman.

In other cases, however, the wage policy is much better organized, and definite procedures are set up for the evaluation of the individual and the granting of merit increases. Some companies have periodic rating periods, at which time each supervisor must consider the work of each of his subordinates and make recommendations for merit raises. In some cases this is done individually, according to the time a person started with the company, so that a new employee is rated, for example, at the end of his third, sixth, and twelfth months of service, and annually thereafter. In other cases the entire company goes through a rating procedure at fixed dates, so that everyone is judged, and all raises given, at the same time.

Merit raises, no matter how they are handled, usually cause disturbances in the status relationships in the work group. By giving one worker a nickel raise for merit, even though deserved, and withholding it from another, the foreman or management is saying, in effect: "Joe, you are a better man than Jim, more valuable to us, and we think more of you." And Jim feels not only that Joe has received recognition but that, in a sense, he himself has been criticized, that his quality and worth have been questioned. When Joe tells his wife that he got a raise because of good work, she tells the neighbors proudly and repeats what the boss said to Joe about his value to the company. Jim's wife, on the other hand, wonders why he did not get a raise and is ashamed to tell the neighbors. She scolds Jim for telling her that he has been getting along all right, or she takes it out in being mad at the company and at his boss for not giving him proper recognition; and she is sure that that fellow Joe with the "snooty" wife must have a "pull" somewhere.

In theory, if raises are given for improved performance, then pay cuts could be given for poor performance. Actually, such pay cuts are very rare unless the individual is so poor that he is demoted to another job. This means that, as long as he stays on the same job, a worker will maintain whatever pay level he has reached. While this is not very logical from the point of view of costs, the sentiments are so strong against such penalties that few companies attempt to use them. A practice of giving cuts regularly would probably upset the morale of the entire group, since a cut in pay is a very serious blow to an individual's feelings of worth and to his status, relative to others in the group.

Another basic difficulty in the systems of merit increases is the implicit assumption that supervisors or management can make an accurate evaluation of the performance of an individual, relative to either his past performance or the performance of his fellows. Such an evaluation assumes that they have all the facts concerning his actual work and will consider the difficulties he encounters and the many factors which affect his work. It assumes that they can be very wise and just in their evaluation of the total situation and completely fair in their decisions. It assumes that they will not be influenced by prejudice, personal likes or dislikes, or friendships and that decisions will be based upon what a man does, not on whom he knows. Unfortunately, it rarely works that way, because there are always many intangible things which influence judgment and decisions; it is always easier to decide in favor of one person rather than another; and it is always difficult to make decisions which are completely fair to all those involved. And for the person who does not get a merit raise, even a fair decision is painful and difficult to accept.

There is, furthermore, in most work groups a certain measure of distrust of the ability of management to administer a merit-rate system fairly and satisfactorily. In some cases there is a strong distrust of the intentions of management, a feeling that no plan proposed by management would ever work to the benefit of the workers. The common complaint against almost any system of merit raises is that the foremen fail to evaluate people properly, that they play favorites or overlook the people who do not complain and make demands, that they do not take the proper factors into account, or that their superiors have these failings when they overrule a foreman who is trying to be fair. In other words, they do not trust their superiors as all-wise judges able to decide fairly for all.

In general, merit-increase systems are much more popular with top management than with foremen and other lower supervisors. Frequently, the big bosses are people who have come a long way on ability and merit. They believe firmly that an individual should be able to get ahead by hard work and application and that one who does do better than his fellows should be properly rewarded. Furthermore, since many of them have been motivated by a desire to get ahead, they often think that all others either do or should have the same drive and that they will respond enthusiastically to an opportunity to gain recognition. As a result, they believe that a merit system will be welcomed by the majority of workers and that it will offer management a powerful tool by means of which they can motivate their people to build a more effective organization.

Foreman's Point of View

For the foreman, however, it is often a different story, especially when he does not have final authority on raises. He would like to be able to reward his people properly at his own discretion; but he knows that final decision is in the hands of his superiors, who are often more concerned with costs than with rewarding the faithful. He realizes that wages play an important part in the status equilibrium of his work group and that careless adjustment of wages may create serious problems, problems with which he may have to deal for months to come. He knows that, no matter how conscientious he may be in granting raises, there will always be some who see only their own side and are critical and dissatisfied. Many foremen, in fact, would rather not have a merit system, since it so often engenders complaints and criticisms. One company, for example, had regular rate reviews at six-month intervals, when the foremen made their recommendations for raises. If times were bad and only a few raises were given, the workers who did not get them felt that it was unfair; if times were good and raises were generous, there were less complaints, but there were always some who felt that the foreman had been unfair in the amounts given, even if there was a general uniform increase for the whole group.

The Union Preference

As a result of all the complications and attitudes toward merit raises, it is quite common for unions to oppose such systems. In some cases, as one of its first moves, a newly organized union tries to force management either to do away with the system or to set up careful controls over merit raises. Even where merit raises have been in use for years, union officials usually respond to the flood of complaints after every raise period by demanding either drastic modifications in the system or its elimination. In its place they usually prefer a system in which raises are based upon service and are not dependent on a foreman's judgment. In such a system the progress of the individual within the rate range for his job is a matter of "right," and he does not feel that he has to play up to his boss in order to get ahead. Obviously, such a plan lacks the incentive features which are supposed to lie in the merit increases, but it is simpler from the point of view of the foremen and generally more satisfactory for the workers.

PIECEWORK SYSTEMS

Piecework is another wage system which is often in high favor with management. It is just what the name implies: a worker is paid according to the amount of work turned out, and the more he produces, the more he is paid. Such a system should provide the maximum of direct monetary incentive to spur workers on to greater and greater effort. In its simplest form, management establishes the amount it will pay for each unit of output, or each piece; and measurement of the output of the individual determines his earnings. It is very simple and direct in its basic principles, but it becomes very complicated in actual application.

This system has considerable appeal to certain of our ideas of what is fair, and especially to the idea that the individual who works hard and produces should be rewarded. As we have seen, to reward these hard workers through merit increases is a very difficult problem, and it is inadvisable to punish those who do not produce. All this is solved theoretically by piecework; when they work hard they get paid for it, and when they do not work hard they do not get paid. Each member of a work group will work out his position in the wage system without being dependent on the judgment or good will of his boss. Furthermore, the system itself is supposed to supply all the necessary incentive, so that the boss does not have to stand over his people and by weight of authority, threats, or kind words struggle to get them to do a fair day's work.

From the point of view of management, this system has the advantage of not only stimulating output, which it actually does, but of being an effective control of labor costs. When a rate is set for a given job, that fixes the amount which will be paid to the workers. Thereby the labor cost can be known before the work is actually done and will not be dependent upon the ability of the foreman to get the work out of his people. In actual practice it is not, of course, quite this simple; but, on the whole, it provides a much simpler control over labor costs than other methods. With such a system, however, there can be no savings in labor costs by improving the efficiency of the workers without cutting the rates, but that is a problem to be discussed later.

Piecework Variations

There are a number of variations of piecework systems. In the simplest of these, there is a price set for each unit of output; the output of each worker is measured, and he is paid accordingly. The rate itself is usually based on a determination of the expected output per hour of an average worker and the hourly rate for jobs of that level of skill. If, for example, it is estimated that an average operator can turn out ten units per hour, and if it is a semiskilled job for which you would pay $1.80 an hour, then the rate would be set at 18 cents per unit; and if the worker turned out twelve units, he would earn $2.16. Although all workers have an hourly rate which applies when they are not working on piecework, it does not affect their earnings on a piecework job of this kind. The $1.50 man who turned out twelve parts an hour would earn just as much as a $2.00 man who turned out the same amount. Thus the high-rated, experienced machine operator who was placed on a bench assembly job might actually earn less than the low-rated girls with nimble fingers who habitually worked on bench assembly. From the point of view of labor costs, with such a system it does not matter whether the worker is on a job fitted to his particular level of skill; but it does matter to the worker. Therefore, the machine operator usually insists that he be given jobs with rates such that he can earn more than the girls on bench assembly, so that he can maintain his proper place in the status system. In other words, the operators will not allow the piecework system to function so as to reduce the wage differentials between the top and bottom of the job hierarchy.

In most piecework systems today the operators are guaranteed their hourly rates. That is, they will be paid their hourly rates no matter how low their output. This protects them in case there are changes in the job, poorly set rates, or in case they are changed to new jobs. It puts a floor under their take-home pay and relieves some of their anxiety over changes which would lower output. It also sets a minimum level of performance as a goal for the foreman to shoot at. Since his labor costs will be high until his workers are earning their hourly rates, he prods the workers whose piecework earnings are below; and if they do not improve, he will want to get rid of them. In some plants there is a rule that a worker who does not reach this acceptable level of output within a certain period will be discharged.

Another variation of the piecework system is group piecework. Here the group, rather than the individual, is the unit for measurement of output and payment. Although each job may have a rate on it, no record need be kept of the work of each individual but only for the group as a whole. In calculating the earnings, the group is credited with all the work turned out, and this is distributed among the workers in proportion to their hourly rates and time worked. Thus, every member of the group shares with the others and is interested in the way the group as a whole works. This is expected to encourage group unity and co-operation and to develop group discipline over slow or lazy workers. In this system the hourly rates become important because they directly affect earnings; the earnings of each individual in the group are determined by this hourly rate, relative to the others, rather than by his efficiency.

Another variation is the use of "time" rates, in which the rate is set in units of time rather than in units of money. In the preceding illustration, for example, the rate which was set at 18 cents per unit under money rates, would be 0.1 hour per unit under time rates. If the operator turned out twelve units per hour, he would receive credit for 1.2 hours of output and would be paid 1.2 times his hourly rate. In this system the hourly rate again directly affects earnings, since the $2.00 man who turns out twelve units will earn $2.40, while the $1.50 man turning out the same amount will earn only $1.80. This protects the high-rated worker who may be placed on low-rated jobs and maintains the differentials in earnings between low- and high-rated people.

Limiting Piecework Earnings

It might be supposed that piecework would provide an opportunity for the worker to increase his earnings far beyond the normal level of pay for his particular job. Actually, however, this is not the case, because on most piecework jobs there is a clearly defined ceiling beyond which the worker does not attempt to push his output and earnings. From the point of view of management, there are two concepts operating to prevent unlimited increase of piecework earnings. In the first place, the worker on straight daywork is expected to do a fair day's work, which is somewhere near the upper limits of his capacity. Piecework is looked on as a device for stimulating him to give that extra push, to extend himself to the limit; and the limit should be only a moderate increase over what can be expected of him without the extra incentive. In some cases the possible increase is assumed to be only 15 per cent, but in others it is supposed to be 25 per cent.

Furthermore, in keeping with the general point of view concerning labor costs, if a worker on a certain job is earning far above the accepted daywork rate for the kind of work, management is likely to feel that it is paying too much for the job. This is especially true when there is no generally recognized standard of output by means of which management can compare its labor costs for the job with the labor costs of other companies. Since this is true of almost all jobs, there is usually a feeling that you are paying too much if your workers earn a great deal more than workers on comparable jobs in other companies. If other companies can get people to do those jobs for so much less money, there is no need for you to pay more.

Setting the Rates

The key problem in any piecework system is the setting of rates. This may be done in a number of ways, the simplest of which is to have an experienced foreman estimate either what the rate should be or how much hourly or daily output should be expected. If the job is not a new one, the rate can be based on average figures of past performance. Such methods are at best rather inaccurate and are not often used. In order to obtain more accurate rates, methods of time and motion study have been developed by means of which the proper methods of doing a job are determined and the exact time necessary is measured. In theory, proper study will produce an exact rate which is not a product of judgment but is the result of "scientific" measurements. Such rates are supposed to be so exact that all variations in earnings on a job will be the result of differences in skill or effort of the operators. Furthermore, with such accurate rates there should be no cases of excessively high earnings or low earnings, and labor costs can be held firmly in line.

Unfortunately, this ideal of completely accurate and "fair" rates is probably never achieved. There are always what the workers refer to as "fat" or "loose" rates, on which it is easy to make high earnings, and "lean" or "tight" rates, which are hard to make. This is a continual source of dissatisfaction on the part of the workers, since the men fortunate enough to be on jobs with fat rates can earn more with less effort than those on lean rates. This leads to friction and quarreling within the group; and if the foreman controls the distribution of jobs, he is continually being accused of playing favorites in the way he apportions the fat and lean jobs.

This problem of fat and lean rates is a source of concern to management, too. As we have seen, if the rates are too fat, management feels that it is paying too much for the work. This, combined with the friction which arises in the work group, makes foremen and executives all feel that it would be desirable to keep rates "in line," that something should be done about rates which are too fat or too lean. While the workers also feel that something ought to be done about the lean rates, they are bitterly opposed to any change in the fat rates. There is, in fact, a common belief that the principal function of piece rates is to enable management to get more work out of them for less money. As a result, management is always welcome to increase any lean rates, but cutting fat rates is considered a very despicable act. Indeed, rate cutting often leads to strikes and labor troubles and is outlawed in many union contracts. Many piecework systems guarantee no reduction in rates without a change in methods, that is, a change in the way the work is done. This does not prevent management from increasing rates whenever they feel it is necessary, nor does it prevent the workers from asking for increases when they think a rate is too low.

Individual piece rates are likely to require elaborate systems of records and controls. If the work is broken down into simple units, each performed by separate workers, then a rate must be established for each unit. If, for example, the processing of a particular part requires grinding of a rough casting, drilling two holes, and tapping the holes, then the work may be broken down into three operations, each handled by a different operator, and there may be three separate piece rates. Furthermore, it is necessary that the parts each operator processes be inspected to see that the work is done properly and counted in order to determine his earnings. Under some conditions, piece rates may be impractical because of the difficulty and expense of either setting the rates or of maintaining the system.

In group piece work the problems are somewhat different. In some cases, all the group may be on the same type of operation, such as drill presses; but in others the group may perform a sequence of operations on the same objects. In the first case, the rates are set as in individual piecework; but in the second, the rates may be set on the entire sequence rather than on each separate operation. Then the work can be measured and inspected after the final operation rather than at each stage, since the group performs all operations within the sequence. This reduces inspection and counting costs, and the larger the group the cheaper and easier it is to administer.

With group piecework the earnings of the individual and his status in the group are directly affected by his hourly rate. When they are paid on a money rate, however, the distribution of hourly rates within the group does not affect labor costs but affects only the distribution of piecework earnings within the group. Changes in hourly rates can, therefore, be made without affecting costs, and there is a tendency for management to be fairly lenient in giving increases in hourly rates. Any such change does affect relations within the group, however; and when one gets an increase in rate, he increases his earnings at the expense of those who are not increased. With time rates, on the other hand, the labor cost under group piece rates is directly affected by the hourly rates of the members of the group. As a result, management is much more careful in the way it gives out raises, since every raise increases not only the earnings of the individual but also the labor costs of the job. This is considered fairer to the workers, however, since a rate increase for one worker does not penalize the others.

RATE SETTERS

Activities and Functions

In a shop that uses piecework, rate setters have a very important role; and because of their activities and functions, they may be seen as a control group. Rate setting determines labor costs of the products; it has direct effect upon the earnings of the workers; and their piece-rate earnings reports are in many plants an important source of information for management. The man who sets the rates is the one who can keep costs down or let them go up; he makes the rate fat or lean for the workers; and he gets the blame from either side or from both when the system does not work. In large plants there is usually a piece-rate organization which is set apart and functions somewhat like a staff organization. When a new job is brought into the shop, members of this organization are called in to set the rate; and once the rate is set, the accounting routines do the rest without further aid from the piece-rate organization. Thus the rate setter seldom goes into a department where everything is running smoothly and where there are no changes, but spends most of his time where there are new jobs or where rates are in dispute. In effect, his presence is a sign of difficulties or change in the shop.

Relations with the Shop

One of the outstanding features of the relations between the piece-rate organization and the shop is the constant suspicion and antagonism between the two. Interviews with workers show a consistent suspicion of piece rates and rate setters. This is so widespread that it seems almost to be one of the attitudes which is transmitted from parent to child among workers and is not necessarily learned from experience in the work situation. For example, it has been observed that young people on their first factory jobs show concern and slow down their work when a rate setter comes into the department. As a result of this distrust, workers carefully regulate their work pace and work behavior whenever a rate setter is present.

The foreman usually shares the suspicions of his people and sides with them against the rate setters. From his point of view it is important that the rates be fair or even fat, since then his people can make satisfactory wages without difficulty or complaints. He must see that there is slack in the job to take care of delays, breakdowns, or other emergencies without affecting either output or earnings, so that he can make the proper showing on the earnings reports. He is constantly in the position of defending his group against the piece-rate organization. He often feels that he should study every rate before it goes into effect; that he must look for errors in it especially of operations overlooked or difficulties underestimated; and that, if there is too much trouble in making the rate, he must demand a review and insist that it was set too tight. And if the earnings drop on new jobs, he usually excuses himself on this ground, complains that the rates are too tight, and wants his boss to do something about them. As a result, the foreman and his superiors frequently find themselves in conflict with the piece-rate organization.

For his part, the rate setter is prone to be critical and suspicious of the shop. He often suspects that the workers are trying to put something over on him; he feels that he is really looking out for the interests of the company, while the foreman is more concerned with keeping his people satisfied than with keeping costs down. This becomes especially apparent when there is a large piece-rate organization. Then the rate setters can associate with their own kind and sometimes tend to draw away from other organizations, to eat and play in isolation together, and to put up a defensive front toward the whole shop organization.

Rate-Setters' Logics

Every piece-rate organization has a very definite set of beliefs regarding the function of piece rates in general and its own organization in particular. They have firm convictions about economic motivations and the way wage incentives should operate. Usually they accept as self-evident the theory that the desire for more money is the strongest motivating factor for all people, including shopworkers. Furthermore, they usually believe that the proper wage incentive should overcome problems of lack of co-operation, restriction of output, poor morale, and so on. They feel that, since the opportunity to earn more money is such a boon to the workers, piece rates and their services in setting rates should be welcomed by workers and shop supervisors. Therefore, when they meet with antagonism and suspicion, they are likely to think that the shop people are ignorant and uncooperative and "don't know what is good for them." When a rate does not work, that is, when the shop claims that it is too tight and that they cannot make any bonus on it, rate setters are inclined to believe that the failure is due either to the shop supervision, which does not organize the work or keep the job going smoothly, or to the attitude of the workers, who will not co-operate. The fault must be in the shop, never in the rate. Probably most rate setters or wage-incentive men will feel that this is an unfair accusation or even a misrepresentation of their attitudes. They are convinced that they reach their conclusions through sheer logical examination of facts and that the attitude of the worker represents a lack of understanding of piecework and a pigheaded refusal to accept the good intentions of the piecework organization. Among themselves they may admit the existence of tight and loose rates; but according to the logics of rate setting, such rates are mistakes and should not exist. However, in the face of the general suspicion, antagonism, the widespread restriction of output under piece rates, and the frequency with which wage-incentive systems fail to work satisfactorily, it might be well to re-examine some of the logics of human motivation and try to see a more complete pattern of why people act the way they do.

Large piece-rate organizations sometimes develop both a high degree of interaction as a group and a uniformly defensive front toward outsiders. Under such conditions they tend to be suspicious of members who become friendly with outsiders, especially with shop people. A rate setter, for example, who develops very friendly relations with a certain shop department may be suspected of buying this friendship by setting fat rates on the jobs in that department. His superiors may feel that such friendships will prevent him from being objective in his rate setting and will make him prone to accept shop complaints about the rates without examining the merits of the cases critically. In other words, it is often felt that a rate setter cannot be both friendly to the shop and loyal to his own organization. It is probably true, in actual fact, that the rate setter who is friendly with the shop is more sympathetic with the shop's complaints about rates and with their ideas of fair rates than the rate setter who does not like the shop and is suspicious of their ideas.

Such attitudes are, however, contradictory to some of the basic assumptions of piece rates. Piece-rate organizations, as mentioned earlier, usually take the position that rates can be set so accurately that, for a given expenditure of energy, an experienced worker will earn exactly the same amount on different jobs—in other words, that earnings on different jobs will vary directly with the ability and effort of the workers and that there need be no fat or lean rates. This belief is often expressed in the statements that rate setting is a "scientific measurement" of the elements that go into the job and that it is completely "objective." It is thought to be in a class with other forms of measurement which can be reduced to simple operations in which the judgment of the operator plays little part. Unfortunately, and inevitably, with any except the simplest sorts of operations under most uniform conditions, the rate setter introduces into the rate many of his personal judgments regarding such matters as what constitutes an average worker operating at normal speed, what variables to take into account, or what unusual conditions must be allowed for. If rate setting were the completely objective procedure which many claim it should be, furthermore, then there would be no need for concern over friendships between rate setters and the shop, since the work could always be checked by examination of the objective evidence, or another rate setter working independently would always get the same answer.

One effect of the assumption that rates can be set which will be exact and scientifically accurate is to stimulate the search for better methods and for more accurate work. As a result, modern rate setting has moved far from its earlier methods. There have been elaborate studies of the motions required to do certain jobs; there have been detailed measurements of various motions; there have been careful techniques of measurement devised. This has led to more uniformity in rates and has reduced the possibility of excessively fat or lean rates. At the same time, this produces a tendency for the rate-setting organization to increase in size. In their attempts to do a better job they tend to increase the intensiveness of their work and expand their force, adding more specialists along with more elaborate techniques. Thus, as with other staff and control organizations, their preoccupation with their own special field acts as a pressure toward both refinement of techniques and expansion of force. And over a period of time we see that this pressure is blocked by management. At some point the big boss has to say no, and the organization is filled with feelings of frustration and anxiety.

An Illustration

The following excerpt from a study of one factory shows how one wage-incentive organization operates, and illustrates some points of this discussion:

The organization has certain beliefs which it uses to explain its activities; and these have become identified with the organization itself, so that any admission that the concepts are inadequate would be an admission that the organization itself is inadequate. One of these is the belief that piece rates are wage incentives, that they are a means of getting the employee to produce more because he will be paid more. While they recognize that piece rates may be thought of as a cost control, they feel that such functions are incidental to their primary function as wage incentive. Furthermore, the piece rate is regarded as a product of scientific measurement which is something final and absolute; and if the rate setter applies proper techniques, he will arrive at the correct rate for the job.

While they admit within the organization that a rate is "out of line," they always look on such as a failure of techniques rather than as any failure in their basic assumptions. These admissions of failure are found only when rates are "fat." Apparently, no rate considered "tight" by the shop will be admitted to be other than the exact rate for the job. Thus "fat" rates are mistakes, and "tight" rates do not exist as far as the organization is concerned.

The rates in this plant are supposed to be set with a 15 per cent incentive. That is, a group working at maximum efficiency should earn 15 per cent above the base rates. Since there are admitted to be individual differences in skill, there is expected to be a possible variation from this of 10 per cent so that the groups should earn between 5 per cent and 25 per cent. Actually, there is a great variation from this ideal with some groups going "in the hole," that is, earning less than their base rates, and others earning 70 per cent or 80 per cent.

Since these extreme variations are considered to be "wrong," the organization must find acceptable explanations for them. And to be acceptable the explanations must fit the concepts of the organization. For example, a department which was on a fairly new job was running far "in the hole." This was at first explained on the grounds that the group was inexperienced in the work and that the job was poorly organized. As earnings rose gradually over a period of

WAGES AND WAGE SYSTEMS 345

time, this was pointed out to prove that the rates were correct. When improvement stopped with the earnings still below the base rates, the piece-rate organization claimed that the workers and foremen were unco-operative and were not trying to increase earnings.

In another case, there was a group with extremely high earnings on a job which had been running without change for a number of years. Since this suggested that the rates were wrong, the piece-rate organization made a careful study of the job, with the idea of finding changes in methods which would justify changes in rates or else finding an acceptable excuse for the high earnings. The job was such that no changes in method seemed possible; so under company policy the rates could not be changed. The organization prepared an explanation, which was announced to all rate setters. They explained that the workers were all men with long experience on that job and were unusually efficient. Furthermore, they took special pains to learn all the instructions on the job, would even take the blueprints and instructions home and memorize them in their spare time. Thus they could work steadily without stopping to read the instructions or check the prints.

For smaller deviations from what were considered the proper earnings, there were a few stock explanations. When only a little above 20 per cent or 25 per cent, the groups were spoken of as efficient; and if earnings were low, the group was called inefficient in terms of poor organization or supervision or inexperienced workers. When earnings went much above 25 per cent, they explained that there must have been changes in methods of which they had not been notified.

The higher levels in the piece-rate organization kept a close watch over the piecework earnings of every shop department as one of their controls over the functioning of their own organization. If there was any sharp change in earnings for any department, someone from the organization would go to the shop foreman to investigate the cause. Regardless of the explanation given by the shop, it was restated in keeping with the concepts of the piecework organization. For example, in one case there was a sharp drop in earnings in a department having a combination of machine work and assembly work. The foreman explained that the machine rates were tight and the assembly rates loose, so that any change in proportions of work affected the earnings of the department as a whole; and for that month most of the work had been in the machine section. In reporting back to his superior, the investigator said the drop in earnings was due to the relative inefficiency of the group on machine work. Nothing was said about fat or lean rates.

Rate setters are aware of the antagonism of the shop and sometimes remark: "Those guys are lazy and don't like us because we make 'em work." In one case where a group was having trouble in making the rates on a conveyor assembly job, the rate setter pointed out to the foreman that the workers would slow down the conveyor when they could not keep up. He suggested what he called a "slacker-proof" conveyor which could not be controlled by the workers. The foreman replied that the idea might work but that he could get the same results with a horsewhip. The rate setter said he was wasting time trying to help out the shop foreman and might as well give his idea to his superiors and get credit for it.

Another type of defensive behavior was shown when the company decided that the foremen should be given a better understanding of the piecework system. A series of meetings were arranged at which supervisors from the piece-rate organization would explain the system and answer the questions of the shop foremen. In preparation for this the piece-rate organization prepared a series of questions which might be raised, and the higher levels worked out the acceptable answers to these questions. Copies of the questions and answers, which were called "The Bible," were given to the supervisors, who were to attend the foremen's conferences so that they might all give the proper answers to any questions.

16. WAGE INCENTIVES AND RESTRICTION OF OUTPUT

To those who hold to the theory that economic motivations are the principal motivations of all workers, wage incentives—and especially piecework—appear to be the perfect solution to many of the problems which plague management. If one accepts the idea that to each worker nothing is so important as the opportunity to make more money, then any system which would enable him to earn more should be received with enthusiasm. Some theorists have even felt that workers were so "money hungry" that they were likely to overwork themselves on piecework. Actually, such simple faith in the incentive value of piecework has rarely been justified in actual practice, and we are forced to conclude that individual motivation is a much more complex matter than the theories imply.

RESTRICTION OF OUTPUT

Careful observation of many work situations makes it quite clear that restriction of output in some form exists in practically every plant, on all sorts of jobs, and under all kinds of payment systems. It is so common as to be taken for granted by most experienced workers; and one of the first things the man on the new job wants to know is: "How much is a day's work?" The newcomer who does not abide by the accepted standards of the group usually has it called forcibly to his attention. In fact, it often happens that such limitations are much more strictly adhered to on piecework than on daywork.

Concepts and Beliefs

On nearly every job there is some concept of a day's work which serves as a standard of performance for the group. It is rare to find a job on which the only measure is "as much as you can do"; almost always there is some definite amount against which an individual can measure himself. To understand restriction of output, it is necessary to understand how these standards become established and what ends they serve for the group.

One of the most important factors in limiting output is the general suspicion which workers have of the motives of management. Especially when it comes to output, the workers feel that management is primarily interested in getting more for their money. Almost invariably they look on piecework not as a means for them to earn more money but rather as a method by which management can get more work out of them. Such attitudes are usually justified, too, since management does quite consistently look on piecework, or any wage-incentive plan, as a system for increasing the efficiency of the workers. The important thing about these attitudes of workers is that they so often feel that they cannot win in the long run but that they will end up by doing more work without significant gain in wages. Workers believe, too, that if their earnings are too high, their rates will eventually be cut. This is quite consistently believed, even when management has assured them that no rate will be cut without definite change in method. Even where there are union contracts protecting them against rate cutting, workers still cling to this belief; and almost every experienced worker can tell of cases from his own experience when rates have been cut.

In the case of straight day wages or daywork, the fear is that any increase in output over what is customary will make the boss expect them to do more work all the time. If one worker exceeds the others, they all feel that his record will become a goal which they will all be expected to reach. Thus, the more one does, the more is expected of him; he just cannot win.

Establishing Ceilings

Out of all these expectations, quite clear ideas inevitably develop as to how much output is proper or "safe" for any job. On daywork jobs, it is expressed in units of output—so much is a day's work. One executive told how he learned this fundamental truth when he took his first job on the line gang of a telephone company. He said: "The first day I was on the job they put me to digging post holes. I was a young punk just out of college—ambitious, and eager to win approval. So I was really getting those holes dug when an old-timer came over and said, 'Hey, Bub, three holes is a day's work.' So I saw the light and dug three holes, no more."

With piecework, especially where the individual handles a variety of work with different rates, the day's work is usually expressed in terms of earnings rather than in units of output. If $2.00 an hour is considered the proper earnings, each worker will watch to see that his output does not exceed that amount. If he is working an eight-hour shift, then, when his earnings amount to $16.00, he will stop work and kill time; or he will help someone else, or hold over any additional output for the next day.

The way in which these ceilings are established is often not very clear and may involve a number of factors. On any new job, one of the first questions the workers ask of the foreman is how much output is expected. Then, after they have worked on it for a time, there gradually develops some idea of what can be thought of as a fair day's work; usually this is kind of a balance between what the foreman would like to have and what the group finds it possible to do. If they find that they can come up to the foreman's expectations without too much effort, they may soon level off at that point. If his sights are pretty high, they may level off somewhat below that point and may resist any further efforts on his part to increase output. He may then gradually modify his demands until they reach an agreement on what he will accept and what they will do. All this goes on rather under cover—with the foreman prodding them to do more and with the group finding all kinds of reasons for not being able to do it—until finally an agreement, often unstated, is reached.

In many cases the ceiling on piecework earnings grows out of the general idea of a fair wage for the type of work. When earnings rise much above what is generally accepted as a fair wage, the workers begin to wonder what management will think about it; they wonder if they have not gone far enough and soon begin to restrict. A few comments about the possibility of management cutting the rates, and the ceiling is soon fixed.

In some cases the accounting routines have been observed to set a very definite ceiling on piecework. In one piecework system, which was mentioned earlier, it was believed that 25 per cent was good earnings; and anything above that must be due to exceptional circumstances. While a few jobs showed earnings over 50 per cent, they were viewed with considerable concern by the rate setters, who felt that the rates were out of line. They further assumed that any earnings above 100 per cent were impossible; and when the records showed such high earnings, it was assumed that there was either an accounting error or else the worker was putting something over. For that reason, no payment of over 100 per cent could be made without the specific approval of the superintendent, which meant that all such cases would be investigated. As a result, the foremen let the workers know that it was best not to earn as much as 100 per cent; 95 per cent was all right, since it would be paid automatically without discussion; but 100 per cent meant that the superintendent would be asking questions and looking on the department with a critical eye, that the rate setters would be looking the job over, and that the accounting organization would be checking over all records—all looking for something wrong. Inevitably, no worker earned 100 per cent; that was the absolute ceiling and nobody would think of violating it.

Controlling Output

Usually a work group likes to keep the output level at a point where the individual can maintain acceptable production without too much effort. This does not mean that the workers prefer to just loaf on the job. Actually, most workers prefer not to kill time deliberately; but they do not want to be under too much pressure. They also like to feel that, if they have trouble with the job or are not feeling well part of the day, they can speed up and can make up losses later. In other words, they like to have something in reserve for emergencies; and this reserve means a work pace and level of output well below what is easily possible for the fastest workers in the group.

The control of output usually lies in the hands of the work group. They come to an informal agreement as to how much is a day's work and then exert pressure on the individuals to see that they all abide by the limits. As we have seen, a new worker is informed of these limits, and they usually police him to see that he accepts them. If he does not, he will likely become an outcast, will be the butt of jokes and "kidding," may have difficulties with his tools or his work, and will have his life made unpleasant generally. Most workers soon succumb to such pressures and accept the dictates of the group, or else they become so unhappy that they quit the job. The "rate buster" is, in fact, almost always a source of friction and a center of disturbance —so much so, that he is often not even liked by the foreman in spite of his high performance.

In many instances the foreman knows that there is restriction of output and accepts it as a matter of course. In fact, as long as his group is performing to the satisfaction of his superiors in terms of output, costs, or however they judge him, he is not apt to be very concerned over a certain amount of restriction. As long as the group works together smoothly, turns out the work expected of them, and responds to any emergency demands, he is perfectly willing for them to go along at whatever pace suits them best. He himself may, in fact, limit their output if he thinks any increase will call undue attention to the group. Just as in the case where earnings exceeding 100 per cent were investigated, the foreman is ever on the alert to prevent anything from calling excessive and critical attention to his group; and if high output or earnings may do it, he will act to limit them. He may do this directly by telling the operators what the ceiling is, or he may do so by manipulating the work. If he thinks that the high output of a rate buster may call attention to the customary ceiling of the group, for example, he may keep moving the rate buster around on different jobs to prevent his developing speed on any one; or he may give him the jobs with the lean rates or put him on daywork jobs. Such practices are, of course, viewed with horror by higher executives or by rate setters, but they are perfectly natural adjustments to the pressures under which the foreman must operate.

Output Records

The concern of either the workers or the foreman over attracting undue attention to the group often results in the control of output. For one thing, high executives, in watching the various reports, usually question any sharp fluctuation from normal or any changes which run counter to what they expect. Output records based on department or work group are usually watched closely; and in the case of piecework, there may be records of the average earnings of the group. As a result, the foreman is likely to be questioned concerning sharp or unexpected fluctuations in these records. In case of a drop in either output or earnings, he may be criticized for failing to keep the job running smoothly; or in case of a sudden jump, executives may wonder why he has not kept output at these levels before and may expect him to keep it up in the future. To avoid this, he prefers to have the job run pretty evenly with little fluctuation or with only those fluctuations which are obviously due to changes beyond his immediate control and for which he will have adequate alibis. Thus, the "straight-line" output, or earnings, records are to the foreman and the work group the "safest" and the most desirable.

To maintain such straight-line performance is not so difficult on long-running jobs—that is, jobs in which the same operations on the same products are performed day after day. In such jobs, the workers can perform the same operation over and over, and an even work pace can be maintained. On irregular jobs, where different parts or operations are met with daily, there may be a constant shifting of workers and work pace. In any case, the foreman will try to keep some sort of records so that he will know just where he stands with respect to maintaining a straight-line output record. He prefers to have the average work pace at a level where he can, if necessary, call on the group for more output without too much resistance. Under such conditions he can maintain an even record, in spite of difficulties or delays, by taking up a little slack in the system.

A good example of this was observed in a department working on group piecework and making electrical switchboards. The orders were usually for relatively small lots, so that the workers rarely worked day after day on one routine operation but were constantly being changed from job to job. Two important control reports were the monthly piecework earnings of the department and the monthly "fall-down" report, or record of orders not delivered on the date promised. The manufacturing interval on many of the orders was fairly long, and the delivery dates were not very tight; so they did not have to rush each order out as soon as received but could plan the work over several weeks. The foremen in the department always tried to organize their work with these two reports in mind and, during the month, would keep informal records to show where they stood on the orders which had to be delivered that month and where they stood on their cumulative piecework earnings for the month. Thus, if they were falling behind on an order, they might shift a lot of the workers onto that job and let some other less-pressing job wait. In this way, they could make deliveries on time and stay off the "fall-down" report. At the same time, they would watch piecework earnings, especially after the middle of the month; and if it looked as if they were falling behind, they would shift their people onto the simple orders, which could be rushed through in time to clear inspection and be paid for on that month's piecework. Or they would put as many as possible to work on the final stages of work in progress in order to get it finished that month. If they seemed to be ahead on their piecework earnings, they would put the group on the difficult jobs which would not be completed that month; or they would take them off the final stages of work and put them on the beginning operations of jobs just starting. This would stop the movement of finished work into the inspection department and accumulate unpaid-for time in work in progress. By close watch over the details and careful juggling, they were thus able both to make deliveries and to control the piece-work earnings, so as to prevent serious fluctuations.

In another department, the foreman used individual output records as a method of keeping track of what was going on. He had each operator turn in a daily report of all the work he did. Each operator had to show the job he had worked on, the quantity of parts used, and the time spent. This was a sandblasting job on which each operator might work on one job all day or on eight or ten small jobs, each with a different piece rate. The operators had a definite idea of a fair day's work, and before they turned in their output records they would carefully figure their earnings for the day. If too low, they would claim some lost time; or if several were on the same job, the fast workers would let the others have part of their output. If too high, they would either "give it away" or just not report part of the work actually done. This did not affect their earnings, since it was group piecework and since they were paid on the basis of work actually finished and delivered to inspection, rather than on the operators' reports. However, the work shown on the daily reports was never quite what was accounted for by inspection. While they approximated a straight-line output record, they were careful not to show the same earnings day after day. They said that the foreman knew that no one could work at a perfectly even pace on that job; so if they maintained a perfectly even straight-line record, he would know that they were making it "with the pencil" or controlling it in other ways. For that reason they always saw to it that their reports fluctuated slightly from day to day in order to "give the boss what he wanted."

In this same department it was interesting to see how the concept of the proper learning curve for a worker on a new job operated. One old-timer had been brought in from another totally different job and put on sandblasting. He had had experience on sandblasting years before and picked up the work very rapidly. He watched his daily reports very carefully, however, and showed only a moderate increase each day, even though he was well below what was considered a fair day's work and was not working very hard. When asked about the work, he said that he could have reached the average output within three days but was careful not to progress too fast. He explained that the proper learning curve for a new man on the job was one which showed fairly rapid improvement for about a week and then a gradual slowing of progress, so that it would take several weeks to reach average output. He was making his output conform to this proper pattern, since, if he improved too fast, the foreman would know that the group were taking it fairly easy and would try to make them increase their output.

A Study of Restriction

While most of the phenomena which we have been discussing are fairly common knowledge to anyone with much factory experience, there have been few attempts to study them in detail. Probably the most careful study of restriction of output and its related factors is that made at the Hawthorne Works of the Western Electric Company. The following excerpts taken from the detailed report on the Bank Wiring Observation Room, which worked on a group piece-work system, may serve to illustrate this discussion.[1]

In interviews with the operators in the department before the study began, the investigators encountered certain beliefs which the employees seemed to hold in common. Chief among these was the concept of a day's work. This idea kept cropping up in interview after interview. Of the thirty-two men interviewed in the department before the study began, a group which included the nine wiremen later selected for the study, twenty-two discussed rates of output. Of these twenty-two, twenty said that the wiring of two equipments constituted a day's work. The other two men said they were supposed to try to make the bogey, which they correctly stated as 914 connections per hour. . .

From comments such as these it was apparent that the operators were accustomed to thinking of two equipments a day as a day's work. This was verified by the observer, who found that the operators frequently stopped wiring when they had finished their quotas even though it was not officially stopping time. This concept of a day's work was of interest for two reasons. In the first place, it did not refer to the bogey or any other standard of performance officially imposed. . . .

In the second place, the idea of a day's work was of interest because it was contrary to one of the basic notions of the incentive plan. Theoretically, the incentive plan was intended to obviate the problems attendant upon the determination of a day's work. . . .

As the study progressed, it became more and more apparent that the operator's concept of a day's work had a much wider significance than has thus far been implied. The interviewer, while inquiring further into this belief, found that it was related to other beliefs which the operators held quite generally. These other beliefs, which incidentally are quite common and more or less

---

[1] F. J. Roethlisberger and W. J. Dickson, *Management and the Worker* (Cambridge, Mass.: Harvard University Press, 1939), pp. 412, 414, 416–17, 419–20, 421, 422, 423, 428–29.

familiar to everyone, usually took the form: "If we exceed our day's work by any appreciable amount, something will happen. The 'rate' might be cut, the 'rate' might be raised, the 'bogey' might be raised, someone might be laid off, or the supervisor might 'bawl out' the slower men." Any or all of these consequences might follow. . . .

Statements like these indicate that many apprehensions and fears centered around the concept of a day's work. They suggested that the day's work might be something more than an output standard, that it might be a norm of conduct. The data obtained by the observer provided additional evidence in support of this interpretation. He found that men who persisted in exceeding the group standard of a day's work were looked upon with disfavor. This was manifested in subtle forms of sarcasm and ridicule. . . .

W6 and W2 were the first in output and it was toward them that most of the group pressure was directed. W6 was designated by such terms as "Shrimp," "Runt," and "Slave." Sometimes he was called "Speed King," a concession to his wiring ability. W2 was called "Phar Lap," the name of a race horse. W1 was nicknamed "4:15 Special," meaning that he worked until quitting time. W5 was also called "Slave" occasionally.

One of the most interesting devices by which the group attempted to control the behavior of individual members was the practice which they called "binging." This practice was noticed early in the study. The observer described it as follows:

"W7, W8, W9, and S4 were engaged in a game which they called 'binging.' One of them walked up to another man and hit him as hard as he could on the upper arm. The one hit made no protest, and it seems that it was his privilege to 'bing' the one who hit him. He was free to retaliate with one blow. One of the objects of the game is to see who can hit the hardest. But it is also used as a penalty. If one of them says something that another dislikes, the latter may walk up and say, 'I'm going to bing you for that.' The one who is getting binged may complain that he has been hurt and say, 'That one was too hard. I'm going to get you for that one.' . . ."

In addition to its use as a penalty and as a means of settling disputes, binging was used to regulate output of some of the faster workers. This was one of its significant applications and is well illustrated in the following entry:

W8 (to W6): "Why don't you quit work? Let's see, this is your thirty-fifth row today. What are you going to do with them all?"

W6: "What do you care? It's to your advantage if I work, isn't it?"

W8: "Yeah, but the way you're working you'll get stuck with them."

W6: "Don't worry about that. I'll take care of it. You're getting paid by the sets I turn out. That's all you should worry about."

W8: "If you don't quit work I'll bing you." W8 struck W6 and finally chased him around the room.

Obs (a few minutes later): "What's the matter, W6, won't he let you work?"

W6: "No. I'm all through though. I've got enough done." He then went over and helped another wireman. . . .

Another idea frequently expressed, directly or indirectly, by the employees in the interviews was that their weekly average hourly output should show little change from week to week. This does not mean that all of them should try to achieve identical average hourly outputs each week. It did mean that each of them should try to be fairly consistent week after week irrespective of differences in the absolute levels of their outputs. Their reasons for this were similar to those they advanced for not exceeding their day's work. They felt that if their output showed much change either from day to day or from week to week "something might happen." An unusually high output might thenceforward become the standard their supervisors would expect them to maintain. The men felt it would be a way of confessing that they were capable of doing better. On the other hand, they felt that a low output would afford their supervisors an opportunity to "bawl them out." If output were kept fairly constant, they thought, neither possibility could happen. . . .

The department permitted employees to claim daywork for unusual stoppages which were beyond their control. It did not, however, define what an unusual stoppage was or attempt to state which stoppages were and which were not beyond the employees' control. Such a definition would have been difficult to make because practically all delays were in some sense subject to employee control. Moreover, if the wage-incentive plan functioned as it was supposed to, there was no need for such a definition. It was assumed that the employees would resent any stoppage which interfered with their work and, as long as the opportunity to do piecework was present, that they would never either deliberately bring about a situation in which they could get only daywork or claim more daywork than they were entitled to. Yet that is exactly what happened. Some of them claimed more daywork allowances than they were entitled to or contrived to bring about occurrences which would justify their claims. The interesting thing about these claims is that they meant nothing to the operators in terms of payment. The operators were addressing themselves not to financial gains but to the security they felt came from uniform output curves. They said, of course, that the more daywork they were allowed, the less output they would have to produce in order to maintain a given output rate.

RATE CUTTING

Rate cutting is generally considered "unfair" by both management and workers, and it is clearly recognized that attempts to cut rates on high-earning jobs kills any incentive which the worker may have to try to increase his earnings. In order to convince the workers that management is trying to be fair and will give them the benefits of any increase in output and efficiency, it is often necessary to make a formal guaranty of the rates. This may be given merely as a statement of policy or may be incorporated into union contracts. In any event, management reserves the right to establish rates on any new job or on an old job in which there is a significant change of method. Thus, a change in method of drilling holes in a part, so that, instead of drill-ing each hole separately on a single-spindle drill press, they can all be drilled at one time on a multiple-spindle press, would call for a new piece rate. Thus, as a result of rapid technical development in tools and methods and of changes in design, piece rates are apt to be con-tinually changing. Since these technical developments are originated by management or by its technical experts, the engineers, the shop often interprets the changes as a method by means of which the rates can be cut if earnings prove excessive. In many cases, not only work-ers, but foremen and other shop supervisors as well, actually claim that, whenever piecework earnings on a job go too high, the engineers will look it over as a good place to show savings by a change in meth-ods. No doubt an engineer who is trying to make a showing by im-proved job methods will look for the spots where changes are likely to show the most results. A good chance for savings occurs at any spot where labor costs appear to be high. This does not mean that engi-neers devote their attention only to the jobs where piece-rate earnings are high, but in many cases it is undoubtedly a factor in their decisions as to what to work on.

Furthermore, it is usually true that, when a very fat job is re-engi-neered, it comes out much leaner. This all combines to convince the workers that the most they can expect from an incentive system, in the long run, is a moderate increase over what they would earn on straight daywork and that they will probably work much harder for it. As a result, the assurances of management that they want the work-ers to work hard and earn as much as possible seldom really convinces them that they gain anything by extending themselves to the utmost. The changing of rates with improvement in methods also tends to discourage the workers from trying openly to make improvements in the job. If they figure out some short cuts, develop better tools or fixtures, or improvise better ways of doing the job, they must keep the improvements hidden, or sooner or later a new rate will be set. As a result, they may work out improvements that will help them do the job better but keep them hidden from the eye of the foreman or the engineers.

On jobs which have run steadily over a period of years without change in methods or rates, it is often found that the earnings have increased gradually until they have reached a level very much above what is customarily thought of as high for that particular plant. In these cases the ceilings have apparently been moved upward over a period of years until quite a high level is accepted by management and considered "safe" by the workers. These high earnings on such jobs are often the result of a combination of factors, one of which is the acceptance of the fact that nothing will happen to the job because of the high earnings. Also, in many cases there may be gradual improvements in the quality of the parts or materials used, and conditions which formerly slowed down the job may no longer exist. Furthermore, over a period of years the workers develop a high degree of skill on the one job, learn all the tricks and short cuts, memorize the instructions, and generally improve their efficiency.

On completely new jobs, especially those which require considerable dexterity, it is often impossible to set rates until the workers have developed the necessary skills. In such cases the rate setters prefer to wait until the workers have reached what is assumed to be a normal level of output and are stabilized there, before timing the job. As a result, the workers often restrict their output and slow down the rate of learning the job, since they feel that if they level off at a comfortable working pace the rate will be set on that basis. They hope that this will give them a fat rate on which they can make fair earnings without much effort. This presents a problem to rate setters, of course, since they do not know whether the workers have actually reached a high degree of skill and are giving a reasonable output for the job or whether they have restricted their work at a low level in order to get excessively fat rates. At the same time, supervisors and workers may be demanding that the rates be set promptly on the new jobs so that they can have the advantage of piecework earnings as soon as possible.

This feeling that they must protect themselves from the rate setters is almost universal among workers, as pointed out earlier. If a rate setter just appears in a shop department, the whole tone of the place is likely to change. When he actually times a job, the worker tries to give the impression that he is working steadily at an even pace, so that he cannot be accused of stalling on the job. At the same time, he is very careful to follow every detail of job instruction, avoiding all short cuts, and putting in a few inconspicuous extras, if possible, to slow him down. Experienced rate men, however, are usually familiar with all these devices and are inclined to cut a bit off the actual timing when it comes to setting the rates. In one case, a group, who worked together in assembling a complicated and large-sized steel framework, had worked out a system to be used only when the rate setter was present. They found that, by tightening certain bolts first, the frame would be slightly sprung and all the other bolts would bind and be very difficult to tighten. When the rate setter was not present, they followed a different sequence; and the work went much faster. As a result, they never had any trouble in making high earnings on that job; but they were always careful not to go too high lest the engineers make a careful study and figure out their trick.

THE MERITS OF PIECEWORK

In view of this discussion, it might seem that piecework has no virtue whatever as an incentive. In spite of all the difficulties and the consistent restriction of output, however, experience has shown that a sound piecework system usually does increase efficiency and actually gets more output per man than a straight daywork system. In fact, some experts claim that the use of piecework will increase output as much as 50 per cent over daywork. This does not actually mean that the workers work 50 per cent harder, but only that output increases that much as a result of a lot of changes in the total work situation. When properly introduced, a sound piecework system does serve as some incentive to the workers; and they will make added efforts to increase their efficiency even while they are careful to restrict their output and earnings within certain limits.

Another factor in the improvement of output under piecework is that the work group generally gives more attention to keeping the job running smoothly. On daywork, if there is some time lost waiting for materials, or for setup men, or because of machine breakdowns, the operator may take it as a matter of course. If he is on piecework and this lost time threatens his earnings, he is likely to complain to the foreman and put pressure on him to prevent these losses.

Piecework earnings of groups or departments often serve, too, as one of the important records which top management uses as an index of shop performance. As one executive explained:

When I look at the records of a department and see that the piecework earnings are going along at what is felt to be a fair level and without much fluctuation from month to month, I know that they are getting the work out and there will probably be no serious delays in delivery of orders. Also, I know that the people will probably be pretty well satisfied, as any serious trouble would affect earnings and any sharp drop in earnings would cause dissatisfaction.

If I see a sharp drop in earnings, I know I can expect trouble with employees and probably trouble from other sources where people are affected by the drop in output in that department.

When looked at in this way, the piecework earnings reports are a potential threat to the foreman. He knows that, if he allows anything to slow down the job or otherwise cut down the earnings of his group, his superiors will be demanding explanations. This really keeps him on his toes in planning and organizing the work so that there will be few delays. It also stimulates him to put pressure on the employees to maintain their efficiency. On the whole, this can prove to be a very powerful pressure upon the foreman, and in some cases it seems to be the real source of improved performance under piecework. As one foreman put it, "Piecework isn't so much an incentive for the workers as a whip over the foremen."

This aspect of piecework was especially apparent in a plant where a number of new jobs were being put on group piecework. Before the groups, mostly new workers, had really developed their skill on the jobs, the rates were set at the level it was expected they would ultimately attain. In some cases this was far above the present level of output, and as a result the groups showed losses on the piecework earnings reports; that is, their piecework earnings did not equal the daywork rates which they were guaranteed. In many cases the difference between what they were actually producing and what they would have to produce to make any piecework earnings was so great that the workers all felt that they could never hope to make the rates and did not try very hard. The foremen, however, were under terrific pressure to get the earnings out of the red. In spite of the indifference of the workers, the foremen managed to get improved performance until the groups were just about breaking even. By this time, the workers were getting the feel of the jobs and began to see some prospects of piecework earnings. This served as a stimulus and gradually they came up to where they were earning a few per cent over their daywork rates. This was not enough for higher supervisors, however, who insisted that the job should earn between 15 per cent and 20 per cent; so the pressure was still on the foremen. They, in turn, kept the pressure on the workers and continued to try to improve the planning of the job and the flow of work so that there would be as little waste motion as possible. They gradually pushed the earnings up until they reached the desired 15 per cent. The pressure was then off, and the earnings stabilized there. If left to their own devices, the workers would have leveled off their output even below the daywork rates; they were forced to go higher only because of the insistence and assistance of the foremen.

17. UNIONS AND
THEIR STRUCTURE

A LABOR union is ordinarily thought of as something extraneous, an excrescence upon the structure of industry, rather than as an integral part of it. Actually, a union can be as much a part of the total structure as an engineering or accounting organization. Probably the fact that it usually arises out of the desires of the workers rather than as a decision of management leads to the belief that it is something apart and outside. From our point of view, however, whatever organizations or groupings exist within any given plant organization are all equally parts of the structure of that plant. This does not mean that the plant could not function without any one of its parts. The fact is that the one basic relationship in a factory is probably that of workers at work, producing goods. All other organizations and relations are built upon this; but they are, nonetheless, integrated parts of the whole plant structure.

Internal Structure

The internal structure of the large labor organizations, such as the Congress of Industrial Organizations or the American Federation of Labor, is quite complicated; but the structure of the local unit in any one plant is usually fairly simple. In one medium-sized plant, for example, the local union consists of four status levels: the chairman, members of the executive board, stewards, and all other members (Fig. 17-1). All of the offices are elective, and all are held by regular shop employees. Any complaints or grievances may be taken directly to the stewards, members of the executive committee, or the chairman. Since all the officers are working in the shops, they all have direct contact with the other workers. In fact, each one, regardless of his position in the union hierarchy, functions as the steward for the shop department in which he works.

A complaint from a worker is generally handled first by his steward, who takes it up with the foreman. If it cannot be settled at that level, the steward may contact the next level of supervision directly. But if it is necessary to go higher, the complaint is turned over to the executive board, who carry it higher up, according to the procedure agreed on in the contract between the company and the union. In some cases the chairman may delay formal action and may take up

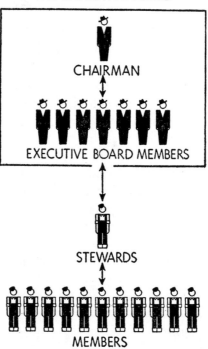

THE EXECUTIVE BOARD

CHAIRMAN

EXECUTIVE BOARD MEMBERS

STEWARDS

MEMBERS

FIGURE 17–1.—The Structure of a Union Local

the complaint unofficially with the higher levels of the company in order to give supervision time to work out some satisfactory settlement.

The Functions of a Union

Union organization often develops as a result of management's limited point of view and of restricted communication within the structure. In the supervisory ranks the whole focus of attention is upon getting the job done and upon conditions affecting the job. This leads to a habit of thinking of the workers as merely tools, merely means to the real goal—production. The attitudes and problems of workers are likely to be treated as unimportant compared to the job, and workers feel that management is indifferent to them. They feel that their future, their rewards, and their satisfactions are controlled by a management which is basically indifferent to them and their desires. Furthermore, because of their subordinate position at the bottom of the hierarchy, they feel blocked and helpless to get anyone to listen to them. The line of authority is their one accepted means of communication with management. This means that their immediate supervisor, the foreman, is the one to whom they have to take their grievances. The way in which the complaints are handled and the satisfactions they receive are dependent upon the effectiveness of the immediate supervisor in carrying them up the line. If he is indifferent, they do not feel free to take their problems above him except as a most reckless venture. If he is sympathetic, they know that he may be blocked by the indifference of those above him.

With a union, however, the situation is considerably altered. The union is the workers' own organization; it is concerned with what they think is important; the focus of its attention is on the workers, not on the work. The existence of a union gives the workers a feeling of unity as a group, which makes them feel protected and courageous. As individual workers, they hesitate to stand up for their rights against their bosses; and when one does occasionally, the others look upon him as brave, but foolhardy. But as union members, with a group behind them to back them up and protect them, they can speak without fear. Furthermore, their immediate supervisors are not then the only ones to whom they can go with their complaints; they can take their grievances to their union representatives and expect to get some action.

Some of the situations and worker feelings which stimulate demands on the union are shown in the following statements by employees:

1. I feel so badly I could scream. With my service and the way I'm pushed around! I complained to the union representative and he said he was going to take it up with the big boss. I'm not wasting my time talking to any supervisors any more, because they don't do a thing for you.

2. I didn't get a raise this time. I sure was hurt about it. They never call me up and tell me anything about the job; yet I don't get a raise. I come in every morning; I'm never late; but I never get anything for it. I'm going to talk to the shop steward.

3. I'm back here and it sure gripes me. There are still men over me there with shorter service than I have, but they transfer me. It means a cut of $5.00 a week for me. I saw my union steward this morning and complained to him.

In all these statements the employees feel that they have been unfairly treated and that they must look to the union to defend their interests. In the first statement the employee feels that his superior cannot or will not correct the situation and that the union will take the complaint to the Big Boss. In the second statement the operator seems to feel completely ignored, since he gets neither a raise nor any recognition for his faithful service. As these statements suggest, the attitude of employees toward the union and the extent to which they feel the need of a union is frequently closely related to the effectiveness with which the line handles work dissatisfactions.

Even those who are not especially ardent union members recognize that it is only as a group that they dare to stand up to the boss. As one worker said,

I ain't too sure about the union. I guess it's all right for some, but I can't see it does me much good. Of course, if you've got a complaint it's better to have the union to go to the boss with you. It's hard sometimes to get the boss to listen when you have to go to him all alone and lots of people are afraid to do it. With the union, you know he will pay some attention and not push you around.

The Union as a Bargaining Agent

Not only does the union defend the rights of the individual to work, but also it represents them as a group in negotiating with management. In this, one of its very important roles, the union acts for the workers in their transactional relation with management. The union leaders meet with management to negotiate:

1. The wages to be paid.
2. The hours to be worked.
3. The working conditions.
4. The rights of workers in their relations with the company, supervision, etc.
5. The procedure by which any problems can be dealt with.

In these negotiations they endeavor to reach an agreement which can be spelled out in the form of a contract binding on both groups.

Since the union is representing all the workers it must make demands which are satisfying to all groups in its membership and not merely benefiting a few. This means that it must strive to find a set of principles or logic to justify differences in wages which will be acceptable to the group as well as management. When some groups within the union feel that their particular interests are not being protected, they are apt to try to withdraw and join some other union.

As a result of negotiating with unions over wages, management has been forced to develop systematic wage structures with clearly defined logic to support wage differentials between types of jobs. This leads to elaborate methods of job evaluations, often with scoring systems which make allowance for skills required, physical effort, responsibility, and so on.

Once the bargaining is over and the terms are settled, the union then becomes the watchdog protecting the agreement in general as well as the rights of the individual worker. It is to his shop steward that the worker turns if he feels he is not receiving what is due him under the contract, or that unfair demands are being made on him, or that he is being subjected to working conditions which are "illegal." Thus, through the union and its contract with management many facets of the transactional relationship between workers and the company are formally expressed. Without the union many of these remain as informal understandings rather than clearly prescribed rights and responsibilities.

Union Communication

Besides its roles in representing the individual worker and giving them the feeling of strength as a group, most important, it has highly formalized procedures by means of which it can bring its demands (the workers' demands), directly to top management, if necessary, and thrust its point of view upon them without being delayed and blocked by intermediate supervisory levels. Through its stewards and other officials, it serves as another channel of communication through which information can move up through the structure even as far as top management. Unlike other channels, however, communication through the union is not controlled by management. The union is not trying to give management only the "good news"; and it is not trying to protect itself from management's criticism. On the contrary, union communication is seldom simply for the purpose of keeping management informed, but it is predominantly concerned with bringing *to* management criticisms of the way line organizations are functioning and demands for changes. In this respect, the union is unique in the industrial structure. In all the other organizations in the structure the great bulk of communication takes the form of information moving *up* and criticisms and demands moving *down*. Communication upward through the union, however, serves to put pressure on management and supervision and sets in motion changes in activities in a way that other forms of communication fail to do. Significantly, however, the union cannot make the decisions or actually take the action necessary to solve the problems about which it complains and makes demands. It acts largely as a mechanism for getting supervision's attention to employees' interests, insisting on decisions, and speeding up action. Decisions and final action must come down the line from above.

Union communication may cover a wide range of subject matter and is, in fact, almost as versatile as the line of authority in this respect; but unlike the line, it is always directed toward the workers' interests rather than toward the job and the effect of things upon the work. A foreman reporting to his boss on some difficulty in the shop is thinking mostly in terms of what it means to the job; a shop steward reporting on the same incident to the union is thinking of the workers' attitudes and feelings about it. When both of these reports are passed on to management, one through the line and one through the union, then management must examine the situation both from the point of view of the work and from the point of view of the workers.

The union, too, serves to speed up action on worker requests and complaints, either by speeding up communication upward through the structure or by "short-circuiting" the line. In many cases, as we pointed out in an earlier discussion of communication, worker requests move very slowly up the line; and waiting for action may seem interminable. The request or complaint is viewed with less and less interest as it goes up the line and gets farther removed from the work situation; each level of supervision feels that it is rather unimportant, and each one either neglects to act on it or passes it on to his superior without making a decision. In all such cases the entrance of the union into the situation speeds up the processes of communication and decision. The union does not have to wait for things to move up the line through the normal routes, but can go directly, without waiting, to any level. This fact speeds communication up the line especially at the lower levels of supervision, where they do not have the authority to make the decisions. If the union should go to a higher authority with a request which has not already come up the line, then the lower levels are "on the spot" for not having kept their superiors informed. For that reason, the moment a case goes to the union, the news is passed up the line in a hurry. For example, a worker feels that he deserves an upgrading to a higher grade of work, and he requests it of his foreman. The foreman feels that the change is not justified, or at least that it will not benefit the job, and so he refuses, or puts it off and forgets about it. The worker, however, is not satisfied and he goes to his shop steward. The steward sees the foreman and says that he thinks the request is justified. The foreman then either grants the request, refuses it, or says that he will have to con-

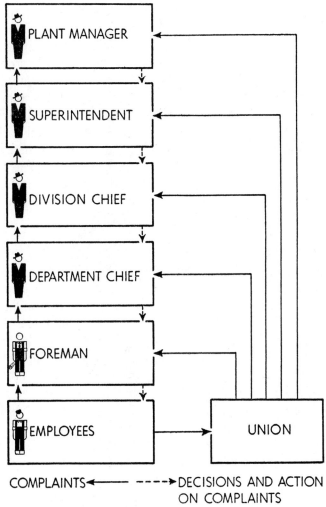

FIGURE 17–2.—Communication through the Union

sult with his boss, depending on his authority in the matter. Unless he has the authority to allow the change and does allow it, he will inform his boss of the incident, presenting his side of the story and his excuses for not acting sooner. This is imperative, because his boss must be informed before the union goes to him with the request. At higher levels, or whenever the supervisor can make the decision and is merely "stalling" because of indifference or lack of attention, the union may serve to hurry his decision, not necessarily by actually going above him, but sometimes merely by the fact of having the ability to go above if he does not act.

The functions of union communication, as compared with communication through the line of authority, can be diagramed as in Figure 17–2. Solid line arrows indicate the channels through which information and complaints may pass up the line; dotted arrows show decisions and action moving down. With a union, the employee is not limited to communication up through the line but may go to either his supervisor or his union representative with his problems. The union can go directly to any level and force it to deal with problems which might never get through the line; and when there is delay or blockage at one level, the union can short-circuit the line and take problems to the next level. It will be noted, however, that decisions and action do not come from the union but from management and are passed down through the lines of authority.

Union Organization

The union has relationships and internal problems of organization quite different from the other organizations. In the first place, there is little of the concept of authority in union relationships. The chairman is not the "boss." He does not give orders or make decisions which can be imposed on those below him. He does not directly control the distribution of rewards or recognition for the individuals. In contrast to the line, where supervisors are selected by their superiors, union officials are elected by, and are therefore responsible to, those below them in the union hierarchy. Besides this, or perhaps because of it, the union also lacks the elaborate system of rewards and punishments which a line organization usually has available. The average union member accepts the union activities as useful but incidental to the work. His daily life, his hopes, and expectations are centered much more around his job than around the union. His eye is on his boss for approval or criticism, not on his steward. He may be critical of his steward, but he does not especially care what the steward thinks of him; recognition from the steward does not give him the same satisfaction as recognition from his boss; and criticism from the steward only makes him mad.

For the most part, workers judge the union by results; and the individual worker often thinks in terms of satisfaction for himself, more than for workers as a group. In many cases, workers complain that the union is incompetent or lacks the power to get effective results for them. In other cases—and this is one of the severest criticisms—they believe that the union is indifferent to them and does not try to get results. These critical attitudes toward the union are illustrated in the following quotations from dissatisfied workers:

1. If anyone such as a union steward comes around, I'm going to mention that I'd like a transfer. A. doesn't pay any dues because she doesn't belong, but I pay my $2.00 a month and don't get a thing out of it, and she gets a good job.

2. I don't even make $45.00 a week after all my service. That's no salary for a man with a family. We had a union meeting last night about the percentage here. It's no good. All the fellows are kicking. I didn't go myself, didn't feel as though I wanted to. How can a fellow support a family on a salary like that? They ought to do something about me. What good does it do to complain, though? They don't do anything about me.

3. The steward was down to see me and said the superintendent was going to fix me up with something good. I said he doesn't even know me; he walks through here and never recognizes me. As far as I'm concerned X and his union can go to hell! I'm a fool for paying them $2.00 a month!

4. We're supposed to hear something from the union this week. I suppose we'll get knocked off on it. I don't think they can do us any good. I think we were foolish to make a kick at all. They just sit around and talk about it; it doesn't make any difference to them. They don't seem to care whether they help us or not.

5. That damn union is no good. We took our kick up to them and got nothing. In fact, they made it worse for us.

The union does not, of course, spend all its time on the complaints and grievances of individual workers but is constantly keeping an eye on company policies and practices and suggesting or demanding changes to benefit workers as a group. Besides this, the union is always pressing management for uniformity in practices. Thus the union seeks uniform wages for comparable work throughout a plant, and it asks for uniform methods in upgrading, transfers, and so on. If one department introduces rest periods, the union may request them for the entire plant; if one group changes its starting time, the union may ask that others do the same. This pressure for uniformity becomes especially noticeable when one union has organized several plants of one company. Then, any change in one plant may lead to requests for similar changes in the others. Under such conditions, management is very careful about making any changes or improvements in one location which it is not willing to consider for all the others.

Foremen and the Union

The ability of the union to go over his head on any problems or complaints puts the foreman in a difficult position. Since he is the one who has the most direct contact with the workers and who is constantly controlling and directing them, many of their complaints and dissatisfactions arise out of his actions and decisions. Without the union these dissatisfactions usually have no effective outlet and are not an immediate threat to the foreman, since few workers have the temerity either to "tell off" their boss or to go over his head with their complaints. The foreman can, therefore, concentrate on getting the work done and does not have to worry much about how the workers feel. Once the union comes in, however, he is forced to think in terms of satisfying both his superiors and his subordinates. He has to give attention to the workers as well as the work, and neglect of either may bring criticism from above. Thus he is, in a way, caught in the middle between his superiors and his subordinates. This situation often gives a foreman feelings of great insecurity; he feels that he is losing his authority and control. If many of his decisions are taken up by the union and then overridden by his superiors, or if the union gets favorable action on requests which he has turned down, he feels that his superiors are not backing him up and that the union is running his job. He is likely to feel, too, that his superiors will listen to the union while they ignore him, which is certainly true in many cases. Such situations and attitudes make the foreman's position an unhappy one, especially if he is having difficulties with the job or has an aggressive steward.

It should not be assumed, however, that blockages or difficulties with the union always occur at the foreman level or that they occur only at that level. In some cases the foremen, and even higher supervisors, are aware of employees' sentiments and do whatever they can at their level. Sometimes, however, the foreman himself feels frustrated in his attempts to get higher levels to recognize the workers' problems and help to solve them satisfactorily. Then he may recognize the fact that the union is more effective than he is in overcoming blockage in the line and getting the attention of higher levels. This is illustrated in the following statements by supervisors:

1. These guys had quite a kick. They took it up to the union and argued about it. They talked to me about it first, but there wasn't anything I could do about it. After all, there's a limit to my authority; so I told them that's the way things are; so they went to the union with it. After all, what've they got a union for?

2. I suppose you've heard about the rumpus we've been having. What the union is asking for is that we increase their rates. That sounds reasonable enough to me, but it's up to the guys upstairs to approve it. I can't get Mr. X to approve it because he's leaving and says it's Mr. Y's job, but Mr. Y won't do it until he takes over. As a result we are getting pushed around by the union, and, of course, we can't tell the union what's holding it up. They would be shocked to learn that the bigshots are handling it like that.

In some cases, where a department chief is being dilatory or indecisive, the foreman can get action by merely mentioning that the question has been referred to the union. In other cases, foremen deliberately let complaints that might easily be settled by the line go to the union because they believe that the union can get action more quickly and easily. In extreme cases they may even encourage the union to take up matters which would not ordinarily interest them, or about which workers have not complained much. For example, a foreman may think that his shop needs better lights, but he has been unable to get his superiors to approve the expense of the change. A discussion with the shop steward about the "lousy lights we got" and a little complaining about not being able to get anything done about it, and soon the union may present a complaint about the lights. The idea of foremen using the union in this way will probably be shocking to management, but it does happen sometimes. And when it happens, it can always be traced to some blockage in the line which prevents the foremen from getting things done through the regular channels.

Management and the Union

It will be apparent from this discussion so far that the union differs sharply from other organizations in the industrial structure in several ways, most particularly in its relations with management. To begin with, the union's orientation and point of view is opposed to that of management, of staff and control organizations, and of most supervisory levels in the shop organization. All of the union person-

nel—its members and its officials—are workers; and all of its attention and activities are directed toward worker interests; whereas all
the other organizations or groups are oriented toward satisfactory
production of goods or some special phase of it. In the second place,
the union has quite different procedures for communicating its point
of view to management. We have seen how each of the other organizations struggles to get the attention of top management, each working through the lines of authority, each striving to force its interests
on its superiors, while the executives weigh, select, eliminate, or pass
on the demands. The union, on the other hand, working through the
formalized contract negotiations and grievance procedures, can bring
its demands to bear directly upon top management without censor-
ship or control by the intermediate levels. This is true whether they
are dealing with particular cases in grievance procedures or with general principles.

Unlike the other organizations, then, the union is not controlled
by management and management cannot protect itself from the union. In the other organizations, the hierarchies and lines of authority
serve not only as channels of communication but also as layers of insulation by means of which top management protects itself from
many problems and demands originating at the bottom of the structure. A request for a new machine in the shop, for example, seldom
reaches top management via these channels. The request is either
granted or denied at a lower level, and there is usually no recourse,
no formal procedure by means of which it can be carried to higher
authority. In contrast to this, the union offers a relatively open pathway to the top, and management cannot be insulated against it.

The chief function of the union is to force management to consider the effects of company policies and practices upon the workers.
It is the function of management, on the other hand, to decide on
these policies and practices and to give orders about them. In this
role, top management may be seen as dictator; and it often assumes
an attitude of complacent omnipotence, passing down decisions and
orders with the assurance that there can be no repercussions from
below, since it is safely insulated from any backfire up the lines of
authority. In view of this, it is not surprising that management is often
reluctant to accept either the union's point of view, its ability to
short-circuit the line, or its pressures. In many cases, top management believes that consideration for the worker, his attitudes and
satisfactions, is irrelevant and even detrimental to the main objective

of getting the work done cheaply and well. Even when it is recognized that worker satisfaction is essential to maintaining efficient production, management often resents having the fact "rammed down its throat" or decisions forced upon it by the union.

Once top management has accepted the point of view and powers of the union, however, it usually sees the union organization as a useful part of the total structure. If worker attitudes must be considered, management usually finds it simpler to have one organization which can present a composite of these attitudes. And it is easier, too, to deal with a small group of union officials than with a mass of individual workers when discussing complaints, company policies, or changes in practices. In this particular the union can function like the other organizations in the structure, assembling and selecting from a mass of detail the significant matters to be presented to management, and aiding in the interpretation because of its knowledge of these details. Even here, however, there is an important difference between the union and the other organizations. When the others have brought information to top managment and helped to interpret it, then management makes the decisions and gives them back down the line as "orders." The union, however, does not take orders from management. When union officials take information to top management, they are "consulted," they may make suggestions, and may even be asked for advice. Thus, management can say to the union: "We are planning to make these changes. How will they work from the employees' point of view?" Or the union can say to management: "There are certain practices which are hurting morale, and something should be done about them."

The union is also expected to help management in carrying its decisions back down to the workers. When management and the union have come to an agreement about a matter, the decision or statement of changes is passed down from management to the work level through the regular channels. But the union is expected to explain and justify the decision to the individual employees and to smooth the way for its acceptance. Since the union officials are elected by the workers and are the workers' representatives, management quite naturally expects, too, that the workers will accept the decisions about which the union has been consulted and has agreed. If, for example, through the collective bargaining process, management and the union have reached an agreement as to wages, seniority rights, or shop practices, it is expected that the union will explain the agreement and that the workers will accept it. Unfortunately, this does not always happen; and either individual workers or groups sometimes refuse to accept the agreements, especially if they mean a compromise for the workers. (One is reminded of our state and national legislative processes, and of how often people refuse to accept and abide by the laws which are passed by their elected representatives.) When workers do refuse to accept these joint decisions, management is usually outraged, not only at the individual offenders, but at the whole union setup. Once a matter has been settled with the union representatives, management feels it should be settled for good and all. For this reason, management often prefers to deal with a "strong" union which has the backing of most of the workers, which is, in reality, representative of the workers and which can actually smooth the way for acceptance of union-management agreements.

Union Officials

Union officials are an interesting factor in the effective functioning of the union, both in its relation to the workers and in its relations with management. Just as the effectiveness of the line in dealing with problems of the work or workers is in large part dependent upon the receptivity of supervisors at each level and their ability to make decisions or carry the problems on up, so the effectiveness of the union is largely dependent upon the ability of its individual representatives. And just as a worker's attitudes and relations with his foreman often set the tone for his feelings toward the whole company, so his attitudes toward his steward often determine his evaluation of the union as a whole. Thus the steward who is indifferent to the complaints or requests of his people often arouses antagonism, not just toward himself, but toward the whole union organization. As the irate worker quoted above said, "As far as I'm concerned, X and his union can go to ———!"

Unlike supervisors in the other organizations, the union officials, as we have pointed out, do not have either the authority or the status of the boss. The workers, whether union members or not, do not have to take orders from the officials, and, for the most part, are quite indifferent to them unless they have some grievance. Furthermore, except for a relatively small group of full-time officials, the union does not offer a way of life, a job with a pay check, to which the individual can devote all his energies, and it does not offer economic rewards or status. The union official is just another employee, with his own job and his own problems and career to think about. His duties to his fellow workers as their union representative do not make his personal situation as a worker any less pressing, but may, in fact, add to his difficulties.

All these factors have a significant influence upon the kind of individuals who become active in the union. Generally, the ambitious worker who is progressing satisfactorily, and especially the one who expects or hopes to move into supervisory ranks, feels little need of union support or protection and may even sympathize and identify himself with management instead of the union. Some believe, too, that to be active in the union will antagonize their superiors and lessen their chances of promotion. These ambitious ones make very poor stewards, when they do occasionally accept the office out of a feeling of duty. They are more concerned with their own future than with the interests of other workers, and they are reluctant to criticize their superiors or be too aggressive in contacts up the line. One such steward explained his feelings thus:

> I've had a feeling, and I've also heard from a lot of the other stewards, that once you get to be a steward you never get a raise. If I thought there was any truth in that, I would quit this job right away. No sense in me sticking to a steward's job if I can't get a raise out of it. I actually heard a lot of the stewards talk like that. Why is it I can't get something better around here?
> . . . I'd like to get something I really like. After all, I've got twenty years' service and I wouldn't want to stop at $70.00 a week. That's why if I thought being a steward kept me from getting a raise, I'd get out of this as fast as I could.
> . . . . I don't mind the job at all. I've learned a lot on it. But if it is going to hurt me, I'd get out of the union tomorrow.

In other cases, earnest employees, working hard to make a showing on their jobs, feel that they do not have time for union activities. These, too, are ineffectual and promote antagonism to the union if they become stewards. Their preoccupation with their own jobs, their reluctance to discuss union matters on the job, and their concern with proper shop behavior, all tend to keep them away from the people whom they are supposed to represent, and force the other employees to take the initiative in bringing matters to them. One of these stewards explained his position:

> When they brought that thing up to me about the low earnings, I intended to take it up. First three guys came over to me, and then five more, then seven

more, and finally I said, "Hey, let's not have any more of this up here." I told them we could have a meeting over at headquarters, so that's what we decided to do. I figured, let them have their meeting. That way they can raise their opinions and let off steam over there. I haven't got time to listen to that stuff during working hours, especially when they pile over here to see me. That looks very bad on the job.

. . . I don't spend hardly any time on union activities during working hours. I have a lot of new people in here that I should be contacting to try to get them to join up. I just don't feel as though I ought to spend the time on it.

In other cases there are the older, skilled workers who feel that they have made satisfactory progress and who are, in many cases, the spokesmen or leaders of their work groups. They are likely to feel that the union has little to offer them, or, sometimes, that the union is a fine thing for the others but that they themselves do not have time to be active. Like the other indifferent ones, they sometimes accept jobs as stewards through feelings of duty or because they think the wrong people are running the union. Usually they soon grow tired of the duties and drop out "to give some one else a chance."

On the other hand, many stewards and other union officials are very active and enthusiastic members who are aggressive in upholding what they consider the "rights" of the workers, who take seriously their duties as representatives of the workers, and who are very critical of stewards who approach supervisors timidly or not at all. Something of their attitude was expressed by one steward, who said:

It is hard for me to know when they really have something to complain about. After all, I have to go up the line with some of these things, and sometimes I am not so convinced that the employee has a squawk coming. But I carry it along just the same because I feel that I owe it to them because of my job as steward. These guys that are indifferent to their responsibilities give me a pain in the neck.

Often the person who is dissatisfied with his own situation, who is very critical of management and the work generally, who is a "sorehead" or "griper" in the eyes of the foremen and management, is very active in the union and becomes a steward or higher official. The workers often feel that such a person will put up a better fight for their interests than one who is less critical and accepts conditions. Such a steward, however, who is aggressive, antagonistic, and inclined to belligerence, generally rubs foremen and management the wrong way; and they invariably feel that he is prejudiced and unreasonable.

Problems of Stewards

Another problem of union personnel is that the officials change quite frequently, especially the shop stewards. This means that, at any given time, a great many union stewards are novices who have not established relations with the workers as their representatives and who have not devised techniques for dealing with supervisors. It means, too, that supervisors and workers are continually having to deal with new stewards who are unfamiliar with procedures, who do not know what has gone on before, and who, therefore, have a lot to learn before they can function efficiently. Very frequently, neither the union organization nor management have the benefit of a stable group which, over the years, constantly improves its understanding of the problems and its skill in handling them. Each time there is a change in officials in the union, there is a resulting period of tension and adjustment—with the new officials feeling inept; the workers, doubtful and anxious; and management inclined to be irritable—until satisfactory and familiar working relationships are developed again.

Some workers do, of course, remain active in the union over a period of time, and some rise in the union hierarchy. And just as there is a shift in understanding when a shopworker is promoted to foreman, so the union member who becomes an effective and active shop steward changes his point of view. As a mere worker, even though a union member, he generally thinks of problems of the work, or policies, or management's decisions primarily in terms of himself. His attitude toward the whole work situation is personal. If Joe gets a better job on the basis of seniority, Charlie may feel that he is being treated unfairly because he is a better worker than Joe. But as a shop steward, Charlie has to think about Joe's promotion not just in terms of himself but in terms of Joe and all the others in the work group. He has to consider, not just the promotion of Joe, but the matter of policy and fairness for the whole group. If there are complaints, he has to hear the foreman's side of the problem, too, and try to understand it. To be effective, he has to know the foreman's problems, too, as well as the workers'—why the foreman does the things he does and what pressures he is under.

The steward who is conscientious often meets complications in trying to represent a whole work group fairly, and he sometimes gets mixed up in their personal relationships, especially where there is disagreement in the group. As an ordinary worker, he can enter into an argument and take sides; but as a steward, he is likely to be caught with both factions expecting him to represent them. Frequently a suggested change in practice will benefit part of the group and be to the disadvantage of the rest, and the steward has to decide whether or not to press for such a change. For example, in a department working on shifts, the morning shift started at 6:00 A.M. and the second shift ended at midnight. Some of the people on the first shift complained that they had to get up too early in the morning and wanted to change their starting hour to 7 o'clock. This seemed reasonable until the steward discussed it with workers on the second shift. They were strongly opposed to the change because they would not get through work until 1 o'clock instead of midnight. If the steward then officially requested the change, the second shift would be down on him; but if he did not, the first shift would feel that he was not representing them properly. In another case, one group of workers complained that it was unfair for them to be kept on a type of machine which was harder and more disagreeable than a slightly different type of machine which another group used. They requested that all workers be rotated on the different machines. Here, again, the steward had to decide whether to request a change which would improve conditions for part of the work group at the expense of the rest.

After experience in trying to work out problems like these, trying to improve conditions and relieve conflicts, and acting as go-between from workers to management, union officers often begin to change their point of view about the problems and what to do about them. Especially when dealing with a management which is honestly trying to work with the union, the officers sometimes begin to understand management's problems and point of view and are more sympathetic with its difficulties. They begin to see why it is impossible to adjust the system to satisfy each individual demand; they see the limitations of legal restrictions, of wage ceilings; they learn something of the complexities of planning the work so that things go smoothly. And with this broader point of view and understanding, they often find that they have difficulty in explaining their actions to the groups which they represent. They are making decisions based on an understanding which the others lack, and because of this lack the others cannot accept their reasoning. As a result, the officials sometimes become annoyed with the people they represent, begin to think critically of them as dumb or hardheaded, and complain that they are unreasonable. As one steward said, "You know, some of these people are funny. No matter what you do for them, they still blame the union and never give us credit. Some of these guys don't appreciate the position the company is in. The company is really nice to us guys; they give us a lot of consideration."

18. THE INDIVIDUAL
IN THE STRUCTURE

WE HAVE seen that the individual is part of a larger community and society which determines to a great extent his basic sentiments and attitudes. He brings to the job his own personality, his unconscious needs, as well as his conscious goals. Also, he brings to the job many habits and expectations which have been taught him through his life experiences. As a result, he may have an underlying need to dominate others yet expresses it in ways which are common and acceptable to our culture. Thus, the personal satisfaction he attains in his work depends on the extent to which, through his work, he satisfies the complex patterns of unconscious drives and needs, as well as the extent to which he meets his requirements as a social being.

Work Adjustment and Personality

Each individual can be thought of as having a basic psychological personality which is expressed in his behavior, motivations, and desires. Thus, an aggressive, domineering person may be "bossy" in his relations with others, be outspoken with his ideas, and generally seek to be the center of activity and attention. Or the extremely insecure person may be afraid of any change which forces him into new situations or relationships.

This problem of personality as it relates to work behavior and adjustment is extremely complex—too complex to be covered here. It becomes especially complicated when we consider that the person who makes a good adjustment in one work situation may make a poor one elsewhere. For example, an effective salesman may have personality characteristics unsuited for a factory job. Or a man who does well under a strong-willed, decisive boss may do poorly under one who is less firm and clearcut in his orders. Similar differences may be seen in students, some wanting to know exactly what the professor expects of them, and others feeling quite at ease with vague assignments in which they have to figure out for themselves the details of what should be done.

The Meaning of Work

The work itself has great importance to the individual and has many meanings. First, it has social approval in our society. Work is a virtue; idleness is wrong, or even evil. Work is serious and dutiful as contrasted to play—and while play is approved within limits, "playboy" is a derogatory term. So we can assume that working at something is part of our way of life, and everyone in business and industry expects to work.

The work you do provides one of the important definitions of who you are. In the first place, it defines your general status, tells how important you are, and indicates much about your probable way of life. The lawyer is different from the factory worker in importance, in activity, in way of living, in types of friends.

The work implies a definite pattern of activities which differ from one occupation to another. Some jobs mean simple manipulations repeated over and over—the simple, routine factory or clerical jobs. The machine operator deals with objects, the mathematician with abstract symbols, the salesman with people. In fact, in a way, all jobs deal with either things, people or ideas, or usually with combinations of the three. Thus some jobs are largely dealing with things, others are interacting with people, and others are thinking—probably no jobs are exclusively one or the other.

Also, one's job may determine the amount of physical activity, the degree of novelty and change, the contacts with people. Each job provides a setting which offers both opportunities and limitations. At the same time, the organization within which the work takes place becomes the setting of the job and part of the opportunities and limitations.

Significance of the Industrial System to the Individual

To the individual employee, the industrial organization consists of machines, benches, tables, and desks, all of which are symbols of positions and jobs occupied by people. Furthermore, he is aware of a system of technical processes and interrelations between these various positions and functions, which determines (a) the tasks which employees must perform, (b) who shall interact with whom, and (c) under what conditions and circumstances this interaction shall take place.

However, he sees the industrial organization not only as a technical process and a set of relations between specific work tasks but as a social system where the various functions and positions of the system have social meaning and significance to him. To the rank-and-file employee, the boss not only is a functionary who co-ordinates work activity but also is a person in a position of authority who occupies a superior social rank. The social nature of this relationship has much to do with the adjustment which both the rank-and-file employee and the boss will make to the work situation.

In the same way, all of the positions and functions in an organization are socially interpreted and classified by employees and thus take on an aura of significance and meaning, which influences the individual who occupies the position, as well as those who must interact with him. A punch press is not merely a machine but a symbol of the role that the individual employee occupies in the social system of the factory. The employee, therefore, must adjust to the work demands which the machine imposes upon him, not only in a physical sense, but in a social and psychological sense as well. The work routines of the job, the people with whom he works, the boss from whom he receives his orders—all these determine what he can and cannot do and directly influence the conceptualization that he makes of his role in the social structure of the factory.

With these views in mind, the importance and significance of the day-by-day, routine experiences of the employee within the industrial system become apparent. The ordinary job activities of a factory or business are typically so commonplace that we often take them for granted and miss the significance they have for the individual. Yet, these common, everyday activities determine to a surprisingly large extent how the employee feels about his work environment. They set the dimensions within which the employee must adjust his own individual demands and his personal conception of himself. If his daily work experiences run contrary to his self-image, he will feel unhappy and disgruntled. On the other hand, if he is able to integrate his own social needs and demands into his day-by-day job activities, then he will feel satisfied and tend to support and accept the organization that gives him these personal satisfactions.

Because of this tendency among employees to identify and integrate their own personal demands and needs into the system of work activity, change in the organization and system of work may be interpreted by the individual employee as a personal attack on his own personality and ego. Thus, we can see that the job that he does and the daily tasks that he performs are much more to him than a set of routine, technical functions; they are part and parcel of his whole conception of himself and the role that he plays both inside and outside the factory.

Interpersonal Relations and Individual Adjustment

To the average person, some of the most important elements in the job and work situation are the interpersonal relations. The boss or bosses, the people he works with, all those he must contact—all may add or detract from his satisfactions at work. And in this area, the interplay of personalities becomes especially important.

As we have seen, everyone sees the boss as having certain rights to command and supervise. Nevertheless, the individual's reactions to the supervision may vary with his own personality. Some individuals are somewhat (or extremely) rebellious against authority and are disturbed by any signs of authoritarianism. In short, they have a hard time taking orders, and will overreact to direct order and will want an order disguised as a request. Those extremely hostile to authority often resent anyone in position to give them orders and are rebellious against company rules and regulations.

On the other extreme, we find people who are submissive to authority—who not only accept it but are most comfortable when being directed. These can accept even autocratic supervision as being right and expected, and they adjust easily to rules and directives.

The pattern of the individual's reaction to authority will be an important element in his adjustment at work and in his work satisfaction. If he overreacts to authority, a job with close supervision or a demanding autocratic boss may be intolerable. Often the same type of job, but with a different boss or less close supervision, may be completely satisfactory.

In many cases, a person's reaction to superiors is influenced by his feelings of his own importance or by his desire for greater status. For example, a highly skilled toolmaker may easily accept as his boss another skilled toolmaker, but may be extremely rebellious if an engineer is put in charge. In this, he feels that he can take orders from his own kind because they represent the skill he respects; but the engineer is different and has no understanding of his skill. In essence he says: "I can be a subordinate to one who represents the same knowledge and values which I hold, but I cannot tolerate anyone who does not."

An extreme type of case is that of a man who is given a woman supervisor. Regardless of the woman's ability, the man is likely to feel that he loses status by taking orders from a woman. By the definitions of our society, the man should be the superior, and any reversal of this role is disturbing to the man.

Thus we have both the individual's personal reaction to the boss, and to authority, and the social definition of whom he can accept as a boss. To the average person, it is usually easier to be "bossed around" by someone high in the particular hierarchy than by one low. Most people will accept direct orders from the president much more readily than from their immediate supervisor.

To many factory and office workers, the social environment created by the work group provides some of their major satisfactions. For example, a girl who worked on a routine job in a radio assembly line said: "I just love to come to work. All the girls are so friendly. I'd say they are my best friends. We talk and kid each other all day long. We talk about our boy-friends and our dates and all sorts of things. Sometimes the boss tells us not to talk so much, but he's good-natured and doesn't really mind so long as we keep up with our job." Here we have a girl who gets no particular pleasure from the work itself, but her job satisfaction derives from the friendly relations with the other girls.

What one seeks and expects in these situations varies a great deal. Many, as the above girl, seem to seek a warm, friendly group such as the cliques of close friends so common in adolescence—a group in which you find warm acceptance and interest.

In other cases, we find individuals who react competitively to their fellow workers. Some seek to dominate their fellows, try to "boss" them around, show superior knowledge, always try to win arguments, or become competitive in the work. These more aggressive individuals may become leaders and spokesmen in their group, and they become the ones to whom the others look for advice or direction. In other cases, their aggression generates hostility, and they become outcasts—or they are the constant target for jokes and kidding.

The individual's reactions to people are especially significant in jobs which are built around interpersonal relations. A salesman who dislikes meeting people has a hard time calling on customers. Or one who is submissive and unaggressive in presenting his views may have trouble in convincing customers, and will be too quick to accept a refusal. On the other hand, one who is too aggressive and domineering may irritate customers and drive them away. In the same way, an engineer who is ill at ease with shop people may have difficulty in getting their co-operation. Or a staff man who tries to dominate others may create resistance to his ideas.

In terms of personality, we find many people who have problems in relating themselves to others. They may be excessively hostile or competitive. They may be ill at ease and withdrawn. They may be more or less effective with men than with women. Often many of these are more at ease in dealing with objects or ideas. And as a result, they often develop interests or occupations which take them out of contact with people. They may become scientists or engineers, or prefer solitary occupations where they work with tools and are not bothered with people. In this sense, a skilled toolmaker, a trucker, and a pharmacist have this in common: their jobs do not require frequent dealing with people or close working relationships.

PROBLEMS OF ADJUSTMENT

Since each person must adapt himself to his place in the organization, each movement within the structure means a fresh adjustment. Just as we recognize that there is a very extensive adjustment of behavior and attitudes expected of the young man who changes his role through marriage, so every change of place within the factory means readjustment. If an individual is moved from this punch press to that one, he makes only a small adaptation; yet to many workers, even this is so difficult that they prefer to stay on the same machine.

Other types of movement also create serious problems of adjustment. The salesman who becomes sales supervisor or manager must shift his concept of himself and his job. He must learn how to get other salesmen to call on customers and make the sales, and not try to do it himself. He must worry about selection, training, motivation, and supervision, rather than about how to handle a particular tough customer.

The engineer who becomes a shop foreman, the production superintendent who becomes a labor relations man, or the accountant who becomes a production man—all must adjust to new activities, different responsibilities, new problems, and to new concepts of themselves.

Experience and Expectations

While many movements require only slight changes in behavior or in physical activities, many other moves result in decided changes in ways of thinking, in attitudes, and even in the whole orientation of the individual. This is especially true of changes from one level to another in the supervisory hierarchy, such as from worker to foreman, or from department chief to division chief. If an individual moves upward in the structure, he must adjust himself to completely new activities, to new relations with others, and to new ways of thinking. A similar shift is found with changes from one type of organization to another, such as from engineering to manufacturing or to personnel administration. The individual who moves within the structure not only must face new work problems but must learn to think properly for his new position; he must learn to think like a foreman, or a division chief, or a personnel man. This, on the whole, is one of the least understood aspects of the adjustment of individuals to changes in position.

The individual is not an inert plastic being forced into a social mold; he does not automatically change in conformity with each new role. Instead he has been "conditioned" by his experiences in all his different roles in all the different structures; and he brings to his job a complex pattern of behavior, attitudes, and concepts which are a result of his whole life experience. Out of this background of experience, he has developed attitudes and expectations of the job and ideas as to what is expected of him and what he can expect of others. He may have developed habitual ways of acting which are so routine that he is no longer conscious of them; and to change his role and learn new behavior and attitudes may be a slow and painful process.

Furthermore, the individual may be thought of as bringing to his job his own personal set of "demands." He is seeking certain satisfactions; he expects the job to perform certain functions for him; and he judges it constantly in terms of these demands. These expectations are another product of his conditioning; they grow out of the society itself and out of his place and experience in it. Thus the son of a banker, with a college education, has different expectations and makes different demands of his job than the son of a day laborer with a grammar-school education. These differences in expectations and demands mean a difference in the way they each look at the job, a difference in the way they react, and a difference in the meanings they attach to everything that happens in the work situation.

Looking at it this way, we can describe the well-adjusted person as one who finds some balance between the satisfactions he is seeking, between his demands and expectations, and the satisfactions which the job provides. The poorly adjusted individual is the one whose demands are much greater than the satisfactions he receives. The individual who is seeking status and recognition in the community, for example, will be dissatisfied with a low-status job; and the person who is trying to maintain his position in a group of friends with high incomes will be dissatisfied with the pay of a semiskilled shop job. A single girl living at home, on the other hand, may feel that a friendly work group is more important to her than high pay. Neither high wages nor good environment, however, automatically produce satisfied and well-adjusted workers. The adjustment and satisfaction of the individual on the job is not just a simple matter of wages and physical working conditions but also an adjustment within a complex pattern.

Because the satisfactions which the individual is seeking are expressions of his past conditioning in the society and of his present positions in the social structures, there are certain uniformities in attitudes and expectations among people at work. People with similar positions, backgrounds, or experience are likely to have similar expectations of their jobs. Thus, we can make some predictions about the way an individual will react if we know something about his place in various sets of relationships. As pointed out, the son of a well-to-do professional family is not content to remain long on a low-status shop job; and when we see him in such a situation, we can expect his behavior to reflect his disturbance. This is so well known that most employment men hesitate to put such people on shop jobs except for limited periods, such as vacation employment of college students or as a training period.

The patterns of the society itself, the groupings into which people fall in their relations in the home and community, are the basis of many of their attitudes toward their jobs. Men and women, for example, have different roles in the society, and this is reflected in different attitudes toward their jobs. Patterns of behavior and attitudes vary with age, too, and with one's role in the family group, so that a boy does not have the same activities or expectations as an old man, or a young girl the same as a mother. People also fit into groups in the class system of the society on the basis of their status relationships with others, and the members of one class or status group act and think and hope differently from members of the other groups. His place in each of these groupings, and in others, has a part in determining a person's attitudes toward his job and the satisfactions he looks for in it.

Over a period of years, any one individual may be seen to change his attitudes and expectations from time to time. Many of these changes are the result of new experiences; they are expressions of changes in his pattern of relationships or his role in either the work group or the outside society. Some of the changes are so common to all of us that we can say that there are certain phases through which nearly everyone goes which create problems of adjustment.

Furthermore, the adjustment to change is influenced by the personality pattern. Many people show patterns of anxiety and insecurity so strong that they tend to cling to familiar situations. Any change is seen as threatening, and they dread the unfamiliar. In many cases, they will accept the established situation, even though unsatisfactory, rather than face the uncertainties of the unknown.

Sex Differences

Women generally think about their jobs quite differently from men and expect quite different satisfactions. The normal or expected role of the woman in our society is that of wife and mother, and this is supposed to be her primary center of interest. Men, on the other hand, are expected to be the breadwinners, whose lives are centered around their jobs and who are earning a living for their families. This difference is clearly reflected in the attitudes of the two groups, in the things they talk about, the decisions they make, and in their evaluation of jobs and of work situations. Among factory workers, for example, men are more concerned about opportunities for advancement than women. Men do not often refuse a transfer to a more important or better-paying job, while women frequently refuse such opportunities. This contrast is especially clear between young single girls and young single men who are just starting to work in industry. The girls usually look on their jobs as a temporary filler-in from the time they leave school until they marry. Even among groups who will probably spend most of their lives working, the girls think of marriage as a chance to stop work, keep house, and raise a family. Working after marriage, they think, will be only a temporary expedient to help pay for furniture, accumulate savings to help raise a family, or help out in emergencies. With those attitudes they judge their jobs in terms of whether they enjoy the work or the group, whether it provides opportunities for meeting potential husbands, whether or not it interferes with their dates and social activities. Their jobs are judged in terms of immediate satisfactions rather than in terms of future possibilities.

With the young men we see something quite different. As soon as they leave school and start to work, they begin to think of their roles as adult men. They often become concerned over their rate of advancement in both status and pay. They often wonder how long it will take them to be earning enough to get married and keep a family, and how they can get to be recognized as full-fledged adults. They grow impatient with "boys' " or beginners' jobs and with the processes of advancement, often slow in ordinary times. They show much less concern over whether the work group is friendly and worry less about making friends in a new group. When offered a transfer to another job, they want to know whether it is a better job, if it means more pay, if it has more opportunity for advancement.

School versus Factory

Both young men and young women who are just out of school and taking their first factory jobs, find a problem in adjusting to the work routines. In school, as in the factory, they come and go on a fixed schedule; but the school activities during the day are varied. They move from room to room, from subject to subject; they have "gym" and study periods; and there is continual opportunity for contacts with other students. In the factory, they are often put on simple repetitive jobs where they stay at one work position all day long doing the same job over and over, often with little contact beyond the people right around them. This may go on day after day, even after they have learned the job thoroughly and developed considerable skill. In school, not only were the day's activities varied, but they progressed from day to day. They did not work the same problem day after day, or read the same book; as they learned, they advanced to something new and more difficult. In the school, too, the promotions were frequent and the requirements were very clear. At work, however, the situation is quite different. Not only do they go on day after day doing simple routine jobs, but the channels of advancement are not clear; the how and when of getting ahead are not well defined. When they ask their boss how they can get ahead, he can say only that if they work hard, do a good job, behave themselves, and try to learn about the work, eventually they will be given a chance at better jobs. He cannot say that, if they do this and this and this, they will be promoted at the end of so many months as they do in school, because industry does not work that way.

While both boys and girls have been accustomed to the same school system, their adjustment to the job conditions is often quite different and seems to be directly related to the different meaning that work has for them. Most factory girls adjust quickly to the routines; and if the work group is friendly, they do not mind the simple repetitious jobs. They rarely express anxiety about getting ahead or complain about the monotony of the work. To them it is only a temporary interlude until they "get their man." The boys, as we have seen, react quite differently. They often have a hard time settling down to the work; they like to play around; they soon get tired of doing the same thing all day long, and their attention wanders. As soon as they learn one job, they become impatient to get on to something else; they begin to complain about monotony and wonder about getting ahead. In many cases, they have so much difficulty in making this adjustment that they do poor work and quit, and sometimes they are fired from several jobs before they settle down.

Age Differences

The attitudes and adjustment of both men and women vary with age, too. The attitudes and expectations of the older women are much different from those of young girls. Those who have not married finally begin to realize that they may never marry, and they begin to accept the idea that they will work all their lives. This change in attitude usually takes place around the age of thirty, depending on the customary age of marriage for girls from their place in society. In many cases this change involves a period of emotional disturbance and anxiety which disturbs their relationships both at work and outside. Once they have made the change, their expectations of the job become more like the attitudes of men. They become more interested in advancement and more concerned over status and security than the younger women.

Married working women have still a different pattern. Many of them work to help out in the home; they may be widowed or divorced and have children to support, or their husbands may be sick. In such cases the home is still the primary interest and the work is supplemental to it, although working is no longer thought of as a temporary thing. These women, like older unmarried women, often put considerable emphasis on stability and security; but they are less inclined to be ambitious and are less interested in their futures and their careers as workers. Older men, too, are concerned with stability and security. Most factory workers have reached their ceilings by the time they are forty, and after that they are not likely to advance to higher grades of work or learn new skills. They have usually adjusted to the work they are on and are interested in maintaining their position as it is.

Class Differences

When we examine the adjustment of people from various levels of society, we see that the evaluations of the job vary with social position, too. That is, the way a person thinks of jobs—his feelings that certain jobs are "good" or "bad"—depends in part upon his background. The good job to the son of a janitor will seem a poor job to the son of the president. As we have pointed out, the boy from a high-status family usually is dissatisfied with a low-status factory job; the daughter of a prosperous doctor or lawyer cannot bear to work in the shop but must have an office job. Suppose we consider the case of John S., a young college graduate who had difficulty in adjusting to factory work because of his middle-class background.

John S. was raised in an upper-middle-class suburban neighborhood composed of the families of successful doctors, lawyers, businessmen, and top executives. His father was the successful vice-president of a large manufacturing concern, who had worked himself up from the ranks. John, along with his clique of friends from the neighborhood, went off to college where he took a liberal arts degree. When he finished college, his father urged him to take a factory job and work his way up as he himself had done. Although he was not enthusiastic about factory work, John felt that, with his background, it would be just a temporary thing and that he would soon receive recognition and promotion.

At the same time, many of his friends were returning from college and making their choices of occupations. One, whose father was a doctor, studied medicine; and when he returned his father took him into his practice. Another studied law and was taken into a small law firm where he could gain experience and build up his own clientele. Another entered the family business in a minor executive position. Each of these other boys started in jobs which had status; they were doctors or lawyers or businessmen, all occupations comparable to the occupations of their fathers. Even though their earnings might be low at the start, they could all expect fairly rapid improvement; and in the meantime they were developing the skills that they would later use as lawyers, doctors, or businessmen.

In his contacts with his old group, John began to feel ill at ease. When they talked about their jobs, they could talk as professionals of the interesting cases, the problems they must deal with, the decisions they must make. But John could talk only about his difficulties in getting enough speed on the assembly job he was working on, or the way his foreman treated people, or the way the other workers acted. At first he could treat all this as a sort of initiation for future executives, something you had to go through to learn what the work was like and how workers feel, to learn the business from the ground up, but not as an opportunity to learn the skills that you would use later. At first he could hold his own with his group on this basis. He would explain that it was important to get this understanding of the work and that all the big companies preferred to promote people who had actual factory experience.

As months passed, however, he had less and less to talk about, since he was still doing the same job and the newness had worn off. The others were still finding something fresh to talk about—their medical or legal victories, their clever decisions. John began to feel more and more out of it. He often avoided the group or was glum and irritable when with them. His concern over the situation reflected itself in his work. He lost interest and was always willing to stop and talk with anyone who came along. He was indifferent to the others in the work group and did not get along well. He was apt to complain a good deal and frequently said that he was not given an opportunity to show his ability. The foreman thought that he was capable enough but that his attitude was wrong; and he felt that he could not recommend him for advancement unless he settled down to the work.

This case is typical of the problems of executives' sons when they start out in industry. Unless times are very good or they are very fortunate, they will probably have to start at the bottom, and the way up may be very slow. This is especially true of people at the intermediate levels, whose connections are limited to one company or even to one plant, so that they cannot give their sons the benefit of wider contacts at top-management levels, which would make it easier for them to gain recognition and wider opportunities. Thus, these boys cannot inherit their fathers' status; they cannot step into their fathers' shoes, but must start out on their own.

Problems of Getting Ahead in Business

Boys from working class families have different problems. Many of them have only modest expectations in terms of job status and level of earnings, and to them the jobs that John S. would scorn may be very satisfactory. These fellows soon adapt themselves to the routines of shopwork when they reach a level which they consider indicates satisfactory progress. Many of them look to such jobs as toolmakers, machinists, automatic screw machine operators, as being the height of their ambitions; and they try to get special training to prepare for such jobs. Moreover, when they have reached that level, they are generally considered successful in the eyes of their families and friends. On the other hand, many boys from the families of workers are not content to remain at that level but are driven by a desire to rise in status. This ambition, this urge to get ahead, is sometimes a very powerful drive, forcing them to struggle for more education and training and more recognition on the job. They often have many of the same symptoms as the higher-status boys, like John S., who are forced into shop jobs; and they are impatient with the slow progress, bored with the monotony of shopwork, and anxious to know how to get ahead. Thus, there are two groups with quite different backgrounds who react to their jobs in a very similar manner, but the meaning of this urge to get ahead is quite different for the two. To the higher-status person, the shop job is a threat to the position he has known all his life; it upsets his relationships at the level where he feels that he belongs; and all his efforts are directed toward returning to a comfortable equilibrium at that level. The ambition of the lower-status boy, however, is to rise about his former position; he must do better than his father and outstrip his boyhood friends. And, if he succeeds, he must establish an entirely new set of relationships, not only at work, but outside in the community as well.

When a person with this mobility drive does not receive satisfaction through recognition and advancement on the job, he often tries in a variety of other ways to receive satisfactory recognition. He may turn to hobbies or sports and put a great deal of effort into excelling in them. The story is told of one man, now a top executive in a large concern, who took up one thing after another, when he was just a young fellow in a low-status job, and put all his spare time and effort into each until he could excel in it. His need for success was so obvious that his associates interpreted his efforts to excel in such things as tennis or chess as part of his effort to gain the satisfactory recognition which was lacking on the job. In another concern, there was a large engineering staff with many young graduate engineers in the lowest-status engineering jobs. While these were good jobs and fairly well paid as compared to shop jobs, they were, nevertheless, at the bottom of the engineering hierarchy; and advancement was often slow. Among the employees of the company a very active camera club was developed in which many of these young engineers participated; there was a great deal of competition for recognition in photographic exhibits and for positions as officers of the club. Through this camera club they apparently received the recognition which they felt was lacking in their jobs. As soon as they began to advance in the supervisory hierarchy or otherwise gain status on the job, they began to lose interest in the club; they found they "did not have time" to compete in exhibits, and often would practically give up the hobby.

When a person is not able to gain recognition in these activities, he is likely to lose interest in them; and he may become very critical of the hobby club, its members, and the way it is run. In one instance a man who worked very hard at photography, but who had never received any mention at exhibits or at the camera club to which he belonged, was extremely critical of the judgment of others; he claimed that the judges did not know how to judge the work properly and that the other members in the club were prejudiced against him and would not listen to his good advice. In his work he showed a terrific desire to get ahead. He would work very hard at different things in addition to his regular work, thinking that this would show how superior he was to others in his department. He apparently lacked the ability to do an outstanding job, and everything he attempted was coolly received and left him feeling frustrated. Each time he would react with criticism of everyone in the department from his boss on down, and would talk in much the same way as he talked about the members of the camera club.

The mobile group, with their great desire to get ahead, generally have high expectations. They visualize themselves as achieving important positions in the company, as becoming part of management. With these feelings, they tend to have a strong identification with management rather than with the workers. This is especially true of the group from the higher-status background, of course, who have been brought up in the attitudes of the business and professional group and expect to return there. As long as these people feel that they are making satisfactory progress toward their goals, this attitude, this acceptance of management's point of view, is reinforced. When, however, they feel that their progress is blocked and that they cannot obtain the status they are seeking, they tend to turn against management. In these cases they express great dissatisfaction with the company; they become critical of all its policies and suspicious of all its motives. If they are shopworkers, they often turn to the union and become active in it, or perhaps are active in organizing a union. Sometimes through this union activity they find the recognition they have been seeking, just as others find it in other types of organizations. And sometimes the fellows who are effective in union affairs catch the eye of management and receive promotions, which would not have come their way if they had remained unnoticed as mere operators doing their jobs.

"Status Anxiety"

"Status anxiety" is a kind of individual disturbance found frequently at all levels in industry. In these cases an individual expresses concern over his position relative to others. He is disturbed if someone else gets more recognition from the boss than he does; he worries over status symbols; he is concerned if others do not recognize his proper status; and he is worried about advancement and especially about his rate of progress relative to others. This is a common development among those mobile people whose progress has been blocked. Their anxieties may become so extreme that they develop into severe neuroses, accompanied by feelings of persecution, insomnia, inability to concentrate, and other nervous disorders. One striking example of this was the case of an engineer who started in with a large concern soon after he finished college.

Herbert R. was very ambitious, and the first few years he progressed satisfactorily, although not spectacularly. Then the depression reduced the force; and although he was kept on, his progress was stopped for several years. He was moved around to various jobs and was finally put on one which required considerable contact with outside suppliers. He stayed on this for several years with only a little increase in wages or other recognition. He wanted to get onto some other job which would give him more opportunity, but nothing was done about it.

As time went on, he became more and more disturbed about his situation. He became active from time to time in outside organizations but never seemed to get satisfaction out of them. Then the people in his department began to notice erratic behavior. He began to try to attract attention to himself in various ways. He went to department parties, and, after one or two drinks, he would get up on a table and put on acts or make speeches and generally try to dominate the group and hold their attention. Finally, outside suppliers began to comment on his erratic behavior, which seemed to be his way of getting attention and impressing them with his importance. As a result of this, his superiors "bawled him out"; and shortly afterward he had a "nervous breakdown" and spent several weeks in a sanitarium. His peculiar behavior reappeared, however, soon after he returned, and he was moved to another job. Although there was no cut in pay, the job was with a lower-status department and required daily contacts in the shops.

At this point he was extremely disturbed again, could hardly work at all, and could sleep only with the use of sedatives. In fact, he took several times a normal dose of phenobarbital, was still not able to sleep except for brief periods, and would be too dull to work the next day. He believed that his boss was persecuting him, that he had refused to give him opportunity or recognition, and that he had talked against him to other supervisors. He felt that the boss had his favorites who got all the "breaks" and were getting ahead while he was being held back. Now he felt demoted to a really poor job, and he could see no hope of ever getting ahead. He was extremely excited whenever he talked about the way he felt about this job. He told how he hated to have the people with whom he had formerly worked see him at his new job down in a shop location. On one occasion he had gone out in the shop to get some parts to be tested, and as he was coming back with a box under his arm he saw an old friend coming. He was so ashamed to be seen carrying a box of parts that he turned and hid until the friend had left. Formerly he had driven home from work with some engineers from the old department, but now he rode the streetcar because he couldn't bear to go near them. At the same time, he was embarrassed if anyone whom he knew saw him on the streetcar, because he felt it was such a loss of status to be seen with all the shopworkers. In fact, every little thing which could be associated with loss of status was magnified in his thinking and he would brood over each one by the hour.

This case also illustrates the adjustment problem of the mobile individual who has reached what, at least for the time being, is his ceiling. In many of these cases, especially if the ceiling is fairly low in terms of ambitions and expectations, the individuals go through a period of intense disturbance and maladjustment, often lasting several years, until they accept the realities of their limitations.

Another case of this type was that of Albert N., about forty-five, who was a well-paid expert in a special technical field.

Albert N. worked in a small department consisting of about a dozen experts at his level and a miscellaneous group of technical assistants, secretaries, and clerical helpers. He himself had risen from the ranks of the technical assistants with the aid of evening-school study. For a number of years an elderly man approaching retirement age had been the head of the department, and he was very friendly to Albert. For the last two years before his retirement, this department head had been ill a great deal, and in his absence he had delegated more and more responsibility to Albert and generally made him his right-hand man. In this role, Albert was in constant touch with what was going on in the department. He sat in on decisions about the work; he sometimes had to supervise others; and he handled much of the correspondence. During this period he felt that when the chief retired he would be made head of the department, and probably his chief thought so, too.

When the chief did finally retire, however, his superior officers decided against Albert, and brought in a man who had handled similar work in another organization but who had had a better education and broader experience in other phases of the work, This man had been in the department some years before, and Albert had known him then; but he probably did not understand the distinction Albert had attained more recently as informal assistant to the department chief. At any rate, when he took charge, he treated Albert just as he did all the others at his level. Albert was no longer "in the know" on all problems of the department; he no longer was brought into discussions of policy and practices; he did not handle any correspondence for the chief nor take charge of things when he was away. He began to worry about the situation, about his relations with the new chief, and about his own future; and he developed severe anxieties and worried over many little things which he felt indicated loss of status. Whereas formerly he had been the first to see any memos or letters which were circulated to the group, now the new chief had a rubber stamp with the names of the men at Albert's level arranged in alphabetical order; and any correspondence was sent around in that order. Albert was at the bottom of the list and was the last to get the material, so that, instead of being the first to know about any new developments, he was often the last unless he was told by others. Also, instead of discussing all the work problems with Albert, the new chief took up only those pertaining to Albert's own work and never discussed the problems of others with him. Where Albert had previously spent more time with the chief than had any of the others, he no longer felt free to drop in to see the chief; and he actually began to avoid him. Thus, he had lost his former informal status and all the little symbols which went with it, and he had become just one of the group again.

For a couple of years, things went along this way; and although Albert was disturbed by the situation, he was able to handle his work to the satisfaction of his new chief. Gradually, however, he grew more and more discouraged. He complained to his chief about the work, wanted to know what was wrong, and generally showed dissatisfaction. The chief began to feel uncomfortable in his contacts with Albert and began to avoid him. He began to spend more time with the others, drawing them into his confidence and leaving Albert out. Noticing this, Albert began to feel that his superior "had it in for him"; and he spent hours worrying over the cause, which he finally attributed to an incident which occurred when he had been just a young fellow in the department and the present chief had seemed annoyed at a joking remark he had made. He soon reached a stage of feeling quite persecuted. If his chief failed to talk over his work with him, he felt that he was being ignored deliberately; but if the chief did comment on his work, he thought he was being criticized. If he saw the chief talking or laughing with one of the others, he saw in it fresh evidence that he was not liked or wanted. In fact, practically anything the chief did was interpreted in terms of these feelings of persecution.

Along with this, he began to develop insomnia and stomach trouble, and to worry about his health. So when he was not lying awake at night worrying about his status and his relations with his boss, he was lying awake worrying about his health. He felt tired all the time; he would get home at night feeling exhausted; then he would work in the garden so that he would be tired enough to sleep; but he would end up taking a sedative after all. After this, he worried about the possible ill effects of taking so much sedative. He withdrew from his former social activities, refused to play bridge or golf, and would sit around the house in the evening, not wanting to go anywhere or see anyone.

Finally he reached the point where he could hardly do any work at all. He would sit by the hour gazing out of the window or just staring at papers on his desk without seeing them. The boss sent him to the doctor who diagnosed his case as "neurasthenia" and recommended a few weeks' rest in a sanitarium. After a few weeks away from the job, his condition improved; he returned to work; but soon he was as bad as ever again. This recurred several times; each time he would improve after a period away from the work, and then he would have a relapse within a few weeks of his return. He was finally put under special treatment, but it required about a year before he had made a readjustment, before he could accept his situation and carry on his work and personal life in a normal manner.

This adjustment of the individual to his ceiling of attainment is not usually accompanied by such severe symptoms. In the case of Albert, of course, his reactions were accentuated by the fact that the next step had seemed to be so clearly within his grasp and had then been snatched away by forces beyond his control. In other cases, the approach to the ceiling is much more gradual and the individual adjusts his expectations almost without realizing it. Also, it is probable that in most cases the individual has reached a level which gives him a satisfactory status, so that, although he might like to rise higher, he feels no great frustration at his actual level of attainment.

Possibilities for Advancement

All these problems of adjustment are related to the whole problem of upward mobility in the industrial structure. In the first place, we have seen that the structure forms a pyramid with fewer and fewer people at each higher level. This means that it is impossible for everyone at one level to rise to the next. This is especially true for the non-supervisory or worker level, where there are at least ten workers for every foreman or supervisor and there may be fifty or more in some types of work; here only a relatively small portion of the lower group can ever rise into the supervisory ranks. And it also means that only a few from the foreman level can ever move up to higher supervision.

This limitation on movement from the ranks to supervision does not mean, however, that there can be no hope for progress for the mass of the workers. As we have seen, there are highly developed status systems within the work level through which the individual can advance. There are the gradations of jobs into varying degrees of skill and prestige, and the individual may progress from the low-status beginners' jobs to the higher-status and better-paid jobs requiring greater skill and experience. There may also be a wage structure which provides for wage advancement on the basis of merit or service even though the individual remains on the same job. Then there is the possibility of moving from low-status organizations to those of higher status, or from shopwork to office work. In fact, whenever there are status differences in jobs, there is a possibility of some degree of status advancement.

Unfortunately, there is no clearly marked pathway to advancement in most factories; there is no clear-cut plan of action and no timetable by which the beginner can plan his progress. He cannot say, "I will do this and this, and by next year I will have reached that place." While we like to tell the youngster that if he works hard and shows ability he will progress, we must admit that, for the average run of people, chance also plays a major role in his progress. We must not only be ready and able to move on to the next step, but the opportunity must be there.

Within the hierarchy of jobs we do find many cases in which there are certain steps necessary for progress from one level to another. For example, in many of the crafts there is provision for the training of young people through an apprenticeship which they must pass before they can be accepted as a full-fledged mechanic. In such cases there are usually only two or three steps in the system: apprentice and mechanic; or apprentice, class B mechanic, and class A mechanic. When a youngster starts on such a course, he knows pretty clearly what his ceiling will be and about how long it will take him to get there. If he wishes to go farther, he must move out of that particular system entirely. Even in such a system, of course, there are decided limits, since the group usually limits the number of apprentices to the apparent demand for the mechanics (often in depression years no one will be admitted to apprenticeship).

With the vast majority of factory jobs there is no similar road to advancement; the beginner just comes in, takes any job he is put on, and then wonders where he goes from there. In many cases the experience and skill he develops on one job may lead almost directly to a better job of the same type. In such cases the beginner feels that the sooner he learns the job and develops his skill, the sooner he will be able to move to the next level. Unfortunately, any such move also depends upon there being need for additional workers at the next level; and until there is an opening, no matter how good the newcomer may be, he will not be able to advance. Here again the needs of the structure must govern, rather than the desires of the individuals.

In every large plant there are many blind-alley jobs which have but limited possibilities in themselves and do not lead to anything better. Many of these require the development of special abilities or skills which are of no particular value on other jobs. In fact, in many companies there are some jobs which are so specialized that they are unknown outside the one company and thus have no value anywhere else. Sometimes these jobs are fairly well paid, and they may require months or even years to develop a high degree of skill and to rise to the top wage level. An individual on such a job, who is not satisfied to have risen to its top level, often finds himself in a difficult position. In order to advance further he must go to another kind of job where he will have to start all over again at a lower level and learn new skills. Suppose, for example, a man, who has risen to the top level of a specialized job at which he earns $2.00 an hour, is not satisfied and wants to get into toolmaking, which has much greater possibilities. But to do this he will have to start at the bottom as an apprentice in the toolroom at $1.50 an hour. This may seem an unusual case, but it is surprising how many jobs in modern large plants are so specialized that their skills are not transferable to other work. Indeed, the same situation can occur in a retail store, where a topnotch salesman does so well in promoting his own line of merchandise that he cannot afford to accept a lower-paying, but higher-status, supervisory position —even though this offers him greater opportunity for advancement. As a result, many employees find themselves in the position that, no matter how hard they work or how well they learn their jobs, they are not preparing themselves for a step upward.

Problems of Selection

For the ambitious individual, it is unfortunate that all transfers, promotions, or upgradings are directed in accordance with the needs of the organization rather than with the desires or needs of the individuals. When a foreman has a job to be filled, he has to think in terms of who can best handle the job rather than who wants it most. In many cases the one who works hardest or is the best at the lower level is not the one who can do best at the next level. This is especially true where there is no particular relation between the skill at one level and the next. A youngster, for example, who did very well on a routine assembly job, but who did not get along well with other workers might be a very poor choice for a job where he had to keep other workers supplied with parts and materials. Or a file clerk may not make a good secretary. In such cases the boss's selections may seem very unfair to some of the group.

This problem of selection is especially acute in the movements into the supervisory level. The best mechanic or the most efficient operator does not always make the best foreman; the ability to handle a group does not develop naturally out of the ability to handle machines. As a result, the expert machinist or the extremely efficient worker may find that he is being passed over in favor of others with much less skill or knowledge of the work. The highly skilled worker finds that he must take orders from someone who, he feels, does not really understand the job. In addition, management is putting more stress upon getting a different type of foreman from the old-timer who was selected because of his technical skill. Foremen who have more education, who understand management's logic, and who are skilled in dealing with people rather than machines are in demand now. All this makes it harder for the ambitious man to rise by virtue of hard work and skill with his hands.

When selecting a person to fill any position, there are two things which should be considered. The first is the ability to do the job, and the second is the effect of the selection upon the group. The first is rather obvious: if you want a typist, you select someone who can type, and this is, in fact, usually given first consideration. The second is not always so obvious a consideration and is often overlooked, especially when moving people within a work group. Suppose we take a few typical cases:

1. A new and improved press was brought into a printing department. None of the pressmen, mostly long-service men, had had experience with this type of press, and it was decided to train one of them for it. One of the few short-service pressmen, a very alert and capable man, was selected for the new job. The group looked on the job as being a real opportunity in terms of both security and status, since the new press required more skill and might eventually displace some of the older ones. The selection of a short-service man upset all the older men, who felt that, because of their service and experience, they should have been given the first chance at the job.

2. In a shop department the inspector's job was at the top of the informal job hierarchy. When a vacancy occurred, the foreman selected an operator who was a hard worker but who was very unpopular with the group because of his unfriendly attitude and his unwillingness to help the others. The group thought the choice unfair and did everything they could to make the work difficult for this new inspector.

3. A machine department had a large group of old and highly skilled operators. They had group chiefs whose principal duties were of a minor supervisory nature—distributing work, checking upon individual jobs, keeping records, and seeing that raw materials were on hand. When one of these positions was open, a man was transferred in from another department instead of one being promoted from the ranks. The more ambitious men felt that they were being ignored and that one of them should have had the job. The skilled operators were annoyed at having someone over them who was unfamiliar with the work and who did not understand their problems and difficulties.

Sometimes selections are made because the foreman becomes interested in or sympathetic toward one person and thinks only of satisfying that person's needs without considering the effect upon the group. Some one worker talks to him about how much he wants to get ahead, and the foreman feels sympathetic; and the first time there is an opening on a better job, he puts that man in it. He forgets that there may be others in the group who feel just the same way; and because they have not talked to him, they have not caught his attention and interest. Or, again, one fellow may complain that he has not had a raise in some time, that the cost of living has gone up, or that he has more family responsibilities; and if he has been doing a reasonably good job, the foreman is likely to be sympathetic and give him a raise, or extra overtime, or a chance at a better job. Whenever he does this, there are always others who feel they deserve as much consideration and are being ignored. It is out of such incidents that the almost universal belief arises that "it is the squeaking axle that gets the grease."

Because they feel that the supply of foremen and executives cannot be left to chance, many large companies have programs for recruiting and training executive personnel. This usually means that they recruit people just out of college and put them through a special training which is not generally available. In many cases, part of this training consists of a tour of duty in the shops, during which, in theory, they go into the shops and work at various jobs just as any other beginner would. They are not, however, left to their own devices in climbing from there, but are moved around through various jobs and departments in order to give them a wide experience. Then when supervisory or executive jobs are open, they will be filled from this group. They are the privileged group, the "fair-haired boys," who will be the future executives. And the more management relies on such a group to fill their supervisory and executive positions, the less will be the opportunity for others to rise out of the ranks. All such plans for recruiting and training future executives indicate the significance of college training for the higher positions. Most, if not all, of such programs recruit almost entirely from college graduates. And certainly for those ambitious to rise above the rank of foreman, college training, whether in day or night school, is an important asset.

For successful adjustment as a shopworker, on the other hand, a college education seems to be of no help. In fact, the person who has obtained a college education usually has ambitions far beyond a factory job, either because the college training itself stimulates such ambition or because the training is a result of the ambition. Thus the boy from a working family, who makes the effort to get an education, usually does so as a means of rising above his background. He wants to do better than his father, or his family is urging him on. And the boy whose family gives him an education as a matter of course already takes the higher status for granted. As a result, both of these college graduates feel continually frustrated in shop jobs, are always explaining or justifying their position, and generally have difficulty in making adjustment. This condition is so well understood in industry that experienced employment interviewers usually differentiate people as shop types and office types, and they put all those with more than high-school education, unless it is some form of trade or skill training, into the office group. Even when conditions are such that college graduates are willing to take shop jobs, the companies prefer not to have them, because sooner or later they become dissatisfied and, unless there is the possibility of promoting them fairly rapidly, they will become serious problems.

Adjustment to Promotion

The ambitious, mobile people who manage to rise through the structure must, of course, face problems of adjustment somewhat different from those of more stable people who settle down at about one level. For example, when a man is promoted to the supervisory level, he must make much more extensive adjustments than the man who moves from a semiskilled to a skilled job. In the first place, his whole view of the work changes when he becomes a supervisor. He no longer thinks only of his own job, but every job in his group becomes his job and his responsibility, in a sense. Also, he must think of the other workers, not just as his fellows, but as people whom he must direct and supervise, encourage, and discipline. If he is in charge of the group of which he was once a part, he finds that all his relationships with them change. If he continues to be intimate with his old friends, then the others accuse him of playing favorites; if he drops them, they say he is "high-hat." All his social contacts are colored by the fact that he is now the boss, and the others act and talk with him differently because of it. He himself soon develops relationships with other supervisors; they may lunch with him or invite him to their parties, and he is gradually drawn into new circles of social activities.

This sort of adjustment goes on with every major change of rank or status and, to some extent, with every change of organization. This means that the mobile fellow who rises steadily or who is shifted around to gain experience in various organizations is continually adjusting to new concepts and points of view and to new sets of relationships with people. This even extends itself to his relationships in the community outside the plant. While he is a shopworker, he usually lives in a working-class neighborhood and associates with other workers. As he rises through the ranks, he moves to better neighborhoods and associates with different people.

Adjustment at Lower Levels

Fortunately, everyone in industry does not have a strong mobility drive. Many people make good adjustment at even the bottom levels and are able to get satisfaction out of their jobs. This does not mean that they would not want better jobs, or that they will admit to a lack of ambition; but, actually, many are sufficiently well adjusted that they will not make the effort or take the chances necessary for going on to something better. This, however, is counter to the beliefs of many people, especially those who do have strong ambitions, who feel that everyone should be motivated just as they are. Thus, many top executives, who have reached their positions because of their efforts and determination, believe that everyone feels as they do, and that everyone should respond to the same incentives to which they responded. As a result, they believe that by holding out promises of opportunities for advancement they can motivate their people to work the way they have worked. They also tend to view with horror anything like a system of seniority rights which may stand in the way of the rapid advancement of ambitious youngsters; and they think that the bulk of the workers do, or should, feel the same way.

To be well adjusted in the lower-status positions, or even the lowest-status position in a work group, does not mean that the individual is insensitive to status differences. In fact, we continually meet with disturbances due to minor shifts in status relationships and with cases of anxiety over relative status. For example, to give a raise to one individual in a group causes reactions among the entire group, usually accompanied by demands for similar raises and by criticism of that individual and of the foreman. In one such case the men said that they were perfectly content with their wages and would have had no complaint if the foreman had not given one of the group a raise. We see the other side of this when an individual is demoted from supervision to the ranks, is moved to a lower-status job, or has his pay cut. He almost always has a severe reaction, feels ashamed and embarrassed among his group, and may withdraw from contacts with them as much as possible. Sometimes an individual will quit his job entirely, even if it means taking an even worse job elsewhere, rather than face a loss of status within the same work group.

Stability versus Mobility

If we consider the people in industry in the light of what they are striving for, what satisfactions they are seeking, we can see two different tendencies. One, which is especially strong in the mobile individuals, is the desire to move from the position they are in to some other and higher status position in the structure. The other is the tendency to stay put, to retain their present position and protect it against changes; and this is found in those who have made a comfortable adjustment to their present place. Thus, we might describe one group as trying to maintain their established pattern of activities and relationships, and the other as trying to take on a new pattern. Most people, however, are not completely one way or the other, but only predominantly so; and people sometimes change their goals. During his life cycle an individual may pass from one phase to another. He starts out anxious to rise out of the youngster group in terms of job, pay, and status; he moves up a bit in the structure, reaches a level which satisfies his needs and to which he can adjust comfortably, and then stops pushing and settles down. In the first period he will be upset over lack of progress in too stable a situation and will complain about the boredom and monotony when he feels that he is not progressing adequately. After he has settled down, he will prefer stable relations, will not be bothered by routines and monotony, and will be reluctant to make changes. This cycle is often expressed in comments to the effect that young men want opportunity and older men want security.

SYMPTOMS OF DISTURBANCE

Closely allied with the whole problem of the adjustment of the individual is the significance of complaints and grievances. In general, we can say that most complaints are expressions of some disturbance in the individual's relationships either at work or elsewhere. In an exhaustive study of the complaints expressed in interviews with 20,000 employees, Roethlisberger and Dickson found three classes of complaints.[1] The first referred to objects or conditions which could be clearly seen and agreed upon, as, for example, a broken tool or a burned-out light bulb. The second were those referring to experiences or conditions which could not be clearly seen and agreed upon, such as, "The room is too hot," "The light is poor," or "The work is too heavy." The third class were complaints which did not refer to verifiable external conditions but were expressions of the sentiments of the person, such as complaints about wages, supervision, or advancement. They also found that a large portion of the complaints, in fact, the things about which people seemed most disturbed, were in the third group—things that could not be seen and agreed upon and which could not be dealt with directly as you deal with a burned-out lamp. They found, further, that, with any of the complaints, the things complained about were not always the actual causes of the disturbances; they were the symptoms, the outward expressions of some underlying problem or disturbance. Thus, to understand any complaint, it is necessary to understand the latent content of the complaint; it is necessary to know what the complainant is really talking about, what is really "eating on him." This presents a problem in understanding and diagnosis which is a major problem in dealing with these complaints. If a worker complains about his machine when his real trouble is that his foreman is pressing him to turn out more work, it does not do any good to "prove" to him that there is nothing wrong with the machine.

One of the interesting features of complaints about wages is that a surprisingly large number of them are merely symptoms of some underlying conditions, and many of them are not cured by wage increases. We are so prone to take for granted the idea that everyone wants more money that we often fail to look below the surface on

---

[1] F. J. Roethlisberger and W. J. Dickson, *Management and the Worker* (Cambridge, Mass.: Harvard University Press, 1939), pp. 255–69.

such complaints. We forget to ask ourselves, "What is he really grip-ing about?" Yet time and again we meet with cases in which Jim wants more money because Joe got a raise, or because he feels that his fore-man does not give the proper recognition for his years of service, or because in some other way the raise would symbolize status or other satisfaction he is seeking, and not because of any real need for the money. If we try to cure such complaints merely by manipulating wages, we find that we are only treating the symptoms and are not curing the disease.

Often the complaints about the most obvious of external condi-tions may be indicative of some disturbance of the individual. The in-dividual who is satisfied with his job and his life, in general, tends to accept things which to another may seem intolerable. He may take for granted dirty surroundings, poor tools, or other conditions as long as they do not symbolize inadequacies or frustrations in his adjustment either at work or outside. But the frustrated worker may complain about these same conditions which the other takes for granted as part of the work situation. For this reason, it is important to treat com-plaints as symptoms; and even though the thing complained about can be and is corrected, it should not be assumed that the complainant will be satisfied.

Since complaints usually represent some disturbance in the equi-librium of the individual, they appear most often when a person is worried or anxious. Status anxieties, for example, are usually ac-companied by all kinds of complaints about the work and the work situation as well as about relations with other workers and superiors. And though some complaints may be merely expressions of momen-tary or superficial annoyances, many are expressions of serious mal-adjustment and are part of a complex pattern of disturbances.

While a complaint in itself is often unimportant, the conditions of which it is a symptom are of serious import to the individual as a worker. Investigation has clearly proved that anxiety from any cause tends to reduce efficiency of the worker, no matter how satisfactory the job and the work situation may be. Actually, such findings agree with the experiences which most of us have had from time to time. Almost everyone can remember an occasion when anxiety over some home conditions, a quarrel with family or superiors, or worry about some difficult decision has prevented him from putting his full at-tention on his job and may even have reduced him temporarily to a state where he just could not work at all. Thus, any serious disturbance may produce a state of what Roethlisberger and Dickson refer to as "morbid preoccupation," in which the individual is so preoccupied or wrapped up in his worries about some personal situation that he cannot do his work.[2] You might say that his mind withdraws from consideration of the work and goes round and round on this other problem; and in a severe case he may develop other symptoms, such as nervousness, inability to sit still, inability to concentrate enough to read, trembling hands, avoidance of others, loss of appetite, and insomnia.

Such morbid preoccupations are not limited to any level in the organization and are not affected by status and education of the individual. It is often asserted that such behavior is an expression of low intelligence or lack of education and that it is not found, therefore, among college graduates, engineers, and others that have been trained to think. In general, such assertions come from successful executives who have reached a very satisfactory level of attainment and adjustment and are no longer subject to these kinds of disturbances. Actually, such conditions are found to exist at every level and often seem to interefere more with the work of those who work with ideas than those who work with their hands, for many shop jobs are so much a matter of manual routines that they require very little conscious attention.

Since the anxieties and preoccupations are part of a pattern of personal disequilibrium, they may appear whenever an individual must make a new adjustment either at work or outside. And since most work situations are constantly undergoing changes of some sort, they appear to be very productive of anxieties and the accompanying complaints. This is so clear that, knowing what changes will occur, it is possible to predict the areas of disturbance even down to the particular individuals and their probable reactions. Thus, a proposed change in organization, in which a certain department will be removed from one division chief's authority and given to another, will probably make the first one feel that he has lost status and make him wonder if his superior thinks he is not capable of handling such a big job. At the same time, the department chief who is being moved will probably have some anxieties about the new boss and will wonder what he will expect of the department. While in many cases the disturbances are only momentary and adjustment takes place rapidly, nevertheless there is almost always some touch of anxiety or uncer-

[2] *Ibid.*, p. 292.

tainty created by the change. Often the actual emotional adjustment is made before the change itself takes place; that is, the individual is able to adjust his attitudes and expectations toward the new conditions between the time that an anticipated change is announced and the time when it actually takes place. In other cases the adjustment may be very gradual and sometimes it extends over a period of months during which there are continual complaints and anxieties.

Not only are the complaints symptomatic of the anxieties accompanying such changes, but they often seem to play an important role in the adjustment of the individual. Apparently the free statement of the fears and anxieties provides some relief to the individual, and the more effectively he can voice his feelings, the more easily he makes the necessary adjustment. Furthermore, when the change is one affecting the entire group, the "griping" seems to give the individual a feeling of support from his fellows, a feeling that they are all in it together and all feel the same way about it. Then, as the adjustment begins to take place, the complaints begin to dwindle away and the individual gradually fits into the new pattern. There is, in fact, a rough cycle of adjustment which all individuals and groups seem to go through. First, there is the period of disturbance, characterized by a lot of anxiety and complaining. Next, the complaints dwindle, and the individuals begin to talk more constructively about the meaning of the change and to think about the actions they may take in meeting the change. Finally, there is the period of adjustment and settling down to the new equilibrium. In any change, therefore, the complaints should be viewed as part of the normal process and should not be repressed. Instead, they should be brought out into the open where they can be watched for evidence of more serious disturbances than have been anticipated.

19. THE TECHNIQUES
OF ORGANIZATION

As we go from organization to organization, we find that each has its own special personality which gives it a special tone or atmosphere. Thus, status systems and status concerns appear in all except a few very small ones; yet, in some, status anxieties run rampant, and worry over one's relation with superiors overshadows everything. In others, this anxiety is comparatively slight, and other concerns hold the attention of the group.

These differences between organizations are not due to differences in the people but to differences in the way the whole is put together and to the forces acting on it. In order to understand these things better, let us examine some of the techniques of organization and their influence upon human relations.

SYSTEMATIC TECHNIQUES AND METHODS

It is quite apparent that the way an organization accomplishes its goals can range all the way from highly systematized techniques and procedures, to which the employee is supposed to adhere rigorously, to no techniques or procedures at all. Assembly-line factories represent one end of this scale, while "arty" organizations represent the other. In factories, everything is arranged in accordance with standard work practice and well-defined procedures. Deviations from these procedures cannot easily be countenanced. In many cases, an effort is made to control the work habits of the individual employee; he is told how to do the work and is not permitted any individual variations from the routines that have been set up. In organizations where predetermined work routines and procedures have not been established, the employee is permitted a great many more individual choices in how he performs his work. He is not asked to adhere rigorously to precisely defined work practices.

Since we know that large numbers of people react negatively to situations where it is difficult, if not impossible, to express their own individuality, it can be expected that morale will suffer in organizations which have a tight, systematic technology. This certainly has been borne out in studies and observations which the authors have made. Whenever employees are called upon to perform highly routinized, repetitive work in accordance with rigorously prescribed procedures, they begin to feel as though management is treating them like children. "It's like a kindergarten around here," they say.

A distinction should be made here between a highly rigorous technology which is based on scientific knowledge and a technology based entirely on arbitrary procedure. The reactions of employees appear to be partially determined by the extent to which the technology makes sense to them. A technology based on science is reasonable in the sense that the logic of nature confirms it. You can verify what you are doing, either in elaborate experiments or by objective observations in real life situations. An employee in a factory usually is able to make some sense out of what he is doing, particularly after he has acquired a knowledge of mechanics and some notions about time-motion economy and methods engineering. More than that, he can see something very real being accomplished.

A technology based on procedure can be, and often is, purely arbitrary. It is just one way of accomplishing the task; there may be other ways that are equally as effective. As often as not, a procedure is founded in historical precedence; it appears to be the best way of accomplishing a particular task simply because "we have always done it that way."

The purpose of any procedure is simply that of setting up a formal way of accomplishing a particular task in order to reduce to a minimum the need for constant decisions on matters of detail. In one sense, a procedure is to an organization what a habit is to an individual. If we had to think through all of the details involved in getting ourselves dressed in the morning, we would never get to work, so engrossed would we be with buttoning our shirts and tying our shoelaces. In the same way, a procedure in an organization eliminates the necessity for thought about minor matters. Just so long as you follow the procedure, you can be assured that the right people will be notified and the proper records kept. Everything will be conducted in a "business-like" manner.

Overelaboration of Procedures

Carefully worked out procedures can have a practical value in the operation of a business. But there is a strong tendency for many organizations to develop procedures for handling practically every problem situation—to define everything to the point of eliminating all individual decision and initiative. In considering many modern industrial organizations, it would seem almost as though they were being slowly strangled by an overelaboration of procedures and policies. In some organizations, no one dares to breathe unless he first finds out what the procedure is. Everything has been defined. Nothing has been left to the imagination or individual decision. Rigid, unadaptive bureaucracy reigns supreme!

Another feature of procedures which creates poor morale among the employees who are subjected to an overabundance of them is their tendency to persist long after they have outworn their usefulness. Indeed, it appears as though a procedure, once established, seldom dies a natural death; it usually has to be murdered in cold blood if it is to be done away with at all. Probably one reason why procedures are taken for granted and allowed to continue *ad infinitum* is that they were originally set up to eliminate thought. As a consequence, and we are speaking seriously here, they are never thought of again until some inquisitive person happens to ask what this report is used for, or why this procedure is being followed. More important than this, perhaps, is the fact that procedures are generally determined by higher authority. Therefore, no one down the line dare make modifications.

Regardless, however, of the reasons for the persistence of procedures, employees are frequently aware of their purely arbitrary character and feel that they are unnecessary and restrictive. Particularly is this true when employees themselves play no part in determining the procedures. Under such circumstances, they develop the notion that management does not trust them to develop a systematic and intelligent way of handling things. Whenever you hear employees saying, "They do all your thinking for you around here," you can be sure that morale is low, or else on its way down.

Unnecessary Procedures

In many cases management prescribes procedures which are actually unnecessary for the accomplishment of the over-all task of the organization. Many such procedures are set up merely to insure good "business practice" among employees. Gate passes, passes to first aid, procedures for securing gloves or rags—passes and procedures for this, that, and the other thing—all fall into this category. Many of these practices are necessary for an orderly operated organization.

Nevertheless, when they become overelaborated, employees begin reacting against them. Frequently such procedures are set up as though most or all employees would not be businesslike or honest in their work if they were not closely controlled and watched in all situations. While it is true that a reasonable amount of supervision must be exercised, the fact remains that most employees will follow orderly business procedures, once an explanation of the reason for the procedure is given, and particularly if they are permitted to assist in setting up any formal procedure which may be decided upon. It is the implication that management considers them dishonest, irresponsible, or "like children" which creates injured feelings.

One case is so flagrant an example that it bears recording here. The manager of the organization involved was extremely suspicious of subordinate employees. He felt that most, if not all, employees, were essentially irresponsible and interested solely in keeping as far away from work as possible. His own work habits were good, at least as far as the routines were concerned. He came to work an hour early; he stayed late; he was always on the go. He consumed most of his energies during this period, however, wondering what his subordinates were doing and prying, in all sorts of petty ways, into the details of their work and of their personal lives. Since this was a factory organization, the manager had no difficulty finding members of his staff who tended to confirm his views. He enlisted the help of his auditor and a few others in setting up a system of oppressive rules and regulations which had his organization reeling in very short order. First, all the gates were locked, except at specific times, in order to be sure that no employee, once on the grounds, could get out. This was done because it was suspected that a few employees were slipping out for a cup of coffee at unauthorized times. Next, the cafeteria was closed during the morning hours because a small number of employees were using it for coffee during their rest period. Then the guards were instructed to take the name of any employee coming in after the whistle blew. This was done even though employees had to punch a regular time card in their own departments. It was felt that some employees were coming to work early, punching in, and then slipping out for coffee and staying out until after the starting whistle. The lunch periods were reduced in number from three to two in order to gain closer control over employees during this time. It was strongly suspected that employees were slipping downtown to do their shopping at lunch time. Employees began to ask the personnel department when management was going to mount machine guns at the gate. The final blow came when the cafeteria was closed without warning and the door was bolted and barred so that employees could not use the area even to eat the lunches they had brought with them. The ostensible reason for this action was that the company could not afford to clean up after them. The answer to this challenge was simple: the employees refused to go back to work until the cafeteria was unlocked. Actually, what management was expressing here in the establishment of these various procedures was a considerable hostility toward the employees, which the employees quite naturally felt. In such a situation, it is difficult to argue against control because it appears as though you are arguing against virtue and for sin. After all, why should employees slip out for a cup of coffee after the starting whistle? The point is, of course, that the great majority of them do not and that the offenders, and only the offenders, should be punished and controlled.

Reasons for Overelaboration of Controls

An overelaboration of procedural controls frequently develops whenever the economic situation becomes tight. Under such circumstances, management has the vague feeling that "we have to cut out all this tomfoolery; employees have to toe the mark or else. . . ." Some tightening down, of course, is necessary; but, for the most part, this kind of managerial action does far more harm than good to the organization. It would be more intelligent, and certainly more effective, to solicit the help of employees in reducing expenses and increasing output, rather than to lash out at them indiscriminately and arbitrarily in the hope that fear will drive them to greater productivity and increased interest in the welfare of the organization.

Unions, in many cases, tend to stimulate the proliferation of procedures where they did not exist before. Most union-management relations are characterized by a formal definition of rights and privileges. A "legal" situation is created with all that this implies. Management is required to set up formal procedures for handling various matters of mutual concern to management and the union in order to insure adherence to the provisions of the contract. This is particularly true in conflict situations where the union is suspicious of management and watching every move it makes. Another effect of unionization is the tendency to centralize the determination of procedure and policy. The interpretation of the contract is often thought of as a legalistic activity, which indeed it is. As a consequence, many organizations feel safer if this interpreting is done by experts and kept out of the hands of lower-level supervision. This is true, also, of union officials who want all handlings negotiated with their top representatives in order to prevent any concessions which might be granted by less-experienced stewards. There is, therefore, a definite trend toward the centralization of control, even with regard to minor details, on higher and higher levels. This trend tends to reduce still further the opportunities which the individual employee has of participating in decisions which affect him; although on major issues, such as the election of his representatives and the acceptance of the contract, he may have considerably greater opportunities than he had without the union. This is not an argument either for or against unions but is merely designed to show the effects of unionization in increasing the overelaboration of procedures in industry.

The size and complexity of an organization can have a good deal to do with the tendency of management to attempt to control all activities by prescribed procedures. In such cases, management is aware of its lack of control over the various things going on in the organization and attempts to reassure itself by setting up procedures for the handling of details. This is supposed to insure that the job gets done in the proper manner. Anyone familiar with large organizations knows that no amount of procedural administration will guarantee control to management over all parts of the organization.

Management tends to lean heavily on procedural controls whenever, for any reason, it fears that it lacks control over what is happening in the organization. Such fears are especially likely to occur as the size and complexity of the organization increase. Excessive development of procedural control may also result from management's desire for protection from legalistic or other reprisals by the union if certain policies are not carried out, or it may arise from suspicion of the worker and the conviction that he is not co-operating with his bosses in getting the work done. It may get its impetus from fear of economic failure in times of stress or from the fear and anxiety inherent in the personalities of management representatives. But, whatever the cause, an overelaboration of procedural controls is likely to create resentment and bad feeling among employees.

Routine Work and Obsessional Thinking

It is apparent from our studies and observations that a particular technology, or way of accomplishing the work of an organization, influences morale positively or negatively to the extent that it permits individual choice and decision by employees on the job. It is also apparent that employees are more likely to accept a work demand which ties in with actual production than a strictly procedural demand which may be arbitrary and even unnecessary. However, in either case, any work which is routine and repetitive is likely to be a morale liability. It is not that employees cannot stand repetitive work; as a matter of fact, some like the rhythm of the job, the steady hum of machinery, and the chomp-chomp-chomp of the presses. However, repetitive, routine work employs only the muscles and kinesthetic sense of the worker; his mind is free to wander. This, in itself, is not demoralizing to the worker; his reveries may be very useful to him in passing the time. But, with many people, this opportunity for uncontrolled projection of thought opens the way for preoccupation with events occurring in the organization, situations at home, and personal problems. He begins to brood over things that happen and to develop obsessions. The effect of obsessional thinking on the employee's productivity and personal well-being is described in considerable detail in Roethlisberger and Dickson's *Management and the Worker*. Here it is stated:

> The important role repetitive work plays in creating an ideal setting for the development of discontent has been frequently overlooked. Work in modern industrial organizations consists not so much of hard manual labor as repetitive jobs which require a minimum of skilled attention and allow a great deal of time for preoccupation. It is apparent that for many workers engaged in repetitive or semirepetitive tasks the point of proficiency is soon reached; that is, the amount of attention that the job can carry for the worker is less than the amount of attention the operator is capable of giving. In such a situation, where it is no longer possible for the worker either to elaborate or change his job, he can either switch his attention to other things in the immediate surroundings or indulge in revery. In the absence of any real social situation in which to participate, his reveries frequently take the form of brooding futilely about his personal problems.[1]

The rather extensive development of counseling in industry is partly a result of the tendency of employees in repetitive and routine work to become preoccupied with personal problems. Getting the employee to talk about his problems and listening to him with an understanding ear often is sufficient in itself to relieve him of many of his symptoms. In this way, he becomes aware of his overthinking and

---

[1] F. J. Roethlisberger and W. J. Dickson, *Management and the Worker* (Cambridge, Mass.: Harvard University Press, 1939), p. 322.

preoccupations and is able to deal with his real-life problems more objectively and constructively.

Many employees prefer work which permits them to move around rather than tying them to the workplace. They say that the work is more interesting and less boring if they have an opportunity to move about. In one warehouse that was studied, it was found that employees who were tied to one place had higher turnover and lower morale than stockmen who had to move from place to place in carrying out their activities. This has been observed in other organizations as well. In fact, some organizations have made it an administrative policy to shift people around on routine, repetitive jobs in order to give them sufficient variety in their work to prevent boredom and unnecessary personal preoccupation. Apparently this has been done without loss in efficiency, for most employees are quite capable of learning diverse jobs of the same skill level without too much difficulty.

Pressure of Work

Another aspect of technology which can have an effect on the morale of employees is the pressure of the work. Some organizations, like restaurants and assembly-line factories, work under extreme pressure. Any slowing-up of effort at any point in the line can impede the work of the entire organization. As a consequence, employees and supervisors are almost frantic in their drive to get the work out. Pressure of this sort tends to aggravate personal antagonisms, stimulate outbursts of temper, and generally give employees the feeling of futility and frustration which comes with any continuous drive to accomplish the impossible.

It has been our experience that employees prefer a cycle of activity rather than either constant drive or constant inertia. Employees frequently do like a great deal of work. Beating a deadline or meeting a quota can be a stimulating experience. But when they are drawn through a knothole day after day, the situation begins to lose its novelty and, certainly, its stimulating effects.

WORK SIMPLIFICATION AND ITS EFFECTS

One of the basic principles of the industrial engineer is that increased productivity and decreased costs can be obtained by reducing jobs to simpler and simpler work elements. The extreme of this development is seen in the mass-production assembly lines, where the worker performs the same simple operation over and over, day after day. In other cases, the same results are obtained by changes in methods, improved tools, new design, etc., to the end that the level of skill is reduced and the worker does only the simplest operations. In any case, the result is that less-skilled people are needed, the learning period for new workers is lessened, and costs are generally reduced.

Along with the reduction of jobs to their simplest elements in the interests of mass production, there has been a tendency for the determination of work processes to become more and more a function of management staff departments—particularly the engineering and methods departments. The worker is not asked to think about improved methods of performing his job. This is a management function. He is asked only to do the job as he is told to do it, even to the extent, in some instances, of penalizing him if he tries to be ingenious. "After all, you cannot have just anybody messing around with expensive dies and equipment. Better leave that function, too, to somebody who knows something about it!"

Unquestionably, work simplification can be carried too far. Work can be deskilled to the point where it becomes meaningless and actually creates inefficiency and restriction of output. In one factory, where a group of girls were making raincoats, the work was broken down into its simplest possible elements so that each had one small specific task to perform. Management felt that each would develop an unusual proficiency in her own assignment and would, therefore, increase her efficiency and productivity. This particular work unit became, instead, a real trouble spot. Productivity and efficiency failed to come up to expectations, and morale sank. For want of something better to try, management decided to put the job back together again. Each employee was permitted to make a complete raincoat in her own way. The result—increased productivity and efficiency and improved morale.

Another real threat to efficient organization arising from an oversimplification of jobs is the administrative problems it creates. There is reason to believe that, when work tasks have been deskilled to the point of meaninglessness, employees no longer see the connection between their efforts and the end product. The man who does nothing but drill a hole in a piece part, the ultimate destiny of which he is ignorant, is hardly going to see the necessity for careful workmanship and enthusiastic work effort. Artificial stimuli and rigorous supervisory control are the only ways that he can be kept in line. The efficacy of some of these stimuli is discussed in the chapter on wages and restriction of output among employees.

The fact remains that, from an administrative point of view, there is no substitute for a job situation that makes sense to the workers in it. The problem of maintaining a complex system of operations— functionally tied together, but each one by itself meaningless—can become an administrative undertaking of insuperable difficulty in a complex organization. In one medium-sized plant with which the authors are familiar, there are over 25,000 separate operations, each with its own rate. These operations are further broken down into the thousands of distinct elements that constitute them. An elaborate time-study department is working full time to keep up with the rating of jobs. An equally elaborate time-keeping department keeps track of the employees' time on various operations as he moves from job to job. Supervisors spend 75 per cent of their time seeing that the right men are assigned to the right jobs and are properly paid for their various activities, whether in doing a job or sitting in the corner on their thumbs. An expensive labor relations department is maintained to deal with the union, mostly over issues arising out of methods of pay, rates, and job classifications. The employees spend thousands of dollars to insure that they have the proper representation in these negotiations. The entire system is overelaborated, ponderous, and top-heavy. One wonders whether it does not create more problems than it solves.

THE FUNCTIONAL TYPE OF ORGANIZATION

Another notion of administration which has had wide acceptance in management circles is that increased efficiency and productivity can be achieved by lumping together in one department all closely related activities. Like the idea of breaking jobs down into their simplest possible elements, this notion seems to be confirmed by logical deduction and scientific fact. It seems apparent that, if you can bring together all employees performing a particular kind of work, their activities can be better co-ordinated, more closely supervised, and better distributed. The thinking involved here generally follows the pattern of observing, first, that certain departments have employees performing similar tasks and that these employees are not always busy. Next, the efficiency expert conceives the idea that, if all of these employees could be brought together in one department, not only could they be more closely supervised but the work could be systematically laid out so that all of them would be busy all of the time. Unquestionably, the reasoning goes, productivity would be increased because employees would be working continuously on the same jobs. Furthermore, efficiency would be likely to improve because employees would be supervised by a person highly trained in the particular activity of the department and would have an opportunity themselves to gain greater proficiency.

There are, however, certain definite liabilities to this kind of organization. For one thing, it takes employees away from the department which gave meaning to their work. In one organization where this administrative notion was applied, a group of record clerks who formerly maintained perpetual inventory records for individual buyers were physically and organizationally separated from the men for whom the records were maintained. Instead, they were lumped together in one department in order to achieve greater record-keeping efficiency and better utilization of time. In the old setup, the record keeper was an integral and significant part of a small buying unit. Her job made sense to her. She knew why she was keeping the records and what they were used for. Under the new arrangement, she merely maintained a set of meaningless figures day in and day out. Needless to say, the morale of this group was materially reduced.

Another difficulty inherent in this kind of administrative action where functionally related jobs are lumped together is that it considerably increases potential conflict in the organization. Whenever a group of functionally related activities are separated from their mother departments and brought together in a department of their own, the original line departments no longer have control over these activities. This means, of course, that the work of the new department cannot be planned entirely in accordance with the needs and demands of any one of the original line departments but must be accomplished in proper order in accordance with the requirements of all. As a consequence, stresses and strains develop between the original line departments, which are demanding special favors and consideration in order to get their work done, and the new service department, which must maintain some order and system in its work effort. The authors have seen conflict between line departments and service departments time and time again. The line makes special requests for handlings which are refused by the service department on the grounds that they cannot give any special considerations for fear their own work will suffer.

In factories, this functional type of organization is very common. For example, in one factory there may be a series of functional departments, such as punch presses, screw machines, drill presses, milling machines, plating, painting, assembly, etc. Parts in process may move back and forth between departments for every separate operation, making necessary a great deal of handling, checking, and record keeping. Also, each department has its own hierarchy, and in a large plant there may be elaborate management groups for every function.

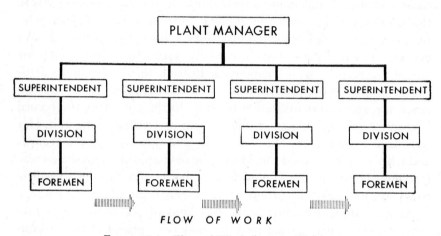

FIGURE 19–1.—Flow of Work between Divisions

In one large factory the functional development was carried so far that the workers were constantly working on parts that had no meaning, and they often had no idea where the parts were used or how their work affected the work of others. At the same time, there was an elaboration of inspection, with parts being inspected and counted after every operation. This meant that the work was not only constantly moving between functional departments but was also passing at every move through the hands of the inspectors.

This organization had developed a fairly elaborate hierarchy with four levels of supervision (Fig. 19–1). As the work moved through the plant, it moved from the jurisdiction of one chain of command to another. Any complaints about the work, such as assemblers complaining that the parts didn't fit well or workers protesting that inspection was unfairly rejecting too much of their output, had to be handled between separate chains of command. Gradually the conflicts between groups became so great that only minor complaints could be settled at lower levels. Anything of any importance would be carried up the line, and division chiefs and superintendents spent much of their time settling such disputes.

Finally, the conflicts and inefficiencies in the system forced the management to reorganize the plant on what was called a "product" basis. Selecting a limited type of product, they organized a shop to produce this one product, so that a single department would have full responsibility for the production of a single product. The department head might have charge of a machine section with a variety of different drill presses, punch presses, welders, milling machines, etc. He might have another section with finishing equipment, plating tanks, paint spray booths, etc. Still another would be the assembly section putting together the product. He would also have inspectors; but instead of their being responsible to an outside department, they were responsible for helping maintain quality so that the final products would pass inspection after they left the department.

In these product shops the chain of command was short, and the responsibility was pushed down toward the bottom. Also, the whole department could identify themselves with the product and develop a feeling of real teamwork in getting it out. The result was better morale and co-operation, better quality and lower inspection costs, and a much more efficient operation.

While such product shops have many advantages, both for the workers and for management, they constitute a significantly different world from that of the functional shops. This difference is especially pronounced in the machine sections.

In a functional machine department, such as a punch-press department, all the presses of every size and type are assembled in one location. The youngster starting work usually begins in some simple job such as a helper or trucker. After a time he is put on a light press; and after learning to operate it, he begins to help the setup men and to learn to set up the press. Then he moves on to bigger presses and more skilled jobs, until gradually he may become familiar with every machine and type of work. From there, he might advance to become a setup man and even on to become a foreman.

In such a system, the young man is thrown into contact with the older skilled men; he learns the lore of the job from them; and he becomes familiar with the more skilled jobs without the need of a special training program. Thus, he is placed in a system in which his daily activities, contacts, and observations help prepare him for advancement. He can see clearly the route to advancement and, at the same time, recognize the skills and abilities of the older men who have moved up the path ahead of him. It is such a system that develops the foremen who can boast that they know every job and every machine and can step in and handle them all. And in such a system the foremen are respected for that knowledge.

Now, in the product-type shop, the big functional groups are dispersed. A machine section rarely has a complete hierarchy of skills but exhibits only a collection of special skills. Here the young man may be put on one simple machine, but its mastery does not lead anywhere. No matter how skilled he becomes on a drill press, he does not graduate from it to a milling machine. Any shift may mean that he starts learning a new type of job and starts from scratch. The pathway to success is not clear; there is no simple logic of skills and advancement which everyone can see. So, the individual often feels trapped—doomed by forces he cannot control to live out his days on one job and in one status position.

This also creates a special problem for management in providing the necessary skilled mechanics. The skilled people cannot rise gradually to the top, through the normal processes of the work, but must be specifically trained. Under such a system, management must develop special training methods, often regular schools, in order to teach people much of the skills which they would spontaneously acquire in the other type of organization.

Another difference lies in the characteristics of the supervisors. In the product shop, the foreman must be a man who can organize the work and keep it moving. He cannot hope to master all the skills; so he must be able to use and direct the skills of others. Also, he cannot hope to hold the respect of the skilled mechanics through his superior knowledge in their specialty. He must retain leadership through skill in dealing with people rather than through mastery of machines. This means that the foreman will be a different kind of person, in terms of background and experience, and often will be selected from outside the work group.

Thus, the two types of shops are, in effect, two different worlds. In one, all skills are related and the workers and supervisors are integrated in terms of the particular skill; prestige is related to the job knowledge and experience; and progress is along the lines of the skill hierarchy. Often the work of one department is unrelated to the work of another, and there is no integration, or even need for much co-operation, in terms of the product.

In the other type of shop, everything focuses on the product and the integration of the jobs and skills in terms of producing the product. Thus, co-operation and teamwork can be developed around the goal of production, and the failures or poor performances of one of the group will directly affect the work of others. Furthermore, if the product shop is not too large, the individual has some understanding of the entire sequence of operations and sees how things fit together and how he fits in. In this way, there can be a goal which he can understand and a team of which he can be a part. These two types of organization may exist in every factory or business, or some firms may be almost completely organized on one plan or the other. Some small firms are entirely functional in their activities. For example, there are concerns which only manufacture screw machine products, and the whole shop is a functional organization operating a variety of screw machines. The shop may turn out thousands of different products on these machines—all parts to be used by other manufacturers. In some other small firms making a few special products, the whole factory may be a product shop with only general functional divisions into groups, such as the machine shop, assembly, office, etc.

However, except in very large organizations or in special types of organization, the variation between the two types is a matter of degree. Most organizations have some of the characteristics of both, depending on the types of processes, the kind of business, and management's ideas as to the best way to build an effective organization.

THE "TALL" VERSUS THE "FLAT" ORGANIZATION

In most treatises on organization, there is considerable emphasis on the "span of control." Out of experience in military organizations have evolved firm beliefs as to how many subordinates should report to a superior—that is, how many others one man can supervise. These beliefs have been given supposedly scientific backing by mathematical calculations which show that the possible combinations of interpersonal relations in any group of over a dozen people will run up into the thousands and will be too great for any supervisor to deal with. However, such reasoning, though mathematically correct, bears no relation to the realities of human relations.

In spite of this, there has been developed fairly general acceptance of the ideas that one supervisor for 12 to 15 workers is a reasonably correct ratio in most factory operations and that, at higher levels, an executive should not have over 4 to 7 people reporting to him.

Application of these concepts of the span of control, then, forces the development of a certain pattern of supervisory and executive structure. If a plant has 300 workers, it should have 20 foremen, 4 department heads, and a superintendent. If it increases to 1,500, then it needs 100 foremen, 20 department heads, 4 superintendents, and a manager to supervise the superintendents. If it goes to 7,500, it increases accordingly and will require 4 managers and a general manager to supervise them. Fortunately, business executives are never this rigid in their thinking about organization and usually fit the structure to the realities of what will work best rather than to a mathematical formula.

However, in these theories of the span of control are certain unstated assumptions concerning the supervisor's or executive's job. If it is assumed that the job of the department head is to know all about what is going on, to check on every action or decision of his foremen, to know how they stand on every job, and to be able to answer any question his superior might ask, then he can only handle a small department and four or five foremen. If he does this, he can be said to be in control of the situation, can prevent any mistakes, and can keep his superior completely informed.

Now, if this is his concept of his job, how does he work? First, he spends a lot of time on the job, watching the work and talking with his foremen. His presence makes it easy for the foremen to discuss things with him, to ask his advice, and to go to him with problems or information. Also, he keeps his eye on the details of the work so that he can ask them endless questions as to why they do this or that.

In addition, he may spend a lot of time going over records. He watches production reports, earning reports, and what not. From these he gleans further things to ask the foreman or information to pass on to his superior.

He also spends time with other departments, straightening out any difficulties, checking to see if they will have parts ready for him, etc. Finally he devotes time to his superior, partly just to keep him informed and partly to ask his advice and get his approval on decisions.

When functioning in this way, the smaller his department the more completely he can enter into every decision and can know about everything that happens. But, if he has a large department—say 10 foremen—then he is lost. He cannot be constantly available to give advice on instructions; he cannot keep track of every detail; and he cannot discuss everything with his superior. And he will feel that he has lost control, that things will go wrong, and that the foremen will make mistakes for which his boss will criticize him.

Now, observation shows that the span of command and the nature of the supervisory hierarchy vary a great deal from organization to organization. Furthermore, in the same type of business, some units function efficiently and profitably in one way and some in another. And we also see that, in practice, there are two types of structure. One we call the "tall" organization, which has a hierarchy with several levels, conforming roughly to the hierarchy which evolves from the theory of limited span of control. The other, which we can call the "flat" type of organization, has fewer levels and more people reporting to each superior.

In this flat organization, the steps from top to bottom are fewer, the chain of command is short, and the direct attention the superior can give to each subordinate is limited. You might say that supervision is spread thin and that each must handle his job without looking to his superior for detailed guidance. Such an organization can work well only if the supervisory groups know their jobs, are able and willing to stand on their own feet, do not hesitate to make decisions and accept responsibility for their mistakes, and can run their jobs as part of the whole system.

With persons who are poorly trained, whose judgment is poor, who are afraid to make decisions, or who want to do things their own way without regard for the rest of the organization, such a structure is hazardous. It does not provide the tightness of control necessary to prevent serious mistakes, to support the dependent or those with poor judgment, or to keep the unruly in line. In effect, such an organization depends on individual ability at all levels, with a minimum of control from above.

On the other hand, the tall structure depends on tight, and even autocratic, control. As James C. Worthy says:

Many businesses closely resemble the authoritarian state in the sense that all direction, all thinking, all authority tends to flow from the top down. While the top administrator may delegate certain parts of his responsibility and authority, the delegation is largely in terms of those at lower levels of the organization merely implementing and effectuating policies and directives which have already been set up. While the over-all directive may be broken down into a series of parts and parcelled out to different people, and while these people may be expected to show initiative, drive and judgment in executing their work, their activity is essentially that of merely carrying out an order.

To make such an organization work, management is forced to set up a rigorous system of controls to see that things get done and to insure that people do not make too many mistakes in carrying out their orders. In other words, a minimum of reliance is placed on the people in the organization, and the system depends primarily on the initiative and judgment of those at the top.

A corollary to this tendency is the elaboration of staff organizations, because if the exercise of judgment and skill is largely reserved to top administrators, they must be assisted by specialized advisory staffs. The result is a further extension of the system of controls through the efforts of the staff departments, as well as a considerable complication of the organization structure, thus leading to the necessity for more controls to hold the whole organization together and make it work. At the same time, because of the necessity for operating the controls and because people at each successive level must be closely supervised and directed in their work, the supervisory hierarchy becomes more and more extended.[2]

In these tall organizations, certain characteristics tend to develop to a greater degree than in flat ones. With the extended hierarchy and close supervision and control, worry and concern over what the boss thinks and expects increases. With the boss on hand all the time, the subordinates will naturally devote a great deal of attention to his personality and to his likes and dislikes, and, in general, to the problem of responding correctly to him at all times. Furthermore, this concern will exist even where the general morale is high and the attitudes toward the company and superiors are friendly. Thus, this anxiety and worry is accepted as normal and inevitable by people in such organizations, and members adapt to it without doing much to change it.

Another problem in tall organizations is that of communication. The more steps in the chain of command, the more the flow of information or ideas from the bottom up is censored and retarded. Also, with close control, all decisions and all initiation of action tends to be pushed up the line. Thus, if a foreman wants to make some change but feels he has to clear it with his boss, and his boss must discuss it with *his* boss, etc., it may take days to get it done. This tends to discourage the foreman from attempting to try new ideas, until finally he just sits back and follows instructions from above.

The tightly controlled organization is frequently the product of strong, autocratic leadership at the top. The president who wants

---

[2] James C. Worthy: "Democratic Principles in Business Management," *Advanced Management*, March, 1949.

things done his way, who is sure that he is right and doubts his subordinates, wants an organization which carries out his decisions to the minutest detail. Under this sort of pressure, every level acts in the same way: all are concerned with knowing the commands from above and trying to make a showing by obediently carrying them out. This forces more and more decisions up the line, stimulates the development of detailed systems of controls and of rules and regulations, and increases the subordinate's fear of acting on his own without the approval of his superiors. In such a system, nobody "sticks his neck out"; the rule is never to take a chance.

Not all these tightly controlled organizations are headed by autocratic leaders. Some develop this pattern because of acceptance of the theory that this is the most effective structure and that such close control is necessary or leads to greater efficiency. In such cases, you often hear expressed the theory that there is always one best way of doing anything—whether it is setting up an organization, answering a phone call, supervising a work group, or what not. Therefore, management, often with the help of experts, decides what that one best way is and then gets everyone to use it. Such "one-best-way" thinking leads inevitably to rigidity of form and methods, to elaborate rules and instructions, to controls, and to policing to see that the "best way" is followed.

Once the pattern of the organization is established, it tends to become stabilized and to maintain itself. New members take on the behavior typical of that organization and are rapidly trained in what is proper. If a young man, unaccustomed to worrying about what the boss will think, speaks up freely or attempts to go ahead without checking with the boss, he soon learns that that is not the way to act. When others say, "You stuck your neck out on that," or "You've sure got nerve to talk up the way you did," or "Better be careful," he soon becomes conscious of these things. Thus, he rapidly learns what the group thinks should or should not be done, even though his superior may not be critical at all. In fact, in an organization where such apprehensions are strong, a new executive will receive from his subordinates the same concern, the same deference, and the same expectations as his predecessor. And unless he is unusually alert to these things, he rapidly fits into the pattern of going into details, making minor decisions, and letting his subordinates depend on him.

Certain kinds of activity tend to develop in the tall organizations much more than others. In general, manufacturing lends itself readily to the concepts of the tall organization with tight controls. This is partly due to the need of proper timing and integration of activities so that the work flows smoothly. Thus, the greater the need of co-ordination and co-operation, the greater the tendency to try to achieve this through close supervisory control. In many cases, the growth of an elaborate hierarchy can be observed in new plants when under pressure to get the job started. For example, one case was observed of a large new factory opened just after World War II. The company was struggling to get the new plant into production promptly and staffed it with experienced supervisory personnel from their other plants. However, with new products, new equipment, and with new and, often, inexperienced workers, they had a lot of difficulties. When the foremen complained that they just couldn't keep on top of all the problems, the management gave them assistant foremen. When the department heads felt they were losing control of the job, management gave them assistants, and so on, until three levels had been added in the chain of command.

One episode showed clearly how this worked out. A machine broke down and tied up one small production line supplying parts to the main assembly. The assistant foreman called the foreman, who called a setup man. He found a broken part on the machine, and it was taken to the machine shop for repairs. As it was a rush job, the machine-shop boss put one of his best mechanics to work on it. Within a few minutes the assistant department head came by, saw the shutdown, and questioned the foreman, who explained the trouble and described what was being done. However, the assistant department head had to see for himself; so they both went to the machine shop, talked to the boss, and interrupted the mechanic to see how he was getting on. Shortly, the department head came by and went through the same routine, and following him was the superintendent and a couple of engineers. In short, everyone was maintaining control over the job by checking and rechecking. Yet not one of these executives did anything essential; in fact, they merely wasted the time of those actually getting the job done.

Now, some organizations meet such conditions without extending the chain of command. If a foreman is swamped, instead of subdividing the group under assistant foremen, management gives him help in another way. If too much of his time must be spent in training in-experienced workers, he is given a skilled worker to help him train others. This worker is not a supervisor but is there to help the others learn their jobs. If there are a lot of interruptions because of poor scheduling or missing materials or parts, management gives the foreman someone to help check on those things and to help keep them moving. By skillful delegation of such things, the foreman can keep on top of the job and really be a supervisor rather than a combination of errand boy, expeditor, mechanic, etc., with no time left to supervise.

In sales organizations or department stores, the flat organizations are more common. In these, the activity of an individual member of a sales department can go on independently of other salesmen or other departments. Thus, the high degree of co-ordination and supervision is not so necessary, and the tendency toward elaborate controls is not so great.

20. MINORITY GROUPS IN INDUSTRY

THE GENERAL PICTURE

A N IMPORTANT element in the pattern of American industry is the continual process of introducing and assimilating new groups into the structure. For many years there was a constant flow of European immigrants into American industry, as one nationality group after another followed the promise of the New World. As each group arrived, it began to move into the industrial pattern as a new and strange minority seeking to make its way in an industrial structure dominated by the older groups. And in time each of these became an older group into which still newer groups were intruding.

In the industrial areas, each of these newcomers followed a similar pattern. Each new group tended to move in at the bottom of the community structure. The latest comers always had the lowest status; they moved into the poorest districts; they were looked down upon by all the older groups and were considered the poorest, dirtiest, least intelligent, and least desirable group in the community. Each new group formed its own neighborhood, speaking its own language and living its own culture, and generally formed a little island separated from the groups around it. The passage of time, however, gradually reduced this separation and its barriers. The children learned new ways and moved to new neighborhoods. And, as each group began to adjust itself to the new life and move upward in the occupational structure, there were still newer groups pushing in beneath them—people, again different in language and culture, starting at the bottom of the heap. On these new groups, in turn, were directed all the criticisms which the others had faced.

In spite of some increase in immigration since the end of the war, the major flow of European immigrants has been halted. As a consequence, many of the sharp differences between groups have disappeared, at least as far as industry is concerned; so that it is no longer necessary to pick foremen with an eye to their nationality background or their command of foreign languages, or to consider the ethnic composition of a group when hiring new workers. At the same time, with the shutting-off of European immigration, there is no longer the continual stream of new foreign groups to move in beneath the old, to take the heavy, dirty, unskilled jobs, and to be a new bottom layer whom everyone can scorn as ignorant, incompetent, "dumb laborers." These low-status, low-paid jobs must then be filled by members of the older groups or by their children and grandchildren. But the urge for improvement, the stimulus of better education and greater assimilation in the American life, with its traditions of getting ahead, has made these young people unwilling to accept these low-status jobs. Thus, we see forces operating to reduce the supply of workers who will freely accept the lowest jobs, and at the same time we have an increasingly large portion of the old group who are acutely dissatisfied when restricted to this occupational level. From management we hear complaints that the younger generation is not what it ought to be or what its parents were. Formerly, executives spoke disparagingly of the "dumb polaks" or "bohunks" who were good for nothing except the lowest sort of jobs and who were content to spend their lives in them. Today these same executives speak with nostalgia of these same workers and recount their virtues, their faithful plodding service, their willingness to accept whatever job was offered, their interest in a steady job and modest income. In contrast, they point to the restlessness of the next generation, their unwillingness to take the hard and dirty jobs, their grasping for the symbols of mobility, and their spendthrift ways.

This occupational impasse has to some extent been averted, and at the same time been complicated, by recent migrations within this country. The need for workers in different parts of the country, especially during the war and in recent years, has stimulated an internal movement of people from rural areas to industrial centers, much of which has been from the rural South. The movement of southern whites and Negroes has been so extensive that they may, in fact, be considered the latest immigrants into industrial areas. Simultaneously, women have been moving into industry in increasingly large numbers and are now employed in many industries and occupations previously closed to them. Each of these new groups has faced problems similar to those of new nationality groups. Each has had to come in at the bottom of the industrial structure starting as common labor in unskilled jobs, and each has spread upward through the structure only slowly. Each has had to accept a subordinate role; each has been ridiculed and criticized by the superior groups and has had its work scorned: "That is only woman's work," "That job is only fit for niggers." As these minority groups begin to press toward the better jobs and higher status, they find barriers raised against them—barriers of tradition, of beliefs concerning their incompetence, of reluctance to accept them into other groups. And like the other groups when they were new, they are the ones who have the least security in the system and the ones who will fill the ranks of the unemployed during times of depression.

Another force is complicating this aspect of the industrial scene. The increase of automation for routine, repetitious jobs and the use of machines instead of human muscle is rapidly making the common laborer obsolete. Our construction jobs, whether roads or buildings or industrial plants, are no longer done by swarms of unskilled laborers. Now huge machines in the hands of skilled operators do the heavy work. This is in sharp contrast to the practices of the past, still prevalent in less-industrialized countries such as China, Southeast Asia, and Africa.

With machine power replacing muscle power and automation replacing the semiskilled worker, the need for a supply of unskilled low-paid labor is vanishing. Now the need is for a labor supply with considerable technical skill and education. This means that the newcomer, whether from the rural South, Puerto Rico, or Latin America has a tremendous handicap in his lack of education and industrial skills. As a result, not only does he move in at the bottom of the status heap, but finds the opportunity to escape through hard work and on-the-job learning almost closed.

As this trend continues, and it has been accelerating in the last decade, we can postulate that the advanced industrial society will no longer represent a world of opportunity to the immigrant from the underprivileged regions. Our great metropolises will no longer be the gateways to a better life where the newcomer can find employment, opportunity, and freedom.

NEGROES: NEW INDUSTRIAL IMMIGRANTS

The movement of southern Negroes to northern and western industrial centers is similar to the migrations of Europeans in some respects. They are culturally and racially different and set apart; they come in at the bottom of the social and occupational structures; they are looked down upon and unwanted either as neighbors or fellow workers; they are considered dirty, dangerous, untrustworthy, ignorant, stupid, and so on. Unlike the European immigrants, however, Negroes are not likely to become assimilated in a generation or two, for the white society maintains a strict caste system with effective controls for keeping Negroes separate and subordinate. Furthermore, the Negro is conspicuous. Whereas the European immigrant could gradually lose his identity and blend with the general population, the Negro is branded by his skin color, so that he cannot lose himself in the mass. This fact is one of the most important reasons why his adjustment in the industrial population is a slower and more difficult process than that of any other group.

The Caste System[1]

The position of Negroes in our society and the generally accepted attitudes toward them produce serious problems in their introduction into a plant or work group. In the first place, there are very common, and very strong, beliefs in the uncleanliness and tendency to disease of the Negro, which are a part of the whole caste system in which he is kept separate and subordinate. Accompanying these attitudes is the reluctance, and even refusal, on the part of white workers to share washrooms, locker rooms, and eating facilities with Negroes. In many cases, open clashes and work stoppages have resulted from trying to bring Negroes into white locker rooms or washrooms or into company restaurants. The whites always explain their attitude and resentment in terms of the uncleanliness of Negroes and fear of disease. Actually, these attitudes are expressions of the social processes by means of which Negroes are kept at a distance and "in their place." No matter how strong the feeling may be, there is never any objection to a Negro acting as janitor or washroom attendant or as cook or dishwasher in the restaurant. It is only when he sits down to eat beside a white, when he washes at the same basin in front of a white, when he undresses at an adjacent locker,

---

[1] Space does not permit a detailed description of this system here. The reader may find a comprehensive discussion of Negro-white relations, the American caste system, and its codes and controls in the following studies of southern communities:

a) Allison Davis, Burleigh B. Gardner and Mary R. Gardner, *Deep South—A Social Anthropological Study of Caste and Class* (Chicago: University of Chicago Press, 1941).

b) John Dollard, *Caste and Class in a Southern Town* (New Haven: Yale University Press, 1937).

c) Gunnar Myrdal, *An American Dilemma* (New York: Harper & Bros., 1944).

it is only when he does these things as a fellow worker and an equal that the whites begin to worry about being contaminated by contacts with him.

Segregation and Discrimination

While these attitudes toward Negroes may be considered irrational, they are so strong that management must take them into account in dealing with the problem. In the past the simplest procedure was to provide separate facilities for Negroes. This avoided the problem and also served to maintain the segregation of Negroes within the plant. In many cases, they were even restricted to certain departments and worked in separate groups. They were also generally limited to the dirty, disagreeable, and low-status jobs, such as laborers, material handlers, janitors, and porters. In this way the problem was solved by perpetuating the caste system within the plant.

From the point of view of management, this worked very well during the prewar period, but during the war the problem became more difficult to solve. In 1940 the federal government began to take steps to prevent discrimination in essential industries. This movement culminated in the Executive Order 8802 and the establishment of a Committee on Fair Employment Practices. This immediately led to actions to prevent any form of discrimination in defense industry because of "race, creed, color, or natural origin." At the same time, the growing labor shortage in industrial areas impressed management with the need to make the fullest possible use of all available workers and not to allow any prejudice against Negroes to prevent their use. Thus, not only was there pressure from the federal government to prevent segregation of Negroes or their restriction to the lowest types of jobs, but also the manpower shortage made it desirable to use them on any jobs for which they could be trained. At the same time, the attitudes toward Negroes still persisted among white workers, supervisors, and management, so that, regardless of the need to use Negroes, the problem of how to use them still remained.

In plants where Negroes were already established in the low-status jobs and with separate facilities, there was the problem of breaking down this established pattern before Negroes could be mixed in with the whites and moved to better jobs. On the whole, this has been more difficult than the problem of introducing them where they had never worked before. Where they are completely new to a plant, there was no need to change established customs but only to overcome the initial resistance and suspicion and fit the Negroes into the patterns customary for any new employee.

Introducing Negroes as Equals

In some cases, management, having decided to hire Negroes and put them on the same jobs as whites, merely issued orders to this effect and expected to have Negroes moved in immediately in large numbers. On the whole, such methods did not work very smoothly; open friction was frequent and the whites often refused to accept the Negroes. The sudden appearance of Negroes in the work groups, especially if they were brought in in considerable numbers, always aroused antagonism and fears as to what was happening to the job and whether Negroes would supplant the whites. The sudden movement of Negroes into positions of equality and close association was always interpreted as a threat to the superior status of the whites, and they reacted accordingly.

Many concerns, on the other hand, went about the change in a more cautious manner. The most generally successful procedure was one in which management first paved the way for the change by having discussions with various levels of supervision and sometimes with union officials. In such discussions, management found it best to take a firm stand to the effect that they had no alternative but to employ Negroes and that they could not segregate nor discriminate against them. Management could then ask the subordinates what they thought the difficulties would be and how they could be worked out. The group was assured, at the same time, that only the "best type" of Negroes would be picked and that careful examinations would be given to be sure that they were free of disease. After these discussions the plants would hire a few carefully selected Negroes and spread them around through the shops, and in some cases a few were put in the personnel organization in clerical or stenographic jobs. Then, as the Negroes began to be taken as a matter of course, more could be brought in gradually without difficulty.

By having these discussions beforehand, the supervisors were prepared for the Negroes and given a feeling that they were being taken into the confidence of management and given a chance to express their ideas. At the same time, management was able to reassure them as to the purpose of the move and the reasons for it. Thus, before the Negroes actually appeared, the supervisors and even the workers were already becoming accustomed to the idea, and the actual appearance of Negroes on the job was not a sudden shock threatening their security. The careful selection of educated, "nice-looking" Negroes, who were quite different from the average concept of the Negro, created a favorable impression which was strengthened when the whites became acquainted and saw that the Negroes could do the work and were pleasant people to work with. This further broke down their ideas as to what Negroes were like; and white workers and supervisors began to see them as individuals to be judged as individuals and not merely as members of an inferior group.

In the last few years we have seen a tremendous crusade by the Negroes to break the patterns and barriers of segregation. In 1963, "the summer of their discontent," they became increasingly militant in their actions, and with picketing, mass demonstrations, and rioting worked for desegregation on all fronts.

Increasingly, in the South as well as North, industry began acceding to this demand, and more and more companies actively promoted or hired Negroes for supervisory, professional, and executive positions.

Unfortunately, just at the time when the old barriers to jobs were crumbling, the Negro was shown to lack the necessary skills and education. It was not enough for companies to agree to hire without discrimination; there must at the same time be Negroes able to qualify. The generally poor level of education in the southern Negro schools, the exclusions from union apprenticeship training, the lack of openings in white-collar jobs, meant that most of the Negroes were ill prepared to take advantage of the new opportunities.

Also, the decline of unskilled jobs hurt them. Once they flocked into Chicago to work in the meat-packing plants, the steel mills, and other industries needing unskilled labor, but in 1963 these jobs were vanishing. At a time when even a lowly foothold in industry could be the first rung on a ladder of opportunity, technological change had cut off the bottom rungs, the only ones most of them could reach.

Thus, in spite of the breaking down of the caste barriers to opportunity in industry, the Negro still finds himself among the disadvantaged. As a result, in order to achieve occupational success he must turn to training and education to give him opportunity. In this problem he is joined by all the migrants from the underskilled and undereducated cultures. The rural poor white, the Puerto Rican, the Mexican, all have the same handicap and the same limited opportunities.

Negro Class Differences[2]

The Negro population as a whole has a much lower average level of education than the white population; their living conditions are poorer, their incomes are less, and their work experience more limited. As a group they have lived in severe poverty in slum areas without education or opportunity to better their conditions. Furthermore, those Negroes who have managed to maintain themselves above this level, who have received more education and training in spite of the general restrictions, have generally not been able to obtain the skilled or white-collar jobs in business and industry. As a result, when industry first started to hire Negroes, they were able to select men and women from the higher-status group, who came from middle-class homes with high-school and even college training. Many of these high-caliber Negroes were eager to break into industry at something above the janitor level and gladly took the ordinary shop jobs. Thus, there were a group of high-status Negroes moving into shop jobs beside the lower-class white workers. The whites recognized this status difference and in general were favorably impressed, in many cases commenting on the intelligence and quality of the Negroes.

As the employment of Negroes spread, however, this group was rapidly exhausted and industry began to bring in lower-class Negroes who more nearly fitted the picture of what Negroes were expected to be like. In this group there was the usual lower-class belligerence and aggression, a tendency to settle arguments by fighting, an inclination to carry knives as weapons, and so on. At the same time, these Negroes had, for the most part, never associated with whites in any position of equality. They had worked *under* whites, never with them. They had attended all-Negro or predominantly Negro schools and had little or no contact with whites either in the schoolroom or on the playgrounds. With this limited interracial experience, they came into a working world which was largely white, and they moved into positions of relative equality with whites. They had had little opportunity to learn, even among themselves, the patterns of co-operation

---

[2] Further discussion of Negro class behavior may be found in the following studies:

a) Allison Davis and John Dollard, *Children of Bondage—The Personality Development of Negro Youth in the Urban South* (Washington, D.C.: American Council on Education, 1940).

b) W. Lloyd Warner, Buford H. Junker, and Walter A. Adams, *Color and Human Nature* (Washington, D.C.: American Council on Education, 1941).

and co-ordination necessary for comfortable and effective group work; and most of them were not accustomed to the steady, routine grind of factory work.

Such a situation is pretty obviously "dynamite." And it is no wonder that there have been many cases of friction between Negro and white workers under these conditions. As already pointed out, the many pressures of the daily work situation often give rise to irritation and friction between individual workers without the added complication of racial differences; and the irritation of the white workers seems to be increased by the Negroes' lack of training and general unfamiliarity with factory work. When white workers expressed their irritation, the Negroes often reacted in typical lower-class fashion, meeting aggression with aggression, profanity with profanity, and threats with threats. In such cases, the whites almost invariably felt that this behavior justified all their beliefs about Negroes. The Negroes, in turn, united against the whites; and the resulting situation was ripe for serious racial conflict and even riot. Generally, tension of this sort can be traced to irritations and difficulties which grow out of the work situation itself; and though they may be accentuated and exaggerated by the racial factor, they are not specifically due to having Negroes on the job. In other words, job pressures, crowded locker rooms, inexperienced workers, and long hours all give rise to irritations and open conflict; and as long as only white workers are involved there are no racial implications. But the moment the difficulty involves both whites and Negroes, the whites conclude that the Negroes are really vicious and dangerous, as they have suspected all along, and should be put back in their place; and the Negroes conclude that the whites do, indeed, have it in for them and that they must stand together against white aggression and domination.

Among the better-educated and higher-status Negroes, who were a valuable addition to the work groups and made an easy adjustment at first, certain problems of a different nature developed later. In the first place, they took the factory jobs with the idea that this was the first step toward an equality in industry both for themselves personally and for Negroes generally. In many cases, they were individuals of considerable education, technical training, or general ability, and they expected that their ability would receive recognition. Like all college-trained men in the shops, they soon became impatient with the normal rate of progress, and their advancement to higher-status jobs was further slowed down by the fact that they were Negroes. This problem became acute when Negroes of lower status and less education were brought in at the same job level as these superior groups. After a period of time, when their excellent performance and high morale brought them no recognition or advancement, these exceptional Negroes became discouraged and restless; and they began to feel that there was no real opportunity for their race in industry, free from discrimination. As this feeling developed, their work deteriorated; and they began looking for other jobs, or turned to union activities for recognition and satisfaction and as a means of fighting against the color restrictions.

WOMEN WORKERS

During World War II, there was a rapid and extensive increase in the employment of women. They moved into plants which formerly had been completely closed to them and into almost all levels of skilled jobs. Special training programs prepared them for jobs as welders, machinists, inspectors, and many other jobs which had been considered strictly men's work. In thousands of cases the jobs were re-engineered to require less skill or strength so that women could do such work, and often the tools and equipment were especially designed to make the work more suitable for women. All this meant not merely an increase in the number of women in industry, but, more important, their spread beyond the accepted categories of women's jobs, and the breaking down of many former beliefs concerning women's lack of mechanical ability and other limitations.

This influx of women into industry was different from the introduction of Negroes or other groups, since it was not accompanied by a wave of migration. Women were not a strange new group but were drawn from the general population. The extensive employment of women in industry did not mean the introduction of a new element in the social organization but meant a change in the role and activity of a group which was already part of the established system. The problem, then, was not one of assimilating a new group which was trying to make a place for itself; it was one of readjusting both industry and the society so that women could function in a new role. To some extent, of course, women had always worked in industry. Certainly at the working-class level of society a large proportion of the women had worked as a matter of course, and many had had to work to support dependents. Nevertheless, the war produced such a rapid increase in their numbers that the readjustment created a considerable problem.

Although women were neither a new group in the society nor wholly new to industry, certain elements in their assimilation were similar to those of Negroes and other new groups. Like the Negroes, they had not as a group been trained for the higher-skilled jobs until recently, and they had not had opportunity to develop their mechanical knowledge and ability. In the past they had been relegated to jobs which had become established as woman's work, and no effort had been made to prepare them for other kinds of work. This is in contrast to the average man going into industry, who is expected to be able to move to higher jobs, who seeks out opportunity to learn these jobs, and who may be assisted in his advancement by older workers or by a system of training or apprenticeship. Like the European immigrants, the women have been considered inferior workers, ignorant and incompetent; and like the Negroes, they have had little chance for advancement.

The Woman's Role

Woman's role in our society has an important effect upon her position in the industrial world. At all levels of society the accepted function of a woman has been that of wife and mother, whose first interest is in the family and the home, and whose most important duties are those of caring for the home and rearing the children. In contrast to this, the accepted function of a man, as a successful father, is that of providing home and sustenance. Thus, while the successful wife and mother is expected to spend her life in the home, the successful husband generally spends his life working outside in order to support the home and family. This difference is sharply illustrated in the different attitudes which young men and young women express toward their jobs. As pointed out earlier (Chapter 18), the average girl taking her first full-time factory job looks upon it as a temporary thing to fill in the time before she gets married and settles down to rearing a family. She is not usually much concerned over advancement or future opportunities in the work but is interested in whether it provides opportunity for meeting single men, whether it will interfere with her social life, and whether it is a pleasant job with a friendly group. A young man, on the other hand, is constantly concerned with the opportunities of the job. How fast can he get ahead, and how long will it take him to reach a level of income where he can afford to marry? In other words, a girl is filling in time while she finds a husband and begins her *real* career, while a boy is establishing himself in his lifework and is wondering if it will soon bring him to his adult role as husband and provider.

"Woman's Work"

Since this is the usual and generally accepted pattern, the woman who does not marry, who instead seeks a career in business or industry, is looked upon as unfortunate, as failing to perform her proper womanly function, and sometimes as a "misfit." At the same time, because younger women starting in industry have been considered only temporary, management has hesitated to develop them for supervisory or executive positions or even to train them for skilled work. As a result, factories have developed a group of jobs which require little skill and training, into which women can come and go without disrupting the work; and these jobs have become accepted as "women's work."

Furthermore, in all things having to do with factory work or machines, women were considered to be less able than men. It was natural, therefore, that women's jobs should be paid less than men. This was reasonable as long as women were restricted to separate and lower-skilled jobs, since the pay differentials could be rationalized on the basis of the difference in the work. In many cases, however, men's jobs which were of no greater skill than the women's jobs were paid at a higher rate; and for jobs which were held by either men or women, the women were usually paid less. This pay differential for equivalent types of work was usually rationalized on the basis that women were poorer workers, that they were lighter and weaker than men and could not work so hard, that they had to be assisted with heavy work, that they did not turn out as much work, and that the quality of their work was poorer. With this precedent, when women began moving into men's jobs, many companies managed to maintain the women in the accepted inferior role by means of a systematic pay differential.

Women in Men's Jobs

These two factors—the inferior status of women's work and the lower rate of pay—give rise to certain difficulties when introducing women into men's jobs. When a woman first comes into what has been considered a man's job, the men on the job almost always react unfavorably. They express doubts as to whether she can do the work; they often ignore her and give her no help in learning the job; they do not try to protect her while she is adjusting to the new work, but stand by and criticize her; they point to every mistake as showing that a woman cannot really handle such difficult work. At the same time, they are often worried by her presence and wonder if women will displace men on the job. If the company pays her the same rate as the men, they feel that they have lost status, since they are worth no more than a woman; and the other men workers may kid them about doing women's work. If the company pays her less for the same job, they worry for fear the company may eventually cut the rate for all of them or replace all the men with the cheaper women. In this very unfriendly atmosphere, with no assistance from the group, the woman worker often fails in her job or gives up.

Women as Supervisors

The advancement of women to supervisory jobs has always been a problem. In the first place, there is the general belief that women make poor supervisors, that they are too emotional and "take things personally," that they cannot command the loyalty and respect of their subordinates nor the co-operation of their equals. In the face of such beliefs, which appear among executives as well as workers, women are rarely given a chance at supervisory positions. And when occasionally one is given such an opportunity, her superiors are always doubtful, as if to say, "We know women don't usually make good supervisors, so we really don't expect you to succeed." At the same time, especially if she is the only woman foreman or supervisor among a group of men, the other supervisors treat her much as the new woman worker is treated by the men on the job. Instead of accepting her as one of them and helping her adjust to the new job, they stand aloof and watch her critically, expecting her to fail. In this atmosphere of distrust and expectation of failure, every move she makes is watched critically. If she asks for help, it shows that she does not know the job; if she does not ask for help, she is acting as if she knew everything; if the strain begins to get her down so that she is irritable and acts annoyed, then she is acting "just like a woman"; and it all goes to prove that women do not make good supervisors. Under such conditions the probability of failure is high.

The fact that women in our society are generally considered inferior and are expected to be subordinate to men also creates problems when placing women in supervisory positions. Most men dislike the idea of working under a woman; and, no matter how competent she may be, they feel a loss of status in taking orders from a woman. Even if the individual man accepts the idea of having a woman for a boss, his friends are sure to make it hard for him, commenting on it and kidding him about it. Among older men, especially those accustomed to ruling their wives and families with an iron hand, subordination to a woman boss is unthinkable. Because of these attitudes management is always reluctant to place a woman over a group of men and usually tries to use them only for groups of women.

Even when placed in charge of other women, however, the woman supervisor has difficulties. For the most part, women themselves prefer to be supervised by men, and few express a preference for a woman as their boss. They usually complain that the woman supervisor is likely to be unfriendly, or too critical, or too concerned with petty details, or too strict a disciplinarian. Sometimes these attitudes and criticisms seem to be expressions of jealousy and competition, but in many cases they are based on real weaknesses in the performance of women supervisors. For one thing, women are often put in supervisory positions without sufficient training, and they do not know how to act as a boss or how to manage those under them. Newly promoted men, too, often have this same handicap; their failures are taken as evidence of individual weaknesses, but the failure of a woman brands all women as poor supervisors. Actually, much of the behavior of women supervisors is typical of new supervisors generally. Any new supervisor who feels unsure of himself, who feels that his boss is watching him critically, is likely to demand perfect behavior and performance from his people, to be critical of minor mistakes, and to try too hard to please his boss. A woman supervisor, responding to the insecurity and uncertainty of her position as a woman, knowing that she is being watched both critically and doubtfully, feels obliged to try even harder. And for doing this she is said to be "acting just like a woman."

In spite of the difficulties, however, it has been found possible in many instances to move women into new kinds of jobs and into higher-status positions. The supposed limitations of women in industry have, in fact, been found to be myths based merely on their inexperience and not on any real evidence or experiment. In the war years the frantic grasping at any straw to relieve the manpower shortage clearly showed that there was not, on the whole, a great difference between the work that men could do and the work that women could do. This was especially true of jobs requiring skill and mechanical knowledge rather than strength and endurance, since it has been clearly shown that, with proper training, women can do even the most skilled work. It has become evident that women succeed or fail in industrial jobs, generally, not so much because of their physical or mental ability but because of the social situations in which they work. Quite simply, women usually succeed in their jobs when they are expected to succeed and helped to succeed and when their supervisors have faith and their work groups are friendly; and they generally fail when they are surrounded by doubt and hostility. Finding or creating the proper social environment should be the first consideration of management when placing women on any new jobs, for women can generally be expected to succeed when the setting is conducive to success.

21. THE PROBLEMS
OF CHANGE

EQUILIBRIUM IN THE ORGANIZATION

IT HAS been pointed out in an earlier chapter that all organizations which have persisted for any length of time tend to achieve a certain equilibrium or balance. All that this means is that people in the organization develop a particular set of relations with the various elements in their environment. They reach a point where they know how to deal with the environment and have made the necessary adjustments to it. While they may not be completely satisfied with the relations which have developed, at least they have the security of knowing what to expect and, in general, how to handle things. Thus, the employee gets up in the morning, dresses, has his breakfast, catches the streetcar at the corner, passes through the gate at work, goes to his workplace, finds things as he expects them, has dealings with the foreman whose moods and attitudes he knows well, gets busy when the big boss comes around, slows down when the time-study man puts in an appearance, jokes with the fellows at lunch, and so on. He develops a certain sense of security, simply because things happens as he expects them to. His environment has been categorized, labeled, routinized, and mapped out to the best of his ability; and he has made a more or less successful adjustment to it. At least, it does not threaten him in any important ways.

Now, when change is introduced into a man's environment, it is apparent that he must make adjustments to it. If his department is moved from one end of the building to the other, he may have to reorganize a considerable part of his work life. Instead of entering at Gate A, he will now have to go in at Gate Z. He can no longer grab his lunch in the little hamburger stand across the street from Gate A. Instead, he has to bring his own lunch; and he loses the conviviality and good fellowship that was a source of satisfaction to him over at Joe's Slop Kitchen. A drinking fountain used to be located right in the department near his machine, when they were situated over near

Gate A. Now, however, he must walk down to the second floor. All these things are petty, little details that do not amount to much; but it is, nevertheless, amazing how many changes occur in a man's life when his department is moved. The adjustments involved for the average employee are sufficient, in fact, to cause some surprising drops in morale unless employees are properly oriented before the change occurs.

In order to understand why morale does drop when changes of various kinds occur in an organization, we have to know something about the psychology of learning. Learning, whether it takes place among rats or men, follows pretty much the same pattern. We tend to repeat those responses which bring us rewarding satisfactions. We inhibit responses which bring us pain and punishment. This process continues throughout our lives, although basic responses and sets are learned very early in life. Whenever we go into a new situation, we learn what responses to avoid and which ones to accept and develop. Those which tend to bring us the most satisfaction or the least dissatisfaction are reinforced and become part of our life pattern. Now, just suppose that, after we have learned a set of responses and a way of behaving which have proved satisfactory to us in a particular work situation, the situation is in some way changed. Suppose that former patterns of behavior and reactions which once brought us satisfactions of various kinds can no longer be followed. Worse still, suppose that responses which once brought us satisfaction and reward now bring us only punishment and pain. It is easy to see that, unless an adjustment to the new situation can be made, we can become frustrated and, in extreme cases, demoralized.

This is exactly what happens in many work situations. Employees are called upon to accept and adjust to changes which are sometimes hard to take. They receive little or no help from management, to whom they look for guidance in assisting them to adjust to the changes; and, as a result, it sometimes takes years for complete readjustment to occur under such circumstances. One situation where such a long, drawn-out adjustment period can occur is with a change of management—one of the most important of the changes which can affect the average employee's work life. Particularly is this true of employees in the middle-management brackets. However, reactions to top management change can run far down the line into the rank and file itself. The pattern of symptoms involved in poor morale resulting from management change is so clear-cut that it can almost be described as a distinct organizational disease. Usually the disease runs a course somewhat as follows: The new manager comes into the organization, all fired up to make a showing for himself. The employees soon get the definite impression that he is not satisfied with them, that their old ways of doing things are no longer adequate. For a time, however, they make some effort to adjust. This initial effort to adjust soon gives way to personal insecurity and anxiety as the employees find that the new manager is not too well satisfied, no matter what they do. There is a growing feeling among individual employees that they, personally, are not measuring up to standard. They think they see the better jobs going to outsiders. They see unfair treatment in every decision involving an old-timer. Then they make the important discovery that a number of other old-timers feel as they do. When this happens, a resistance group develops, which sets itself against the new manager and becomes actively involved in blocking his efforts to get a job done. This group may even go so far as to try to get rid of him by appealing to higher authority in the organization. Usually this pattern of reactions takes from one to two years, or more, to complete its cycle, depending upon the new management's skill and awareness of the problems which are affecting employees in the organization.

Whenever employees in an organization are unable to make the necessary adjustments to changes which occur, the organization can be said to be in a state of disequilibrium, or unbalance. It is very important, therefore, for management to develop the skills needed to maintain the stability of the organization through the variety of changes which can affect employees. This is particularly difficult, since our modern industrial world is characterized by change.

Most industrial and business organizations present a picture of constant changes of one sort or another. There are technological changes of machines and processes, changes in products, changes in organization, changes in personnel, and changes in relationships among individuals. This means that the individual employees are frequently making new adjustments, which vary from that involved in learning a new skill to that of assuming a new position in the status system. As we have seen, every major change in his situation may mean a serious problem of adjustment for the individual; and the ease and speed of readjustment depends largely upon the meaning of the change for the individual and his attitude toward it. Thus, changes which involve loss of status usually result in severe emotional reactions; and adjustment may be slow and painful. Furthermore, many changes which appear to be minor on the surface may be interpreted by the individual as a threat to his status or security; and he may react to them accordingly. Bringing a new, improved machine into a department, for example, may not directly affect the work of the operators of the old machines, but they may look on it as a threat to their positions and skill. Such situations present some delicate problems to either personnel men or supervisors in helping the individuals to adjust.

CHANGES WHICH AFFECT THE EQUILIBRIUM OF THE ORGANIZATION

Any change will affect an employee. However, there are some to which it is easy to adapt. The most important changes affecting employees in modern industrial life are those involving economic fluctuations, social movements and trends, changes in management and key personnel, changes in company policy (particularly with reference to rules and regulations affecting work routines), technological change, and change in departmental location.

Economic Changes

Of these various changes, economic fluctuations can have the broadest and most significant effect upon employees. There is nothing more demoralizing than the loss of a job when the prospect of securing another is remote. It is true that certain groups of employees—particularly those in the lowest working class in our society—are not nearly so concerned with the loss of jobs as higher level groups, at least from a psychological standpoint. Nevertheless, for the average workingman, cutting off his income is a hard economic and psychological blow. For middle-class employees, it frequently happens that loss of job during a depression is taken personally; they feel that some failure on their part must have caused the layoff. With such employees, the psychological effects may be far-reaching. Many men, such as these, never recovered personally from the effects of the Great Depression. This was true also of older men for whom loss of employment meant the end of their work career and dependency in old age.

Almost as important as a loss of job which results from wide swings in the economic activity of the nation is seasonal employment. In industries where the seasonal peaks and slumps are erratic, employees do not know from one month to the next how long they will work. They can make few, if any, plans for the future, and they are forced to lead a more or less hand-to-mouth economic existence. Savings are eaten up rapidly during even short periods of unemployment. Bills acquired during times of good employment become burdensome and threatening when the money is no longer coming in. Some employees practically never get out of the hands of creditors; they pay exorbitant sums to loan agencies in interest for money borrowed to satisfy other creditors who are pressing them for payment of bills. Any personnel manager knows what the average employee goes through from an economic point of view during such periods of unemployment. What he does not see, however, is the loss in prestige at home which the man of the family suffers when he is no longer working. The psychological cost to the unemployed worker is incalculable.

The amount of effort expended by management in attempting to reduce the psychological and economic effects of a layoff are very frequently at a minimum. Many companies announce a layoff no more than twenty-four hours in advance. In unorganized plants, layoffs may be announced on the day on which they are to occur, with no warning at all to the worker. The attitude in many companies is that the problem of layoffs is purely a management consideration. The only role in the situation which employees are asked to play is the passive one of coming to work when asked and going home when no longer needed. It is not commonly felt that employees should be taken into the confidence of management and told when layoffs are impending or likely to occur.

Under these circumstances, it is easy to understand why unions are so much concerned with an orderly procedure for effecting layoffs. With seniority clauses in the contract, employees know at least who is likely to be laid off if a cutback occurs. Furthermore, with plant-wide seniority, the older employees know that they will be kept on, even if they are forced off their regular jobs due to a departmental cutback. In most contracts, also, there are usually protective clauses which guarantee that the employee will receive at least some notice prior to a cutback. The trend is for the length of time of notification to be extended. More than this, there is a definite trend toward guaranteed annual incomes which provide the employee even more security against economic fluctuations.

It is quite apparent that the solution to the problem of layoff and unemployment does not lie in the hands of the management of individual companies. This is part and parcel of our entire economy. Nevertheless, much can be done locally to smooth out production and eliminate seasonal fluctuations. In one small company, during one of the best years of that company's existence, when thousands of dollars in profits were made, employment fluctuated from a low of 875 to a high of 1,200. When you consider that approximately 250 of these employees were a relatively stable group of office and supervisory workers, this meant a fluctuation in factory employment of over 50 per cent during a prosperous year. This is inexcusable from a purely humanistic standpoint; from an economic and morale point of view, it is very costly.

Changes in Company Policy

The importance and significance of economic changes to the stability of an organization are obvious. Less apparent, however, are changes in the rules and regulations of an organization. Changes such as these, when they are not reasonable and where employees are not given proper consideration and notice prior to their effective date, can be very demoralizing. Here, again, the management of many companies does not see the significance of change and its effect on the attitudes of employees. Since the creation of rules, regulations, and policies is primarily a management responsibility and prerogative, employees, often as not, are not permitted to participate in establishing them. The attitude, again, is that employees are merely supposed to follow the rules and that it is part of their job to do so. In fact, any infraction of the rules is regarded as a direct challenge to management's authority. As a result, management in many organizations goes blithely along, setting up new rules and changing old ones with little or no awareness of what this purely arbitrary action is costing in good will among employees. As a matter of fact, the very thing executives are attempting to accomplish among employees, namely, improved discipline and work habits, is being subverted and impeded by this frankly unilateral establishment of work rules and regulations.

The problem of rules and regulations is tied up closely with the problem of work discipline. In every organization, there have to be some rules if it is to operate in a relatively businesslike manner. Employees must come to work at specific times, take their rest periods in an orderly manner, eat at the proper times, smoke only in certain areas, and so on. Without regular procedures of this sort, employees themselves would be confused and the organization would be a chaos of individual wishes and desires. Most employees like to know what they can and cannot do and are more than happy to adhere to rules and regulations, provided that these are fair and reasonable. A few employees are unwilling to comply with any regulation. These constitute a small group of "goldbrickers" and "boondogglers." Furthermore, relatively conscientious employees sometimes indulge in poor work practices for purely social reasons: coffee clubs, smoking groups, and bridge clubs extending beyond the lunch period fall into this classification. In general, however, such employees can be easily brought into line merely by pointing out the effect of such behavior on the work effort. Moreover, some of these practices can be overlooked without too much concern because they can serve as a relatively inexpensive means of keeping employees tied to the workplace.

In some cases, however, management feels that practically all employees are out to take advantage, if they can possibly get away with it. As a result of this highly shortsighted view, rules and regulations are set up as a system of close and rigorous control. Employees begin to feel that they are working either in a kindergarten or a prison. They strongly suspect that management regards them as irresponsible children, requiring definite instructions on practically everything they do. Resentment grows when employees see representatives of management taking advantage of the very rules and regulations which they themselves have set up. Indeed, there is no better formula for wrecking the morale of an organization than setting up a group of arbitrary rules and regulations designed for the sole purpose of keeping employees in line.

Technological Change

Technological change is undoubtedly one of the most important of the changes affecting employees in industry. On the broad historical level, the industrial revolution represents a basic technological change which has required adjustments of major proportions throughout our whole social system. From a rural, agricultural society, we have become an urban, industrial nation within a few generations. This has meant changes in our entire way of life—the kinds of families we have, the way we bring up our children, our work habits, the jobs and skills we have, where we live and under what conditions. There is, in fact, no part of our lives which has not been touched by the massive changes in technology which have occurred during the past hundred years.

On a less epochal level, however, technological change can still be very important in the lives of employees. In his research in Yankee City, Professor W. Lloyd Warner made particular note of the effects of the deskilling of jobs in the shoe industry in Yankee City, resulting from the introduction of complex machinery to take the place of the skills of the craftsman. This decline in skilled jobs, according to Professor Warner, had the effect of reducing the worker's opportunity for upward mobility in the community. The consequent frustration of losing his status in the community with no chance for improvement made the Yankee City worker an easy bet for union organization and mobilization against management. Indeed, Professor Warner sees in this gradual elimination of skill hierarchies through technological change the development, at least in part, of the strong and powerful industrial union organization in this country during the last twenty years.[1]

Within each industrial and business organization itself, minor technological changes are continuously taking place which have a direct and immediate effect on the employee. A simple change in method has an effect similar to the change of procedure which was described previously. The employee who has acquired skill in doing his job one way tends to resist new ways of doing the job. As a matter of fact, he may resist so much that the new way, although actually an improvement in method, may not work out as planned. In some cases, instead of production improving, it actually drops off and declines.

Changes in technology may seriously affect the status of employees in an organization. In one clerical department in a large organization, management introduced a business-machine system for accomplishing the same operation formerly performed by the clerical employees. These employees strongly resented the introduction of the machines —but not because of the threat to their job security, for there were job openings for all that wanted them elsewhere in the organization. What they resented was their loss of status, because they now considered themselves "machine operators" and something below regular office workers.

There is a threat of loss of status in every new change which is introduced. Older employees who are used to a particular way of

---

[1] W. Lloyd Warner and J. O. Low, *The Social System of the Modern Factory* (New Haven: Yale University Press, 1947).

doing things find themselves unable to keep up with new methods. They are, therefore, critical of innovations. "They don't make things the way they used to," said one old-timer. "Why, twenty years ago this stuff really had quality; it was built to last. But now they just throw it together." Actually, this old-timer was simply expressing the rigidity of old age and lack of willingness to adjust. The truth of the matter was that the product to which he was referring was far superior in every respect to the product of twenty years ago. It was not only better designed but better made. The old-timer, however, feared a loss in his own status and the threat to his own, no longer useful, skills.

Technological changes give rise to other adjustment problems. In many companies the engineers are originating a continual stream of changes in products, machines, and processes. These changes are designed to improve the product or reduce the costs, and they generally mean a simplification of processes or the introduction of more automatic machinery. Such changes may affect the individual in a number of ways. They may eliminate his job entirely and force him to learn a new job; they may reduce the number of workers needed and force him out of a job; or they may result in extensive transfers of people, substitution of women for men, or low-skilled jobs for high-skilled jobs. The following example was observed by the authors:

One factory used a large volume of nickel-plated parts, which required many skilled polishers to polish the parts before and after plating. A change in design, which changed the finish on most of the parts to a black enamel instead of nickel plate, eliminated most of the polishers and substituted a few sprayers. This meant that a large group of skilled polishers, some of whom had spent fifteen or twenty years in the work, had to be absorbed into other types of work in other departments. Since most of them were not experienced in other work, they had to be transferred to less-skilled jobs with a cut in rates. As a result, the skill they had spent years in acquiring and in which they took considerable pride was no longer of value. Also, the group in which they had spent years was broken up.

Thus, they had to learn new skills; they had to adjust to lower earnings; and they had to adjust to the change from a work group of which they had been a part for a long time, and in which they had high status because of their skill and experience, to groups in which they were new, inexperienced, and of low status.

Even where technological change does not substitute lower skilled people for the highly skilled, it often substitutes one skill for another.

For example, if, in the manufacturing of an intricate part, die-casting is substituted for machining, skilled die-cast operators may replace equally skilled machine operators. This means that for that particular job the machine operators are displaced even though there might be no actual reduction in the number of skilled workers needed. In some cases, there may actually be a substitution of more highly skilled people for those displaced, although this is rare and usually means a sharp reduction in total numbers needed. In general, we can say that, for a given quantity of goods produced, the technological improvements tend to reduce the average level of skill required and the number of people required.

Personnel Changes

Any change in personnel among employees can create repercussions (even those not involving supervisory personnel). Let us consider, for example, the impact simply of introducing a new employee into a work group. Most modern companies have a procedure for inducting the new employee, acquainting him with company policies and the conditions of employment, and introducing him to his supervisor and fellow employees. However, few of them recognize the problems of adjustment which the older employees must face every time a new face is brought into the work group. Usually, of course, this adjustment process is relatively simple and uneventful, if the newcomer knows his way around and is willing to accept the patterns of social behavior already established. However, if he should get out of line in any important respect, a small-sized volcanic eruption can occur. In retail stores, for example, the introduction of a so-called "hot-shot" salesman can often have dire effects. Most selling departments in retail stores have a fairly well-organized status system which determines, to a great extent, the amount of sales which each employee can or will make. It is apparent that the ability to get sales is very much dependent, not only on sales ability and personal confidence, but also on who is allowed to approach the customers and who is permitted to sell the higher cost items. Higher-status salespersons naturally have all the advantages in this regard. They can compel lower-status employees to defer to them in the choice of customers and in the selection of the better selling areas of the department. If a new employee comes into the department and refuses to recognize this status system, the department will organize to squeeze him out. Even the supervisors will join in attempting to control the newcomer who threatens to wreck the morale of the entire department. Older salesmen will bracket the "hot shot" on the selling floor so that he cannot easily approach a customer coming into the department. The supervisor will give him stock work to do which will keep him off the selling floor. He will be reprimanded for "unethical tactics" if he does not follow the accepted practices in approaching a customer and attempts to beat out others in the department who may already have spotted the prospect. These kinds of social pressures generally are sufficient for the person with average aggressiveness. However, even under these conditions, a few still do not respond and fall into line. Under these circumstances, friction and poor feeling can persist in the department for long periods of time. In many such cases, the "hot shot" finally has to be taken out of the department, in spite of his excellent sales record.

The same kind of adjustment problem occurs in factories when a "rate-buster" is introduced into the department. Here, the technique of control may not be so subtle. The newcomer is simply told by the others what is the accepted "fair day's work" in the organization, and he either responds or lays himself wide open for a variety of social pressures, ranging from joking ridicule to open threats.

The problem of adjusting to a change of personnel on your own, or a lower, level, however, is not nearly so difficult as adjusting to a change in supervision, particularly higher-level supervision in a position to alter established work practices and procedures. Any such alteration is a threat to the established social system of the organization; and anyone who has a stake in that system will be likely to face a new manager or supervisor with considerable anxiety and trepidation. The reaction, however, to a change in management will vary, depending to some extent on the attitudes which employees had toward the former supervisor whose place the newcomer is taking. If there was a good deal of cordial feeling toward the previous boss, the newcomer will be regarded as a usurper; he will be watched closely for shortcomings and weaknesses. If the feeling about the former boss was negative and unfavorable, the newcomer may be received with welcome relief. In a retail store with which we are familiar, a change of management of this order had occurred, with the following results:

The previous manager was thoroughly disliked for very personal reasons. However, the attitudes of employees toward the company in general had remained quite favorable; the feeling was that eventually the disliked manager would be removed and transferred elsewhere. This actually happened; and when the new manager came in to take over, he called all employees together, and said, among other things, "Work can be fun!" Then he spent his first few days in the store simply walking around, shaking hands with everybody. The effect of this procedure was electric, as far as employees were concerned. It keynoted their own feelings; they began quoting the new manager's words as though they were their own, "You know, work can be fun!" Needless to say, the problem of integrating into the store was simple for the new manager.

In another store, however, the reverse situation occurred:

The old manager had been well liked by a large segment of the store. The new manager, who had just come back from a long stint in the army, called employees together and told them that he had been a colonel in the army and, as far as he was concerned, he would continue as such in his new assignment in the store. These may not have been his exact words, but that was the way that employees interpreted them. In any event, he thereupon disappeared into his office and left his anxious and somewhat perturbed people to shift for themselves. Morale swung lower over a period of time. A year later there was a strong resistance group among a number of employees who were actively working against management.

It is apparent from these few comments about change in personnel that the principal problems of adjustment are: (1) the integration of the newcomer's attitudes and behavior with the demands of the work group into which he is moving, and (2) the group's adjustment to the demands of the newcomer if this is necessary, as it is in case of change of supervisor. The adjustment of the group is always more difficult because it involves shaking up, and even destroying, an established status system in which employees have an important personal stake.

Organizational Changes

Another problem of individual adjustment results from the changes in organization or structure which management originates. Management is always interested in changing its organization so that it will work better, or so that it will meet changing conditions of one sort or another. Many of these are changes in formal organization at a level which affects the supervisory structure and may involve the shifting of departments from one division to another without changing the actual work. Changes which have much more direct impact on the work level are those involving reorganization of the work or regrouping of the jobs, change of physical location, and so on. At whatever level such changes take place, it must be remembered that the people, even though they be top executives, must make an adjustment to the new state of affairs.

At the supervisory and executive level, these organizational changes are often interpreted as affecting the status relationships of those involved, and this may result in serious reactions and anxieties. To take a department away from one division chief and place it with another, for example, may be interpreted as loss of prestige for one and a gain for the other; and the one who has lost status may show anxiety over the reasons for the move and about his standing with top management. Even when such moves are obviously logical from the organizational point of view, there will probably be some such reactions unless the superiors give great reassurance. And even if he has been reassured about the meaning of the move, the division chief who has lost a department knows that everyone at his level and below will comment on the change and wonder if it means that he is "slipping."

Reorganization at the higher level often means little to the workers, since such changes can be accomplished without changing the work or the work location. But when the changes mean that the work units are shifted around, they become directly significant to the workers. For example:

One company made a change in its accounting organization which broke up large accounting units in a central location into small units in shop location. This removed the members of the organization from the preferred office location and put them in the lower-status shop environment. It also separated them into small groups isolated from each other, and broke up many of their cliques and social activities which they had carried on as one large group. Furthermore, they were in much less frequent contact with their superiors and felt that they were isolated and ignored. The adjustment to this change required several months, during which time there were continual complaints about the change, about the poor working conditions, the noise and dirt in the new location, the isolation from higher supervisors, anxieties about being lost in the shop, and many similar expressions of disturbance.

The adjustment to all these changes presents a very difficult problem from the point of view of management. In every case where there is serious disturbance, the effectiveness of the individual or even the entire organization is reduced for a time and, in some cases, permanently. Nevertheless, such changes are often unavoidable, and the problem is how to handle them so that there will be a minimum of disturbance and the quickest possible adjustment. Often, by failing to anticipate the disturbance, by thinking of people as though they were inanimate objects which would not react to such changes, management fails to take the reaction into its calculations and does things in such a way as to increase disturbances. In many cases, proper attention to the individuals will reduce anxieties and pave the way for rapid adjustment. In other cases, modification of the proposed changes will remove the features which give rise to the most serious reactions. In general, to announce an important change without preparing those involved beforehand increases disturbances; but if it has been discussed in advance and the subordinates have been able to express their ideas and have had some hand in the planning, then they become adjusted to the idea and accept it more readily. In any case, the superiors should anticipate the way their subordinates will react and give increased attention to them during the change and the period of adjustment. In no case should it be assumed that by giving a simple logical reason for the change the disturbance can be avoided. Explanations play a useful role in the adjustment, but they should be accompanied by increased sympathetic attention from the superiors. Unfortunately, in many cases the intermediate levels, such as department and division chiefs, are just as disturbed as the foremen or workers, and because of their own feelings are unable to give attention to their subordinates and to reassure them.

Change in Departmental Location

Change in departmental location hardly seems like the most important of the changes which can occur in the work life of an employee, and it is not; but the reactions to it can sometimes be so vehement and emotional that some discussion of it seems appropriate. Life, when you think about it, is made up of a set of very elemental, simple routines. None of these routines, in itself, is very important. But picture for yourself the adjustments which you would have to make if, instead of arising at 6:30 A.M., you were compelled to arise at 5:30 A.M. Not much of a change, but your wife has to get up at the same time, or else you get your own breakfast. More important, you have to go to bed before 10:00 P.M. if you want a decent night's rest. And you are hungry as a horse at 11:00 A.M., but you still have to wait until noon to have lunch. Moreover, because you are more tired when you arrive home at night and are, therefore, more irritable, the children wonder whether Daddy really has finally "cracked," as Mamma often said he would. And so it goes, with the change working its way into the very fabric of your life.

In the same way, a change of departmental location requires that employees make a whole series of minor adjustments. Things are never quite the same. The worst part of a change in location, however, is that very often employees are not informed of the change until it is about to happen. Seldom are they taken into management's confidence in planning the change. Indeed, it seems unnecessary to do so. What difference does it make where employees do their work? Space is space, no matter where it is! But the implication of the change is apparent to employees. They think that management does not have the interests of employees at heart; that management does not care whether they have to use the small rear elevator, which is always so "jam-packed" in the morning, instead of the group of larger elevators at the main entrance where the traffic is much lighter; that management does not concern itself with the fact that the new location does not have the window space that the old location had; that the lighting is poorer; and that employees now have to walk half a block to the washroom, and so on.

Very often a change in departmental location has status implications. In this event, the reactions of employees can be very severe, as shown below:

In one organization studied, a small group of employees in a statistical department were moved away from the mother department and top supervision to a location in a separate building. They had built up a good deal of camaraderie in the new location and felt considerable relief in being away from the watchful eyes of the department manager. However, one day, without explanation, they were moved back to the old location. Immediately the question arose, "Why?" Rumor had it that they were being punished for their behavior in the new quarters. Gone was the old camaraderie and good spirit. What's more, employees in the old location avoided them like the plague. Until they were sure of the reasons for the shift, they were not going to put their own security on the block by associating with them. The tension in this department when it was studied was very great.

If the new location is clearly undesirable, employees definitely feel a loss of status. The implication is that their department as a whole does not rate in the organization. Departmental status can, of course, be very important to employee morale. If they feel that they are a part of a going department, one which is accepted and respected in the company, they generally have greater pride and satisfaction in their work. Moving to a poorer location is one sure way to inform employees that their department does not rate and that their supervisor has not enough strength in the organization to protect his people from all kinds of indignities. While this may not be true, of course, it is, nonetheless, a disheartening experience.

Change in Job or Office Location

A change in the place in which you do your job within a department is closely related to a change in the location of the entire department. Here, however, the status implications can be very clear-cut. Particularly is this true in offices where some of the important symbols of status are the type of desk, location of desk, size of office, and location of office. Simply moving an employee from a desk to a table may have serious status implications for him. In some offices, moving an employee from a double-pedestal desk to a single-pedestal desk would constitute a demotion to him as real as though you cut his salary ten dollars a week. Locating a man with a group of women in an office has also created anxiety on many occasions. The following example of the effects of change in office were observed in one large office with which the authors have considerable familiarity:

Every year or so there is a General Moving Day. This shifting about of office personnel is necessitated by the fact, that, because of promotions each year and transfers of key personnel, offices with a good deal of status significance are left vacant. The office that you eventually get constitutes a clear definition of your status. There is always considerable anxiety when a change of this sort is about to take place. Employees on the same general status level talk about those on higher levels, but, of course, they do not talk about themselves. There is considerable effort to relieve tension throughout the entire procedure by joking about it. When it is all over, employee reactions depend on how closely their new office location actually measures up to their own conception of their status in the organization. Sometimes, there are hard feelings, but generally not, because management in this organization is very much aware of the status significance of various office locations and plans the changes carefully.

SUMMARY

The changes which we have been discussing are some of the more common ones which can occur in the typical business and industrial organization. However, it is apparent that any change can affect the feelings of employees. When you consider that our industrial world is characterized by change—indeed, reveres change as a fundamental part of the American system—it is easy to understand that the prob-

lem of helping employees to adjust to change in the work environment should be one of the principal concerns of management. However, it has been equally characteristic of business management that
adjustment to change is regarded as a problem of the individual employee, something which he must work out for himself. As a matter
of fact, employees do make considerable adjustment to change on
their own; after all, even the most rigid humans are unusually flexible
and adaptive. But the cost in employee feelings of anxiety and insecurity and the loss of productive energies and efficiency, engendered by changes affecting the well-being and status of employees,
are significant items of human and economic expense. This is especially true when it is so easy to relieve much of the anxiety caused
by change and do an intelligent job of management in this important
area.

22. BUSINESS AND
SOCIAL RESEARCH

THE TIDES OF CHANGE

SINCE the first edition of this book was published, we have witnessed an unprecedented rate of social and economic change throughout the world. The colonial powers have largely lost their colonies and much of their economic and political status. New countries have emerged and are demanding political and economic independence. Europe is rapidly becoming an integrated economic system free of the former barriers of national boundaries and feelings.

One clear element in the tide of change is the movement away from the traditional societies with their social order based on long-established custom and tradition into more fluid, changeable states. The older binding forces of traditional values and behavior have lost their power, and new values and new ways of life are developing. The child in Africa or Japan or Algeria will not grow up in a clearly defined world where he can know what to expect, where he fits, how he must behave. Neither can he rely on the wisdom and experience of his elders to guide him. Instead he must find his own way in a rapidly changing world filled with new experiences and activities, new demands if he is to survive, and many conflicting values.

Another clear element is the trend toward an industrial society. The emerging nations of Asia and Africa are demanding steel mills and hydroelectric power to accelerate their industrial growth. In many cases these, along with jet airports, are more symbolic of their dreams of industrialization than realistic contributions to immediate progress.

Nevertheless, within the next few decades we will see an almost explosive expansion of industry around the world. Along with this will be the decline of specialization by particular nations as producers of food, of raw materials, or industrial goods. The plains of Argentina will supply beef for Europe for a long time to come; yet within a few years chickens raised in the modern growing plant will feed more Europeans than will Argentine beef.

As a result of this tide of industrialization we can expect increasing consumption of all forms of consumer goods. Probably the United States, with its current high level of consumption, is a model for what we can expect in both goods and quantity. This will mean that gradually the things with which people will surround themselves will become more identical around the world. Every housewife will long for the stoves, refrigerators, and washers which are commonplace here. An inextricable element in the rise of industrialization will be the need for technical skills and knowledge at all levels. Engineers, scientists, skilled mechanics will be in insatiable demand. The untrained and unskilled will find less and less opportunity in this new world. Education will everywhere be increasingly important for even the lowliest industrial worker.

Automation, the replacement of muscle work or repetitious routine by machines, will increase rapidly. In the United States we have reached our present stage of industrial development through large use of manpower and are now beginning to replace this manpower with machines. However, the new nations will not go through our sequence of development. We will supply them with the machines and know-how, so that they will start with our advanced technology. They will build their roads and mills with bulldozers and crawler cranes, not hordes of manual laborers. And the production lines will be automatic machines and skilled operators.

For many nations this means that modern technology and automation will not displace workers, as it does here. Instead, they may never find a place in modern industry. This means that there must be an acceleration of the educational and training processes which prepare illiterate peoples for life in industrial society. Probably new patterns will emerge by which the productive capacities of the new technologies can serve all the people.

A common approach to these problems is through some government ownership, control and direction of the productive capacities of the country. In Russia under communism this has been total ownership, control of all industry and business. Unfortunately this has some built-in tendencies which hamper progress. Such socialization, or even partial socialization, as seen in India and other countries, leads to an elaboration of government bureaucracies. With these all decision making tends to migrate to the top, and local managers have little room for initiative in operations, planning, product innovation, production quotas, and so on. The result is a cumbersome operation which cannot adapt readily to changing conditions.

In such economic systems the individual's success and progress depends upon his adjustment to the requirements of the bureaucracy. In contrast, in our own economic system the success of the individual or organization depends upon his adjustment in an economy built upon transactional relationships. His efforts must produce goods or services which can be exchanged for the production of others.

This is not to say that we do not have our own bureaucracies. A large percentage of our employment is in governmental agencies, and many large corporations develop bureaucratic characteristics. However, we are still dominated by the need to produce for exchange, and even in large corporations the transactional flow must be maintained on almost a daily basis. So far our governmental controls have only tended to set certain limitations on the way the business organization (or the individual entrepreneur) can pursue the goals of effective and profitable exchange.

We in the United States believe that the progress of these other nations will be more rapid if they do not rely on the bureaucratic approach of governmental control. Not only our own experience but also observation of the postwar progress in West Germany and Japan suggest that the entrepreneurial approach tends to be more effective. The energies and abilities of individuals can better be mobilized to get things done under our system. With us, multiple interests ranging from purely profit-seeking aims to idealistic goals can function to create a dynamic and productive society.

Let us now restrict our consideration to the changes we face here. We are caught up in the tide of technological change. The rapid pace of our technology and its elimination of need for unskilled hands means that we can expect a steady change in the distribution of jobs and changes in the human problems. As a nation we face the problem of assimilation of the unskilled and uneducated. This will be a burden for some time to come, and we may have in the next decade a large body of unemployables who will be totally dependent on government aid. It is crucial that we soon develop some fresh, creative approaches in order to solve this problem, for it is clear that the old approaches are not enough.

One effect of this progress will be the change in the character of the working force in any large company. There will be the steady decline in proportion of the blue-collar jobs as compared to white-collar. At the same time many of the white-collar jobs will also decline. For example, a recently organized bank started with accounting and record keeping being handled by a computer. At present they require one part-time computer technician to handle all their volume of accounting, record keeping, monthly statements, interest calculations, and government reporting. They are doing more, and getting it done faster than would be possible under the older methods with half a dozen or more skilled accounting clerks using regular accounting machines.

This means that future editions of *Human Relations in Industry* will have to deal more with the problems of organizations composed primarily of specialists, highly skilled technicians, engineers, and scientists. The humanness of the problems will remain the same, but the nature of the people and the setting will change. Undoubtedly many theories of proper organization will have to be re-examined and new concepts will be developed and tested.

Another change is the rapid move to "bigness." In many fields, especially in manufacturing, the small company can hardly survive. For one thing, the capital investment in modern machines is so great that the very small company has difficulty in financing such machines, yet cannot compete without them. Furthermore, automation can only be effective for large volume, whether it be in production of goods or processing of bank accounts.

This move to bigness is being currently shown in mergers of all kinds, ranging through manufacturers, advertising agencies, and even stock brokers. More and more it appears that growth of the small company beyond a certain point in size is extremely difficult, and below that point life is very hazardous. The sensible solution is to be acquired by a larger company or to merge with other small ones.

For an entrepreneural society this trend to bigness raises some serious problems. Does this mean that no longer is this a society in which the individual can start from scratch and build a substantial enterprise? Or does it merely mean that the kind of enterprise he may build is limited to certain fields of business? Maybe he can no longer create a great, industrial empire as did Henry Ford but can he still build a great merchandising chain or some new service enterprise? These are all questions we can only speculate about, but the signs are clear that the coming generations of entrepreneurs will have to find their opportunities in a different world of enterprise.

SOCIAL RESEARCH

The pace of change today is so fast that there is an increasing need to anticipate what the future will bring. When things changed slowly, the business executive had time to observe and plan. Now the pace is fast, and he must constantly strive to think ahead of change. Also, experience will be a poor teacher, since he will be dealing with conditions which never existed before. As a result, he must be constantly searching for an understanding of the dynamics of change and of the principles involved. He must reason from these into the future and make his decisions and take action before change engulfs him and his company.

We are now caught up in a social system which puts great stress on understanding the nature of the world and on applying that knowledge to the service of man. Out of the laboratories comes a deluge of knowledge, and the engineer and businessman work constantly to apply that knowledge to creating new or improved products, for simplifying tasks, for satisfying consumer interests. This process in turn imposes change on our society. It creates new tasks and eliminates others; it changes social behavior and patterns of consumption (witness the influence of the automobile or the effects of frozen prepared foods).

We can think of this growth of technical knowledge as one of the important forces leading to social change. However, it does not help us to know how to deal with the changes it stimulates. Also, many technical advances or innovations have potential values which often are not recognized by the experts who develop them.

Since World War II more and more corporations, the relatively small as well as large, are turning to research as a tool for maintaining their corporate success. They see a need for new products, for product improvements, for improvements in methods, and are searching for them through increased emphasis on research. The larger ones are even committing sizable budgets to "pure" research whose end results cannot be foreseen. The result is a constant stream of new products which must find their place in the markets.

One result of this has been to shorten the period in which a company can benefit from a new product. A pharmaceutical manufacturer introducing a distinctly new drug formerly could expect it would dominate the market for ten years before any important competitors appeared. Now, its competitors are likely to present similar or even improved versions within three years.

Every change, whether automation or a new product, has its impact on people and on society. The company introducing a new food product must learn how it can get housewives to use it; a machine tool must be accepted by the engineers and production experts. And the new food means a change in buying and eating; the machine tool may mean a change in production-line layout or in the skills required.

In order to anticipate and deal with the human impact of technology, we must turn more and more to the social and behavioral scientists. It is increasingly recognized that as a society we need to increase our understanding of man and his social systems if we are to use our technology to create a better world for people. In fact it is feared that unless our understanding improves we may even make use of knowledge to destroy the world.

In recognition of this need the government and foundations are devoting more and more resources to research in the social sciences. This effort is seen as basic research or else as directed to broad social problems.

Business also is turning more to the social sciences to help with many immediate problems. Consumer research, which has grown rapidly since the war, has become increasingly influenced by the social sciences. In fact, almost every important research department must have its sociologist or psychologist who can apply the behavioral concepts to the study of consumer behavior. At the same time, commercial consulting organizations such as Social Research, Inc. have developed; these are primarily staffed by social scientists and primarily concerned with the application of concepts and methods of the behavioral sciences to a wide range of problems.

As organizations grow larger and the pace of innovation and change increases, the top executives can no longer safely make decisions based on long experience. The president who once felt that from early experience in sales he knew what the present consumer wanted in food, or clothes, or automobiles, is apt to make wrong decisions on products and selling. If he feels that employees today are no different from when he first worked in the mills, he is apt to be wrong in his approach to problems of employee morale and collective bargaining.

It is recognition of these conditions that leads to a growing belief in the importance of a better understanding of the dynamics of human behavior. It is important for modern executives to understand the whole complex of people who make up the human organization and network of relationships essential to the success of the company. It is not sufficient for the company to produce a better product; it must be able to sell it, and selling involves relations with people. It is not sufficient to develop new production machines; the organization must adapt to using them and this, too, is an adaptation of people. In short, with every action and every decision the executive is influencing and adjusting human relations.

In the years ahead it appears that success as a nation, and success of individual business enterprises, will depend upon our ability to anticipate and deal with the human problems, whether international, national, or in the individual business. This need will make it important for us to understand and utilize the growing body of knowledge from the social sciences. At the same time the decision-makers must demand of these social scientists that they learn how their knowledge can be applied to solving problems. It is not enough for them to remain aloof from action and decisions. They must learn to bridge the gap between theory, research findings, and action. Probably what we need is a larger body of "applied social scientists" who have a function similar to engineers in creating a bridge between the technical world of theory and research and the practical world of industry.

INDEX

INDEX

*This book has been set on the Linotype in 11
point and 9 point Janson, leaded 2 points. Part
and chapter numbers and titles are in Craw
Clarendon Book. The size of the type page is 27
by 45 picas.*

DATE DUE